Collins New Primary Maths

Enriching Maths 6

A problem-solving, cross-curricular programme for children working above end-of-year expectations

Peter Clarke

William Collins' dream of knowledge for all began with the publication of his first book in 1819. A self-educated mill worker, he not only enriched millions of lives, but also founded a flourishing publishing house. Today, staying true to this spirit, Collins books are packed with inspiration, innovation and practical expertise. They place you at the centre of a world of possibility and give you exactly what you need to explore it.

Collins. Freedom to teach.

Published by Collins
An imprint of HarperCollinsPublishers
77–85 Fulham Palace Road
Hammersmith
London
W6 8JB

10 9 8 7 6 5 4 3

ISBN 978-0-00-743118-2

British Library Cataloguing in Publication Data
A Catalogue record for this publication is available from the British Library

Cover design by Neil Adams
Series design by Steve Evans and Mark Walker
Cover artwork by Jonatronix Ltd.
Internal design by Steve Evans and Mark Walker Design
Illustrations by Steve Evans, Q2A Media, Mark Walker and Sarah Wimperis
Edited by Gaynor Spry
Proofread by Jan Fisher

Acknowledgements
Peter Clarke wishes to thank Brian Molyneaux for his valuable contribution to this publication.

Printed and bound by Martins the Printers

Contents

Quick reference guide to *Enriching Maths 6*

Strand	Topic	Issue number	Teacher's Notes page number
Counting and understanding number	Whole numbers	1	100
	Negative numbers	2	105
	Fractions	3	109
	Decimals	4	113
	Percentages	5	117
	Ratio and proportion	6	121
	General	7	125
Calculating	Addition	8	130
	Subtraction	9	136
	Multiplication	10	139
	Division	11	144
	Mixed operations	12	149
	Mixed operations – The Financial Issue	13	153
	Calculating with fractions	14	156
	Calculating with percentages	15	160
	General	16	164
Understanding shape	2-D shapes	17	168
	3-D solids	18	174
	Reflective symmetry	19	178
	Rotational symmetry	20	181
	Translations	21	184
	Position and direction	22	187
	Movement and angle	23	191
	General	24	196
Measuring	Length and distance	25	201
	Mass and weight	26	205
	Volume and capacity	27	209
	Time	28	213
	Temperature	29	217
	Area	30	220
	Perimeter	31	224
	General	32	230
Handling data	Organising and interpreting data	33	234
	Probability	34	237
	Statistics	35	242
	General	36	245

Introduction

Enriching Maths aims to provide support in meeting the needs of those children who are exceeding age-related expectations by providing a range of problem-solving and cross-curricular activities designed to enrich children's mathematical knowledge, skills and understanding.

The series has been designed to provide:

- a flexible 'dip-in' resource that can be easily adapted to meet the needs of individual children, and different classroom and school organisational arrangements
- extension and enrichment activities that require children to use and apply their mathematical knowledge, skills and understanding
- mathematical activities linked to the entire primary curriculum, thereby ensuring a range of cross-curricular contexts
- an easy-to-use bank of activities to save teachers time in thinking up new extension and enrichment activities
- an interesting, unique and consistent approach to presenting extension and enrichment activities to children.

The *Enriching Maths* series consists of six Resource Packs, each with an accompanying CD-ROM, one for each year group from Year 1 to Year 6.

Resource Pack

Containing:

- Pupil activity booklets (Issues)
- Teacher's notes
- Resource copymasters (RCMs)

CD-ROM

Containing editable:

- Pupil activity booklets (Issues)
- Teacher's notes
- Resource copymasters (RCMs)

It is envisaged that the activities in *Enriching Maths* will be used by either individuals or pairs of children. However, given the flexible nature of the resource, if appropriate, children can work in groups. The activities are intended to be used as:

- an alternative to the work that the rest of the class is given
- additional work to be done once children have finished other set work
- in-depth work that is to be undertaken over a prolonged period of time, such as during the course of several lessons, a week or a particular unit of work
- a resource for gifted classes, promoting independent thinking and learning
- springboards for further investigations into mathematics based on the children's suggestions.

The National Curriculum (2000) outlines the thinking skills that complement the key knowledge, skills and understanding which are embedded in the primary curriculum.

Enriching Maths aims to develop in children these key thinking skills.

Information processing skills

- locate and collect relevant information
- sort, classify, sequence, compare and analyse part and / or whole relationships

Reasoning skills

- give reasons for opinions and actions
- draw inferences and make deductions
- use precise language to explain what they think
- make judgements and decisions informed by reason or evidence

Enquiry skills

- ask relevant questions
- pose and define problems
- plan what to do and how to research
- predict outcomes and anticipate conclusions
- test conclusions and improve ideas

Creative thinking skills

- generate and extend ideas
- suggest hypotheses
- apply imagination
- look for alternative innovative outcomes

Evaluative skills

- evaluate information
- judge the value of what they read, hear or do
- develop criteria for judging the value of their own and others' work or ideas
- have confidence in their judgement

The activities in *Enriching Maths* also aim to develop children's middle and higher order thinking skills by providing a range of suitable extension and enrichment activities.

Bloom's Building Blocks to Thinking

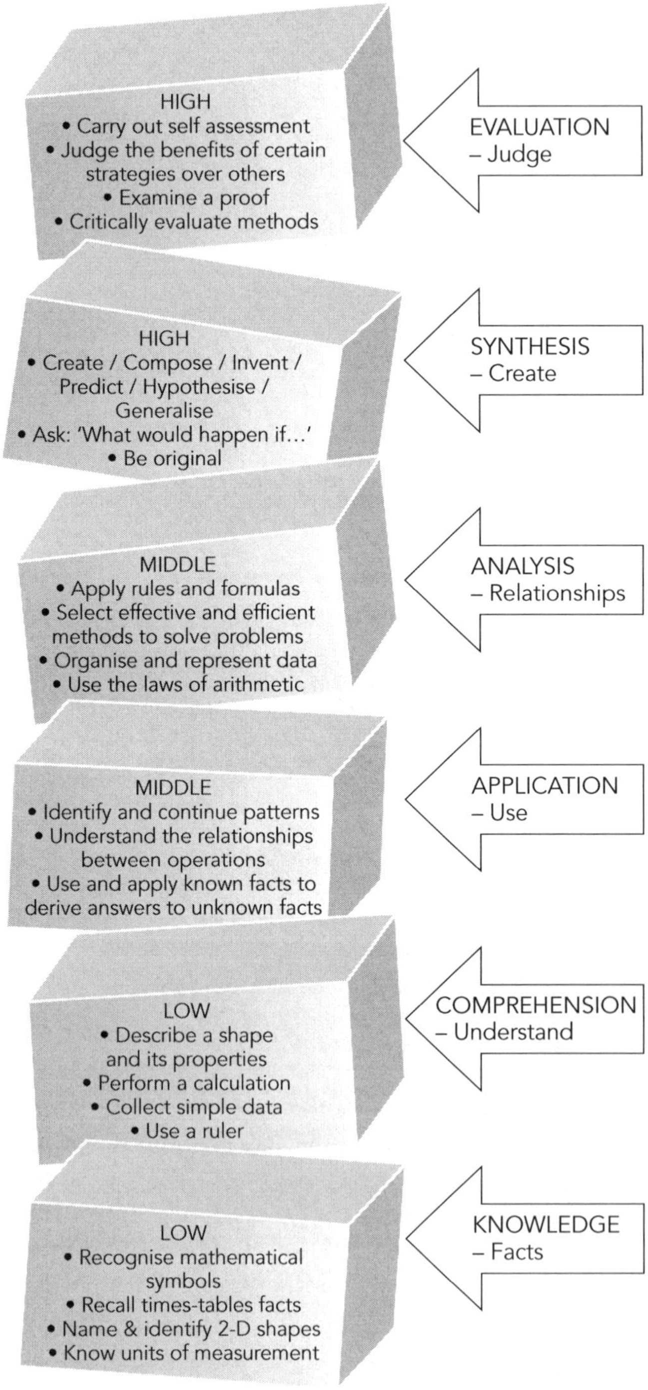

HIGH
• Carry out self assessment
• Judge the benefits of certain strategies over others
• Examine a proof
• Critically evaluate methods
EVALUATION – Judge
HIGH
• Create / Compose / Invent / Predict / Hypothesise / Generalise
• Ask: 'What would happen if…'
• Be original
SYNTHESIS – Create
MIDDLE
• Apply rules and formulas
• Select effective and efficient methods to solve problems
• Organise and represent data
• Use the laws of arithmetic
ANALYSIS – Relationships
MIDDLE
• Identify and continue patterns
• Understand the relationships between operations
• Use and apply known facts to derive answers to unknown facts
APPLICATION – Use
LOW
• Describe a shape and its properties
• Perform a calculation
• Collect simple data
• Use a ruler
COMPREHENSION – Understand
LOW
• Recognise mathematical symbols
• Recall times-tables facts
• Name & identify 2-D shapes
• Know units of measurement
KNOWLEDGE – Facts

Source: Bloom

Mathematically gifted children

Some characteristics of gifted children

The following characteristics are not necessarily proof of high mathematical ability, however they may provide an indication of a pupil's level of ability.

Mathematically gifted children may:

- be inquisitive and ask searching questions
- grasp new concepts quickly
- be imaginative
- be logical
- show unusual and original responses
- have an ability to work things out in their head very quickly
- approach problems from different perspectives
- be persistent
- make generalisations
- easily identify patterns and relationships
- use mathematical symbols confidently
- develop concise logical arguments
- have good memories
- be quick thinkers
- be very articulate for their age
- give quick verbal responses
- prefer verbal to written activities
- communicate well with adults – often better than with their peer group
- have a wide general knowledge
- be interested in topics which one might associate with an older child
- have a range of interests, some of which are almost obsessions
- be self-taught in their own interest areas
- have strong views and opinions
- have a lively and original imagination / sense of humour
- be very sensitive and aware
- focus on their own interests rather than on what is being taught
- be easily bored by what they perceive as routine tasks
- show a strong sense of leadership
- not necessarily be well-behaved or well-liked by others.

The identification of gifted children

Research suggests that up to 20% of pupils can be identified as being either more or exceptionally able. Before effective provision can be made for these children the identification of such children needs to be undertaken.

Schools have the discretion to decide how best to identify gifted children, but are likely to obtain the best results by drawing on a wide range of sources, including both qualitative and quantitative information.

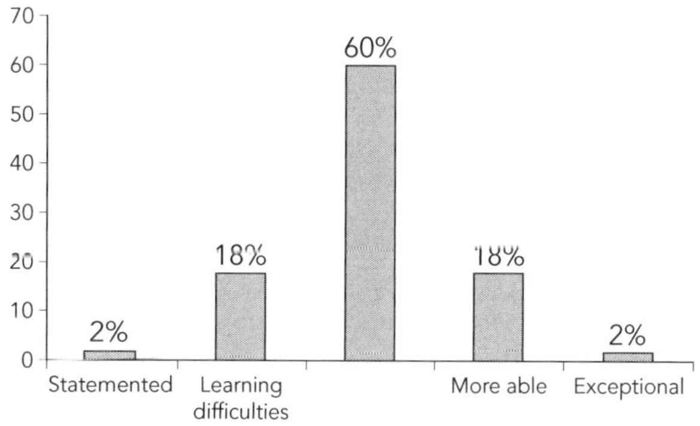

Source: OFSTED

A range of popular methods for identification include:

- teacher nomination
- checklists
- testing
- assessment of children's work
- peer or self nomination
- parental information
- discussions with children
- community resources, e.g. educational psychologists

The key principles of identification are that it is:

- a continuous process
- a systematic whole-school approach
- based on a portfolio approach, using a range of qualitative and quantitative measures
- to be vigilant for the 'hidden gifted', such as underachievers, EAL children, those with specific learning or physical disabilities, those from different cultural or disadvantaged socio-economic groups
- a process that involves all educators, pupils and parents/carers.

Providing provision for gifted children

The most important aspect of meeting the needs of gifted children is the day-to-day experience in the classroom. This can be achieved through a combination of the following:

- incorporating breadth across the whole curriculum
- increasing depth within the subject
- accelerating the pace of learning
- promoting independence in thinking and learning
- providing opportunities for autonomous learning
- encouraging high expectations in both educators and children
- creating an appropriate, challenging and supportive environment where all children can achieve their full potential.

The features of *Enriching Maths*

Pupil activity booklets (Issues)

- Each of the 36 issues in *Enriching Maths 6* consists of a four-page A5 pupil activity booklet (to be printed double sided onto one sheet of A4 paper).
- The 36 issues cover the different attainment targets, strands and topics of the primary mathematics curriculum (see pages 15 to 22).
- The issues have been designed to resemble a newspaper, with each of the issues consisting of between four and twelve different activities, all related to the same mathematical topic.
- The terms 'Issue' and 'Volume' have been used rather than 'Unit' and 'Year group' because they are in keeping with the newspaper theme, and means that an issue can be used in whichever year group needed, rather than being confined to one particular year group.

Types of activities

- All of the activities in the *Enriching Maths* series are designed to enhance children's use and application of mathematics. There are four different types of 'using and applying' activities in the series:

  What's the Problem? The Puzzler

  Looking for Patterns Let's Investigate

- Alongside developing children's problem-solving skills, the series also provides activities with cross-curricular links to other subjects in the primary curriculum. The following shows the *Enriching Maths* features and its corresponding primary curriculum subject.

Curriculum subject	***Enriching Maths* feature**
English	The Language of Maths
Science	Focus on Science
ICT	Technology Today
Geography	Around the World
History	In the Past
	Famous Mathematicians
Art and Music	The Arts Roundup
Design and Technology	Construct
Physical Education	Sports Update

- As well as the features mentioned above, other regular features in *Enriching Maths* include:

  Money Matters At Home (home-school link activities)

- A chart showing the link between the issues, the *Enriching Maths* features and cross-curricular links can be found on pages 23 and 24.
- Please note the following symbols that occur beside an activity when appropriate.

  Denotes that children are likely to need access to a computer.

  Denotes that children are likely to need access to a computer with internet access.

- Enriching Maths Uncovered (EMU) is a recurring feature of the series. In each issue there is an emu holding a mathematical word or symbol. Children locate the emu and write about the meaning of the word or symbol.

Teacher's notes

Each of the 36 issues includes a set of teacher's notes, including answers.

Issue number

Prerequisites for learning

Lists the prerequisites for learning that children need to have acquired prior to this issue.

Lists the associated knowledge and skills that contribute to understanding the issue topic.

Resources

To aid preparation, the resources needed for the issue are listed.

Extensions

Where appropriate, offers suggestions for extending children's understanding if you feel they are developing a good understanding of the main mathematical ideas.

Simplifications

Where appropriate, offers suggestions for supporting children who may be experiencing difficulties understanding the main mathematical ideas.

Assessment for learning

Each issue includes a list of questions specifically designed to assist in assessing pupils' understanding of the issue topic.

Answers

These are provided where appropriate.

Mathematics topic

Teaching Support

Provides teaching points for each of the activities in the issue. These may be helpful when introducing the issue to the children, or when children experience difficulty whilst working on a particular activity.

Almost all of the activities in *Enriching Maths* can be undertaken either individually or in pairs (or sometimes in small groups). Where an activity is particularly suitable for pairs to work on, this is denoted by 👥.

When children are likely to need access to a computer, this is denoted by 💻.

When children are likely to need access to a computer with internet access, this is denoted by (www).

Issue 5
Percentages

Issue 5 Percentages

Prerequisites for learning

- Understand percentage as the number of parts in every 100
- Express tenths and hundredths as percentages
- Express one quantity as a percentage of another
- Recognise approximate proportions of a whole and use percentages to describe and compare them

Resources pencil and paper; RCM 2: My notes (optional); RCM 3: Pupil self assessment booklet (optional); ruler; pair of compasses; protractor; newspapers, magazines and catalogues; data-handling software; calculator (optional); computer with internet access

Teaching support

Page 1
Let's Investigate

- Discuss with the children all the different regular activities they do in a weekday. Encourage the children to organise all the activities into six to ten different categories. This will make it easier for the children to draw their pie chart.
- It is advised that children create their pie chart using ICT.
- Children draw their pie chart using a pair of compasses, a protractor and a ruler.

The Puzzler

- Ensure children are familiar with magic squares.

Ask the children to create a 4 × 4 magic percent square.

Focus on Science

- Children will need to use the internet for this activity.

Page 2
The Language of Maths

- Briefly introduce the children to the terms 'deposit', 'down-payment' and 'balance'. Ensure that they are secure in their understanding of these terms before setting them to work on the activity.

117

Issue 5
Percentages

Page 4 continued
Technology Today

- To be able to answer this problem, children need to be able to express successfully one quantity as a percentage of another.
- Work through one or more examples with the children. If appropriate, provide the children with a calculator.

e.g. 58 out of 80.

$\frac{58}{8\not{0}} \times \frac{10\not{0}}{1} = \frac{580}{8} = 72{\cdot}5\%$

AfL

- What did you find out? What does it mean? How did you go about this?
- How did you go about working out the percentage? How would you do this on a calculator?
- What calculation did you do? What does the answer tell you?
- Approximately what percentage of the pie chart is this sector? Why do you think it is that percent?

Answers

Page 1
Let's Investigate Results of the investigation will vary.

The Puzzler

60%	10%	80%
70%	50%	30%
20%	90%	40%

The magic percent is 150%. Other solutions are possible.

Focus on Science A humidity meter measures the amount of moisture in the air. RH% refers to the percentage of relative humidity in the air. Relative humidity is the amount of water vapour in the air expressed as a percentage of the maximum amount of water vapour that can exist in the air at that temperature.

Page 2
The Language of Maths Results of the investigation will vary.

Let's Investigate Results of the investigation will vary.

119

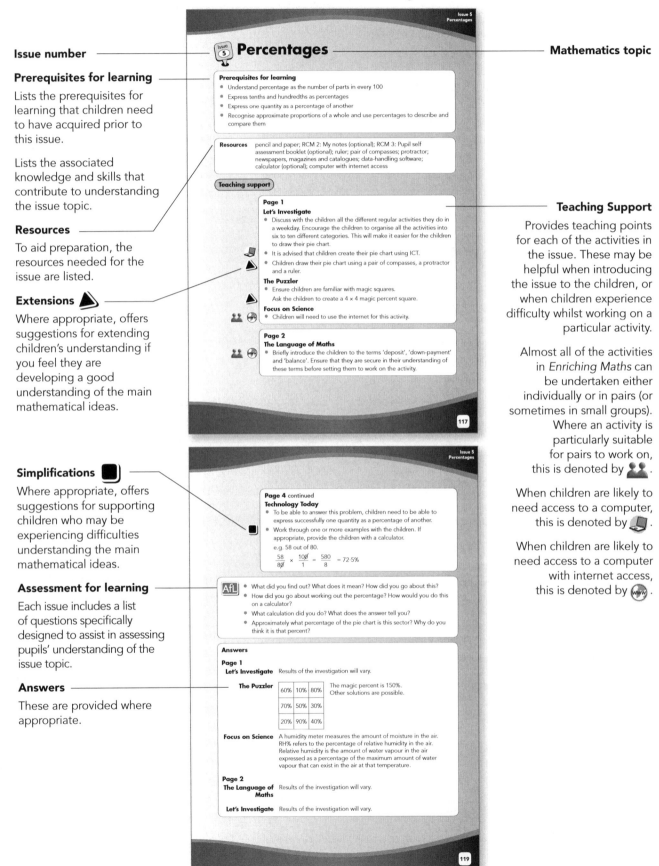

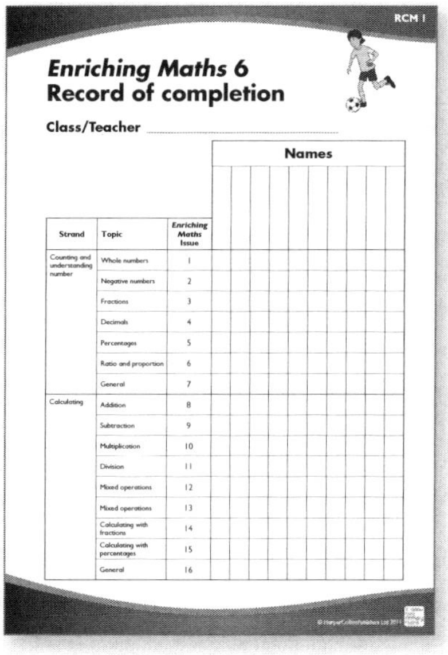
RCM 1

Enriching Maths 6
Record of completion

Class/Teacher ....

Strand	Topic	*Enriching Maths* Issue	Names									
Counting and understanding number	Whole numbers	1										
	Negative numbers	2										
	Fractions	3										
	Decimals	4										
	Percentages	5										
	Ratio and proportion	6										
	General	7										
Calculating	Addition	8										
	Subtraction	9										
	Multiplication	10										
	Division	11										
	Mixed operations	12										
	Mixed operations	13										
	Calculating with fractions	14										
	Calculating with percentages	15										
	General	16										

© HarperCollinsPublishers Ltd 2011

Record of completion

To assist in keeping a record of which issues children have completed.

Once a child has completed an issue you could either put a tick or write the date in the corresponding box.

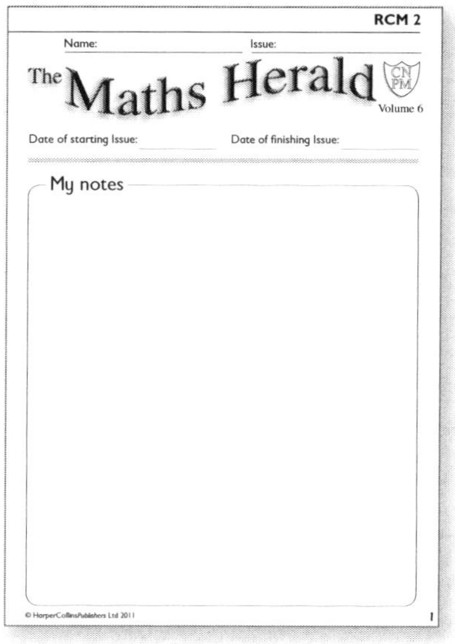
RCM 2

Name: Issue:

The Maths Herald

Volume 6

Date of starting Issue: Date of finishing Issue:

My notes

© HarperCollinsPublishers Ltd 2011

1

My notes

The pupil activity booklets have been designed to resemble a newspaper. This means that there is insufficient space in the booklets for children to show their working and answers.

You may decide to simply provide children with pencil and paper to record their work. Alternatively, you could provide them with a copy of the A5 booklet: 'My notes' (to be printed double sided onto one sheet of A4 paper). This can then be kept, together with the child's copy of the issue and, if appropriate, their 'pupil self assessment sheet'.

Whichever method you choose for the children to record their working and answers, i.e. on sheets of paper, using a 'My notes' booklet, in an exercise book, or any other method, children need to be clear and systematic in their recording. For ease of marking and discussion of their work at a later stage, it is recommended that you instruct the children to write the issue number and *Enriching Maths* feature, for each activity, clearly beside their working and answer.

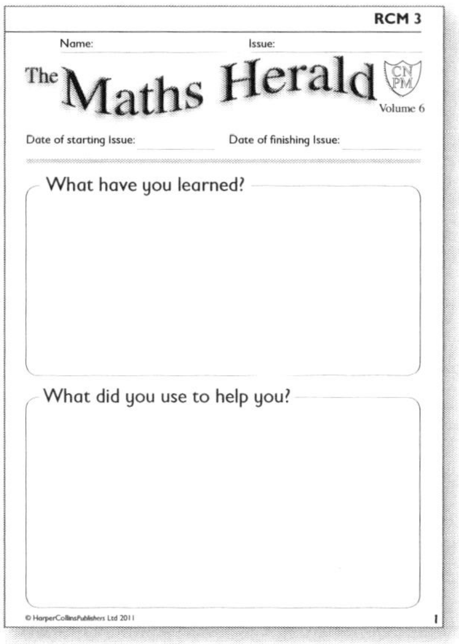
RCM 3

Name: Issue:

The Maths Herald

Volume 6

Date of starting Issue: Date of finishing Issue:

What have you learned?

What did you use to help you?

© HarperCollinsPublishers Ltd 2011

1

Pupil self assessment booklet

Each Resource Pack in the *Enriching Maths* series includes an age-appropriate pupil self assessment A5 booklet (to be printed double sided onto one sheet of A4 paper).

This booklet is a generic sheet that can be used for any, or all, of the 36 issues in the Resource Pack.

The booklet is designed to provide children with an opportunity to undertake some form of self assessment once they have completed the issue.

After the children have completed the booklet, discuss with them what they have written.

This can then be kept, together with the child's copy of the issue and their working out and answers, including, if appropriate, 'My notes'.

Other resource copymasters (RCMs)

For some of the activities, children are required to use a resource copymaster (RCM).

These are included both in the back of this Resource Pack and on the CD-ROM.

A possible *Enriching Maths* teaching and learning sequence

As the diagram on the right illustrates, the process of learning about mathematics can be thought of as the interrelationship between knowledge, understanding and application.

A suggested teaching sequence for working with children based on this model and using the activities in *Enriching Maths* is given below.

A complete sequence may occur during a particular lesson if the activity given is designed to be completed during the course of the lesson. Alternatively, the teaching and learning sequence may extend for a longer period of time if the activities are to be completed over the course of several lessons, a week or during a particular unit of work.

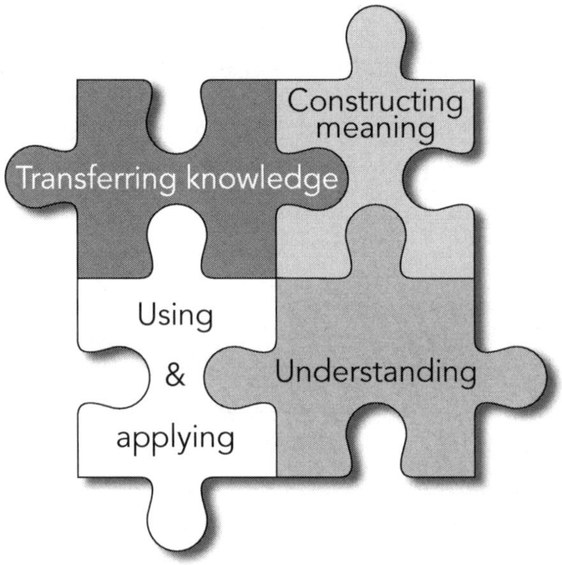

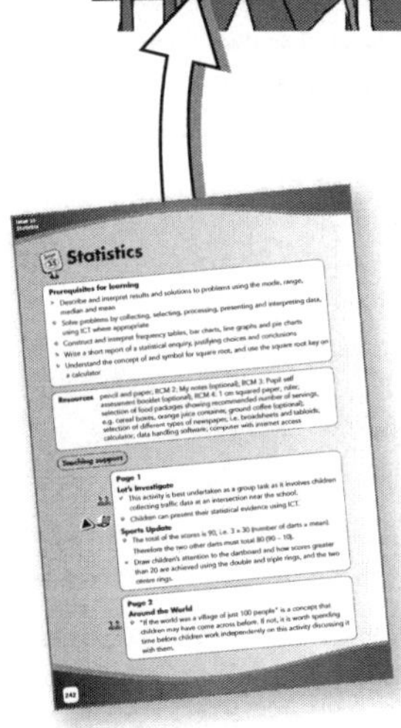

Briefing

The teacher:

- introduces the topic
- checks prerequisites for learning
- introduces the activity
- checks for understanding
- clarifies any misconceptions
- ensures there is easy access to any necessary resources.

Working

- Children work individually, in pairs, or if appropriate, in groups.
- Teacher acts only as a 'guide-on-the-side'.

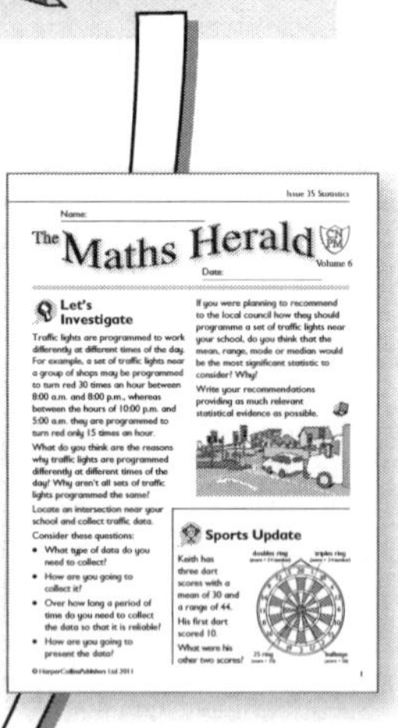

De-briefing

The child / children:

- reports back to others
- reflects on their learning
- identifies the 'next step'.

The teacher evaluates learning.

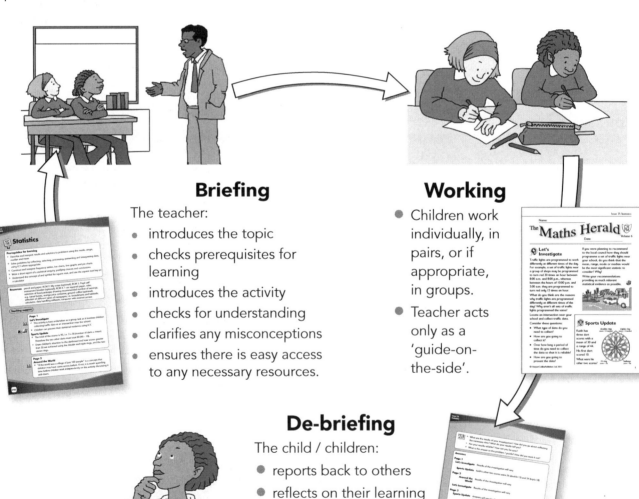

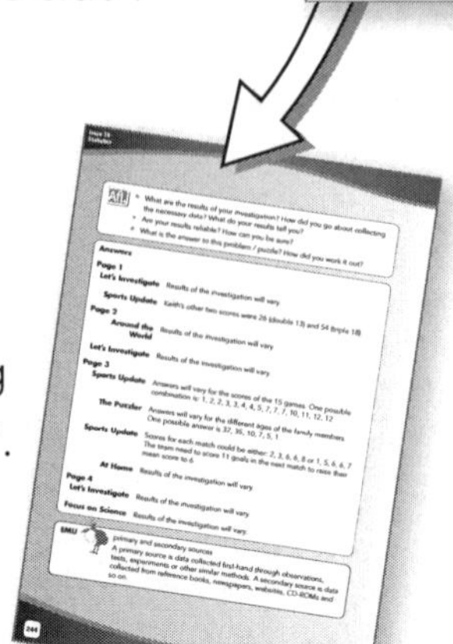

Enriching Maths 6 and Assessing Pupils' Progress (APP)

Assessing Pupils' Progress (APP) is a structured approach to periodically assessing mathematics so teachers can:

- track pupils' progress
- use diagnostic information about pupils' strengths and weaknesses.

Using APP materials, teachers can make National Curriculum (NC) level judgements for each of the following Mathematics Attainment Targets (ATs):

- using and applying mathematics
- number and algebra
- shape, space and measures
- handling data.

APP identifies particular Assessment Focuses (AFs) which are based on the National Curriculum programmes of study and level descriptions.

Using AFs helps teachers to:

- see how pupils' work on a small number of teaching objectives can contribute to the bigger picture of their progress and attainment
- give more precise feedback to pupils
- refine learning targets for individual children and groups within the class
- identify gaps in teaching and learning and adjust planning accordingly
- plan next steps based on the diagnostic information that emerges.

Overall, the information gained from the APP approach:

- provides diagnostic information on pupils' strengths and weaknesses
- enables forward planning based on group and individual pupil needs
- makes the most of pupils' learning experiences across the whole curriculum.

Part of the *Collins NEW Primary Maths* series is an *Assessment Pack* for each year group.
Each *CNPM Assessment Pack* consists of:

- Adult Directed Tasks
- Pupil Self Assessments
- Tests or Individual Assessment Sheets.

All three of these components can assist teachers when making periodic teacher assessment judgements using the APP approach.

The Adult Directed Tasks from the *CNPM Assessment Packs* can also be used as a diagnostic assessment tool to assist with identifying individual pupils' strengths and weaknesses, and when making the decision to provide extension work to individuals or groups of children using *Enriching Maths*.

The following chart shows the links between the 2006 Primary *Framework* strands, the NC Attainment Targets, the APP AFs for mathematics and the issues within *Enriching Maths 6*. This chart, along with the NC referencing charts on the following pages, will help formalise your assessments of pupils' mathematics into level judgements.

2006 Primary *Framework* Strands	**National Curriculum (NC) Attainment Targets**	**Assessing Pupil's Progress (APP) Assessment Focuses (AFs) for Mathematics**	***Enriching Maths 6***
Using and applying mathematics ➜	Ma1 Using and applying mathematics ➜	Problem solving ➜ Communicating ➜ Reasoning ➜	*Incorporated within each issue*
Counting and understanding number ➜	Ma2 Number and algebra ➜	Numbers and the number system ➜	Issue 1: Whole numbers Issue 2: Negative numbers Issue 7: Counting and understanding number (General)
		Fractions, decimals, percentages and ratio ➜	Issue 3: Fractions Issue 4: Decimals Issue 5: Percentages Issue 6: Ratio and proportion Issue 7: Counting and understanding number (General) Issue 14: Calculating with fractions Issue 15: Calculating with percentages
Knowing and using number facts ➜		Operations and the relationships between them ➜	Issue 8: Addition Issue 9: Subtraction Issue 10: Multiplication Issue 11: Division Issues 12 and 13: Mixed operations Issue 14: Calculating with fractions Issue 15: Calculating with percentages Issue 16: Calculating (General)
		Mental methods ➜	
Calculating ➜		Solving numerical problems ➜	
		Written and calculator methods ➜	
Understanding shape ➜	Ma3 Shape, space and measures ➜	Shape ➜	Issue 17: 2-D shapes Issue 18: 3-D solids Issue 19: Reflective symmetry Issue 20: Rotational symmetry Issue 21: Translations Issue 24: Understanding shape (General)
		Position and movement ➜	Issue 22: Position and direction Issue 23: Movement and angle Issue 24: Understanding shape (General)
Measuring ➜		Measures ➜	Issue 25: Length and distance Issue 26: Mass and weight Issue 27: Volume and capacity Issue 28: Time Issue 29: Temperature Issue 30: Area Issue 31: Perimeter Issue 32: Measuring (General)
Handling data ➜	Ma4 Handling data ➜	Processing and representing data ➜ Interpreting data ➜	Issue 33: Organising and interpreting data Issue 34: Probability Issue 35: Statistics Issue 36: Handling data (General)

Links to the Mathematics National Curriculum (2000) Attainment Targets and Levels, and the Primary National Strategy (2006) *Framework* objectives and strands for Year 6

	Enriching Maths Issue																																			
National Curriculum Attainment Target: Ma1 – Using and applying mathematics **Primary National Strategy Strand:** Using and applying mathematics	1	2	3	4	5	6	7	8	9	10	11	12	13	14	15	16	17	18	19	20	21	22	23	24	25	26	27	28	29	30	31	32	33	34	35	36
• Solve multi-step problems, and problems involving fractions, decimals and percentages; choose and use appropriate calculation strategies at each stage, including calculator use (NC Level 4)	●	●	●	●	●	●	●	●	●	●	●	●	●	●	●	●	●	●				●	●	●	●	●		●	●	●	●	●	●	●	●	●
• Tabulate systematically the information in a problem or puzzle; identify and record the steps or calculations needed to solve it, using symbols where appropriate; interpret solutions in the original context and check their accuracy (NC Level 4)	●	●	●	●	●	●	●	●	●	●	●	●	●					●				●	●	●	●	●	●	●	●	●	●	●	●	●	●	●
• Suggest, plan and develop lines of enquiry; collect, organise and represent information, interpret results and review methods; identify and answer related questions (NC Level 4)		●		●					●		●	●	●	●	●	●	●		●	●	●	●			●	●	●		●		●	●	●	●	●	●
• Represent and interpret sequences, patterns and relationships involving numbers and shapes; suggest and test hypotheses; construct and use simple expressions and formulae in words then symbols, e.g. the cost of c pens at 15 pence each is $15c$ pence (NC Level 4)	●	●	●				●	●	●	●	●	●	●				●	●	●	●	●	●	●	●	●	●	●	●	●	●	●	●			●	●
• Explain reasoning and conclusions, using words, symbols or diagrams as appropriate (NC Level 4)	●	●	●	●	●	●	●	●	●	●	●	●	●	●	●	●	●	●	●	●	●	●	●	●	●	●	●	●	●	●	●	●	●	●	●	●

National Curriculum Attainment Target: Ma2 – Number and algebra **Primary National Strategy Strand:** Counting and understanding number	*Enriching Maths* Issue 1	2	3	4	5	6	7	8	9	10	11	12	13	14	15	16	17	18	19	20	21	22	23	24	25	26	27	28	29	30	31	32	33	34	35	36
• Find the difference between a positive and a negative integer, or two negative integers, in context (NC Level 5)		●																				●														
• Use decimal notation for tenths, hundredths and thousandths; partition, round and order decimals with up to three places, and position them on the number line (NC Level 4)				●																																
• Express a larger whole number as a fraction of a smaller one, e.g. recognise that 8 slices of a 5-slice pizza represents $\frac{8}{5}$ or $1\frac{3}{5}$ pizzas; simplify fractions by cancelling common factors; order a set of fractions by converting them to fractions with a common denominator (NC Level 5)																																		●		
• **Express one quantity as a percentage of another, e.g. express £400 as a percentage of £1000; find equivalent percentages, decimals and fractions (NC Level 4)**					●																				●								●	●		●
• Solve simple problems involving direct proportion by scaling quantities up or down (NC Level 4)						●																														

National Curriculum Attainment Target: Ma2 – Number and algebra **Primary National Strategy Strand:** Knowing and using number facts	1	2	3	4	5	6	7	8	9	10	11	12	13	14	15	16	17	18	19	20	21	22	23	24	25	26	27	28	29	30	31	32	33	34	35	36
• **Use knowledge of place value and multiplication facts to 10 × 10 to derive related multiplication and division facts involving decimals, e.g. 0·8 × 7, 4·8 ÷ 6 (NC Level 4)**				●						●	●	●	●			●														●					●	
• Use knowledge of multiplication facts to derive quickly squares of numbers to 12 × 12 and the corresponding squares of multiples of 10 (NC Level 4)												●					●																			
• Recognise that prime numbers have only two factors and identify prime numbers less than 100; find the prime factors of two-digit numbers (NC Level 5)																																				
• Use approximations, inverse operations and tests of divisibility to estimate and check results (NC Level 5)								●			●				●																					

NOTE: Key objectives are in **bold**.

National Curriculum Attainment Target: Ma2 – Number and algebra **Primary National Strategy Strand:** Calculating	*Enriching Maths* **Issue** 1	2	3	4	5	6	7	8	9	10	11	12	13	14	15	16	17	18	19	20	21	22	23	24	25	26	27	28	29	30	31	32	33	34	35	36
• Calculate mentally with integers and decimals: U·t ± U·t, TU × U, TU ÷ U, U·t × U, U·t ÷ U (NC Level 4)							●	●	●	●	●	●	●			●	●								●	●	●			●	●				●	
• **Use efficient written methods to add and subtract integers and decimals, to multiply and divide integers and decimals by a one-digit integer, and to multiply two- and three-digit integers by a two-digit integer (NC Level 5)**				●					●	●	●	●	●			●									●	●	●			●	●					
• Relate fractions to multiplication and division, e.g. $6 \div 2 = \frac{1}{2}$ of $6 = 6 \times \frac{1}{2}$; express a quotient as a fraction or decimal, e.g. $67 \div 5 = 13{\cdot}4$ or $13\frac{2}{5}$; find fractions and percentages of whole-number quantities, e.g. $\frac{5}{8}$ of 96, 65% of £260 (NC Level 5)			●		●								●	●	●	●																				
• Use a calculator to solve problems involving multi-step calculations (NC Level 4)		●							●				●	●	●	●									●	●										
National Curriculum Attainment Target: Ma3 – Shape, space and measures **Primary National Strategy Strand:** Understanding shape																																				
• Describe, identify and visualise parallel and perpendicular edges or faces and use these properties to classify 2-D shapes and 3-D solids (NC Level 4)																		●						●												
• Make and draw shapes with increasing accuracy and apply knowledge of their properties (NC Level 4)																		●	●	●	●		●	●												
• **Visualise and draw on grids of different types where a shape will be after reflection, after translations, or after rotation through 90° or 180° about its centre or one of its vertices (NC Level 5)**																			●	●	●			●												
• Use coordinates in the first quadrant to draw, locate and complete shapes that meet given properties (NC Level 4)																																				
• Estimate angles, and use a protractor to measure and draw them, on their own and in shapes; calculate angles in a triangle or around a point (NC Level 5)																							●													

NOTE: Key objectives are in **bold**.

	Enriching Maths Issue																																			
National Curriculum Attainment Target: Ma3 – Shape, space and measures **Primary National Strategy Strand:** Measuring	1	2	3	4	5	6	7	8	9	10	11	12	13	14	15	16	17	18	19	20	21	22	23	24	25	26	27	28	29	30	31	32	33	34	35	36
• **Select and use standard metric units of measure and convert between units using decimals to two places, e.g. change 2·75 litres to 2750 ml, or vice versa (NC Level 4)**				●																					●	●			●			●				
• Read and interpret scales on a range of measuring instruments, recognising that the measurement made is approximate and recording results to a required degree of accuracy; compare readings on different scales, e.g. when using different instruments (NC Level 4)																									●	●			●			●				
• Calculate the perimeter and area of rectilinear shapes; estimate the area of an irregular shape by counting squares (NC Level 4)																														●	●	●				

National Curriculum Attainment Target: Ma4 – Handling data **Primary National Strategy Strand:** Handling data	1	2	3	4	5	6	7	8	9	10	11	12	13	14	15	16	17	18	19	20	21	22	23	24	25	26	27	28	29	30	31	32	33	34	35	36
• Describe and predict outcomes from data using the language of chance or likelihood (NC Level 4)																																		●		
• **Solve problems by collecting, selecting, processing, presenting and interpreting data, using ICT where appropriate; draw conclusions and identify further questions to ask (NC Level 5)**																							●			●			●				●		●	●
• Construct and interpret frequency tables, bar charts with grouped discrete data, and line graphs; interpret pie charts (NC Level 4)					●																								●				●		●	●
• Describe and interpret results and solutions to problems using the mode, range, median and mean (NC Level 5)																										●									●	●

NOTE: Key objectives are in **bold**.

Links to the Mathematics National Curriculum (2000) Attainment Targets and Levels, and the Primary National Strategy (2006) *Framework* objectives and strands for Year 6 Progression to Year 7

	Enriching Maths Issue																																			
National Curriculum Attainment Target: Ma1 – Using and applying mathematics **Primary National Strategy Strand:** Using and applying mathematics	1	2	3	4	5	6	7	8	9	10	11	12	13	14	15	16	17	18	19	20	21	22	23	24	25	26	27	28	29	30	31	32	33	34	35	36
• Solve problems by breaking down complex calculations into simpler steps; choose and use operations and calculation strategies appropriate to the numbers and context; try alternative approaches to overcome difficulties; present, interpret and compare solutions (NC Level 5)	●	●	●	●	●	●	●	●	●	●	●	●	●	●	●	●	●	●				●	●	●	●	●		●	●	●	●	●	●	●	●	●
• Represent information or unknown numbers in a problem, e.g. in a table, formula or equation; explain solutions in the context of the problem (NC Level 5)	●	●	●	●	●	●	●	●	●	●	●	●	●					●				●	●	●	●	●	●	●	●	●	●	●	●	●	●	●
• Develop and evaluate lines of enquiry; identify, collect, organise and analyse relevant information; decide how best to represent conclusions and what further questions to ask (NC Level 5)		●		●					●		●	●	●	●	●	●	●		●	●	●	●			●	●	●		●		●	●	●	●	●	●
• Generate sequences and describe the general term; use letters and symbols to represent unknown numbers or variables; represent simple relationships as graphs (NC Level 6)	●	●	●				●	●	●	●	●	●	●				●	●	●	●	●	●	●	●	●	●	●	●	●	●	●	●			●	●
• Explain and justify reasoning and conclusions, using notation, symbols and diagrams; find a counter-example to disprove a conjecture; use step-by-step deductions to solve problems involving shapes (NC Level 6)	●	●	●	●	●	●	●	●	●	●	●	●	●	●	●	●	●	●	●	●	●	●	●	●	●	●	●	●	●	●	●	●	●	●	●	●

	Enriching Maths Issue																																			
National Curriculum Attainment Target: Ma2 – Number and algebra **Primary National Strategy Strand:** Counting and understanding number	1	2	3	4	5	6	7	8	9	10	11	12	13	14	15	16	17	18	19	20	21	22	23	24	25	26	27	28	29	30	31	32	33	34	35	36
• Compare and order integers and decimals in different contexts (NC Level 6)				●																																
• Order a set of fractions by converting them to decimals (NC Level 6)																																				
• Recognise approximate proportions of a whole and use fractions and percentages to describe and compare them, e.g. when interpreting pie charts (NC Level 5)			●		●	●	●								●										●					●			●	●		●
• **Use ratio notation, reduce a ratio to its simplest form and divide a quantity into two parts in a given ratio; solve simple problems involving ratio and direct proportion, e.g. identify the quantities needed to make a fruit drink by mixing water and juice in a given ratio (NC Level 5)**						●										●																				
National Curriculum Attainment Target: Ma2 – Number and algebra **Primary National Strategy Strand:** Knowing and using number facts																																				
• Consolidate rapid recall of number facts, including multiplication facts to 10 × 10 and the associated division facts (NC Level 5)				●								●																								
• Recognise the square roots of perfect squares to 12 × 12 (NC Level 5)																●	●																			
• Recognise and use multiples, factors, divisors, common factors, highest common factors and lowest common multiples in simple cases (NC Level 5)	●		●								●			●		●																				
• **Make and justify estimates and approximations to calculations (NC Level 5)**							●				●				●	●										●										

NOTE: Key objectives are in **bold**.

National Curriculum Attainment Target:	*Enriching Maths* Issue																																			
National Curriculum Attainment Target: Ma2 – Number and algebra **Primary National Strategy Strand:** Calculating	1	2	3	4	5	6	7	8	9	10	11	12	13	14	15	16	17	18	19	20	21	22	23	24	25	26	27	28	29	30	31	32	33	34	35	36
• Understand how the commutative, associative and distributive laws, and the relationships between operations, including inverse operations, can be used to calculate more efficiently; use the order of operations, including brackets (NC Level 5)				●					●	●		●																		●						
• Consolidate and extend mental methods of calculation to include decimals, fractions and percentages (NC Level 5)			●	●	●								●	●	●	●																				
• Use standard column procedures to add and subtract integers and decimals, and to multiply two-digit and three-digit integers by a one-digit or two-digit integer; extend division to dividing three-digit integers by a two-digit integer (NC Level 5)									●	●	●	●	●			●									●	●	●			●	●					
• Calculate percentage increases or decreases and fractions of quantities and measurements (integer answers) (NC Level 5)			●		●									●	●																					
• **Use bracket keys and the memory of a calculator to carry out calculations with more than one step; use the square-root key (NC Level 5)**		●							●					●	●	●	●								●	●										
National Curriculum Attainment Target: Ma3 – Shape, space and measures **Primary National Strategy Strand:** Understanding shape																																				
• Use correctly the vocabulary, notation and labelling conventions for lines, angles and shapes (NC Level 5)																	●					●	●	●												
• Extend knowledge of properties of triangles and quadrilaterals and use these to visualise and solve problems, explaining reasoning with diagrams (NC Level 5)																	●					●								●						
• **Know the sum of angles on a straight line, in a triangle and at a point, and recognise vertically opposite angles (NC Level 5)**																																				
• Use all four quadrants to find coordinates of points determined by geometric information (NC Level 5)																					●	●														
• Identify all the symmetries of 2-D shapes; transform images using ICT (NC Level 5)																			●	●	●															
• Construct a triangle given two sides and the included angle (NC Level 5)																	●																			

NOTE: Key objectives are in **bold**.

	Enriching Maths Issue																																			
National Curriculum Attainment Target: Ma3 – Shape, space and measures **Primary National Strategy Strand:** Measuring	1	2	3	4	5	6	7	8	9	10	11	12	13	14	15	16	17	18	19	20	21	22	23	24	25	26	27	28	29	30	31	32	33	34	35	36
• Convert between related metric units using decimals to three places, e.g. convert 1375 mm to 1·375 m, or vice versa (NC Level 5)				●																					●	●			●			●				
• **Solve problems by measuring, estimating and calculating; measure and calculate using imperial units still in everyday use; know their approximate metric values (NC Level 5)**																									●	●	●	●	●			●				
• Calculate the area of right-angled triangles given the lengths of the two perpendicular sides, and the volume and surface area of cubes and cuboids (NC Level 6)																											●			●						

National Curriculum Attainment Target: Ma4 – Handling data **Primary National Strategy Strand:** Handling data																																				
• **Understand and use the probability scale from 0 to 1; find and justify probabilities based on equally likely outcomes in simple contexts (NC Level 5)**																																		●		
• Explore hypotheses by planning surveys or experiments to collect small sets of discrete or continuous data; select, process, present and interpret the data, using ICT where appropriate; identify ways to extend the survey or experiment (NC Level 6)																							●			●							●		●	●
• Construct, interpret and compare graphs and diagrams that represent data, e.g. compare proportions in two pie charts that represent different totals (NC Level 6)					●																		●			●			●				●		●	●
• Write a short report of a statistical enquiry and illustrate it with appropriate diagrams, graphs and charts, using ICT as appropriate; justify the choice of what is presented (NC Level 6)		●																					●			●			●						●	●

NOTE: Key objectives are in **bold**.

Cross-curricular links to the Primary National Curriculum (2000)

Strand	Topic	*Enriching Maths* Issue	Cross-curricular link and *Enriching Maths* feature													
			Mathematics				English	Science	ICT	Geography	History	Art and Music	Design and Technology	Physical Education	Links to money	Links with home
			What's the Problem?	Looking for Patterns	The Puzzler	Let's Investigate	The Language of Maths	Focus on Science	Technology Today	Around the World	In the Past / Famous Mathematicians	The Arts Roundup	Construct	Sports Update	Money Matters	At Home
Counting and understanding number	Whole numbers	1	●	●	●	●					●	●		●		
	Negative numbers	2		●		●		●	●	●						●
	Fractions	3	●	●	●	●					●	●				
	Decimals	4		●	●	●	●								●	●
	Percentages	5			●	●	●	●	●						●	
	Ratio and proportion	6	●		●	●	●							●		●
	General	7				●	●		●	●					●	
Calculating	Addition	8		●	●	●	●				●	●				
	Subtraction	9	●	●	●	●				●	●					
	Multiplication	10		●	●	●		●		●					●	
	Division	11		●	●	●		●		●						●
	Mixed operations	12	●	●	●	●								●		
	Mixed operations	13													●	
	Calculating with fractions	14			●	●				●	●				●	
	Calculating with percentages	15	●		●			●		●		●			●	
	General	16		●		●	●			●	●				●	

Strand	Topic	*Enriching Maths* Issue	Cross-curricular link and *Enriching Maths* feature													
			Mathematics				English	Science	ICT	Geography	History	Art and Music	Design and Technology	Physical Education	Links to money	Links with home
			What's the Problem?	Looking for Patterns	The Puzzler	Let's Investigate	The Language of Maths	Focus on Science	Technology Today	Around the World	In the Past / Famous Mathematicians	The Arts Roundup	Construct	Sports Update	Money Matters	At Home
Understanding shape	2-D shapes	17	●		●	●					●			●		
	3-D solids	18			●	●					●		●			
	Reflective symmetry	19		●	●					●	●	●	●	●		●
	Rotational symmetry	20		●		●				●		●	●			
	Translations	21		●	●	●					●	●	●			
	Position and direction	22			●	●				●	●		●			
	Movement and angle	23			●	●		●	●	●			●	●		●
	General	24	●		●	●	●		●	●	●	●	●			
Measuring	Length and distance	25				●	●	●		●			●	●	●	●
	Mass and weight	26	●	●		●	●	●		●						●
	Volume and capacity	27				●	●	●		●	●			●		●
	Time	28		●	●	●		●						●		
	Temperature	29		●		●	●	●		●	●					
	Area	30	●	●	●	●					●			●		●
	Perimeter	31	●	●		●	●			●			●			
	General	32				●		●		●	●					
Handling data	Organising and interpreting data	33		●	●	●	●	●			●	●				
	Probability	34			●	●	●						●	●	●	
	Statistics	35			●	●		●		●				●		●
	General	36					●	●		●			●	●		

Resources used in *Enriching Maths 6*

A fundamental skill of mathematics is knowing what resources to use and when it is appropriate to use them. It is for this reason that many of the activities in *Enriching Maths* give no indication to the children as to which resources to use. Although the teacher's notes that accompany each activity include a list of resources, children should be encouraged to work out for themselves what they will need to use to successfully complete an activity.

It is assumed that for each activity children will have ready access to pencil and paper, and any other resources that are specifically mentioned in an activity, for example, computers or other RCMs. However, all other equipment should be left for the children to locate and use as and when they see is appropriate.

A list of all the resources children are likely to need in *Enriching Maths 6* is given below.

	***Enriching Maths* Issue**																
Resource	**1**	**2**	**3**	**4**	**5**	**6**	**7**	**8**	**9**	**10**	**11**	**12**	**13**	**14**	**15**	**16**	**17**
pencil and paper	●	●	●	●	●	●	●	●	●	●	●	●	●	●	●	●	●
RCMs	2,3, 5	2,3, 4	2,3	2,3, 4	2,3	2,3	2,3	2,3	2,3	2,3	2,3	2,3	2,3	2,3	2,3	2,3	2,3, 5
computer		●															
computer with internet access	●			●	●	●	●				●						
data handling software					●												
ruler		●		●	●			●		●		●					●
calculator		●		●	●			●	●	●	●	●	●	●	●	●	●
range of different theatre plans	●																
bowl of ice and thermometer		●															
empty frozen food packages		●															
fraction wall			●														
selection of newspapers / magazines / catalogues				●	●												
material for making a poster, e.g. card, felt-tip pens …				●		●											
cheques from a range of different banks				●													
pair of compasses					●												
protractor					●												
recipe books						●											
dominoes								●									
map of the local area and a contrasting area															●		
set square																	●
matchsticks																	●
at least six circular objects, all different sizes																	●
tape measure																	●

	***Enriching Maths* Issue**																		
Resource	**18**	**19**	**20**	**21**	**22**	**23**	**24**	**25**	**26**	**27**	**28**	**29**	**30**	**31**	**32**	**33**	**34**	**35**	**36**
pencil and paper	●	●	●	●	●	●	●	●	●	●	●	●	●	●	●	●	●	●	●
RCMs	2,3	2,3, 5	2,3, 4, 7–9	2,3, 5,7, 8	2,3, 4,5, 7	2,3, 4,5, 7, 8–10	2,3, 4–10	2,3, 4	2,3, 4	2,3	2,3	2,3	2,3, 7	2,3, 4,7	2,3, 4	2,3, 4	2,3	2,3, 4	2,3, 4
computer			●																
computer with internet access		●		●	●	●	●	●	●	●		●		●	●	●		●	●
data handling software																●		●	●

	***Enriching Maths* Issue**																		
Resource	**18**	**19**	**20**	**21**	**22**	**23**	**24**	**25**	**26**	**27**	**28**	**29**	**30**	**31**	**32**	**33**	**34**	**35**	**36**
ruler	●	●	●	●	●	●	●	●	●				●	●	●	●		●	●
calculator								●	●	●	●	●	●		●	●		●	●
pair of compasses		●	●			●	●	●								●			●
protractor						●										●			●
scissors	●		●	●									●						
collection of different polyhedrons	●																		
straws and joiners and / or commercially produced skeletal construction kit	●																		
six paper squares (per child), ideally each a different colour	●																		
interlocking cubes	●																		
cardboard	●			●															
1–6 dice	●																		
postcards, travel brochures, books, magazines and wallpaper samples showing examples of reflective symmetry		●																	
camera		●	●																
coloured pencils	●	●	●	●			●												
sticky tape				●															
geoboard and elastic bands				●									●	●					
map of the local area					●														
floor robot, magnetic / orienteering compass; coin, 1–6 dice, 1–8 digit cards; random number generator, e.g. Number Spinners Interactive Teaching Program (ITP) or similar; torch						●													
chessboard						●	●												
tape measure						●		●			●								●
trundle wheel								●						●					
selection of maps showing different scales								●											
material for making a poster. e.g. card, felt-tip pens …					●				●	●									
selection of food packages									●									●	
collection of cylinders; 100 ml can; sand or rice; measuring cylinder with scale in cubic centimetres; water; collection of small solid objects										●									
Telling Time Interactive Teaching Program (ITP) or similar; digital clock; mirror											●								
stopwatch											●								●
thermometer												●							
newspapers													●			●	●	●	●
range of measuring equipment													●						
world atlas or globe														●	●				
road atlas															●				
matchsticks														●					
string															●				
dice; spinners; material for making board games; selection of different types of books																	●		
electricity bill																			●

Sports Update

The final score of a football match was 4 – 3.

How many different possible half-time scores could there have been?

What are they?

If you know the final score of a football match, what is the rule for calculating how many possible half-time scores there could have been?

The Puzzler

Find a three-digit number, so that when the digits of the number are added together the total is equal to the product of the digits.

Can you find more than one three-digit number?

Find a three-digit number, so that when the digits of the number are added together the total is one-fifth of the product of the digits.

Can you find more than one three-digit number?

In the Past

When writing numbers we use the Hindu-Arabic numeral system.

Roman numerals are an example of a different number system.

I	II	III	IV	V	VI	VII	VIII	IX	X	L	C	D	M
1	2	3	4	5	6	7	8	9	10	50	100	500	1000

28 = XXVIII   634 = DCXXXIV   2449 = MMCDXLIX

Investigate different number systems, both past and present.

Write a set of numerals for each system to demonstrate how the number system works.

Name:

The Maths Herald

Volume 6

Date:

Looking for Patterns

Which of these sequences will be the first to reach 1000 or more?

A = 1, 4, 9, 16, 25, …

B = 1, 3, 6, 10, 15, …

C = 0, 1, 1, 2, 3, …

D = 1, 2, 4, 8, 16, …

How did you work it out?

Which term in each sequence is the first to reach 1000 or more?

What is the rule or name of each of these sequences?

The Puzzler

Consecutive numbers are numbers that follow each other, e.g. 1, 2 and 3, or 27, 28 and 29.

The proper factors of a number are all its factors except 1 and itself.

75 and 76 are a pair of consecutive numbers that have only four proper factors each. There are two other pairs of consecutive numbers less than 100 that also have only four proper factors each. What are they?

Let's Investigate

Which prime numbers less than 100 are also prime numbers when their digits are reversed?

Let's Investigate

3 and 5 are prime numbers. They are also consecutive odd numbers.

What other pairs of consecutive odd numbers between 100 and 200 are both prime numbers?

Looking for Patterns

Look at these rows of greenhouses.

In the first row there is only 1 greenhouse – with a total of 5 sides.

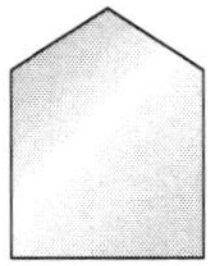

In the second row there are 2 greenhouses – with a total of 9 sides.

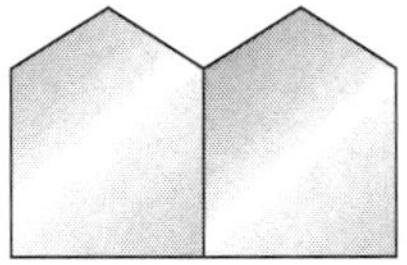

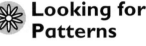

In the third row there are 3 greenhouses – with a total of 13 sides.

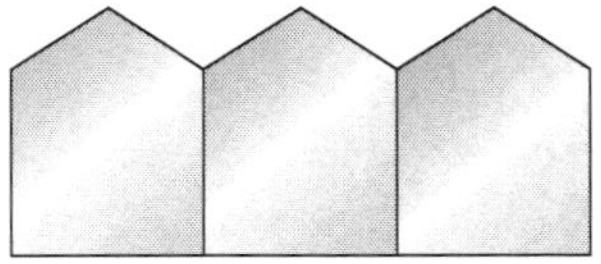

How many sides would there be for a row of 10 greenhouses?

Write a formula for finding the number of sides for a row of any number of greenhouses.

Looking for Patterns

What are the next two numbers in this sequence?

6, 24, 60, 120, 210, …

Explain in words the rule for the sequence.

Write a formula for finding any number in the sequence.

Looking for Patterns

Look at the units and thousands digits in each of these four-digit numbers. What do you notice?

2112
4554
6666

What about the tens and hundreds digits?

Each of these numbers is also divisible by 66.

How many other four-digit numbers are multiples of 66 and have the same units / thousands and tens / hundreds patterns?

The Puzzler

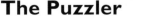

Arrange all the digits 1 to 9 to make four square numbers, using each of the digits once.

How many different ways can you do it?

What about arranging all nine digits to make three square numbers?

The Arts Roundup

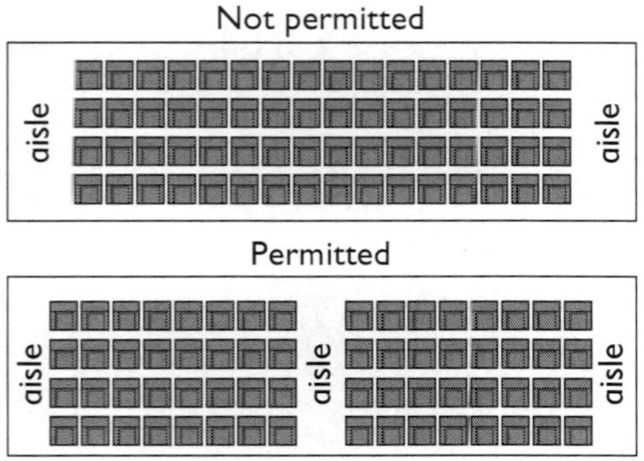

An architectural firm has been asked to design a new performing arts complex consisting of two different auditoriums.

The requirements are as follows:

- The Theatre must have a seating capacity of 840 people and must all be on one level.
- The Concert Hall must have a seating capacity of 1260 people and must be spread over two levels – the stalls and the dress circle.
- All seats must have excellent views of the stages.
- For health and safety reasons, no row can contain more than ten seats without an aisle. See the example above.

Design a seating layout for the Theatre and Concert Hall. As these are architectural designs they need to be as detailed as possible.

Looking for Patterns

The number 84 has 12 factors (including 1 and itself). These are:

1, 2, 3, 4, 6, 7, 12, 14, 21, 28, 42, 84

Which other two-digit numbers have exactly 12 factors?

What's the Problem?

1, 2, 3, 4, 6, 7, 8, 9, 12, 14, 16, 18, 21, 24, 28, 36, 48, 56, 63, 72, 84, 112, 126, 144, 168, 252, 336, 504, 1008

The numbers above are all factors of 1008.

Are all the factors included in this list or are there any missing? Can you explain a quick way of finding out?

You should be able to use your method to check that you have all the factors for any number.

Around the World

Inari is an area in northern Finland.

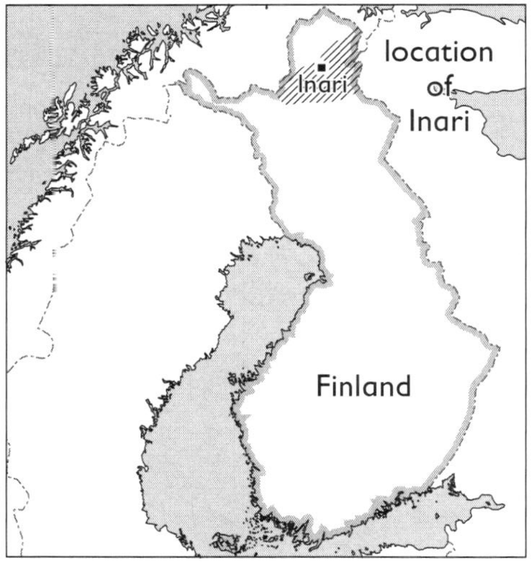

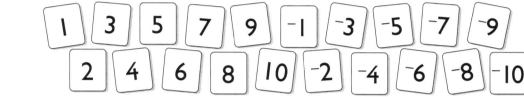

The line graph below shows the maximum and minimum average daily tempertaure in Inari.

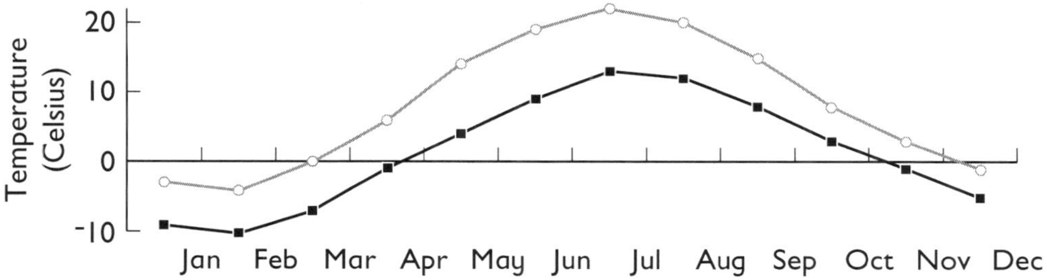

Write a report detailing the seasonal differences in temperature in Inari. Describe in your report the average temperature for each season and how this compares with the yearly average.

Looking for Patterns

Using only these numbers, write down all the pairs of numbers that have a difference of 0·2.

⁻0·3 | 0 | ⁻0·5 | 0·2 | ⁻0·1 | ⁻0·4 | 0·1 | ⁻0·2

Name:

The Maths Herald

Volume 6

Date:

Let's Investigate

1 | 3 | 5 | 7 | 9 | ⁻1 | ⁻3 | ⁻5 | ⁻7 | ⁻9

2 | 4 | 6 | 8 | 10 | ⁻2 | ⁻4 | ⁻6 | ⁻8 | ⁻10

Choose any three numbers. Using some or all of these numbers, investigate how close to zero you can get. If you're able to make zero, record your calculation on a number line.

For example,

Choosing the numbers ⁻2 ⁻5 7 can give ⁻5 + 7 + ⁻2

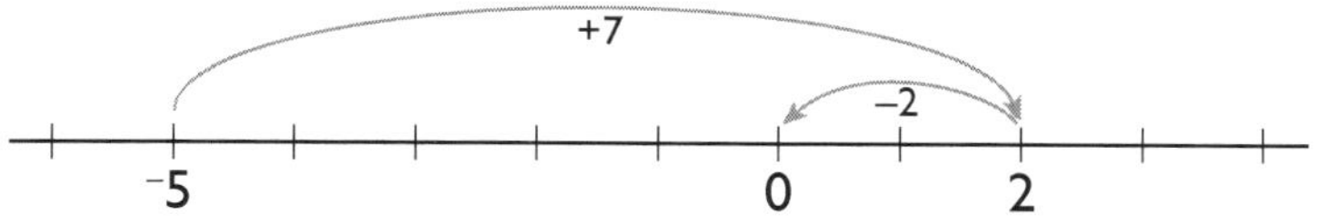

What about choosing four numbers?

Focus on Science

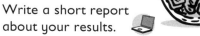

For this experiment you need a bowl of ice and a thermometer.

Measure and record the temperature of the bowl of ice.

After 15 minutes, once again measure and record the temperature of the ice.

Keep doing this every 15 minutes for 5 hours.

Record the results in a chart or graph.

Write a short report about your results.

Let's Investigate

Look at this equation:

$a + b = 12$

If *a* and *b* stand for either a positive or negative whole number, investigate possible values for *a* and *b*.

What about for these equations?

$a - b = 15$

$a + b = {}^{-}8$

$a - b = {}^{-}16$

Technology Today

Look at each of these calculations.

$7 + {}^{-}3$ $\quad {}^{-}4 + 7$ $\quad {}^{-}6 + {}^{-}9$

$10 - {}^{-}6$ $\quad {}^{-}12 - 5$ $\quad {}^{-}16 - {}^{-}14$

$8 + {}^{-}3 + 7 + {}^{-}9 + {}^{-}4$

${}^{-}7 + 4 - {}^{-}8 + 11$

${}^{-}10 - {}^{-}5 + 7 + {}^{-}9$

Design a poster that gives a set of instructions showing how to use a calculator to find sums and differences of combinations of positive and negative numbers. Be sure to provide examples.

At Home

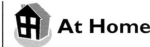

Investigate frozen foods at home or at the supermarket.

All frozen foods have a recommended temperature at which they should be kept frozen.

Is this temperature the same for all types of frozen goods, for example, vegetables, ice cream, meat and seafood?

Does the suggested recommended temperature vary depending on the recommended use by' date?

What else can you find out about frozen foods?

Around the World

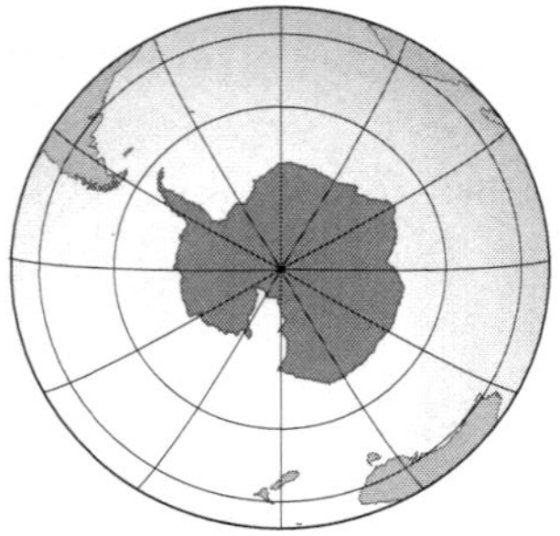

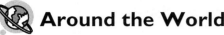

Antarctica is Earth's southernmost continent.
It is, on average, the coldest, driest and windiest continent.

This table shows the average minimum and record minimum temperatures in degrees Celsius on Stonington Island, Antarctica.

	J	F	M	A	M	J	J	A	S	O	N	D
Average minimum (°C)	-3	-4	-8	-10	-14	-17	-16	-19	-16	-13	-9	-3
Record minimum (°C)	-12	-11	-35	-27	-36	-37	-36	-37	-39	-29	-20	-13

Draw one line graph showing both the average minimum and record minimum temperatures on Stonington Island, Antarctica.

Write a report about the average minimum and record minimum temperatures on Stonington Island.

Looking for Patterns

Fill in the missing numbers in each of these sequences:

37, □, 13, 1, □, -23, □, □, -59, -□, -83

□, □, -25, □, -9, -1, □, 15, □

150, □, 10, □, □, -200, -270, □

□, -117, -80, □, -6, □, 68, □

What is the rule for each sequence?

Make up two number sequences of your own involving negative numbers.

Looking for Patterns

On Monday, Mrs Rollo took the weekly school assembly.

At the end of the assembly she told one more than half of all the children in the hall to walk quietly back to their classrooms.

Once these children had left the hall, she told one more than half of all the children that were remaining to go back to their class.

Once these children had left the hall, once again she told one more than half of all the remaining children to go back to their class.

She did this three more times.

At the end, there was only one child remaining in the hall.

How many children were in the hall at the start of the assembly?

What's the Problem?

Approximately, what fraction of your life so far, have you spent:

- asleep?
- eating?
- in school?

Choose another aspect of your life and work out approximately what fraction of your life so far, you have spent doing it.

Name:

The Maths Herald

Volume 6

Date:

Famous Mathematicians

Euclid was a Greek mathematician who lived from about 330 to 275 BC.

He discovered a method for finding the highest common factor (HCF). This is known as "Euclid's Algorithm".

Use Euclid's Algorithm to reduce these fractions to their simplest terms.

$\frac{162}{189}$ $\frac{68}{153}$ $\frac{65}{91}$ $\frac{38}{95}$ $\frac{72}{135}$ $\frac{424}{477}$

Euclid's Algorithm

1. Divide the larger number (dividend) by the smaller number (divisor).
2. If there is a remainder, divide this into the divisor.
3. Continue dividing the divisor by the remainder until the remainder is 0.
4. The final divisor is the HCF.

The Puzzler

Cut this pie into quarters, so that each piece contains two cherries and no cherry is cut.

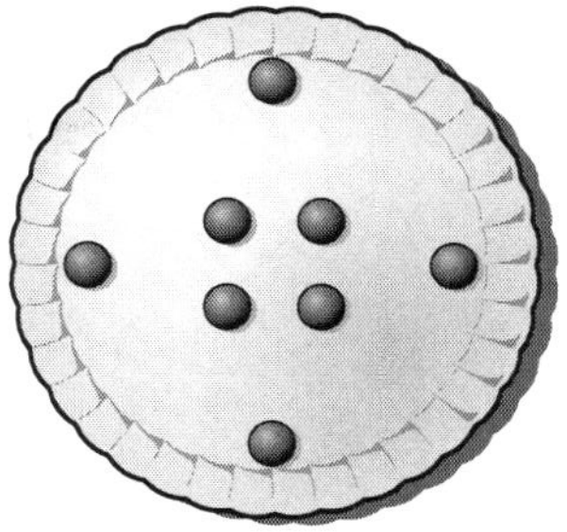

The Puzzler

Arrange all the digits 1 to 9 to make a fraction that is equivalent to $\frac{1}{3}$.

Looking for Patterns

Ordering a set of decimals is easy. But fractions aren't so easy.

A man called John Farey investigated sequences of proper fractions in order of size – they are called 'Farey Sequences'.

The first three Farey sequences (Fn) are:

$F_1 = \frac{0}{1}, \frac{1}{1}$

$F_2 = \frac{0}{1}, \frac{1}{2}, \frac{1}{1}$

$F_3 = \frac{0}{1}, \frac{1}{3}, \frac{1}{2}, \frac{2}{3}, \frac{1}{1}$

Notice the following:

- In F_1 the denominators are all 1, in F_2 the denominators are either 1 or 2, and in F_3 the denominators are 1, 2 or 3.
- The series all start with $\frac{0}{1}$ and end with $\frac{1}{1}$ and the fractions are in ascending size.
- The fractions that have been added to each new sequence all the same denominator:

$F_1 = \frac{0}{1}, \qquad \qquad \qquad \frac{1}{1}$

$F_2 = \frac{0}{1}, \qquad \frac{1}{2}, \qquad \frac{1}{1}$

$F_3 = \frac{0}{1}, \quad \frac{1}{3}, \quad \frac{1}{2}, \quad \frac{2}{3}, \quad \frac{1}{1}$

Write down F_4.

Which additional fractions are in F_4 which weren't in F_3?

Write all the fractions in F_5 and F_6.

There is a formula for checking the order of fractions in a Farey sequence. This is done by calculating each entry in terms of the previous two entries.

If $\frac{a}{b}$ and $\frac{c}{d}$ are the two known consecutive fractions, and $\frac{x}{y}$ is the next fraction, then

$$\frac{c}{d} = \frac{(a + x)}{(b + y)}$$

For example:

$F_3 = \frac{0}{1}, \frac{1}{3}, \frac{1}{2}, \frac{2}{3}, \frac{1}{1}$

So $\frac{a}{b} = \frac{0}{1}$

$\frac{c}{d} = \frac{1}{3}$

$\frac{x}{y} = \frac{1}{2}$

$$\frac{1}{3} = \frac{(0 + 1)}{(1 + 2)} \qquad \frac{1}{3} = \frac{1}{3}$$

Check your sequences using the formula.

What's the Problem?

Taylah and Cloe are sisters. They each get less than £7 pocket money each week.

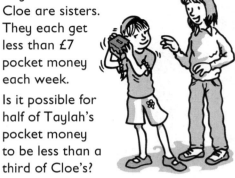

Is it possible for half of Taylah's pocket money to be less than a third of Cloe's?

If half of Taylah's pocket money is less than a third of Cloe's, suggest two possible amounts of pocket money for each sister.

If half of Taylah's pocket money is equal to a third of Cloe's, suggest what pocket money they might each be getting.

Let's Investigate

Choose any four numbers less than 10.

Using these numbers write as many fractions as you can with one-digit numerators and denominators.

How many different fractions can you make?

- Which is the smallest fraction?
- Which fractions are less than 1?
- Which fractions are equal to 1?
- Which is the largest fraction?
- Which fractions are greater than 1?
- Write the fractions in order of size.

Organise your fractions into groups.
What criteria have you used?
How else could you group them?

Investigate fractions for other sets of four numbers.

The Arts Roundup

One-eighth of The Reggio Opera Company are technicians. Two-thirds are singers. The other five members are musicians.

- How many technicians are there?
- How many singers are there?
- How many people are there altogether in The Reggio Opera Company?

The Puzzler

Samir has put a total of £10 into five envelopes.

Envelopes A and B together have a total of £5.20. Envelopes B and C have a total of £4.30; envelopes C and D a total of £3.40; and envelopes D and E have a total of £3.

How much money is each envelope?

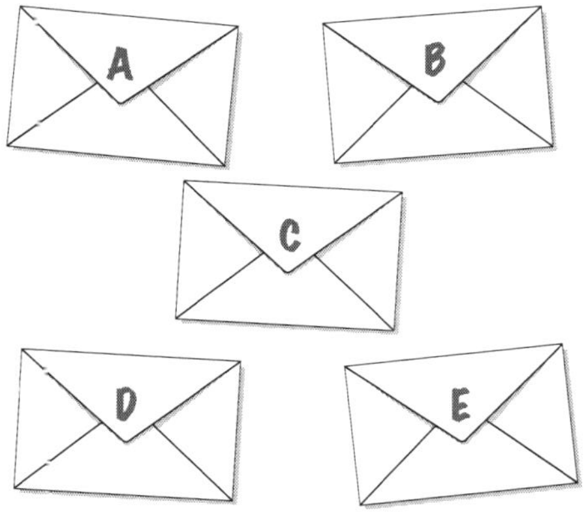

The Puzzler

Arrange each of these numbers so that the sum of each column, row and diagonal is the same. What is the common total?

0·1 0·3 0·2 0·5 0·7 0·6 0·4 0·8 1 0·9 1·1 1·3 1·2 1·4 1·5 1·6

Name:

The Maths Herald

Volume 6

Date:

Money Matters

When goods are imported or exported their prices are affected by exchange rates.

What are exchange rates?

What is the exchange rate today between the British pound and other major currencies?

Compare these exchange rates with the exchange rates for last week. Are they the same? If not, how are they different?

What does all this mean for the price of imported and exported goods?

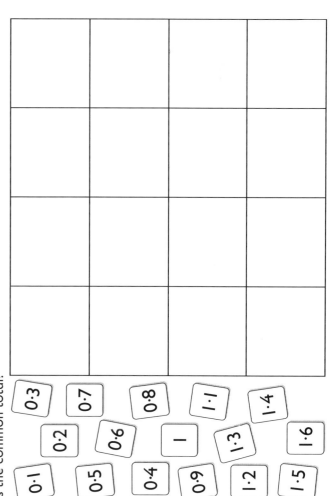

Let's Investigate

Choose any four digits less than 10.

Write as many decimals as you can using two, three or four of these digits.

- Write the decimals in order of size.
- Arrange all your decimals into three different groups. What criteria did you choose?
- How else could you group all your decimals?

Investigate decimals for other sets of four digits.

Let's Investigate

$\frac{1}{2}$ is a *unitary* or *unit* fraction (meaning it has a numerator of 1).

0·5 is $\frac{1}{2}$ expressed as a decimal.

When converted to a decimal $\frac{1}{2}$ *terminates*.

$\frac{1}{6}$ is another unitary fraction.

When $\frac{1}{6}$ is converted to a decimal it is 0·1666666 …

When converted to a decimal the fraction $\frac{1}{6}$ *recurs* (it goes on and on – it does not terminate).

Using a calculator, investigate unitary fractions where the decimal terminates.

Can you find all the terminating fractions from $\frac{1}{2}$ to $\frac{1}{100}$?

Money Matters

One of the ways that we pay for the goods and services that we want is by using cash – notes and coins.

Another method of payment that people use are cheques.

What is a cheque? How do cheques work?

What are the advantages and disadvantages of cheques over other methods of payment?

Look at some cheques from different banks.

How are they the same? How do they differ? What are the things that all cheques have on them?

Imagine your school has formed a bank.
What name will you give your bank?
Design your bank's cheque book.

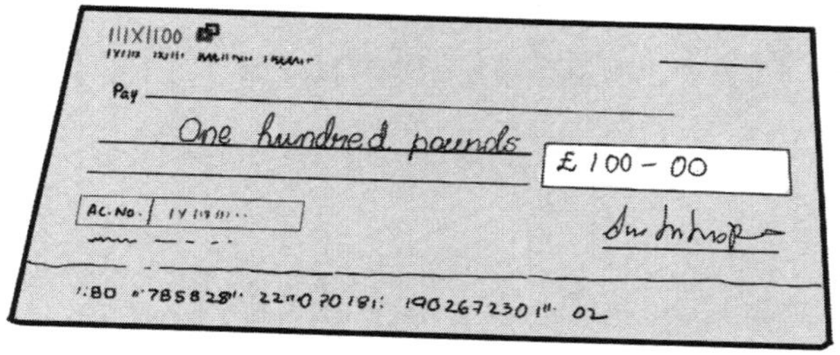

At Home

Look for any examples of decimals at home.

Organise your examples into three lists:

- Numbers with one decimal place
- Numbers with two decimal places
- Numbers with three or more decimal places

The Language of Maths

DECIMAL

What does the word 'decimal' actually mean?

Let's Investigate

0·2 0·2 0·2 0·2

Only using four 0·2s or fewer, make as many other numbers as you possibly can.

Here are some examples:

$0{\cdot}8 = (0{\cdot}2 \div 0{\cdot}2) - 0{\cdot}2$ $0{\cdot}04 = 0{\cdot}2 \times 0{\cdot}2$ $1{\cdot}4 = (0{\cdot}2 + 0{\cdot}2) + (0{\cdot}2 \div 0{\cdot}2)$

Make your answers as varied as you can.

What about using these numbers: 0·2, 2, 2·2, 22?

What if you started with a digit other than 2?

Looking for Patterns

One of the most common uses and applications of decimals is when measuring.

For example:

235 cm = 2·35 m 14 cm 8 mm = 14·8 cm
1600 g = 1·6 kg 1500 ml = 1·5 *l*

To convert metres into centimetres we multiply by 100
e.g. 2·5 m × 100 = 250 cm

To convert centimetres into metres we divide by 100
e.g. 650 cm ÷ 100 = 6·5 m

Design a poster explaining how to convert between different metric units for length, mass and capacity. Be sure to include at least one example for each.

The Language of Maths

centimetre millimetre milligram millilitre

These are words we commonly use to describe measures.

What do the prefixes 'centi' and 'milli' mean?

What about the prefix 'deci'?

centigram decimetre centilitre decilitre

What do each of these measures equal?

Money Matters

When shops have sales, they often publicise the discount as a percentage.

Why do you think this is?

What are the 'normal' percentage discounts that shops offer?

Again, why do you think this is?

Technology Today

Hector and Gomez are twins. Except on Sundays, they spend every afternoon playing their favourite computer game – Solar Seize. Below are their scores for last week.

Hector	
Monday	58 out of 80
Tuesday	22 out of 50
Wednesday	7 out of 20
Thursday	6 out of 10
Friday	49 out of 60
Saturday	31 out of 40

Gomez	
Monday	25 out of 40
Tuesday	45 out of 60
Wednesday	12 out of 20
Thursday	7 out of 10
Friday	60 out of 80
Saturday	24 out of 50

58 out of 80 means that on Monday Hector played a total of 80 games and won 58.

- On which day did Hector win the highest percentage of games?
- On which day did Hector win the lowest percentage of games?
- On which day did Gomez win the highest percentage of games?
- On which day did Gomez win the lowest percentage of games?

Name:

The Maths Herald

Volume 6

Date:

Let's Investigate

Write down all the different things that you do on a normal weekday.

Can you group these activities into different categories?

Over the course of one day, keep a detailed log of the things that you do in each of these categories.

Let's suppose that one whole day, 24 hours, is 100%.

Work out what percent of your day is spent on each of the categories.

Then draw a pie chart to represent your day.

How would this compare to a Saturday or Sunday? Investigate!

The Puzzler

In a magic square the sum of each column, row and diagonal is the same – this is the magic number (or percent).

Complete the magic square.

What is the magic percent?

Make up a magic percent square of your own.

	10%	
70%		
		40%

Focus on Science

What is a humidity meter?

What does RH% refer to?

What does it mean?

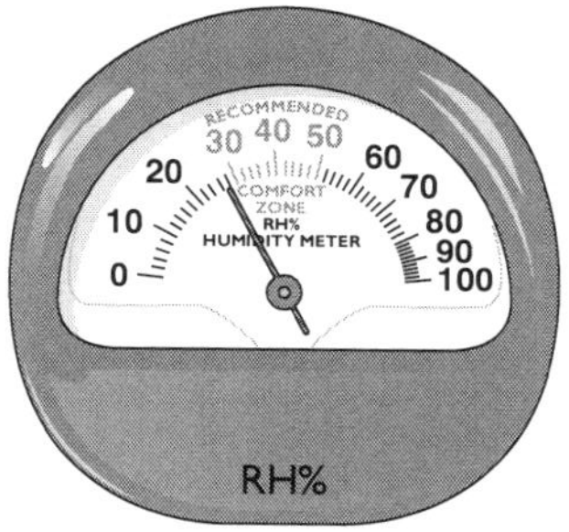

The Language of Maths

The words *deposit* or *down payment* refer to an amount of money that is paid as a first instalment that secures the purchase of something you wish to buy later. The *balance* is the amount of money that is paid later when you actually take ownership of the thing you are buying.

In most cases a deposit is required on large purchases such as a holiday, a car or a house and is a percentage of the full price.

Investigate deposits. What other purchases allow a deposit? What percentage of the full amount is required as a deposit? What are the other conditions of the deposit?

Let's Investigate

What percent of your class are boys? What percent are girls?

Use percentages to make eight other comparisons between all the children in your class.

Think about interesting things to make comparisons about.

Don't just compare two groups within the class, like boys and girls.

Try making comparisons between three, four or more groups.

Money Matters

What do the letters VAT stand for?

What does this mean? How does it work?

What is the current rate of VAT in the UK?

How do you calculate the VAT on goods and services?

Choose some items in a magazine or catalogue that *do not* have VAT added. Calculate the new price of each item once VAT has been added.

If something already includes VAT, what is the calculation required to find the price before VAT?

Choose some items in a magazine or catalogue that already have VAT added. Calculate the price of each item before VAT was added.

Money Matters

Many countries in Europe also have systems similar to VAT (although they are not referred to as VAT).

Investigate the current rates of VAT in different countries in Europe.

Illustrate through various examples the difference in Euros (€) you would pay for a range of goods and services bought in different countries throughout Europe.

The Language of Maths

Write a percentage for each sector of the pie chart.

Make your percentages as accurate as possible.

What might this pie chart be representing?

Write a key to explain the chart.

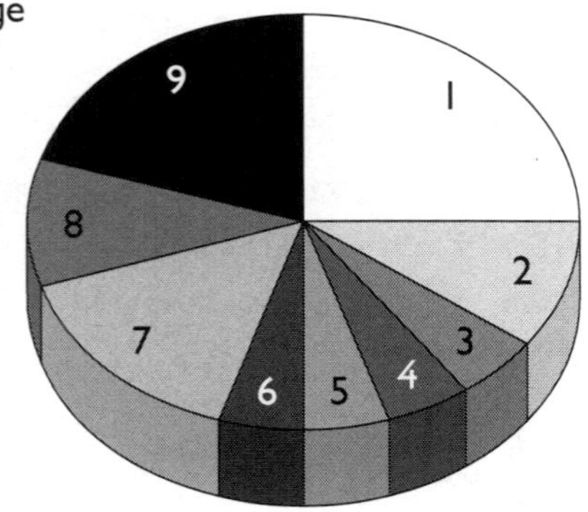

Money Matters

Percentages are often used in the financial pages of a newspaper.

Look through several newspapers and cut out any references to percentages.

Find out what these percentages mean.

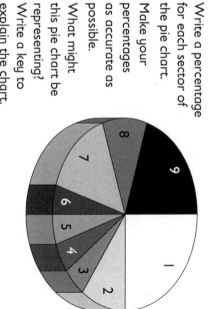

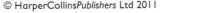

What's the Problem?

On average, how many children a day in your school have school dinners?

Imagine that you are the school cook.

Below are a list of the ingredients needed to make a main dish and a dessert.

Calculate how much of each ingredient you would need to use to cater for all the school dinners.

Show all your working.

Courgette Tart

(For 6 people)

365 g courgette

1 large onion

$\frac{3}{4}$ cup grated cheese

1 cup self-raising flour

$\frac{1}{2}$ cup oil

5 eggs

pinch each of salt and pepper

Banana Cake

(For 8 people)

125 g butter

175 g soft brown sugar

2 eggs

280 g plain flour

1 tsp bicarbonate of soda

pinch of salt

125 ml milk

3 medium ripe bananas

1 tsp vanilla extract

The Language of Maths

What is ratio?

What is proportion?

How are they related?

What words and symbols are associated with ratio and proportion?

Design a poster showing what ratio and proportion mean.

Provide different examples on your poster.

Name:

The Maths Herald

Volume 6

Date:

The Puzzler

Which drink tastes stronger:

7 parts orange juice mixed with 3 parts water *or*

8 parts orange juice mixed with 4 parts water?

How did you work it out?

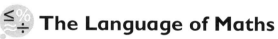

At Home

Make a list of all the members of your extended family.

What proportion of your family is female?

What is the ratio of males to females in your family?

Write three more statements about your extended family. Describe your family using the vocabulary of ratio and/or proportion.

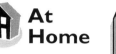

The Language of Maths

Direct proportion means that the increase in one amount or number relates to the increase in another amount or number.

Inverse proportion means that the increase in one amount or number relates to the decrease in another amount or number.

Solve these problems involving inverse proportion:

- It takes 12 hours for 8 men to construct a fence around a sporting field. How long would it take 6 men?
- 4 friends go on a trek. They take 5 containers of water with them which lasts them for 9 days. How long would the same amount of water last them if 6 friends had gone on the trek?
- Walking at 5 kph, it takes Dipo 45 minutes to walk home from school. How long would it take him if he walked at 6 kph?

What's the Problem?

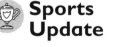

All the guest rooms at the Harriet Hotel are being refurbished. There are a total of 120 rooms, all of which are identical. It took 12 men 5 days to lay new carpet in 60 of the rooms.

- How many men would be needed to lay carpet in all 120 rooms in 8 days?
- How many days would it take 16 men to lay carpet in all 120 rooms?

Explain in writing how you worked out the answer to each of the problems.

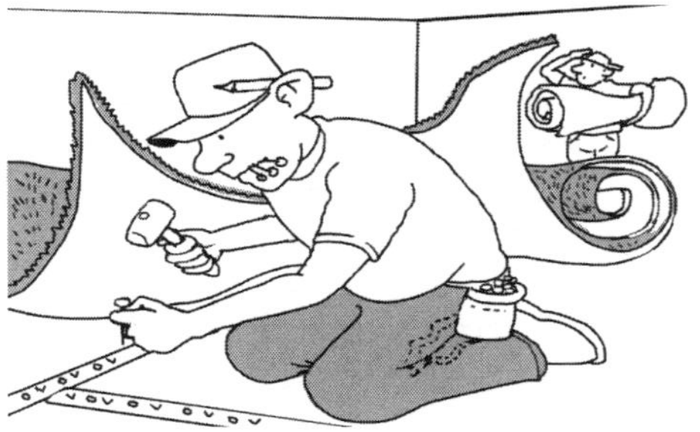

What's the Problem?

Once a month the remote town of Wombat Village is visited by the mobile library unit.

The mobile library carries books, CDs and DVDs for people to borrow.

This month altogether the library has a total of 1976 books, CDs and DVDs.

The ratio of the number of books to CDs to DVDs is 5 : 1 : 2.

How many books, CDs and DVDs does the unit have this month?

Sports Update

Nawra Rovers are playing at home to Berry Rangers.

7 out of every 8 people in the stadium are Nawra Rovers supporters.

Of the Nawra Rovers supporters, 1 out of every 9 are season ticket holders.

There are a total of 91 Nawra Rovers season ticket holders watching the match.

How many people are in the stadium?

Let's Investigate

Your class is going to have a party.

Here is the shopping list.

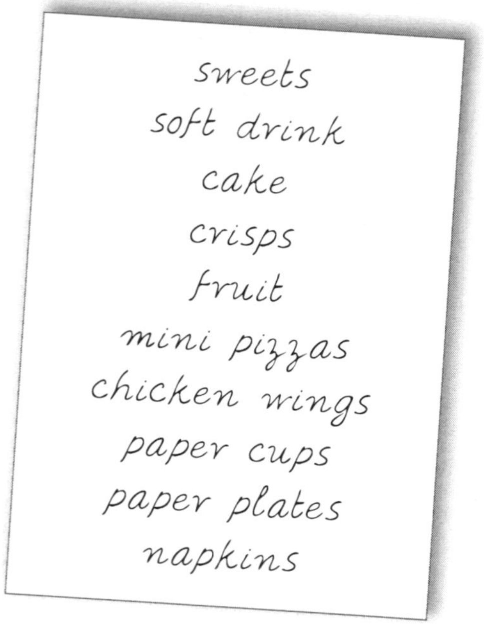

Work out how much of each item you need to buy.

Be as accurate as possible – you don't want to be short of anything, and you want to have as little waste as possible.

Think carefully about:

- the quantities that each person is likely to need
- those items that will need sharing between everyone in the class.

Be prepared to justify your decisions with numerical evidence.

Once you have calculated how much of each item you will need to buy, work out an approximate costing for each of the items. Then work out the approximate total bill for the party and the cost per person.

Let's Investigate

Find a recipe that sounds tasty.

Choose one that has around 8 to 10 ingredients.

How many people is the recipe for?

Rewrite the quantities of each ingredient needed for a different number of people.

Rewrite the quantities of each ingredient needed for another different number of people.

Around the World

Look at the flags of different countries.

Using fractions, decimals and/or percentages, write a sentence describing the proportion of the different colours used in each flag.

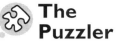

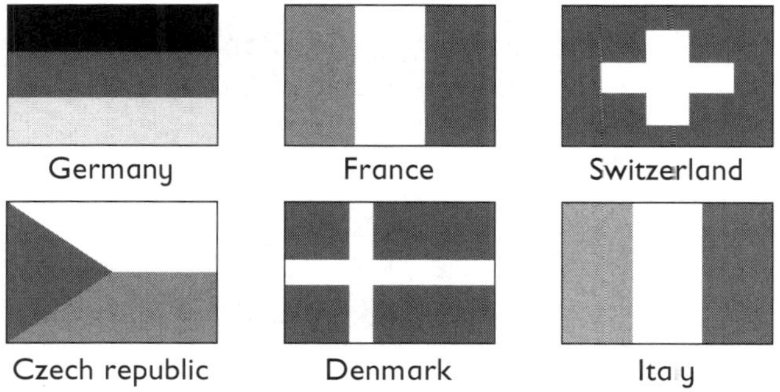

The Puzzler

What mathematical symbol can you place between the numbers 1 and 2 to make a number greater than 1, but less than 2?

1 × < % ÷ □ + = π ≠ > ≥ √ ○ £ 2

The Language of Maths

Counting is an important and fundamental ski l not only in mathematics, but also in so many different aspects of life. When you started to add, subtract, mu tiply and divide, you did so using the skills of counting.

Often counting needs to be accurate, for example, when using money, when taking the class register, finding out how many school dinners there are.

But sometimes the numbers involved are just too large to get a precise number.

Write about how you would get an approximcte number for each of these:

- pebbles on a beach
- grains of sand in a sand pit
- hairs on your head
- stars in the sky.

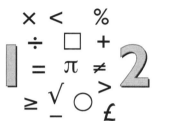

Name:

The Maths Herald

CN PM

Volume 6

Date:

The Language of Maths

Our number system is based on the number 10. It is called the *decimal numeral system* and has 10 as its base. That is why is it referred to as a *base 10* number system.

However number systems can be based on other numbers.

The *ternary numeral system* has 3 as its base. So it is referred to as *base 3*.

The table on the right shows the numbers 1 to 12 written in both base 10 (decimal) and base 3 (ternary).

base 10	1	2	3	4	5	6
base 3	1	2	10	11	12	20

base 10	7	8	9	10	11	12
base 3	21	22	100	101	102	110

Can you work out what the numbers 13 to 20 are in base 3?

Investigate different based numeral systems.

What are the numbers 1 to 20 written in these bases?

Technology Today

The *binary numeral system* is the number system used in computing.

Investigate the binary numeral system.

Technology Today

In a division calculation, a remainder can be expressed in different ways, for example as a fraction, a decimal or a whole number. In computing, the *modulo* operation finds the remainder of division of one number by another number.

Given two positive numbers, x (dividend) and y (divisor), x modulo y (abbreviated as x mod y) can be thought of as the remainder of the division of x by y.

Look at these examples involving modulo 3:

Example 1	**Example 2**	**Example 3**
7 mod 3 = 1	9 mod 3 = 0	14 mod 3 = 2
because 7 ÷ 3 leaves a remainder of 1	because 9 ÷ 3 leaves a remainder of 0	because 14 ÷ 3 leaves a remainder of 2

Choose other numbers between 1 and 20 and calculate their value in modulo 3.

Choose a set of 10 numbers between 1 and 20. Calculate the value of each of these numbers in modulo 4 and modulo 5.

Look at the values of each number in mod 3, mod 4 and mod 5.
What do you notice?

Let's Investigate

This triangular pattern of numbers is referred to as *Pascal's Triangle*.

What is the rule?

Write the next two rows of Pascal's Triangle.

Now rewrite Pascal's Triangle replacing each of the numbers with its value in modulo 3 (see Technology Today activity).

Investigate the different patterns that arise.

Can you predict what the next two rows of Pascal's Triangle will be written in modulo 3 values?

1
1 1
1 2 1
1 3 3 1
1 4 6 4 1
1 5 10 10 5 1

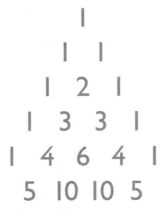

Around the World

Most people, in very different jobs, rely on the use of whole numbers, fractions, decimals, percentages and / or ratio and proportion in order to be able to do their jobs properly.

Make five lists.

1. whole numbers
2. fractions
3. decimals
4. percentages
5. ratio and proportion

For each list, write down which jobs in particular use that type of number. How do they use the numbers? Why are they so important to what they do?

Which jobs belong to more than one list?

Around the World

A census is an official count or survey of a population, where various details are recorded.

In 2010, China, the country with the most people in the world, conducted a census.

Find out what the Chinese census surveyed.

Write a report about some of the results of the census.

Money Matters

In 1992, the Australian government decided to withdraw the use of the 1¢ and 2¢ coins from circulation.

The smallest monetary unit now used in Australia is the 5¢ coin.

What would be the implications of removing all 1p and 2p coins from circulation in the UK?

Make two lists: one list detailing how it would affect businesses, the other list how it would affect consumers.

Looking for Patterns

6 + 7 = 13 8 + 9 = 17 4 + 5 = 9

What do you notice about the numbers that have been added together to produce each of the answers?

What other answers can you get by adding pairs of numbers like these?

What answers can you *not* get by adding pairs of numbers like these?

What answers can you get by adding three numbers like these together?

What about four numbers like this?

What about five numbers?

What patterns do you notice?

Choosing a number, for example 18, can you decide whether or not the number can be written in one or more of these ways?

Let's Investigate

Arrange nine dominoes so that the sum of the dots is the same in each horizontal and vertical continuous line. How many different arrangements can you find?

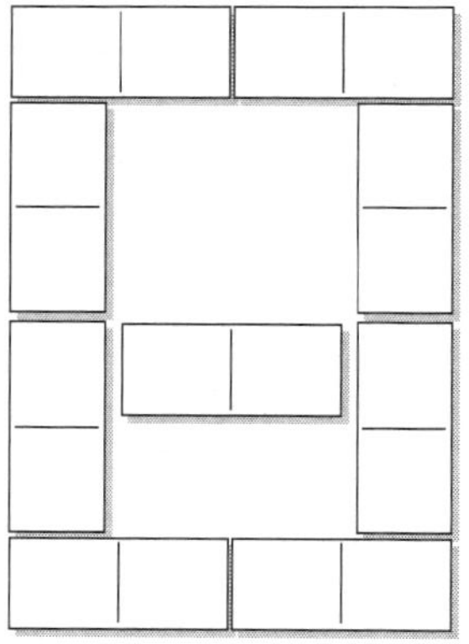

The Puzzler

Complete this August calendar so that the sum of the Saturday dates is a multiple of 15.

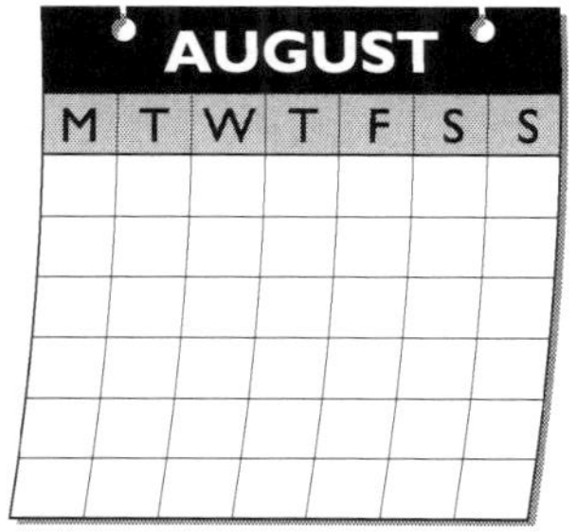

Complete this September calendar so that the sum of one of the full weeks is a multiple of 23.

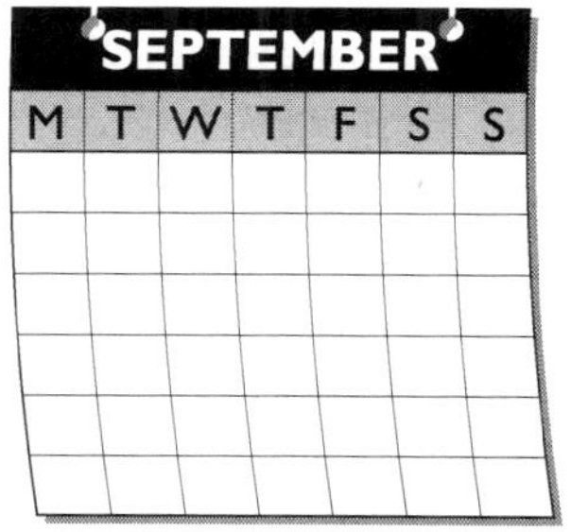

Write down how you did it.

Name:

The Maths Herald

Volume 6

Date:

Looking for Patterns

In each of these grids, shapes have replaced digits.

Work out the value of each shape.

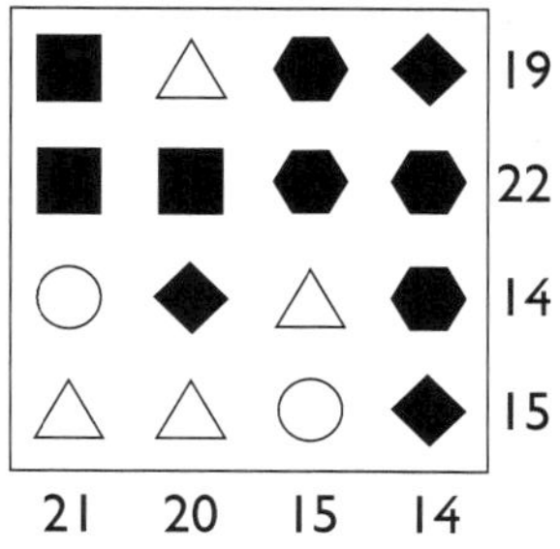

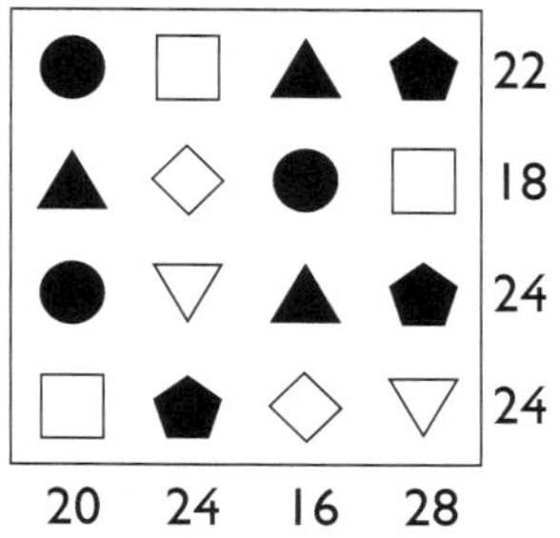

The Puzzler

Write a different number in each triangle so that the four triangles on any one of the three circles add up to 30.

Invent a similar problem of your own. Instead of using interconnecting circles, what about trying rectangles or a different polygon.

The Puzzler

The sum of 9 consecutive odd numbers is 225.

What are the numbers?

Write about how you discovered what the numbers are.

The Puzzler

This is a 3 × 3 magic square.

Complete the magic square using only prime numbers.

The sum of each column, row and diagonal is 111 – this is the magic number.

	37	

The Language of Maths

A *tautonym* is a word that has two or more identical parts. For example, DODO, PAPA.

To work out a *numerical tautonym*, we first give each letter a value that is equal to its numerical position in the alphabet, so A = 1, B = 2, C = 3, … Z = 26).

A numerical tautonym is a word which, when split into two or more equal parts and the letter values of each part added, has the same total for each part.

For example, the word 'WALL' can be split in half: the letters W and A

total 24 (23 + 1), and the letters L and L also total 24 (12 + 12). The two parts have the same total. Therefore, 'WALL' is a numerical tautonym.

Can you find other four-letter numerical tautonyms?

Can you think of any six-letter numerical tautonyms?

What about eight-letter numerical tautonyms?

Let's Investigate

A *palindrome* is a word or number that reads the same backwards as forwards. For example, 'MADAM', 'NURSES RUN', 575, 2002.

The steps on the right show how to make a palindromic whole number.

Does this work in exactly the same way for decimal numbers?

Give examples to justify your conclusions.

Step 1
Write down any number with two or more digits (e.g. 23)

↓

Step 2
Reverse the digits in the number (e.g. 32)

↓

Step 3
Add these numbers together (e.g. 23 + 32 = 55)

↓

Step 4
Is the answer a palindromic number?

yes → Stop

no → Repeat Steps 2, 3 and 4

Famous Mathematicians

This triangular pattern of numbers was discovered in 1653 by a French mathematician named Blaise Pascal.

What is the rule?

Investigate other rules for producing triangles of numbers.

1

1 1

1 2 1

1 3 3 1

1 4 6 4 1

1 5 10 10 5 1

Let's Investigate

Look at this set of 5 numbers:

{1, 2, 5, 7, 8}

14 can be made by adding together some of the numbers (7 + 5 + 2).

Using a digit only once in a calculation, can you make 10? 16? 20?

Which numbers less than 20 can't be made?

Make a set of five numbers that will make every number from 1 to 21 and none over 21.

The Arts Roundup

Morcella Manor is holding an open-air concert.

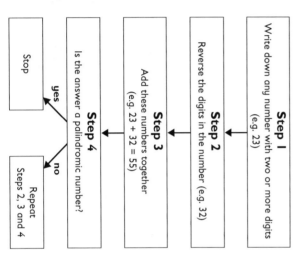

When they opened the gates, 200 people entered the grounds.

During each hour after that, the number of people who entered the grounds was 200 more than the number already in the grounds.

At 9:00 p.m. when the concert began, there were 6200 people in the grounds.

At what time did Morcella Manor open the gates?

Write down how you worked out the answer.

Let's Investigate

Here is another method for subtracting pairs of numbers.

$$\begin{array}{r} 845 \\ -\ 577 \\ \hline \end{array}$$

Step 1: Subtract each digit of the minuend (the number from which the subtrahend is to be subtracted) from 9.

8 → (9 – 8) → 1   4 → (9 – 4) → 5   5 → (9 – 5) → 4

Step 2: Add the answer to the subtrahend (the number to be subtracted).

$$\begin{array}{r} 154 \\ +\ 577 \\ \hline 731 \\ \hline \end{array}$$

Step 3: Subtract each digit of the answer from 9. The result is the answer.

7 → (9 – 7) → 2   3 → (9 – 3) → 6   1 → (9 – 1) → 8

Using combinations of three-digit and four-digit numbers investigate whether this method always works.

Does this method work for decimals?

Provide examples to justify your reasoning.

Do you like this method? Is it a method that you might regularly use? Explain why or why not.

What's the Problem?

867 – 635   7362 – 4073

£57.66 – £34.71   £687.34 – £199.99

If you were to answer each of these subtraction calculations which method would you use? Would it be either of the Let's Investigate methods mentioned in this issue, or would it be a different method? Would you use the same method for all four calculations? Justify your reasoning for using particular methods.

Name:

The Maths Herald

CN PM
Volume 6

Date:

Around the World

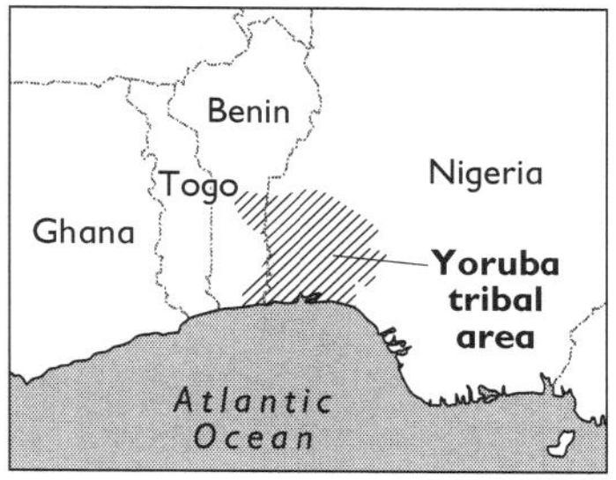

The Yoruba people are one of the largest ethnic groups in West Africa, mostly in Nigeria.

The Yoruba number system is based on the number 20 (*vigesimal*). Wherever possible, it uses subtraction to express numbers.

According to the Yoruba system, the numbers 11 to 14 are written by adding to 10 (i.e. 11 = 10 + 1, 12 = 10 + 2, …).

However, the numbers 15 to 19 are written by subtracting from 20 (i.e. 15 = 20 – 5, 16 = 20 – 4, …).

Similar to the numbers 11 to 19, the numbers 21 to 24 are written by adding to 20, and the numbers 25 to 29 are written by subtracting from 30.

Each number after 30 is written as a multiple of 20 plus or minus tens and units. This pattern is repeated for numbers up to 200, then the system becomes irregular.

For example:

33 = (20 × 2) – 10 + 3

45 = (20 × 3) – 10 – 5

71 = (20 × 4) – 10 + 1

107 = (20 × 6) – 10 – 3

Can you find all the numbers 1–100 using the Yoruba number system?

Try using subtraction rather than addition wherever possible.

What about all the numbers to 200?

Let's Investigate

3 and 5 is a pair of consecutive primes that have a difference of 2.

Find other pairs of consecutive primes less than 100 that have a difference of 2.

What about pairs of consecutive primes less than 100 that have a difference of 4?

Famous Mathematicians

DR Kaprekar (1905–1986) was an Indian mathematician.

He discovered this interesting mathematical constant.

Step 1: Choose a three-digit number (but not one with the same digits).

738 ✓ 444 ✗

Step 2: Rearrange the digits to make the smallest three-digit number possible. Then find the difference between these two numbers.

$$\begin{array}{r} 738 \\ -\,378 \\ \hline 360 \end{array}$$

Step 3: Rearrange the digits in the answer to make the largest and smallest numbers possible. Then find the difference between these two numbers.

$$\begin{array}{r} 630 \\ -\,36 \\ \hline 594 \end{array}$$

Repeat **Step 3** until you get the same calculation repeating itself.

$$\begin{array}{r} 954 \\ -\,459 \\ \hline 495 \end{array}$$

Starting with the number 738 there are three subtraction calculations needed before the calculation starts repeating itself.

What is the largest number of subtraction calculations needed before the calculation starts repeating itself? Choose different three-digit numbers to find out.

What happens if you start with a four-digit number?

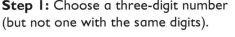

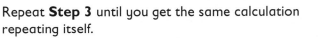

Looking for Patterns

Write a prime number in each shape so that the answer is zero.

The numbers in the circles are consecutive prime numbers.

□ – ○ – ○ – ○ = 0

How many different calculations can you make?

Once again write a prime number in each shape so that the answer is zero.

However, this time the numbers in the circles are *not* consecutive prime numbers.

□ – ○ – ○ – ○ = 0

How many different calculations can you make?

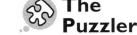

The Puzzler

Write a subtraction calculation where each of the three numbers (*minuend, subtrahend* and *difference*) contains each of the nine digits, 1 to 9.

□□□□□□□□□
– □□□□□□□□□
□□□□□□□□□

The Puzzler

Find a one-digit number where the difference between its square and square root is 14.

Find a two-digit number where the difference between its square and square root is 1290.

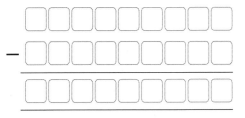

Let's Investigate

Look at this method for subtracting pairs of numbers.

$$\begin{array}{r} 583 \\ -\,396 \\ \hline \end{array}$$

Step 1: Subtract each digit of the subtrahend (the number to be subtracted) from 9.

$(9 - 3) = 6 \quad (9 - 9) = 0 \quad (9 - 6) = 3$

Step 2: Add the answer to the minuend (the number from which the subtrahend was subtracted).

$$\begin{array}{r} 583 \\ +\,603 \\ \hline 1186 \end{array}$$

Step 3: Look at the answer. Cross out the most significant digit (the digit with the largest place value) and add it to the 'new' number. The result is the answer.

~~1~~186
186 + 1 = 187

Using combinations of three-digit and four-digit numbers investigate whether this method always works.

Does this method work for decimals?

Provide examples to justify your reasoning.

Do you like this method? Is it a method that you might regularly use? Explain why or why not.

Looking for Patterns

A *power* tells us how many of the same number are multiplied together.

6×6 is shortened to 6^2, where 2 is the power.
We say: "6 to the power of 2" or "6 squared".

$$6^2 = 6 \times 6 = 36$$

$6 \times 6 \times 6$ is shortened to 6^3, where 3 is the power.
We say: "6 to the power of 3".

$$6^3 = 6 \times 6 \times 6 = 216$$

6^2 and 6^3 are both examples of index notation.

Look at these calculations involving index notation.

$$6^2 \times 6^3 = (6 \times 6) \times (6 \times 6 \times 6) = 6 \times 6 \times 6 \times 6 \times 6 = 6^5 = 7776$$

$$6^5 \div 6^3 = (6 \times 6 \times 6 \times 6 \times 6) \div (6 \times 6 \times 6) = 6 \times 6 = 6^2 = 36$$

What is the rule for multiplying and dividing numbers in index form?

Check your rule using a calculator.

Write several more examples similar to those above.

Let's Investigate

The numbers 57 and 63 are both three away from the same multiple of 10, i.e. 60.

57 is three less than 60, and 63 is three more than 60.

Look at this method for multiplying pairs of numbers that have the same difference from the same multiple of 10.

$$57 \times 63 = (60 - 3)(60 + 3) = 60^2 - 3^2 = 3600 - 9 = 3591$$

Investigate this method by choosing pairs of two-digit numbers that have the same difference for the same multiple of 10, e.g. 88 and 92, 36 and 44.

Does this method work when multiplying similar pairs of three-digit numbers?

What about similar pairs of four-digit numbers?

Be sure to justify your conclusions with examples.

Issue 10 Multiplication

Name:

The Maths Herald

Volume 6

Date:

The Puzzler

$41 \times 51 = 2091$

Use this to help you calculate 41×52.

What about 42×52?

What did you do?

$17 \times 202 = 3434$

Use this to help you calculate 34×202.

What about 34×404?

What did you do?

The Puzzler

n! means $n \times (n - 1) \times (n - 2) \times \ldots \times 2 \times 1$

So, 3! means $3 \times 2 \times 1 = 6$

What is 4! ?

What about: $4! \times 2$

$(4 \times 2)!$

Focus on Science

Light travels 299 792 km each second.

It takes the light of the Sun 8 minutes and 9 seconds to reach Earth. How far is the Earth from the Sun?

Light from the Sun takes 3 minutes and 13 seconds to reach Mercury, its nearest planet. How far is Mercury from the Sun?

The Sun's light takes 6 minutes and 1 second to reach Venus, its second nearest planet. How far is Venus from the Sun?

Money Matters

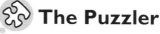

The thickness of a £1 coin is just over 3 mm.

Lucinda wants to buy a new mobile phone costing £174.

If Lucinda was to build a tower of £1 coins, how high in centimetres would it have to be to pay for the phone?

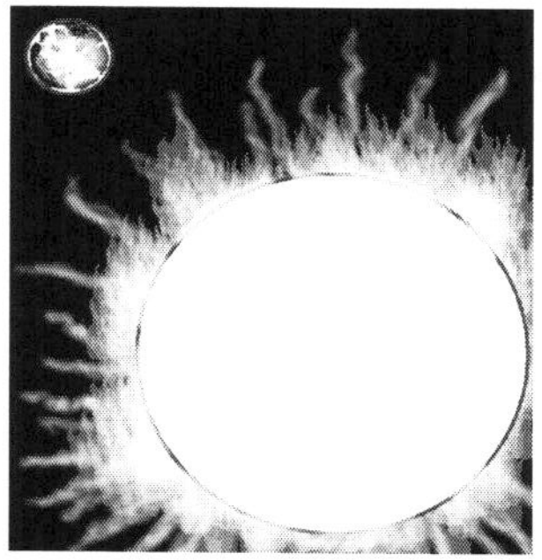

Around the World

Both the Chinese and Hindus invented a clever way of multiplying numbers.

Look at the two examples below.

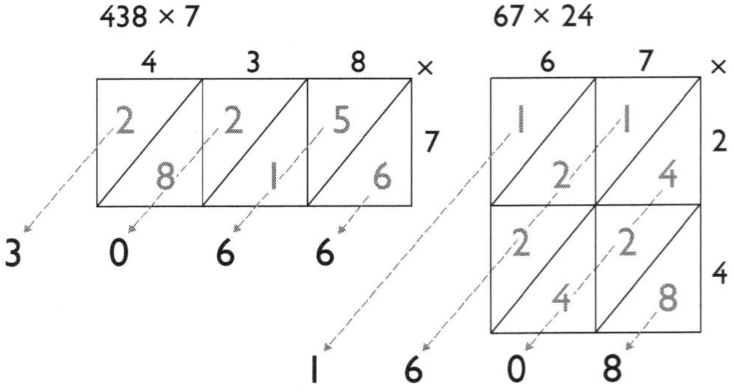

Use this method to work out the answers to the following calculations.

83×76 537×49

886×356 $73{\cdot}9 \times 34{\cdot}6$

Let's Investigate

Using *only* the digits 2, 3, 5 or 7, how many different multiplication calculations can you make?

Rules:

- You can use some or all of the digits.
- You can use each digit more than once in a calculation.
- The digits must form the two numbers being multiplied together as well as the answer.

Here is one: $5 \times 7 = 35$

Looking for Patterns

Replace each star (★) with a digit.

			★	★
×			★	★
	2	8	8	0
		3	3	6
	3	2	1	6

			★	★
×			★	★
	★	★	5	★
		★	★	7
	4	★	★	★

For each calculation, write a statement explaining how you worked out what digits the stars represented.

Let's Investigate

Use the digits 1, 2, 3, 4 and 5 only once to make two or more numbers.

For example:

125 and 34 *or* 15 and 34 and 2

Multiply these two numbers together.

For example:

$125 \times 34 = 4250$ *or* $15 \times 34 \times 2 = 1020$

Using other combinations of the digits 1 to 5, what is the greatest product you can make?

Looking for Patterns

Step 1: Write the digits 1 to 9 in order, leaving out the number 8, to form an eight-digit number.	12 345 679
Step 2: Choose any one-digit number.	7
Step 3: Multiply the digit by 9.	$7 \times 9 = 63$
Step 4: Multiply the product by 12 345 679.	$63 \times 12\,345\,679 =$ ☐

What do you notice?

Repeat choosing different one-digit numbers.

Can you predict what the answers will be for each of the nine digits?

Predict what will happen if you do this using other numbers up to and including 18.

Investigate.

Were your predictions correct?

The Puzzler

What is the smallest two-digit number (x) that leaves a remainder when it is divided by 2, 3, 4, 5 or 6, but *not* 7?

$x \div 2 =$ ☐ R?

$x \div 3 =$ ☐ R?

$x \div 4 =$ ☐ R?

$x \div 5 =$ ☐ R?

$x \div 6 =$ ☐ R?

Write a puzzle similar to this of your own.

Looking for Patterns

Write a digit in each box to complete the following calculations.

Clue: Each of the products share the same two-digit factor (☐☐).

☐☐ × ☐☐ = 1972

☐☐ × ☐☐ = 816

☐☐ × ☐☐ = 2686

☐☐ × ☐☐ = 2244

At Home

Remember, the term *population density* refers to how many people there are for each unit of area.

To work out human population density, we divide the population of a region by the area of that region.

What is the *approximate* human population density of your neighbourhood?

What do you need to know to be able to calculate this?

You will probably need to make several assumptions. What are they?

What are your assumptions based on?

Name:

The Maths Herald

Volume 6

Date:

Focus on Science

Light travels at 299 792 km per second.

Calculate the approximate time it takes light to travel from the Sun to each of the planets.

Write about how you calculated your approximations.

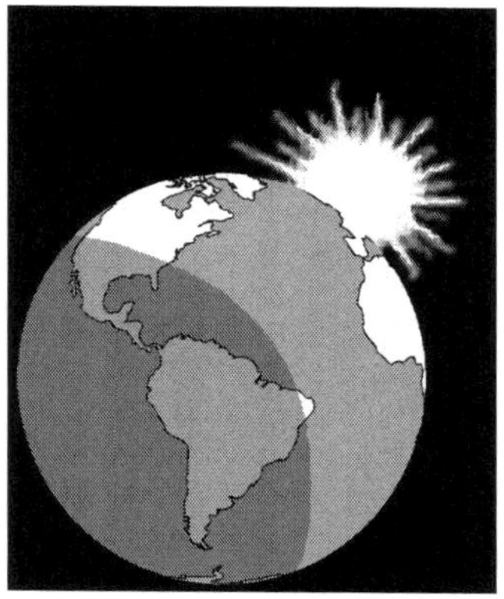

Planet	Average distance from Sun (km)
Mercury	58 million
Venus	108 million
Earth	150 million
Mars	228 million
Jupiter	778 million
Saturn	1·4 billion
Uranus	2·9 billion
Neptune	4·4 billion
Pluto	5·9 billion

Let's Investigate

Investigate whether the following statement is true or false.

When you reverse the digits of any two-digit number to make a new two-digit number and find the total of the two numbers, your answer is always divisible by 11.

What happens if you use pairs of three-digit, four-digit or larger numbers?

The Puzzler

1, 2, 3, 4, 5

× ÷

Using each of the above digits and operations only once, what is the smallest whole number you can make?

Around the World

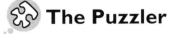

Population density is the term used to describe how many people there are for each unit of area.

To work out the worldwide human population density, we divide the world's population by the Earth's total area.

So, if the world's population is 6·8 billion, and Earth's total area (including land and water) is 510 million square kilometers, then the worldwide human population density is 6·8 billion ÷ 510 million = 13·3 people per km^2. If only the Earth's land area of 150 million km^2 is taken into account, then human population density increases to 45·3 people per km^2.

Look at the figures below. Use them to calculate the population density for the different countries, rounded to the nearest person.

Country	Population	Area (km^2)
Australia	22 456 552	7 682 300
India	1 188 650 000	3 287 240
Jamaica	2 719 000	10 991
United Kingdom	62 041 708	243 610
United States	310 440 000	9 826 675

How do the population densities of each of these countries compare with the worldwide human population density figures?

Find out which countries have the greatest and smallest population densities.

The Puzzler

0 1 2 3 4 5 6 7 8 9

Using each of the digits 0 to 9 only once, it is possible to make two one-digit numbers and four two-digit numbers that are all multiples of 3.

What are the six numbers?

It is also possible to make three one-digit numbers, two two-digit numbers and one three-digit number that are all multiples of 3.

What are these six numbers?

The Puzzler

- Write down any three-digit number. 527

  Write it down again to create a six-digit number. 527 527

  Divide this number by 7. 75 361

  Divide the answer by 11. 6851

  Divide this answer by 13. ☐

  What do you notice?

  Repeat with other three-digit numbers.

  Can you explain why this happens?

- You can make a puzzle very similar to the one on the left.

  Here's how to begin.

  Write down any two-digit number. 68

  Write the number twice more to create a six-digit number. 686 868

  Divide this number by ○. ☐

  Divide the answer by ◇. ☐

  Divide this answer by △. ☐

  What is the rest of the puzzle?

  Can you explain why?

Looking for Patterns

We know that all numbers ending in 0, 2, 4, 6 and 8 are divisible by 2. We can say that this is a *divisibility test* for 2.

We also know these tests of divisibility:

- If a number ends in 0 or 5, then it is divisible by 5.
- If a number ends in 0, then the number is divisible by 10.

Write divisibility tests for 3, 4, 6, 8 and 9.

Can you write divisibility tests for 7, 11 and 12?

Provide proof that your tests work by giving examples.

Looking for Patterns

Algebra is where letters and other symbols represent numbers in a formula or equation. Mathematicians and scientists use algebra to explain complex concepts.

- Think of a number.
- Add 3.
- Double it.
- Add 2.
- Halve it.
- Subtract your original number.

What number do you get? Do this three more times. What do you notice?

This number trick can be explained using algebra.

• Think of a number.	Make n the number you think of.
• Add 3.	$n + 3$
• Double it.	$2n + 6$
• Add 2.	$2n + 8$
• Halve it.	$n + 4$
• Subtract your original number.	4

Use algebra to explain this number trick.

- Think of a number.
- Add 5.
- Multiply the result by 2.
- Subtract 4.
- Halve it.
- Subtract your original number.

Try making up some number tricks of your own. Make sure you can explain how it works using algebra.

What's the Problem?

In each of these calculations, the grey digits are in the correct place. The black digits are not.

Move the black digits so that each of the calculations is correct.

78 + 5 = 56	67 – 6 = 84
38 × 2 = 892	171 ÷ 6 = 12
74 + 51 = 386	98 – 54 = 710
32 × 24 = 231	264 ÷ 68 = 81

Now write down how you worked out where the digits belonged.

The Puzzler

The product of each pair of oval numbers is in the rectangle between them. Complete the puzzles.

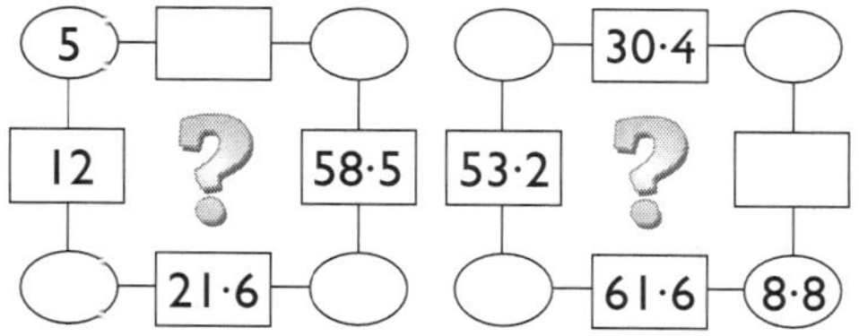

5
12
58·5
21·6
30·4
53·2
61·6
8·8

slide rule

Name:

The Maths Herald

Volume 6

Date:

Sports Update

There are ten teams in the Morcella Football League.

During the season, every team plays every other team twice (once at home and once away).

How many matches are played altogether throughout the season?

Write a formula for finding the total number of games played for any number of teams.

MORCELLA CUP

Sports Update

The Shoalhaven Tennis Club is organising a singles elimination tournament. An elimination tournament means that if you lose the match you are out of the tournament.

In the under-8 girls' tournament there are 12 entrants.

How many matches are played altogether in the under-8 girls' tournament?

Write a formula for finding the total number of matches played for any number of entrants.

Let's Investigate

Start with a two-digit number.

Square each digit and add the answers.

Keep doing this until the answer is a one-digit number.

Investigate doing this for different two-digit numbers.

What if you started with three-digit numbers?

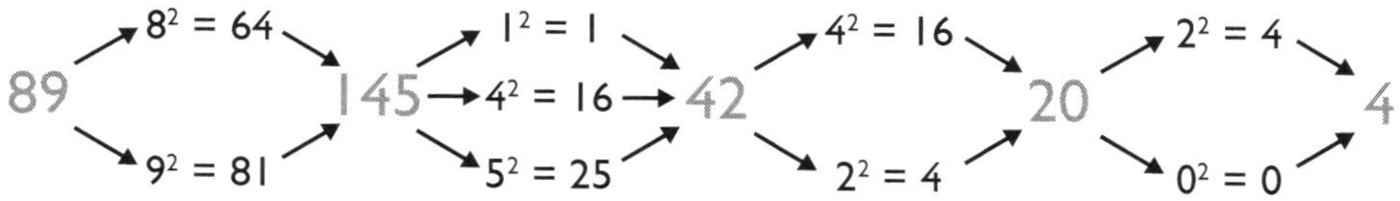

89
$8^2 = 64$
$9^2 = 81$
145
$1^2 = 1$
$4^2 = 16$
$5^2 = 25$
42
$4^2 = 16$
$2^2 = 4$
20
$2^2 = 4$
$0^2 = 0$
4

Sports Update

Calories measure the energy value of food.

The first table shows the recommended daily intake of calories for boys, girls, men and women.

To stay the same weight, you need to use the same amount of calories that you consume.

Referring to the second table, design four different daily programmes (one each for a girl, boy, man, woman), which are designed to use approximately the same amount of calories as the recommended daily intake of calories.

Take into consideration normal daily calorific usage, for example walking, as well as a period of exercise.

Are your programmes realistic?

If not, modify them so that they are. Be prepared to justify your modifications.

Age	Recommended daily intake of calories
girls under the age of 18	between 1000 and 2600
boys under the age of 18	between 1000 and 3200
females aged 31–50	between 1800 and 2200
males aged 31–50	between 2200 and 3000

Calories used in 30 minutes	
walking normally	83
walking the dog	123
walking briskly	142
running	282
aerobics	211
cricket	178
swimming	211
tennis	246
cycling	280
football	292
cleaning the house	123
gardening	176
dancing	158
sleeping	-25
sitting	-30

Let's Investigate

If a calculation involves more than one operation then the calculation must be done in the following order.

1st	B	BRACKETS	( )
2nd	O	OF	power of, e.g. 4^2
3rd	D	DIVISION	÷
4th	M	MULTIPLICATION	×
5th	A	ADDITION	+
6th	S	SUBTRACTION	–

Example 1
$(8 \times 7) - 13$
$= 56 - 13$
$= 43$

Example 2
$(9 \times 4) - (24 \div 6)$
$= 36 - 4$
$= 32$

Using only the digits 2, 4, 5, 6, 7 and 9, make each of the numbers below.

Can you find different ways to make each of these numbers?

Don't forget to use brackets!

41 59 87 93 120

Let's Investigate

In an algebraic expression, letters are often used as substitutes for numbers.

If $a = 5$, $b = 7$ and $c = 10$, investigate what answers you get from the following algebraic expressions.

$(a + b) - c$ $a + b + c$
$a + (b - c)$ $a - (b + c)$
$(a - b) + c$ $(a + b) \times c$
$a \times (b - c)$ $(a - b) \times c$
$(a \times b) - c$

What's the Problem?

In an algebraic expression, if a number is written as $3a$ it means $3 \times a$, and if a number is written as $\frac{a}{3}$ it means $a \div 3$.

Find the value of the following expressions if $c = 5$ and $d = 8$.

$3c - d + 24 =$

$34 + 5(d - c) =$

$4d - 84 + 8c + 68 =$

$12(d + c) - 7(d - c) =$

$\frac{40}{d} - \frac{15}{c} =$

$6(4c - 2d) + 6d - 6c =$

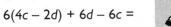

Continued from page 3

When a company makes a profit, the shareholders receive a share in the profits as well. These are called a *dividend*. Dividends are calculated as a percentage of the nominal value of the shares.

Example 1

A company issues 4000 shares with a nominal value of £5 per share and sells them for a market price of £4.20 a share.

a. What is the total nominal value of shares?

4000 × £5
Total nominal value = £20 000

b. What is the total market price of shares?

4000 × £4.20
Total market value = £16 800

c. Are the shares sold below par, at par or above par?

The shares are sold below par.

d. What is the difference between the nominal value and the market price?

£20 000 – £16 800
The difference between the nominal value and the market price = £3200.

Example 2

A shareholder has 600 shares in a company. If the company offers 6% dividend on shares with a nominal value of £8 per share, how much money does the investor receive?

Div dend on 1 share
= 6% × £8 = £0.48

Div dend on 600 shares
= 600 × £0.48 = £288

- A company sells 10 000 shares with a nominal value of £2 at par. How much money is raised?
- Fatima has 1200 shares in a company. They have a nominal value of £4 each and pay a dividend of 2·75%. How much is the total dividend she gets?
- Tayo has 500 shares in a company. The shares pay a dividend of 3·5% and she receives £350. What is the nominal value of each share?
- 000 shares, each with a nominal value of £30, pay a dividend of 5·5%. What is the total dividend?
- A company sells 15 000 shares, with a nominal value of £25 each, at £5 above par. What is the total amount of money that it raises?

Name:

The Maths Herald

CN PM
Volume 6

Date:

Money Matters

When you put, or *deposit*, a certain amount of money into a bank it is called the *principal*. The bank pays you interest on this money. The amount of interest you get depends on the rate that the bank is paying. The interest is usually paid as a percentage per year or *per annum* (p.a.).

Often, people put their money into a *fixed term deposit*. This means they deposit a fixed sum of money, or principal (P), at a fixed rate of interest (R) for a fixed length of time (T). The amount of interest earned on a fixed term deposit is called *simple interest* (I).

To calculate simple interest you use the following formula: $I = \frac{PRT}{100}$

The *amount* (A) is the sum of the principal and the interest earned.
To calculate the amount you use the following formula: A = P + I.

Example

Calculate the interest a person will earn if they deposit £5000 for a period of 4 years at a rate of 3% per annum.

P = £5000, R = 3%, T = 4 years

$= \frac{5000 \times 3 \times 4}{100}$

$= \frac{60\ 000}{100} = £600$

P = £5000, I = £600

£5000 + £600 = £5600

= £5600

What will be the amount at the end of the 4 years?

Use the simple interest formula to calculate the simple interest for each of the following people.

Name: Mr J Brown
Principal: £2000
Rate: 3% per annum
Time: 2 years

Name: Mr T Kanu
Principal: £12 000
Rate: 6% per annum
Time: 3 years

Name: Mrs A Williams
Principal: £4000
Rate: 5% per annum
Time: 4 years

Name: Mrs B Andersen
Principal: £30 500
Rate: 6·5% per annum
Time: 5 years

continued on page 2

continued from page 1

Use the amount formula to calculate the total amount each of the four people will receive at the end of their fixed term.

Look in a newspaper for details on savings.

What are the different options that are on offer? Which do you think is the most favourable option?

If someone had £10 000 to save, which option would you suggest they take? Why?

Money Matters

Sometimes companies or individuals borrow money from banks or other financial institutions. The money borrowed is called a *loan*, which must be paid back over a given period of time. The bank or other financial institution charge *interest* (I) on the money that is borrowed. The rate of interest (R) often depends on how much money is being borrowed (P) and for how long (T).

In most cases, when a bank or other financial institution lends money, they require that the borrower repays a fixed amount of the loan each month, as well as the interest, until the total amount of the loan has been repaid. The time it takes to repay the loan in this way is called the *life of the loan* (T).

To calculate the amount of interest you pay over the life of the loan, use the following formula: $I = \left(\frac{PRT}{100}\right) \div 2$

The total *amount* (A) is the sum of the principal and the interest paid.

To calculate the amount use the following formula: $A = P + I$.

To calculate the amount of money paid each month (M), you divide the total amount (A) by the number of monthly repayments. Use the following formula:

$$M = \frac{A}{T \times 12}$$

Example

A man borrows £15 000 for 5 years at a rate of 4% per annum.

a. What is the amount of interest he will pay over the life of the loan?

P = £15 000, R = 4%, T = 5 years

$$= \frac{(15\,000 \times 4 \times 5)}{100} \div 2$$

$$= \frac{300\,000}{100} \div 2$$

$$= 3000 \div 2$$

$$= £1500$$

b. What is the total amount he will have to pay?

P = £15 000, I = £1500

= £15 000 + £1500

= £16 500

continued on page 3

continued from page 2

c. How much money will he need to pay back each month?

A = £16 500, T = 5 years

$$= \frac{£16\,500}{5 \times 12}$$

$$= \frac{£16\,500}{60}$$

$$= £275$$

For each of the following, calculate:

a. the amount of interest to be paid over the life of the loan

b. the total amount to be paid back

c. how much money will need to be paid back each month.

Name of borrower:	Mr Charles
Principal being borrowed:	£93 000
Rate of interest:	4%
Life of the loan:	2 years

Name of borrower:	Net Works
Principal being borrowed:	£1 500 000
Rate of interest:	9%
Life of the loan:	25 years

Name of borrower:	Mr & Mrs Lee
Principal being borrowed:	£360 000
Rate of interest:	6%
Life of the loan:	12 years

Name of borrower:	Crystal Pools
Principal being borrowed:	£900 000
Rate of interest:	7%
Life of the loan:	20 years

Look for details of loan offers in a newspaper.

What are the different options that are on offer? Which do you think is the most favourable option?

If someone needed to borrow £50 000, which option would you suggest they take? Why?

Money Matters

Many companies raise money by issuing *shares* in their company.

These shares can be bought by anyone who then becomes part owners in the company. People who buy shares in a company are called *investors* or *shareholders*.

When a company issues shares they set a price for each share which is called the *nominal value* or *face value*.

The price that each share is sold for is called the *market price*. This may be the same as the nominal value or above or below it.

If a share is sold for the nominal value it is said to be at *par*.

If a share is sold above the nominal value it is said to be above par or at a *premium*.

If a share is sold below the nominal value it is said to be below par or at a *discount*.

continued on page 4

Let's Investigate

It is easy to subtract fractions if they have the *same denominator.* We just subtract the numerators and reduce the fraction to its simplest terms.

Example 1 $\frac{9}{10} - \frac{3}{10} = \frac{6}{10} = \frac{3}{5}$ *Example 2* $\frac{7}{9} - \frac{5}{9} = \frac{2}{9}$

If we are subtracting fractions that have *different denominators* we:

1. find a common denominator (using what we know about LCM to find the lowest common denominator)
2. convert each fraction to an equivalent fraction with the common denominator
3. subtract the numerators to find the numerator of our answer
4. write the numerator over the common denominator
5. reduce the fraction to its simplest terms.

Example 3

$\frac{6}{7} - \frac{2}{3}$ (LCM of 7 and 3 is 21)

$= \frac{18}{21} - \frac{14}{21}$ ($\frac{6}{7} = \frac{18}{21}$ and $\frac{2}{3} = \frac{14}{21}$)

$= \frac{4}{21}$

Example 4

$\frac{4}{6} - \frac{2}{9}$ (LCM of 6 and 9 is 18)

$= \frac{12}{18} - \frac{4}{18}$ ($\frac{4}{6} = \frac{12}{18}$ and $\frac{2}{9} = \frac{4}{18}$)

$= \frac{8}{18}$

$= \frac{4}{9}$

Choose pairs of fractions of your own and investigate subtracting fractions. Start with simple fractions, such as $\frac{1}{2}$, $\frac{1}{4}$ and $\frac{3}{4}$.

What about subtracting pairs of mixed numbers such as $3\frac{2}{5}$ and $2\frac{4}{7}$?

Let's Investigate

To multiply a mixed number by a mixed number: $3\frac{3}{5} \times 2\frac{2}{3}$

1. Change both mixed numbers into improper fractions.
2. If possible, simplify the numerators and the denominators by cancelling. $= \frac{\not{18}^{6}}{5} \times \frac{8}{\not{3}_{1}}$
3. Multiply the numerators to get the numerator answer.
4. Multiply the denominators to get the denominator answer. $= \frac{48}{5}$
5. Reduce the answer to its simplest terms and change an improper fraction to a mixed number. $= 9\frac{3}{5}$

Choose pairs of mixed numbers of your own and investigate multiplying pairs of mixed numbers.

Name:

The Maths Herald

CN PM
Volume 6

Date:

Let's Investigate

This diagram shows $\frac{1}{2}$ of a $\frac{1}{2}$:

$\frac{1}{2} \times \frac{1}{2} = \frac{1}{4}$

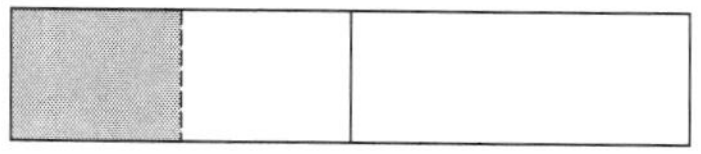

This diagram shows $\frac{1}{4}$ of a $\frac{1}{2}$:

$\frac{1}{4} \times \frac{1}{2} = \frac{1}{8}$

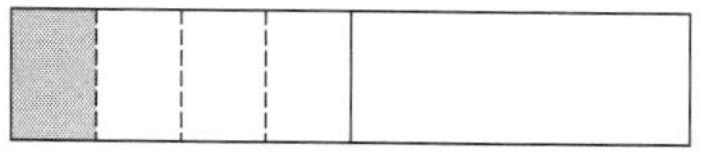

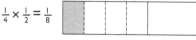

Look at the two examples below which show how to multiply a fraction by a fraction. Explain how the method works.

Example 1

$\frac{2}{3} \times \frac{3}{4}$

$= \frac{\not{2}^{1}}{3} \times \frac{3}{\not{4}_{2}}$

$= \frac{3}{6} = \frac{1}{2}$

Example 2

$\frac{7}{12} \times \frac{4}{9}$

$= \frac{7}{\not{12}_{3}} \times \frac{\not{4}^{1}}{9}$

$= \frac{7}{27}$

Use your method for multiplying a fraction by a fraction to answer these questions.

$\frac{3}{5} \times \frac{5}{6}$ $\frac{1}{4} \times \frac{7}{8}$

$\frac{2}{3} \times \frac{5}{9}$ $\frac{5}{8} \times \frac{6}{7}$

Can you use your method to answer this question?

$\frac{5}{6} \times \frac{1}{4} \times \frac{3}{8}$

Money Matters

Mrs Farringdon has two children – Lucy and Melinda. She has just given each of them their pocket money. However, she has made a mistake and hasn't given each of them the same amount as she normally does.

So Lucy and Melinda have decided to fix it so that they each receive the £6 as they normally do.

This is what they do:

- Lucy gives Melinda twice as much money as Melinda has already.
- Melinda gives Lucy a third of her money.
- Lucy then gives Melinda the same amount of money as Melinda already has.

Now the girls each have the same amount of pocket money.

How much pocket money did Mrs Farringdon give Lucy and Melinda by mistake?

Around the World

Endwintor Road is $62\frac{1}{2}$ miles long. It starts at Endwintor Manor in the west, passing through Endwintor Worthing and Endwintor Havering, and ending at Endwintor Grantham in the east.

The distance between Endwintor Manor and Endwintor Worthing is the same as that from Endwintor Havering to Endwintor Grantham and one-third of that from Endwintor Worthing to Endwintor Havering.

How far is Endwintor Havering from Endwintor Grantham?

The Puzzler

Complete the number chains by writing the mixed numbers that belong in the squares.

START $3\frac{1}{2}$ + ☐ − $3\frac{1}{4}$ + ☐ − $2\frac{3}{4}$ = 3 FINISH

START ☐ + $4\frac{2}{5}$ + ☐ − $1\frac{4}{5}$ − ☐ = $6\frac{1}{2}$ FINISH

Let's Investigate

Draw diagrams to represent each of these fraction statements.

$\frac{3}{4} - \frac{1}{4} = \frac{1}{2}$ $2 \times \frac{1}{2} = 1$

$\frac{1}{2}$ of $\frac{1}{2} = \frac{1}{4}$ $\frac{4}{4} = 1$

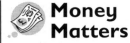

Money Matters

Greg went shopping. He spent £6 more than half of his money in the supermarket. His dry cleaning cost him one-third of what he had left, plus £4 more. He spent £14 at the florist. This was half of his remaining money. How much money did Greg start with?

Let's Investigate

It is easy to add fractions if they have the *same denominator*. We just add the numerators and reduce the fraction to its simplest terms.

Example 1

$\frac{3}{5} + \frac{4}{5} = \frac{7}{5} = 1\frac{2}{5}$

Example 2

$\frac{3}{8} + \frac{1}{8} = \frac{4}{8} = \frac{1}{2}$

If we are adding fractions that have *different denominators* we:

1. find a common denominator (using what we know about LCM to find the lowest common denominator)
2. convert each fraction to an equivalent fraction with the common denominator
3. add the numerators to find the numerator of our answer
4. write the numerator over the common denominator
5. reduce the fraction to its simplest terms.

Example 3

$\frac{2}{3} + \frac{3}{5}$ (LCM of 3 and 5 is 15)

$= \frac{10}{15} + \frac{9}{15}$ ($\frac{2}{3} = \frac{10}{15}$ and $\frac{3}{5} = \frac{9}{15}$)

$= \frac{19}{15}$

$= 1\frac{4}{15}$

Example 4

$\frac{6}{7} + \frac{3}{14}$ (LCM of 7 and 14 is 14)

$= \frac{12}{14} + \frac{3}{14}$ ($\frac{6}{7} = \frac{12}{14}$)

$= \frac{15}{14}$

$= 1\frac{1}{14}$

Choose pairs of fractions of your own and investigate adding fractions. Start with simple fractions, such as $\frac{1}{2}$, $\frac{1}{4}$ and $\frac{3}{4}$.

What about adding pairs of mixed numbers such as $3\frac{2}{5}$ and $2\frac{4}{7}$?

In the Past

Apart from $\frac{2}{3}$, the Ancient Egyptians only wrote fractions with a numerator of 1 (unitary or unit fractions).

They wrote fractions as a sum of different unitary fractions.

So, for example, $\frac{3}{4}$ might have been written as $\frac{1}{2} + \frac{1}{4}$.

How might the Ancient Egyptians have written fractions with a numerator of 2, i.e. $\frac{2}{n}$, such as $\frac{2}{5}$ or $\frac{2}{7}$?

If you can, try and write them as the sum of just two different unitary fractions.

Explore fractions with different numerators such as $\frac{3}{n}$, $\frac{4}{n}$, $\frac{5}{n}$, … and consider how the Ancient Egyptians would have represented these as sums with the least number of unitary fractions.

Focus on Science

The Earth is 149 596 208 km from the Sun.

Mercury is only 57 859 856 km from the Sun. Approximately what percentage of the Earth's distance from the Sun is Mercury's distance from the Sun?

Venus is 108 224 912 km from the Sun. Approximately how far is Venus from the Sun as a percentage of the Earth's distance from the Sun?

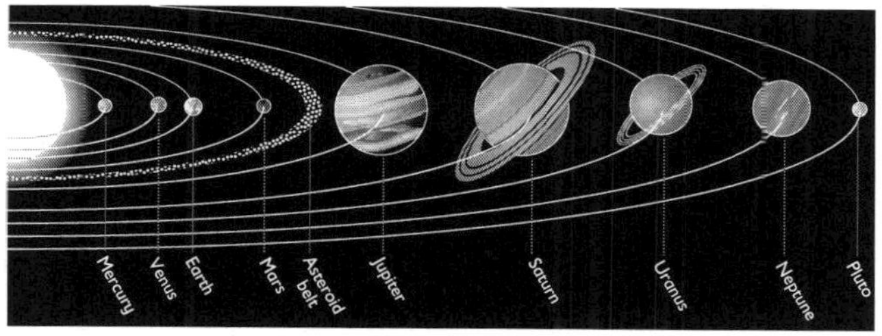

The Arts Roundup

An orchestra consists of 40 male and 30 female musicians.

16 of the male musicians and 40% of the female musicians also belong to other smaller ensembles.

What percentage of the orchestra members also perform with smaller ensembles?

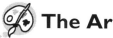

What's the Problem?

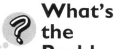

The land area of the Earth is 148 300 000 km^2 and this is approximately 30% of the Earth's surface. Approximately what is the total surface area of the Earth?

What surface area of the Earth is covered by water?

The Puzzler

Complete each of these statements in at least two different ways.

5 is ◯ % of ☐

12 is ◯ % of ☐

18 is ◯ % of ☐

55 is ◯ % of ☐

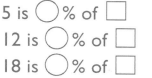

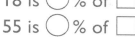

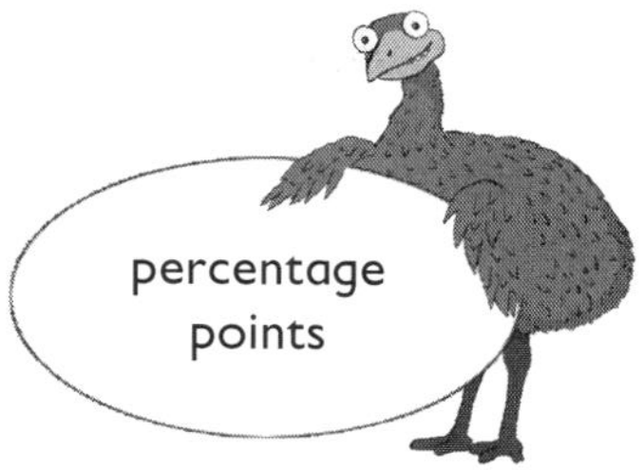

Name:

The Maths Herald

Volume 6

Date:

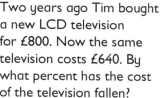

Money Matters

When a price is increased, a certain amount is added to the original price. This is called an *increment* of the original price. This is often expressed as a percentage of the original price.

To calculate the percentage increase, divide the increment by the original price and then multiply by 100%.

$$\text{Percentage increase} = \frac{\text{increment}}{\text{original price}} \times 100\%$$

When a price is decreased, a certain amount is taken off the original price. This is called a *discount* of the original price. This is often expressed as a percentage of the original price.

To calculate the percentage decrease, divide the discount by the original price and then multiply by 100%.

$$\text{Percentage decrease} = \frac{\text{discount}}{\text{original price}} \times 100\%$$

Work out the percentage increase or decrease of each of the following.

During a sale the price of a pair of shoes has been discounted from £60 to £42. What is the percentage discount?

In the past five years, the price of installing a new washing machine has increased from £150 to £225. How much of a percentage increase is this?

The price of a monthly train ticket has increased from £280 to £322.
By what percent has the price increased?

Two years ago Tim bought a new LCD television for £800. Now the same television costs £640. By what percent has the cost of the television fallen?

Look through newspapers and magazines to find the prices of a range of different items.

Imagine that you are the retailer. You decide to offer a discount on some of the products, and raise the prices on others. What percentage discount or increment will you put on each product? What will this mean to the price of each product? As a retailer, what types of products are good for offering a discount on? What types of products are good for including a price increase? Why?

Money Matters

Some businesses need people to help them sell their goods. These people are known as dealers, salespeople or agents. Sometimes these people are not paid a regular salary. Instead, they are paid a percentage of the value of the goods that they sell. This type of payment is called a *commission*.

To calculate a commission in pounds:

Percentage of the commission × value of goods sold

To calculate a commission as a percentage: $\frac{\text{commission received}}{\text{value of goods sold}} \times 100\%$

Example 1

An agent received £750 commission on £15 000 worth of goods sold. What was the agent's commission as a percentage?

Commission received: £750

Value of goods sold: £15 000

$= \frac{£750}{£15\ 000} \times 100\%$

= 5%

Example 2

A salesman was paid 7% commission on all the goods he sold. If he sold £92 000 worth of goods, how much commission did he receive?

Value of goods sold: £92 000

Percentage of the commission: 7%

= 7% × £92 000

$= \frac{7}{100} \times £92\ 000$

= £6440

Complete this table.

Agent	Value of goods sold	Commission as a percentage	Commission in pounds
D Rogers	£34 000	6%	
M Quincy	£194 000		£9700
A Leech	£29 500		£2360
W Ali	£67 800	4%	
C T Adams	£45 350	3%	

Imagine that all five agents work for the same company. Who is the company's best agent? Why? Who is their worst agent? Why?

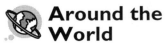

Around the World

Consult a map of your town or the local area.

Calculate the approximate percentage of land that is allocated to:

- housing
- sporting and recreational areas, and open spaces
- commerce and industry
- other uses.

Compare your figures with other towns.

Write about how you arrived at your approximations.

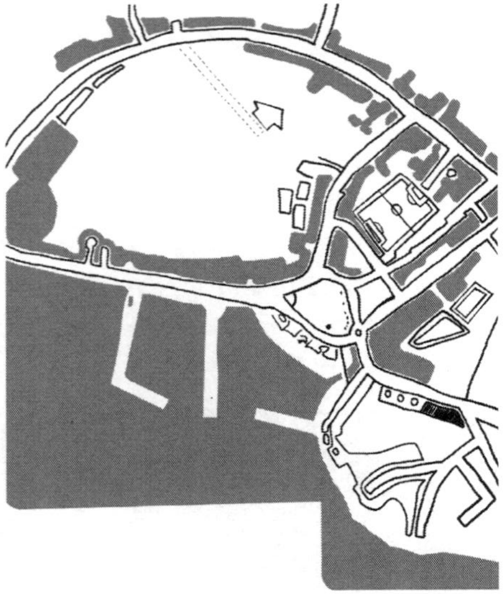

Focus on Science

Your skin is the largest organ of the body.

The average adult has approximately 2000 cm^2 of skin. The average teenager approximately 1500 cm^2 and a child about 800 cm^2.

The diagram on the right shows what percentage of the body's total surface area of skin covers different parts of the body.

Use this information to calculate the surface area of the different body parts for an adult, a teenager and a child.

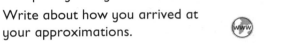

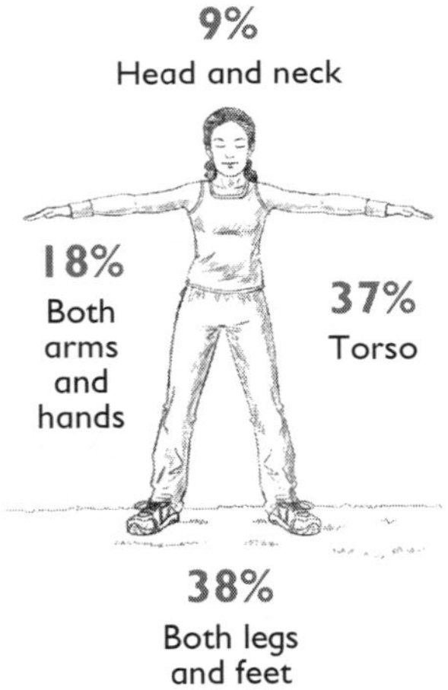

Focus on Science

The human adult has 32 teeth.

There are four different kinds of teeth:

molars: 6 pairs

incisors: 4 pairs

bicuspids: 4 pairs

canines: 2 pairs

What percentage of an adult's teeth are:

- molars?
- incisors?
- bicuspids?
- canines?

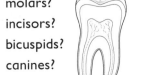

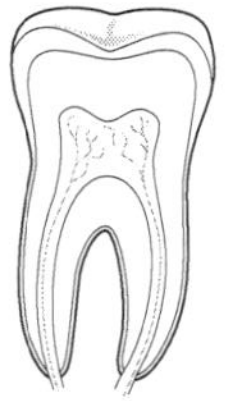

The Language of Maths

7×7 can be written as 7^2 and is read as *seven squared* or *seven to the power of 2*.

The *power* or *index* is 2.

$7^2 = 49$

$4 \times 4 \times 4$ can be written as 4^3 and is read as *four cubed* or *four to the power of 3*.

The *power* or *index* is 3.

$4^3 = 64$

Find the value of each of the following:

3^5 5^3 2^7 8^5 7^4

Money Matters

A percentage of the money that people earn is paid to the government in the form of *income tax*. This money is collected by the government and is used to build and maintain roads, schools, hospitals and other public facilities, and to pay the salaries of government employees such as nurses, teachers and the police.

A part of a person's income is tax free. This is called an *allowance*. After this money has been deducted the remaining income is taxable. The rate of tax is determined by the government. Below is the personal allowance that all tax payers in the UK are allowed, as well as the different rates of income tax.

Personal allowance
£6475

Band	Taxable income	Rate
Basic rate	£0 – £37 400	20%
Higher rate	£37 401 – £150 000	40%
Additional rate	Over £150 000	50%

Example:

Calculate the income tax payable for someone who earns £48 000 per year.

£48 000 – £6475 = £41 525 (earnings – personal allowance = taxable income)

Amount of tax due on £41 525 = (£37 400 × 20%) + (£4125 × 40%)
(taxable income = basic rate + higher rate. Note: £41 525 – £37 400 = £4125)

Total income tax = £7480 + £1650 = £9130 (£37 400 × 20%) + (£4125 × 40%)

Use the tables above to calculate the income tax payable by someone earning:

£56 000 per year £82 000 per year £195 000 per year

Name:

The Maths Herald

Volume 6

Date:

Let's Investigate

The *square root* is a number that when multiplied by itself gives the stated number. √ is the abbreviation for square root.

$\sqrt{49} = 7$

So, the square root of 49 is 7, because $7 \times 7 = 49$.

A square root is the opposite of a square number. $7^2 = 7 \times 7 = 49$

One way to calculate the square root is to divide the number by prime numbers in order to reduce the number to 1.

Example 1

$\sqrt{484} =$ $\sqrt{484} = 484 \div 2$
$= 242 \div 2$
$= 121 \div 11$
$= 11 \div 11$
$= 1$

So, $484 = 2 \times 2 \times 11 \times 11$
$= (2 \times 11) \times (2 \times 11)$
$= 22 \times 22$
$\sqrt{484} = 22$

Example 2

$\sqrt{729} =$ $\sqrt{729} = 729 \div 3$
$= 243 \div 3$
$= 81 \div 3$
$= 27 \div 3$
$= 9 \div 3$
$= 3 \div 3$
$= 1$

So, $729 = 3 \times 3 \times 3 \times 3 \times 3 \times 3$
$= (3 \times 3 \times 3) \times (3 \times 3 \times 3)$
$= 27 \times 27$
$\sqrt{727} = 27$

Use the prime number method to find the square root of these numbers.

$\sqrt{576}$ $\sqrt{676}$ $\sqrt{841}$
$\sqrt{961}$ $\sqrt{1225}$ $\sqrt{1444}$

Looking for Patterns

Which pair of two-digit numbers have:

- a total of 89?
- and a difference of 35?
- and a product of 1674?

Which pair of three-digit numbers have:

- a total of 799?
- and a difference of 247?
- and a product of 144 348?

Write about how you worked out what the pairs of numbers are.

Make up a similar problem of your own for a friend to solve.

Famous Mathematicians

Heron of Alexandria was a Greek mathematician and engineer who lived about 75 AD. He discovered a formula for finding square roots.

Heron's method for finding the square root of a number

Step 1. Make an approximation of the square root.

Step 2. Divide the number you are trying to find the square root of by your approximation.

Step 3. Add the answer to your approximation.

Step 4. Find the average of this number by dividing it by 2.

To get a more accurate answer repeat Steps 2 to 4.

Example

$\sqrt{53} \approx$

Step 1. 7 (because $7 \times 7 = 49$)

Step 2. $53 \div 7 = 7\frac{4}{7}$

Step 3. $7\frac{4}{7} + 7 = 14\frac{4}{7} = \frac{102}{7}$

Step 4. $\frac{102}{7} \div 2 = \frac{102}{14} = 7{\cdot}28$

Use Heron's method to find the approximate square root of each of these numbers. Give your answers to two decimal places.

$\sqrt{28}$ $\sqrt{39}$ $\sqrt{46}$ $\sqrt{88}$ $\sqrt{73}$ $\sqrt{62}$

Money Matters

You are going to make 180 cupcakes for the school fair.

How much of each ingredient will you need?

What will be the approximate cost to make 180 cupcakes?

If you sell all the cupcakes at 75p each, how much money will you take?

How much profit will you make?

Cupcakes *(makes 24)*

110 g butter
110 g sugar
2 drops vanilla essence
2 large eggs
110 g self-raising flour
1 teaspoon baking powder

250 g butter	£1.10
1 kg sugar	95p
28 ml vanilla essence	£1.20
6 large eggs	£1.20
1 kg self-raising flour	£1.50
170 g baking powder	85p

Around the World

Look at this Chinese method for finding square roots which involves subtracting odd numbers.

Chinese method for finding the square root of a number

Step 1: Subtract 1 from the number.

Step 2: Subtract 3 from the difference.

Step 3: Subtract 5 from the difference.

Step 4: Subtract 7 from the difference.

Steps 5 to ?: Continue the pattern until you reach 0.

Count the number of steps.
That is the square root.

Example

$\sqrt{64}$

64
− 1
63
− 3
60
− 5
55
− 7
48
− 9
39
− 11
28
− 13
15
− 15
0 So $\sqrt{64} = 8$

Use the Chinese method to find the square root of each of these numbers.

$\sqrt{289}$ $\sqrt{576}$ $\sqrt{361}$ $\sqrt{529}$ $\sqrt{961}$ $\sqrt{784}$

What are the limitations of this method?

Let's Investigate

Write down five different three-digit numbers.

Work out the square root of each of the numbers using any of the following methods:

- the prime number method
- Heron's method
- the Chinese method.

Then check your answer using a calculator.

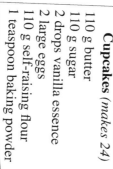

Which method do you prefer to use? Why?

Famous Mathematicians

Pythagoras was a Greek philosopher (569–500 BC). He made many important discoveries in mathematics, particularly in geometry. One of Pythagoras' greatest discoveries is called the *Pythagorean theorem*.

The longest side of a right-angled triangle, the side opposite the right angle, is called the *hypotenuse* (labelled *c*).

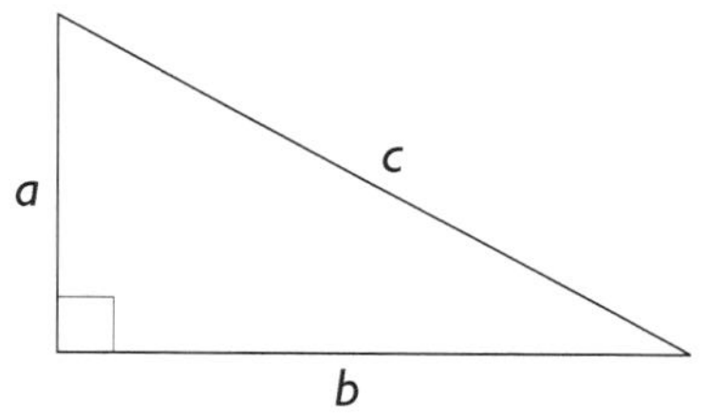

Pythagoras' theorem states that, for any right-angled triangle, the square of the length of the hypotenuse is equal to the sum of the squares of the lengths of the other two sides.

Pythagoras' theorem $c^2 = a^2 + b^2$

Use Pythagoras' theorem to answer the following questions.

Draw a diagram to explain each of your answers.

- You run due north for 5 miles, then due east for 12 miles. What is the shortest distance you are from your starting point?
- A 5 m ladder leans against a wall with its foot 3 m away from the wall. How far up the wall does the ladder reach?

Sports Update

It can be said that a person doing push-ups, when in the upper position, has formed a right-angled triangle.

Draw and label right-angled triangles using the lengths in the table, which are approximates of the triangles formed by five people doing push-ups.

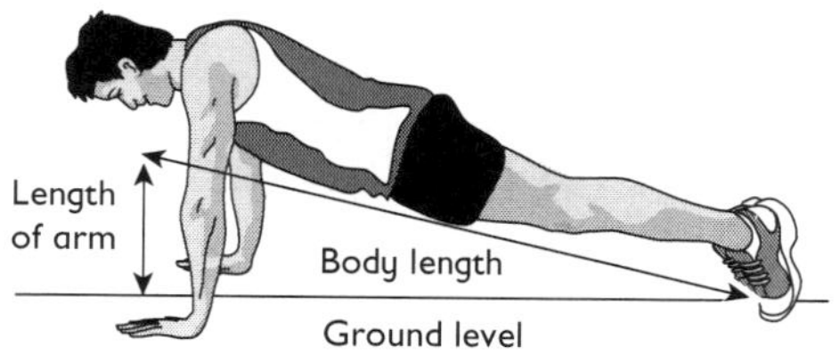

Use a scale of 1 cm to 20 cm for your triangles.

For your drawings:

- calculate the length of the ground level line
- use a ruler, pencil and set-square
- use a sharp pencil
- be as accurate as possible.

	Arm length (cm)	Body length (cm)
Lisa	42	102
Don	64	150
Michelle	36	84
Joseph	48	112
Ian	58	136

Name:

The Maths Herald

Volume 6

Date:

Let's Investigate

Look at the circles below. They show how many line segments (chords) there are in circles with 2 points, 3 points, 4 points and 5 points.

What patterns do you notice?

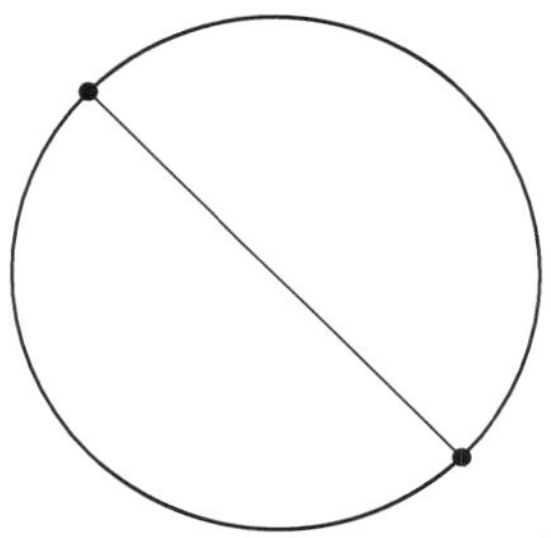

2 points = 1 chord

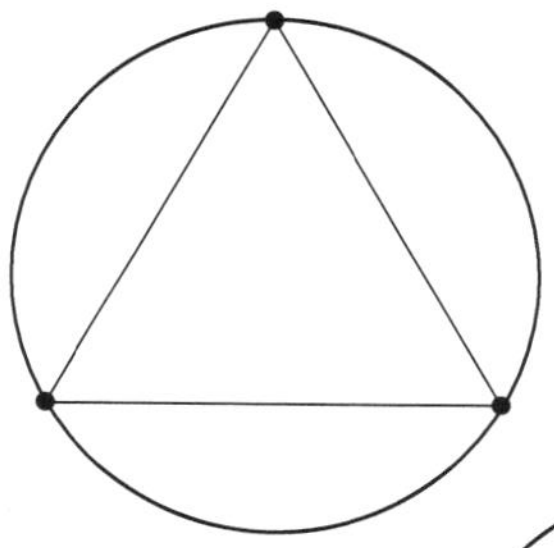

3 points = 3 chords

4 points = 6 chords

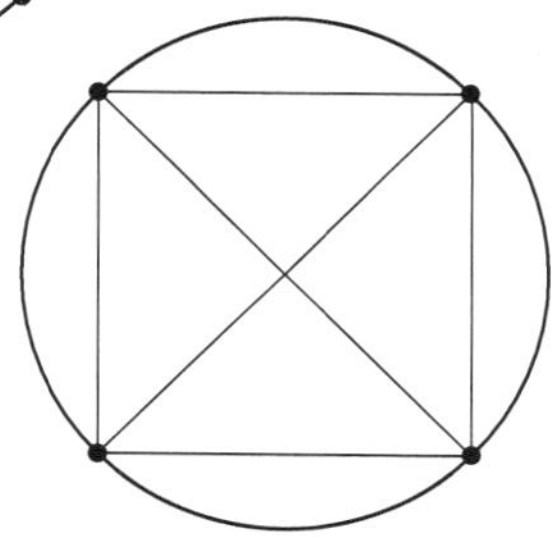

5 points = ? chords

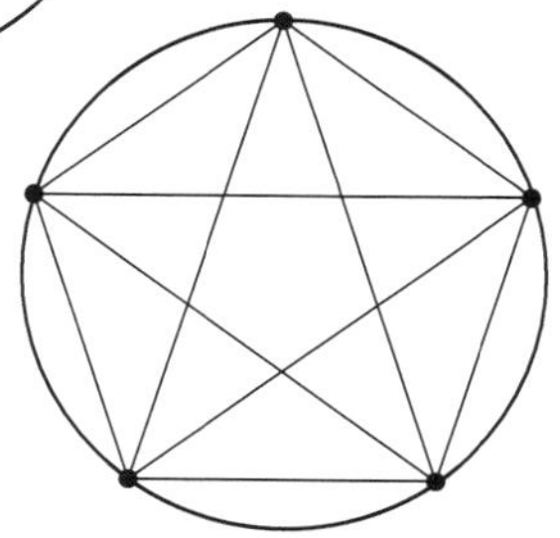

How many chords are there in a circle with:

- 5 points?
- 6 points?
- 7 points?
- 8 points?

Look at the pattern in the number of chords for circles with 2, 3, 4, 5, 6, 7 and 8 points.
What do you notice?

Write a formula for finding the number of chords in a circle with any number of points.

Apply your formula to find out how many chords there are in the circle with 24 points, shown here.

Let's Investigate

Mathematicians have calculated that the circumference of a circle is about 3·14 or $3\frac{1}{7}$ ($\frac{22}{7}$) times the diameter. They call this number *pi* (after a letter in the Greek alphabet) and it is written: π.

Gather together a collection of at least six circular objects, all different sizes. For example, plates of different sizes, wastepaper basket, analogue clock, geometric circular shape.

Using a tape measure, measure the diameter and circumference of each of the objects. Record your measurements.

Now divide the circumference of each object by its diameter.

Finally find the average of all of the answers you have just calculated.

How does your average compare with the value of pi?

The *circumference* is the distance all the way round a circle: the boundary line.

The *diameter* is a straight line drawn through the centre of a circle. It divides the circle into two halves.

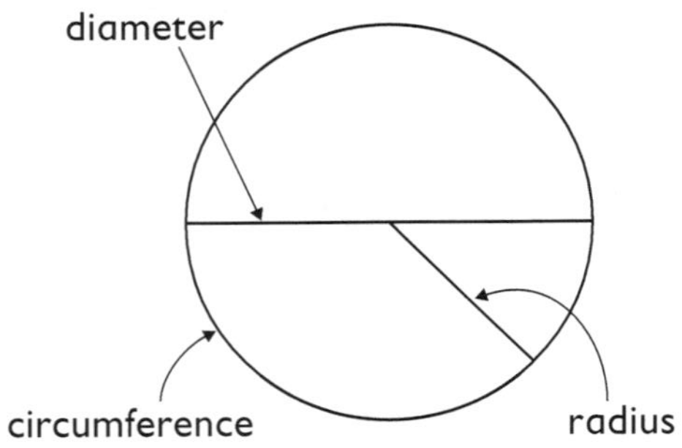

The *radius* (or 'radii' for plural) is the distance from the centre of the circle to its circumference. All radii of a circle are the same length.

Let's Investigate

A square can be cut into four congruent pieces in different ways.

For example:

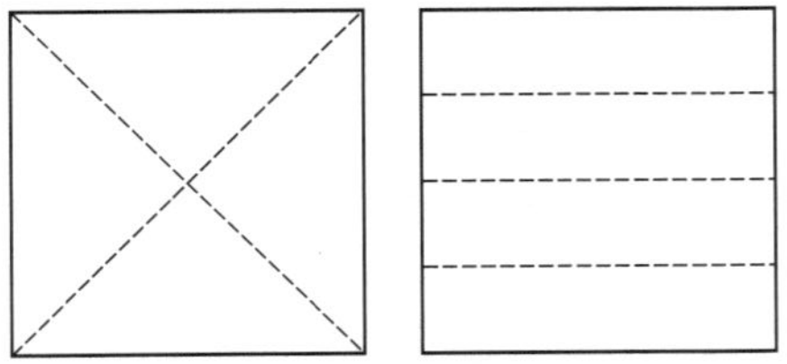

Using squared paper, draw as many different ways as you can.

The Puzzler

What is the diameter of this circle?

Write an explanation about how you worked out the answer.

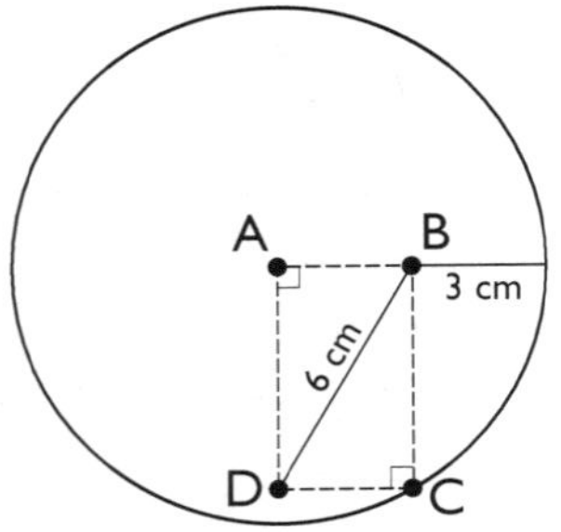

What's the Problem?

Remember: Pi (π) is the ratio of the circumference of a circle to its diameter and is equal to approximately 3·14.

The formula for calculating the circumference of a circle is:

circumference = π × diameter

$c = \pi d$

So, the diameter of a circle is:

diameter = circumference ÷ π

As the diameter is twice the radius, the formula for calculating the circumference of a circle from the radius is:

circumference = 2π × radius

$c = 2\pi r$

So, the radius of a circle is:

radius = circumference ÷ 2π

- Calculate the circumference of a circle with a diameter of 18 cm.
- Calculate the circumference of a circle with a radius of 6 cm.
- To the nearest centimetre, calculate the diameter of a circle with a circumference of 173 cm. What is its radius?

Gather together a collection of at least six circular objects, all different sizes. For example, plates of different sizes, wastepaper basket, analogue clock, geometric circular shape.

Using a tape measure, measure the diameter or radius of half of the objects, then calculate the circumference of each object.

Now measure the circumference of the remaining objects, then calculate the diameter and radius of each object.

The Puzzler

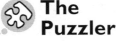

Arrange nine matchsticks like this:

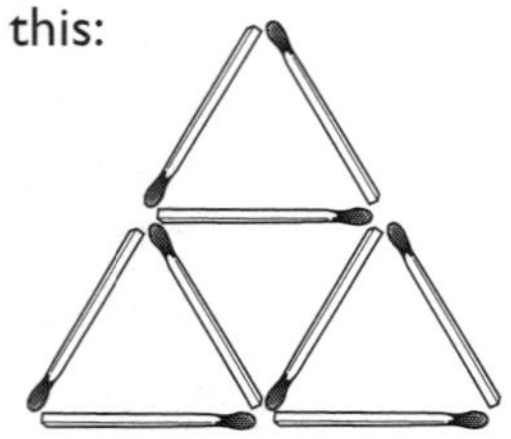

- Remove 4 matches to leave 2 equilateral triangles.
- Remove 3 matches to leave 2 equilateral triangles.
- Remove 2 matches to leave 2 equilateral triangles.

Draw your result.

Now arrange 12 matchsticks like this:

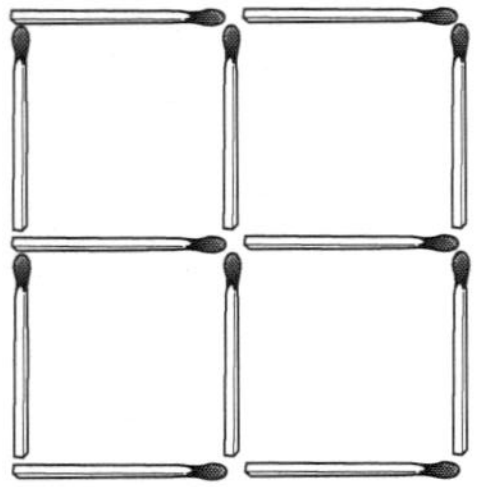

- Move 4 matches to make 2 squares.
- Move 4 matches to make 3 squares.
- Move 3 matches to make 3 squares.
- Remove 2 matches to leave 2 squares.

Draw your result.

The Puzzler

The digits 1 to 6 are written on the faces on a cube.

The three illustrations below show the cube in three different orientations.

This is what the cube looks like as four different nets.

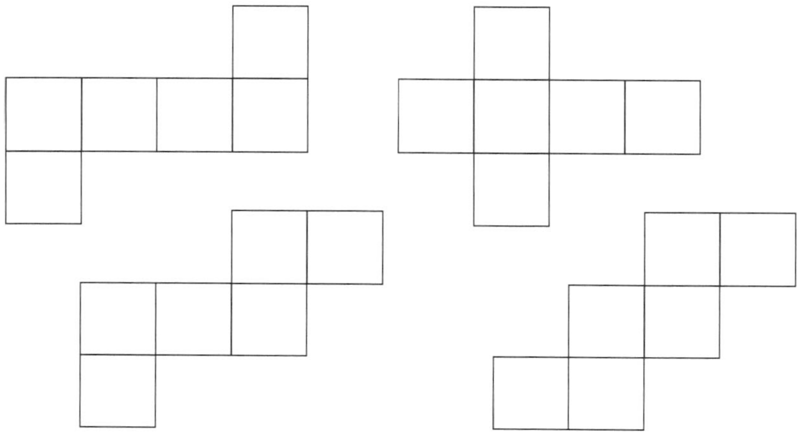

Write the digits in the correct places on each of the nets.

Let's Investigate

How many different $2 \times 2 \times 2$ cubes can you make using four interlocking cubes of one colour and four cubes of another colour?

Draw them.

Investigate using different numbers of each colour.

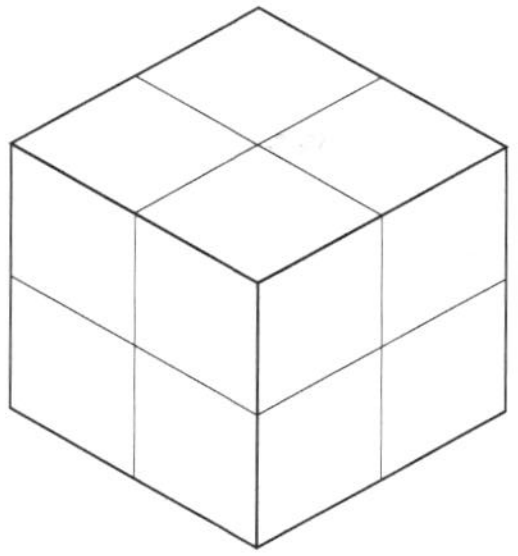

Name:

The Maths Herald

Volume 6

Date:

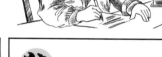

Famous Mathematicians

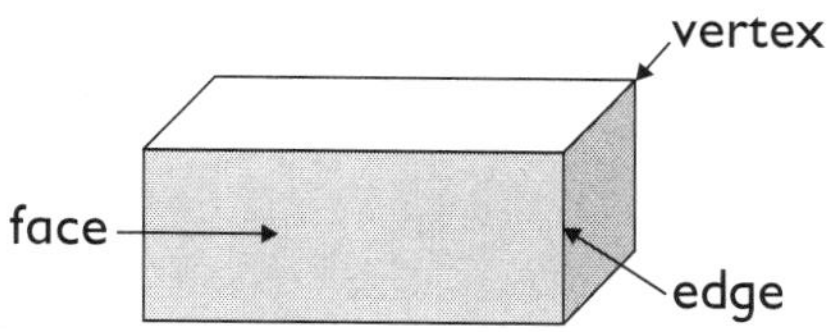

3-D solids are made up of faces, edges and vertices (or corners).

A *polyhedron* is a solid shape with four or more faces.

In the 18th century, Leonard Euler (pronounced Oiler), a Swiss mathematician, discovered a formula giving the relationship between the number of faces, edges and vertices for polyhedrons.

Complete the table to discover Euler's formula. Try to use the letters F, V and E to express your formula.

Polyhedron	Faces (F)	Vertices (V)	Edges (E)
cube (hexahedron)	6	8	12
cuboid	6	8	12
triangular-based pyramid (tetrahedron)			
square-based pyramid			
triangular prism			
octahedron			
dodecahedron			
icosahedron			

A football is not a sphere. It is actually a truncated icosahedron. It has 90 edges and is made from 32 polygons: 12 regular pentagons and 20 regular hexagons. How many vertices does a football have?

Construct

How many different model skeletons can you make using up to 12 straws and 8 joiners in each model?

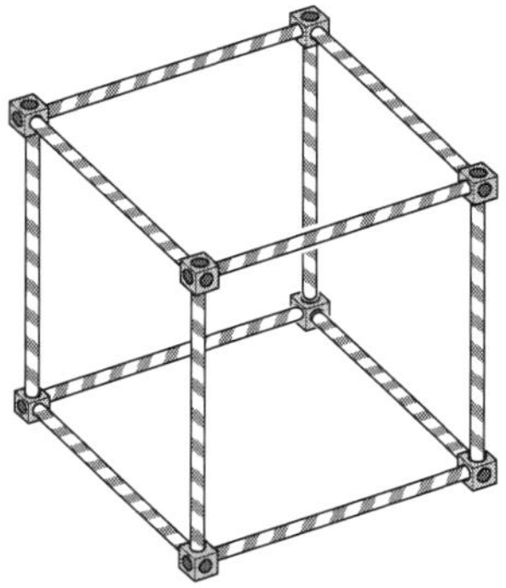

Let's Investigate

Look at this 2 × 2 × 2 cube.

How many small cubes make up the large cube?

Imagine that the large cube was painted yellow so that it was yellow on all the outside faces. How many small cubes have:

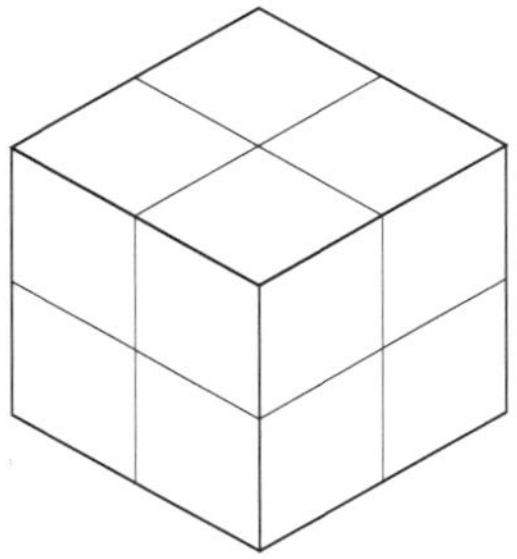

- 3 yellow faces?
- 2 yellow faces?
- 1 yellow face?
- 0 yellow faces?

What do you notice about your answer to the first question and your answers to the second question?

Imagine a 3 × 3 × 3 cube. Answer the questions above for a cube this size.

This time imagine a 4 × 4 × 4 cube. Now answer the questions above for a cube of this size.

What similarities do you notice about all your results?

Construct

This calendar is made from two cubes and three cuboids (only one of the cuboids is displayed).

Between them the three cuboids have the 12 months of the year written on them. The cubes have numbers on them that can be moved around to display the correct date.

Look at the two cube nets below. Write digits on all the faces of both nets so that when put side by side, they will display all the numbers from 01 to 31.

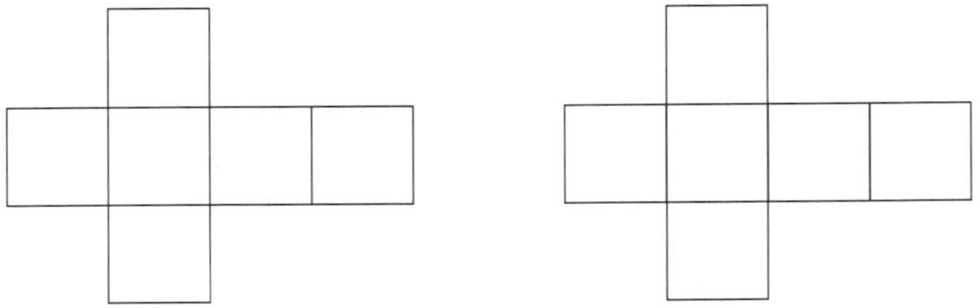

Construct

Make an origami cube. You need six paper squares, ideally each a different colour.

Step 1:
Take one piece of paper and fold it in half to form a crease.

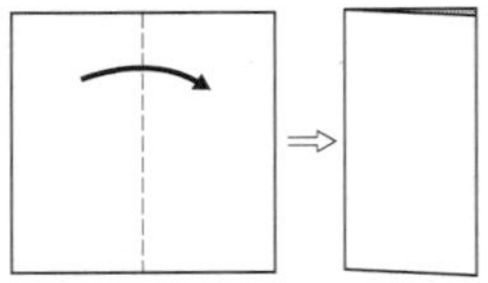

Step 2:
Open the square and fold both sides in towards the centre crease.

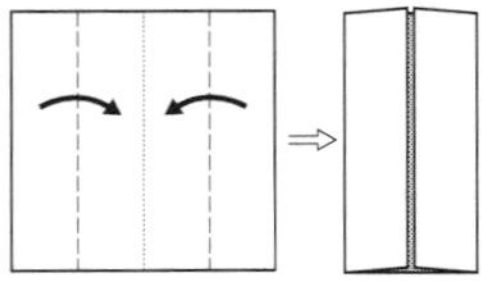

Step 3:
Make a fold from point A to point B. Then open out to step 2 again.

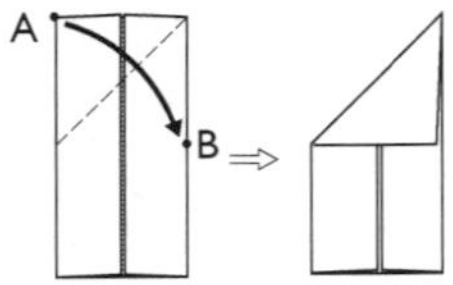

Step 4:
Fold point C under, along the diagonal fold.

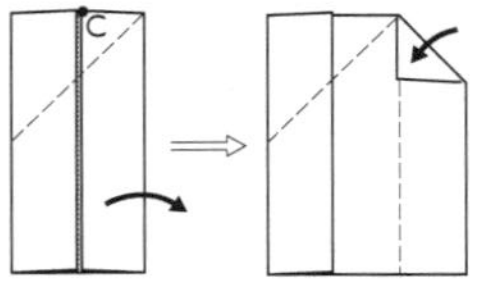

Step 5:
Fold the left-hand flap under the right-hand flap.

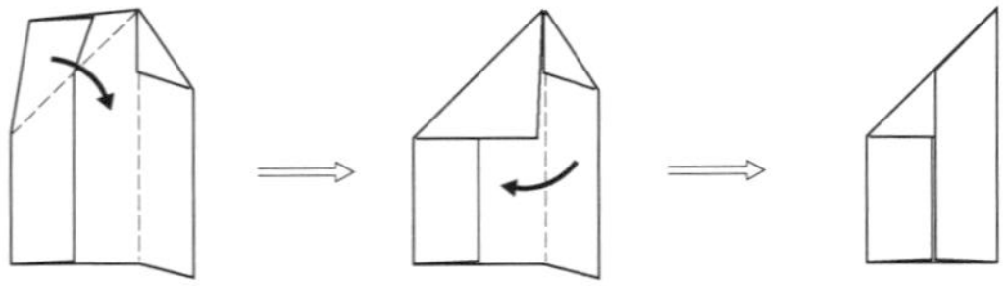

Step 6:
Repeat steps 3, 4 and 5, but this time folding the bottom right-hand flap under the left-hand flap. You should now have two flaps and two pockets.

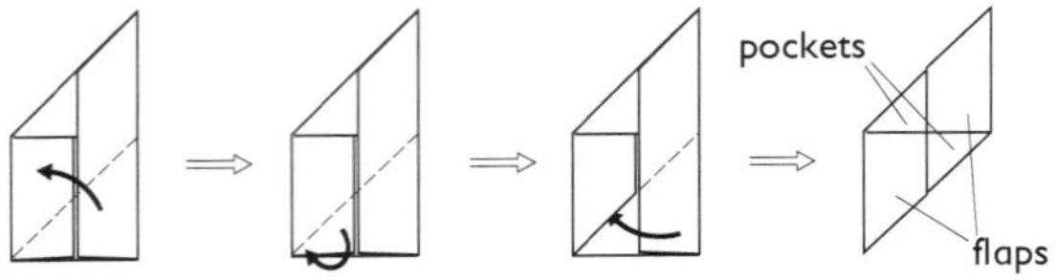

Step 7:
Make two additional diagonal folds.

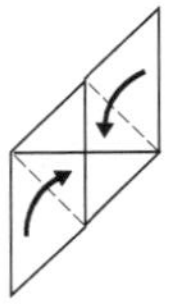

Step 8:
Using the other sheets of paper repeat Steps 1 to 7, five more times, to give a total of six origami pieces.

Step 9:
To assemble the cube, take two origami pieces and insert a flap from one piece into the pocket of the other piece. Then insert a second flap into the other side of the same opening. Each opening in each square fits two flaps from other adjoining squares. Keep inserting flaps into pockets until all the sides are connected and a cube is formed.

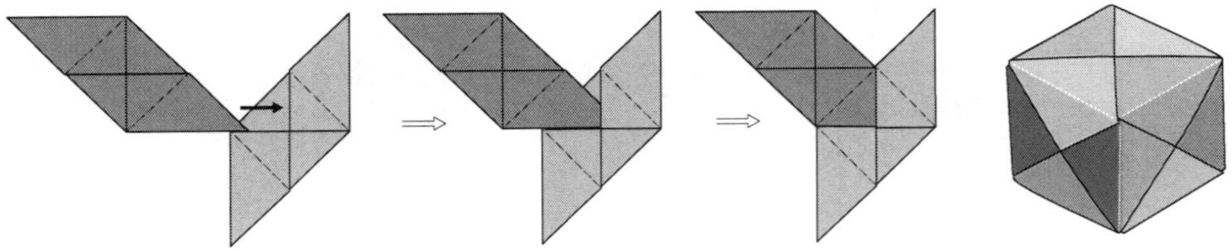

In the Past

Mosaics are pictures or designs made with small pieces of coloured material such as glass or tile stuck onto a surface. Ancient Romans, Greeks and Egyptians, and many other ancient civilisations all produced elaborate mosaics to decorate large homes and important buildings.

Look at these examples of mosaic patterns.

They all show examples of reflective symmetry.

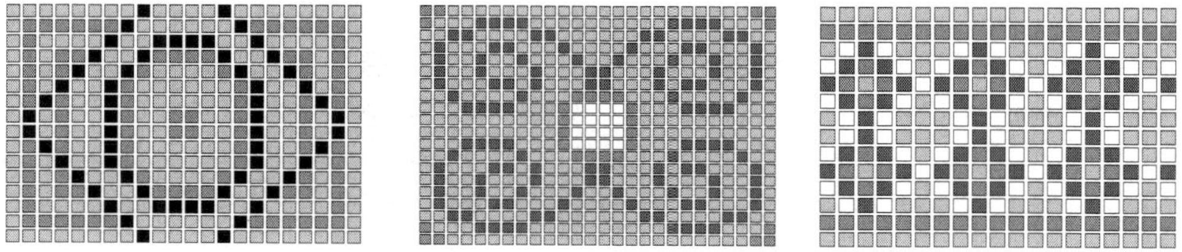

Investigate mosaic patterns.

Draw and colour your own mosaic pattern involving symmetry.

The Puzzler

Draw a reflection of your name in mirror lines placed at different angles relative to your name. For example:

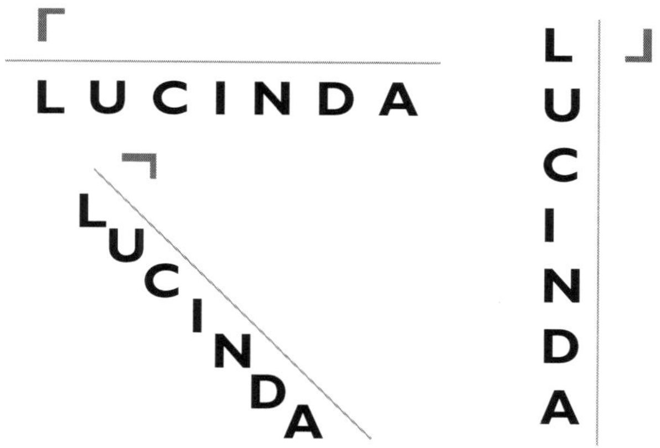

At Home

Many wallpaper designs have examples of reflective symmetry.

Why do you think this is?

Make a collection of different symmetrical wallpaper designs.

Name:

The Maths Herald

Volume 6

Date:

Construct

Throughout history, architects have used reflective symmetry when designing buildings.

Look at these buildings. For each one, find examples of reflective symmetry. Be sure to look for examples in particular architectural features such as columns and windows, as well as in the building as a whole.

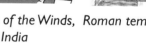

Taj Mahal, Agra, India

St Paul's Cathedral, London, UK

Palace of the Winds, Jaipur, India

Roman temple

Using postcards, travel brochures, books and magazines, make a collection of buildings that show reflective symmetry.

Can you find examples of reflective symmetry in your school or home?

Around the World

The Ndebele are a tribe from Southern Africa. They are known for producing elaborate mural art to decorate their homes, using bright colours with high levels of both vertical and horizontal symmetry.

Investigate Ndebele art. Then design your own Ndebele mural.

Around the World

The Akan are a tribe from Ghana in West Africa. They are known for carving elaborate stools from a single piece of wood.

Some Akan stools also show examples of reflective symmetry.

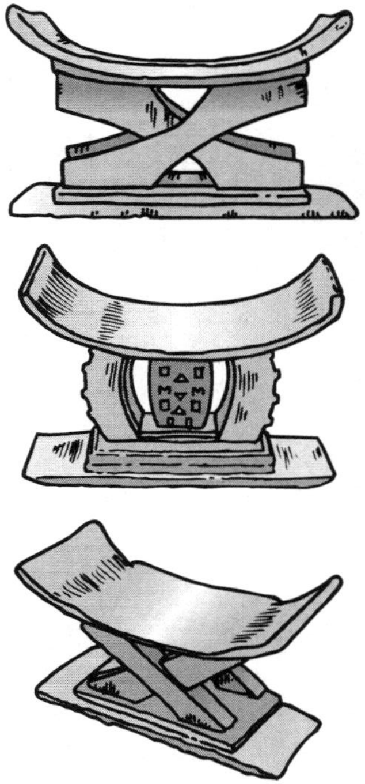

Find out more about Akan stools then draw a detailed design for your own stool.

The Arts Roundup

A common feature of Islamic art is the covering of surfaces with geometric patterns.

Follow these instructions to make an Islamic pattern.

1. Use a pair of compasses to draw a circle.
2. Place the compass point anywhere on the circumference of the circle and move the pencil leg so that a mark is made on the circumference.
3. Then without changing the compass setting, move the point of the compass to the pencil mark and make another pencil mark on the circumference.
4. Do this for a total of six times.
5. Use a ruler to join up the points in sequence round the circle to make a hexagon.
6. Join up every second point to make an equilateral triangle.
7. Join up the other three points of the hexagon to make a second equilateral triangle.
8. Now look at the centre of the pattern you have created – you should see another smaller hexagon.
9. Repeat steps 6 and 7.
10. Now look at the centre of the pattern you have created – you should see an even smaller hexagon.
11. Repeat steps 6 and 7.

Follow the instructions again but this time start with the largest possible circle. How many stars can you make altogether?

When you have drawn the patterns, colour them so that they are symmetrical.

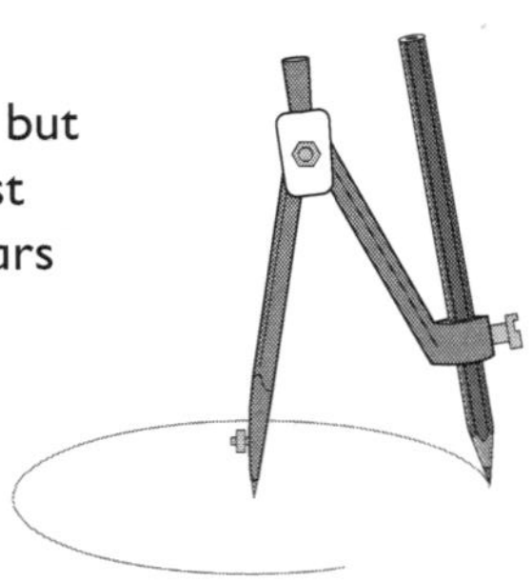

Looking for Patterns

Make a 10 × 10 grid.

Colouring in the squares, design a pattern that shows examples of horizontal, vertical and diagonal symmetry.

You must use six different colours and every square on the grid must be shaded.

When you have finished, write a description of your design, stating its reflective properties.

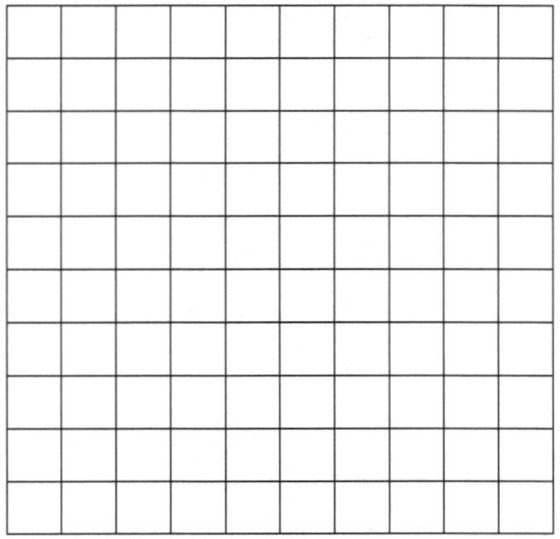

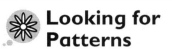

Sports Update

Symmetry is extremely important in the execution of figure skating moves.

Write a statement for each of these moves commenting on the symmetry involved.

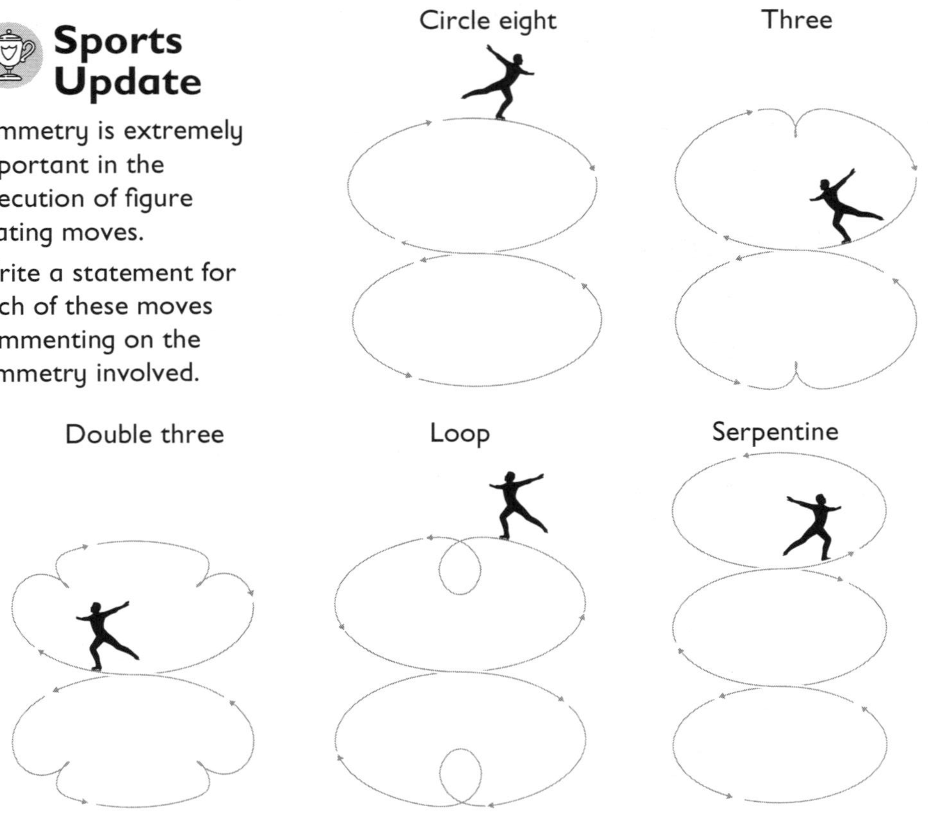

Construct

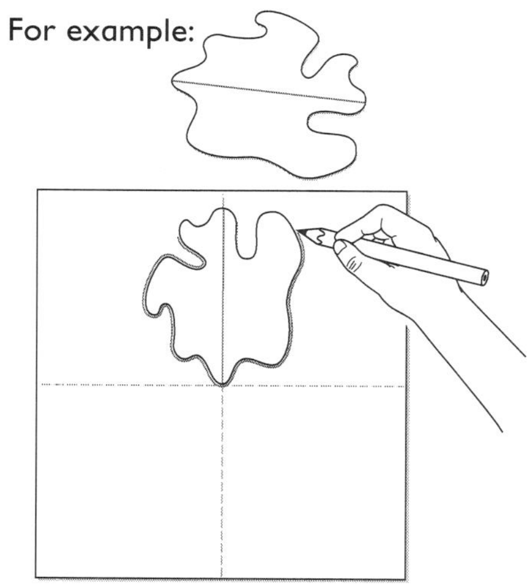

1. Make a template of any odd shape and cut it out. Then draw a straight line through it – anywhere you like.
2. Draw two lines at 90° to each other on a sheet of paper.
3. Place the straight line of the template along one of the lines – with one end of it where the lines cross. Draw around your template.
4. Repeat on each of the four lines, rotating your template each time.

You may want to colour your completed pattern. Look for overlapping shapes.

Try again with a different shape or with lines at different angles, such as:

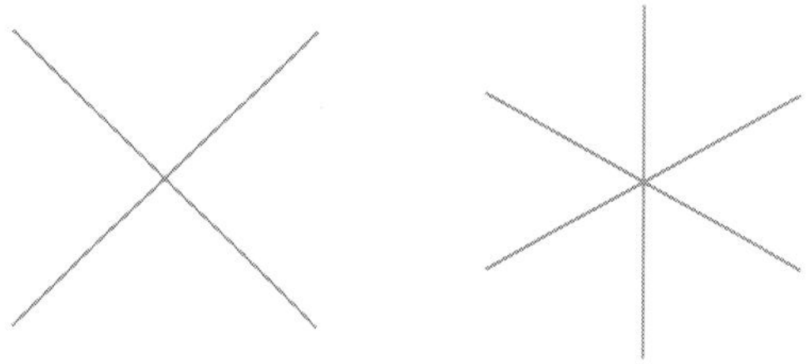

Let's Investigate

What are pentominoes?

Choose a pentomino.

Turn it through 90° about one corner.

Turn it through 90° again and again.

Investigate tessellations of the new shape.

Try with other pentominoes or tetrominoes.

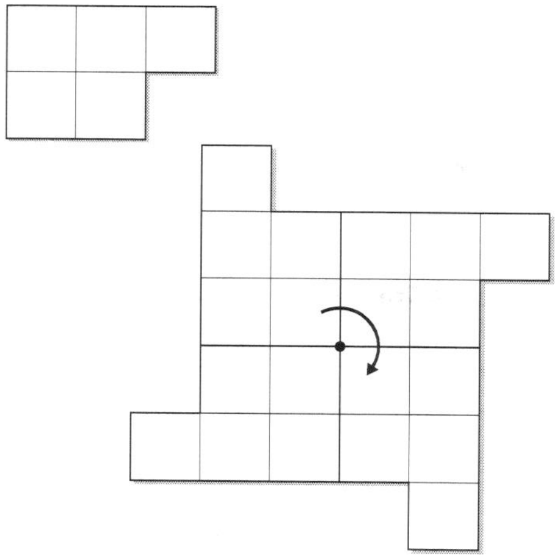

Name:

The Maths Herald

Volume 6

Date:

Around the World

During Diwali celebrations, Hindu families draw colourful Rangoli designs on the floor near the entrance to their home to welcome guests.

Look at these two Rangoli patterns.

They both show examples of rotational symmetry.

Create your own Rangoli pattern.

Be sure to include some rotational symmetry in your pattern.

Looking for Patterns

This shape has been made from isometric paper.

Use isometric paper to draw large triangles like these.

Using four different colours, shade each of the four small triangles a different colour.

Rotate your large triangle about one of its vertices.

Keep rotating your large triangle.

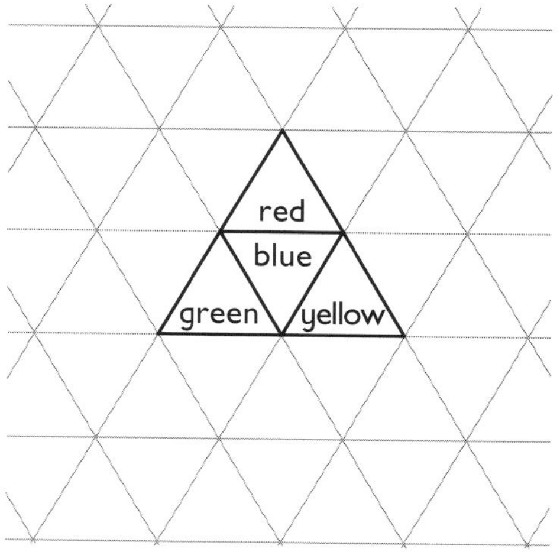

Looking for Patterns

A tessellation is a geometric pattern that fits together without leaving any spaces.

Many tessellations are produced from geometric shapes using a method known as 'half-turn' rotation.

For example:

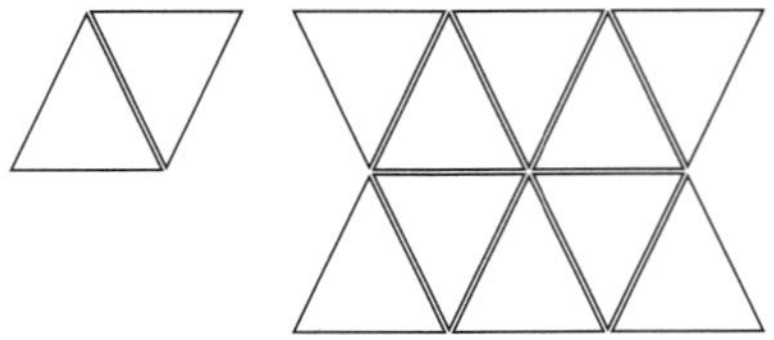

Use the half-turn rotation method to create tessellations from each of these shapes.

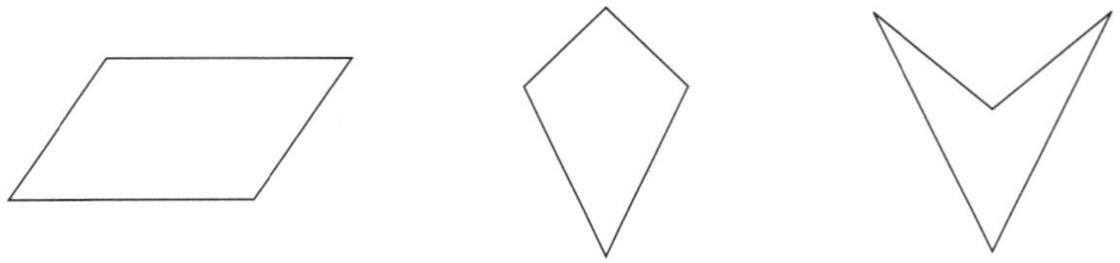

What other shapes can you make tessellating patterns from using the half-turn rotation method?

Let's Investigate

All these hubcaps show examples of rotational symmetry. How?

Investigate the cars in the school car park.

Draw examples of different rotational symmetry.

Explain how each is an example of rotation.

The Arts Roundup

A common Islamic pattern is based on translating a circle along and around a horizontal line.

Follow these steps to make an Islamic circular pattern.

Step 1

Using a ruler draw a horizontal line in the centre of the page.

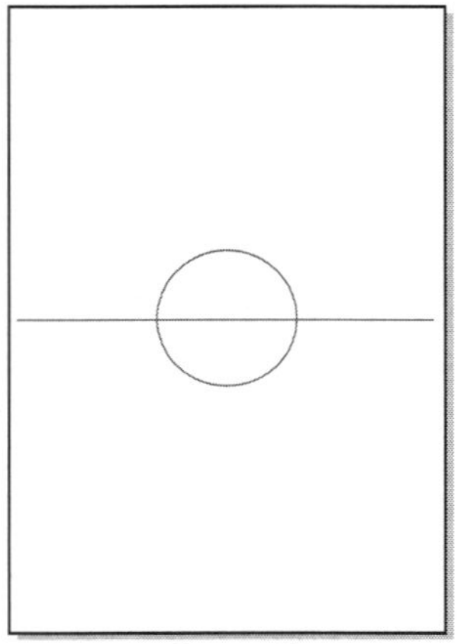

Step 2

Make a circle with a compass point placed in the centre of the line.

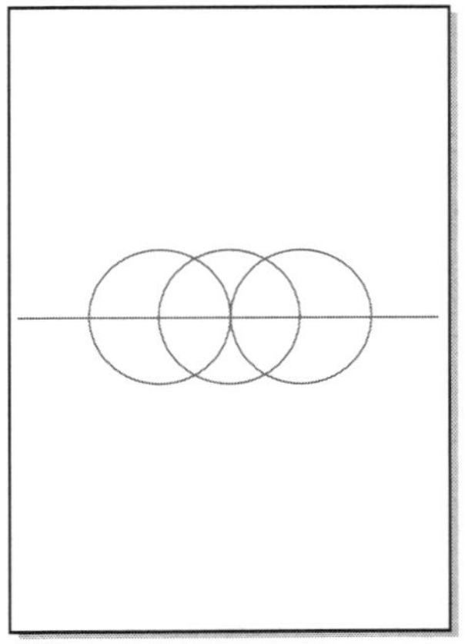

Step 3

Use the two points where the circle intersects with the line to draw two more circles – one on either side of the first circle.

Step 4

Draw four more circles using the new points of intersection as compass points.

Follow the instructions again and keep adding more circles. You will probably need to start with a smaller circle.

When you have drawn the patterns, colour them so that they are symmetrical.

Let's Investigate

Using squared paper, draw a four quadrant coordinates grid. You may wish to extend the *x* and *y* axes beyond ±5 as shown here – perhaps to ±10.

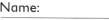

Draw a quadrilateral in the first quadrant of the coordinates grid. Label the shape "A".

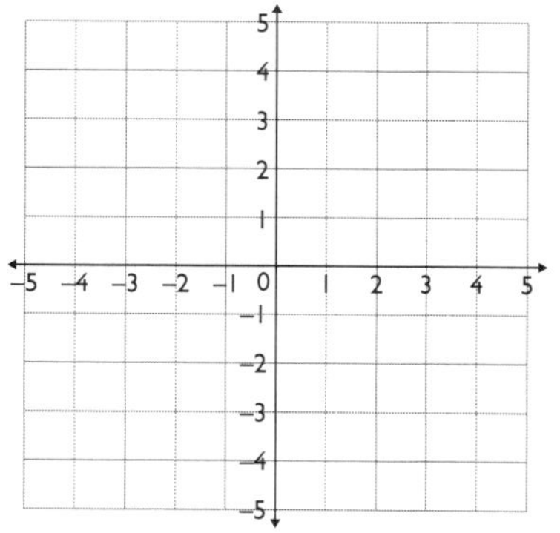

Translate shape A in the first quadrant. Label the shape "A[1]".

Translate shape A:

- twice in the second quadrant (labelled: A^2 and A^3)
- twice in the third quadrant (labelled: A^4 and A^5)
- twice in the fourth quadrant (labelled: A^6 and A^7).

Reproduce the eight quadrilaterals you have drawn on the square coordinates grid onto triangular dot paper.

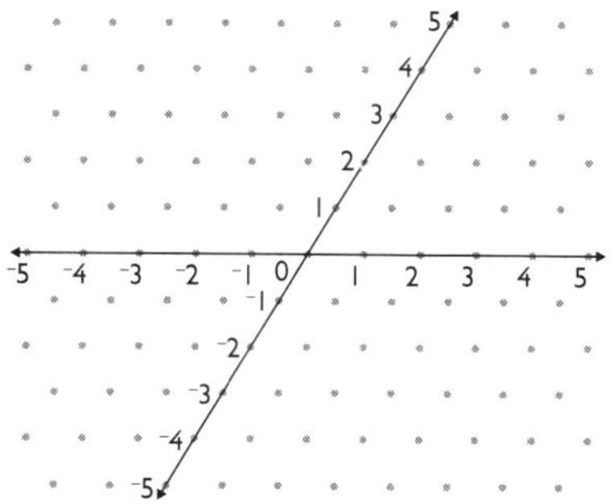

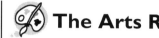

Write about what you notice.

Investigate further by:

- drawing other quadrilaterals and polygons
- using different grids
- using other types of transformations.

The Puzzler

What are all the possible translations of a 1-unit by 2-unit right-angled triangle on a 3 × 3 geoboard?

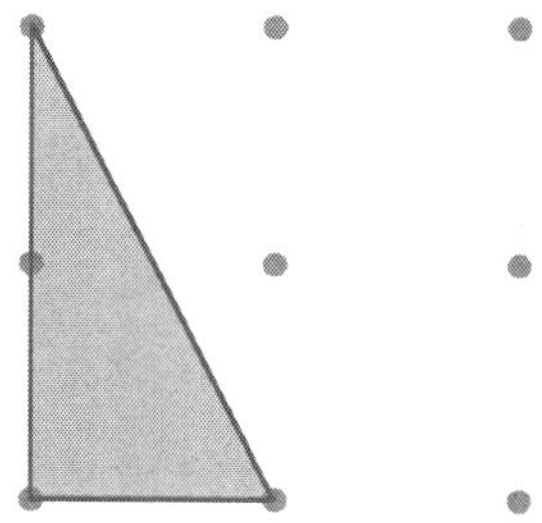

What about on a 4 × 4 geoboard and a 5 × 5 geoboard?

Name:

The Maths Herald

Volume 6

Date:

Looking for Patterns

A tessellation is a geometric pattern that fits together without leaving any spaces.

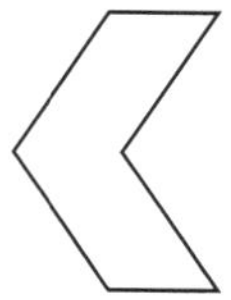

This shape has been translated to make the tessellating pattern below.

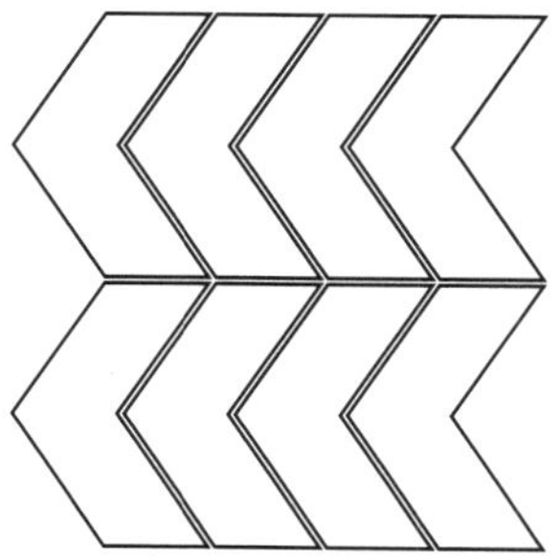

What other shapes can be translated to make good tessellating patterns?

The Arts Roundup

The Dutch artist Maurits Escher used many tessellations in his work. He often used methods based on mathematics.

Make a tessellation using one of Escher's methods.

- Take a square and draw an interesting design along one side.
- Copy this design onto the opposite side and cut it out.

The result will be a tessellating template.

For example:

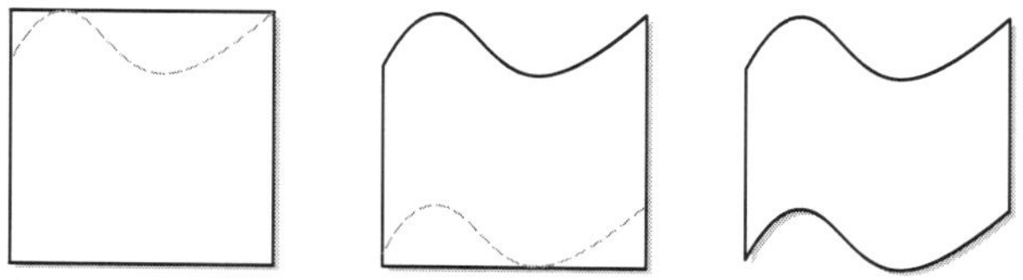

Using your template, make translations to create an interesting tessellation.

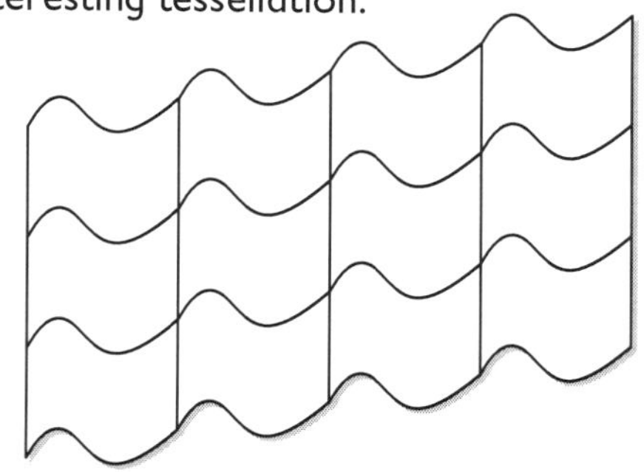

Decorate your tessellation with contrasting colours.

The Arts Roundup

Mauritis Escher was a graphic artist from The Netherlands whose work was heavily influenced by mathematics. He is famous all over the world for his intricate and intriguing designs and drawings which still influence artists, songwriters and filmmakers today.

Investigate the life and work of MC Escher and comment on the mathematics involved in some of his works of art.

Construct

Here is another method for creating tessellating patterns using translations.

- Take a square and change two adjacent sides by cutting out shapes. Try and pass through the corner between them.
- Using the pieces you have cut out, tape these to the opposite sides. The result will be a tessellating template.

For example:

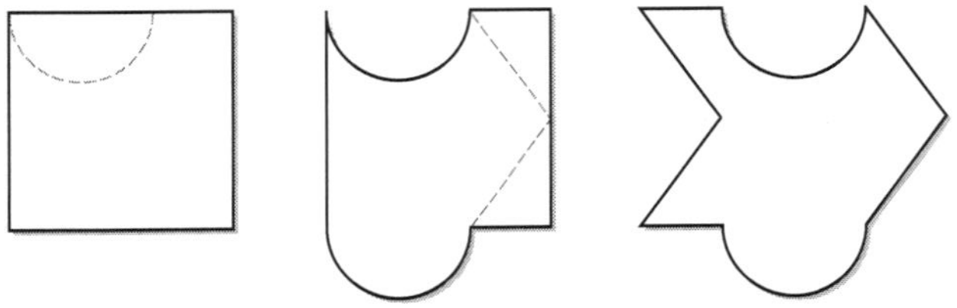

Using your template, make translations to create an interesting tessellation.

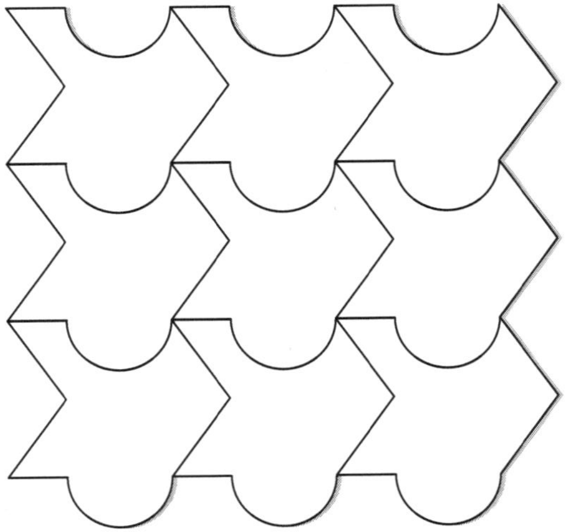

Decorate your tessellation with contrasting colours.

In the Past

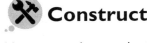

Mosaics are pictures or designs made with small pieces of coloured material such as glass or tile stuck onto a surface. Ancient Romans, Greeks and Egyptians, and many other ancient civilisations all produced elaborate mosaics to decorate large homes and important buildings.

Look at these examples of mosaic border patterns.

They all show examples of translations.

Investigate mosaic border patterns.

Draw and colour your own mosaic border pattern involving translations.

Let's Investigate

Which triangles can the shaded triangle land on exactly after one translation?

What about these shapes?

What about after two translations?

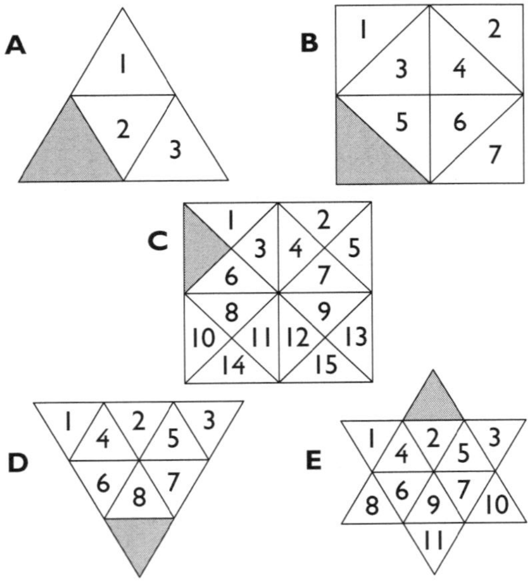

Construct

A *parabola* is the name given to a particular shape of curve. The path of an object thrown in the air is a parabola.

Study the diagram below. Then, using squared paper, copy it to draw your own parabola.

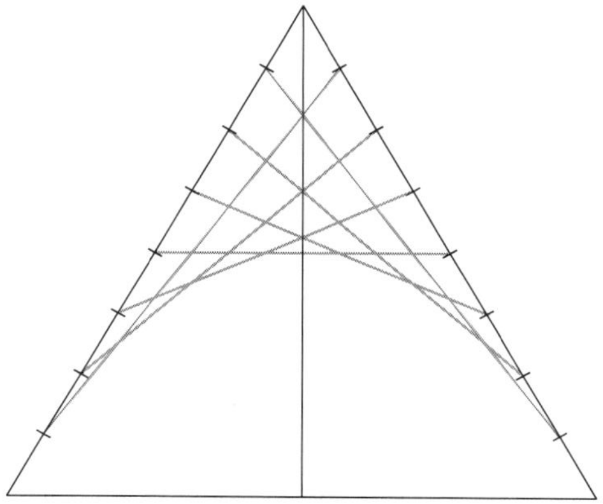

Another way to draw a parabola is by using coordinates.

Using 2 cm squared paper, copy this coordinates grid.

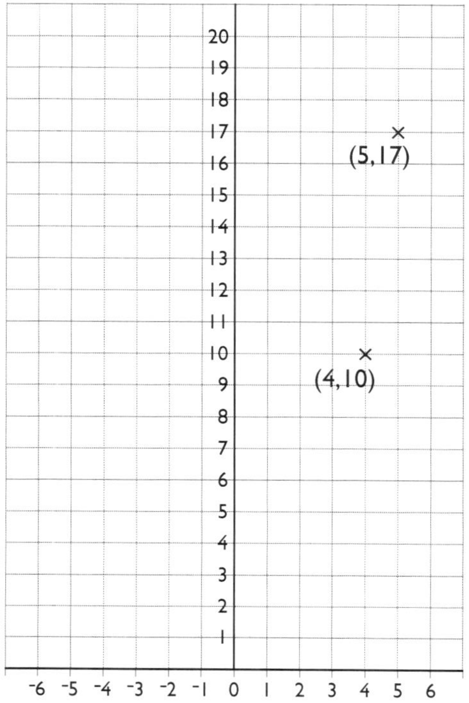

Using as *x*-axis values all the numbers from 5 to ⁻3, use the following formula to work out each of the *y*-axis values.

$$y = (x - 1)^2 + 1$$

Here are the first two pairs of co-ordinates.

(5,17) (4,10)

Label the coordinates of each point on your parabola.

Name:

The Maths Herald

Volume 6

Date:

Famous Mathematicians

Maria Agnesi was an Italian mathematician born in Milan, Italy, in 1718. Agnesi was particularly interested in algebra and geometry.

"The Witch of Agnesi" is a special curve that Maria studied. The name "The Witch of Agnesi" was a misinterpretation of the translation from Italian to English but this mistranslation has stuck!

This is the formula for "The Witch of Agnesi": $y = \dfrac{a^3}{x^2 + a^2}$

A special case of "The Witch of Agnesi" curve is: $y = \dfrac{125}{x^2 + 25}$

Using 1 cm squared paper copy this coordinates grid.

Then using all the points along the *x*-axis, that is, ⁻10, ⁻9, ⁻8, … 0, 1, 2, …10 use the special case formula of "The Witch of Agnesi" to determine the *y*-axis values.

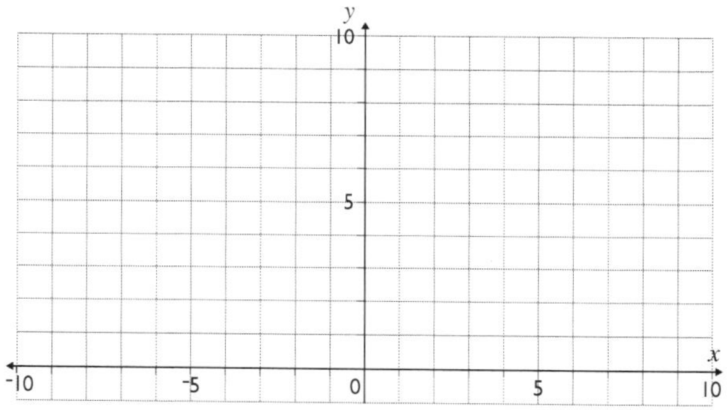

For example:

If $x = {}^{-}10$, then: $\dfrac{125}{{}^{-}10^2 + 25}$

NOTE: Round the *y*-axis values to the nearest tenth.

$$= \frac{125}{100 + 25} = \frac{125}{125} = 1$$

So the coordinates for this point are (⁻10, 1)
Now plot the points on the graph to see the shape of the curve of "The Witch of Agnesi".

Construct

A maze is an area of interconnected paths that it is hard to find a way through. They are usually designed in a garden with hedges between the paths.

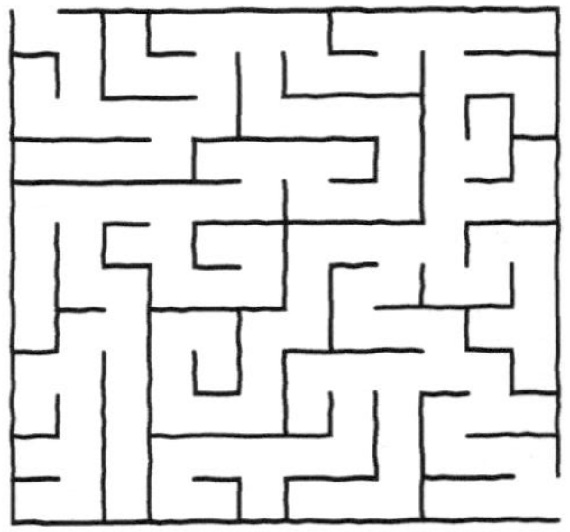

Design your own maze.

Swap your maze with someone else who has designed a maze. Find your way out of their maze!

What makes a good maze? Write some rules for designing a good maze.

Around the World

Satellite navigation systems (satnavs) are devices used for finding specific locations and getting directions to and from places. Many cars and mobile phones now have this system built in as standard features.

Find out all you can about satellite navigation systems. For example:

- Who developed them?
- Why were they developed?
- How do they work?
- How can they be used?

When you have found out as much information as you can about satnavs, design a poster to explain to others what you have found out.

The Puzzler

Robert lives 5 km south west of Becky.

Louise lives 5 km north east of Becky.

Robert lives south of James.

Louise lives south east of James.

How far does James live from Louise?

Around the World

Imagine someone is coming to visit your home for the first time.

Think of a well-known landmark not far from your home.

Write a detailed set of instructions from the landmark to your home.

As well as the instructions, include a simple map for them to follow.

Let's Investigate

Draw a coordinates grid similar to this on dot squared paper.

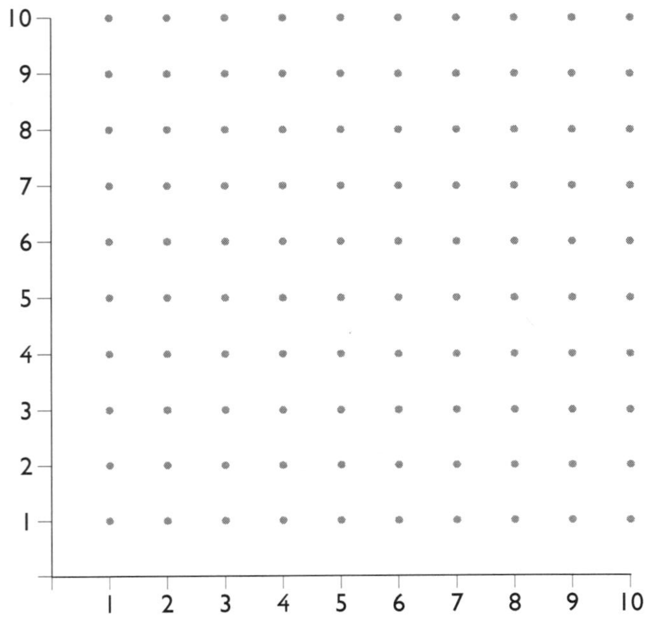

Use the numbers 2, 3, 5 and 8 to make coordinates. For example: (2, 8) or (5, 5).

Use the coordinates to make these quadrilaterals:

- parallelogram
- rhombus
- rectangle
- square
- kite
- trapezium

Let's Investigate

A random trail can be generated by the toss of a coin, the roll of a 1–6 dice or choosing a card from a pack of 1–8 digit cards (reshuffled after each choice).

Coin

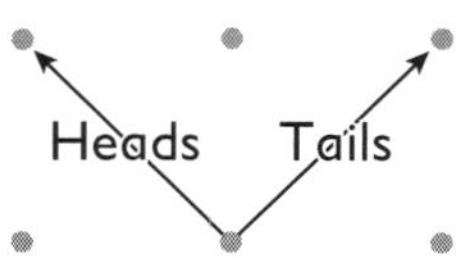

1–6 dice

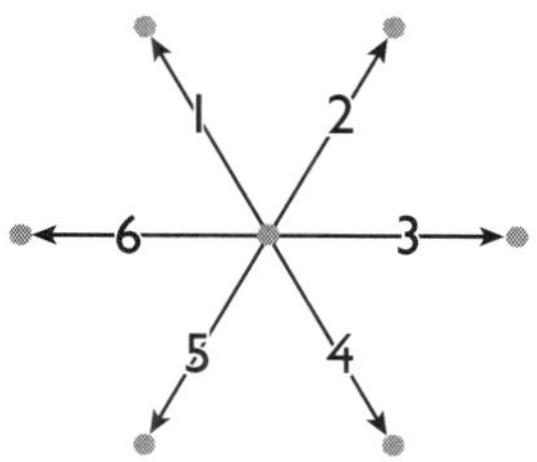

1–8 digit cards

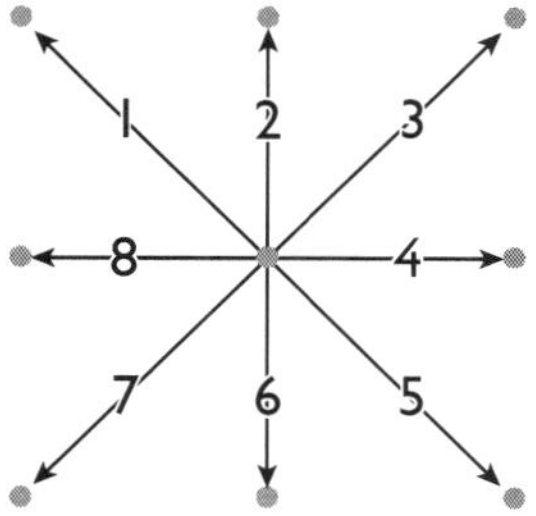

Using different dot paper, investigate the different random paths you can make using a coin, dice and digit cards.

What about if you used a random number generating function on a computer?

Focus on Science

Does the angle of a light source affect the length of a shadow?

Using a torch, design an experiment to find out.

Write a report on your experiment.

Show your results in a graph.

What conclusions can you draw?

At Home

Look around your home and find as many different angles as you can.

Sort the angles you find into the following categories:

- right angles
- acute angles
- obtuse angles

Name:

The Maths Herald

Volume 6

Date:

Sports Update

A British standard pool (billiards) table is 1·82 m long by 0·91 m wide. This means that it is twice as long as it is wide. It has six pockets: one in each corner and one halfway along the length of each side of the table.

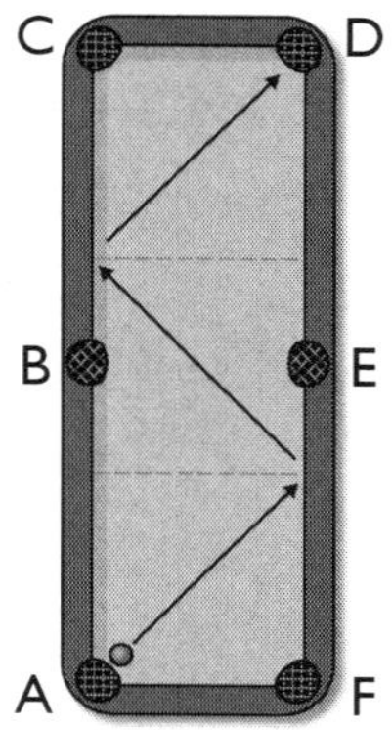

Look at these unusual dimensions for a billiards table.

If a ball is hit from corner A at an angle of 45° to the edge of the table all its rebounds will be 45°.

For a 3 × 1 table, the ball would fall into pocket D.

For each of these tables work out which pocket the ball will fall into if it is always hit from corner A at an angle of 45°.

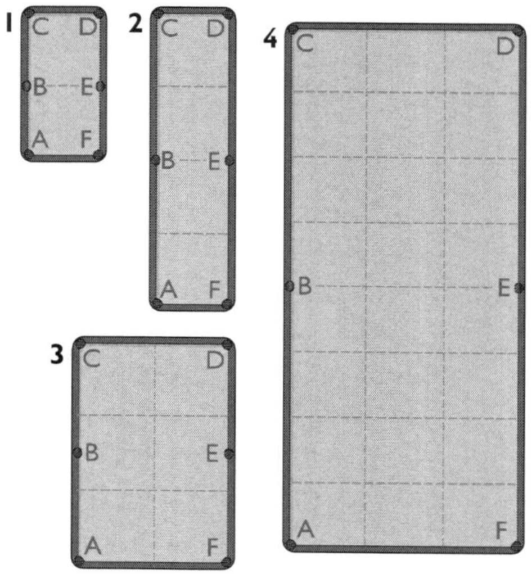

Let's Investigate

If you took three paces forwards, turned 60°, took another three paces forwards and turned right 60°, and kept on doing this, this is the path you would walk.

Write instructions for other shapes.

Then give your instructions to a friend. Can they draw your shapes?

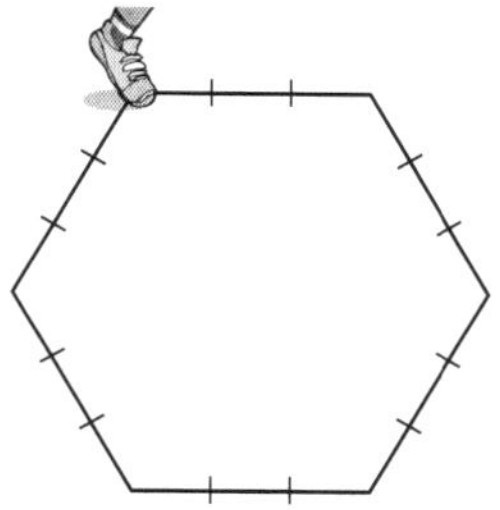

Technology Today

Look at the lists of instructions that you wrote in the Let's Investigate activity on page 1.

Can you recreate your shapes using ICT?

Around the World

One way of giving directions to someone is by using compass directions, for example 'head south' or 'walk in a north-easterly direction'. Another way of giving a compass direction is to give the size of the angle measured from the north as a three-digit number that is always measured in a clockwise direction from north. Such readings are called *bearings*.

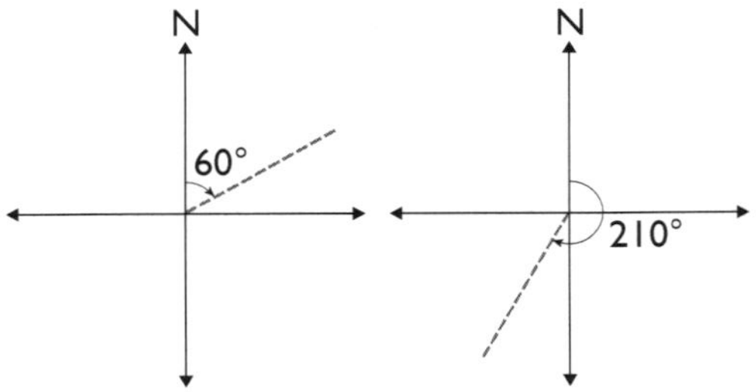

The first diagram on the left shows a bearing of 060°, while the second diagram shows a bearing of 210°.

Bearings are read using a magnetic compass.

How does a magnetic compass work?

Find a spot in the playground. Choose six objects visible from this spot, and read the bearings using the compass.

Construct

Here's how to make the same shape as a 50p coin.

1. Using a pair of compasses, draw a large circle. Make a faint point where the centre of the circle is.

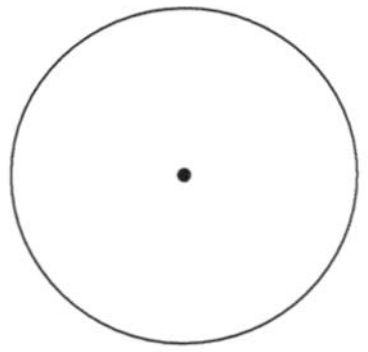

2. Draw a faint line from the centre of the circle to the edge of the circle (i.e. a radius). Label the point 'A'.

3. Draw another six radii. All seven radii need to be equally spaced. As there are 360° in a circle, this means that each angle needs to be about 51° (360° ÷ 7 = 51·428…°). Label the points 'B' to 'G'.

4. Place the point of the compass on point A and increase the angle of the compass to draw an arc from point D to point E.

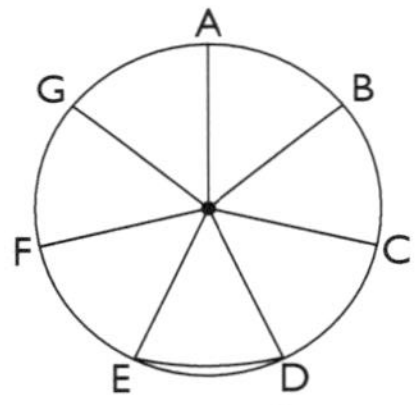

5. Place the point of the compass on point B and draw an arc from point E to point F.

6. Repeat for points C to G.

7. Erase the circle you drew in Step 1 to see the 50p.

The Puzzler

The game of chess has six different kinds of pieces: king, queen, bishop, knight, rook, and pawn. Each piece moves in its own special way. The knight is special because, unlike the other pieces, it doesn't move in a straight line. It makes L-shaped moves, jumping over anything in its way to reach an empty square on a chessboard.

For example, a knight can move two squares forward, then one square sideways, or it can move one square forward, then two squares sideways.

The Knight's Tour is a mathematical puzzle involving a knight on a chessboard. The knight is placed on the empty board and, moving according to the rules of chess, must visit each square exactly once.

Investigate the possibilities of making knight's tours on the following boards.

Record your results on squared paper.

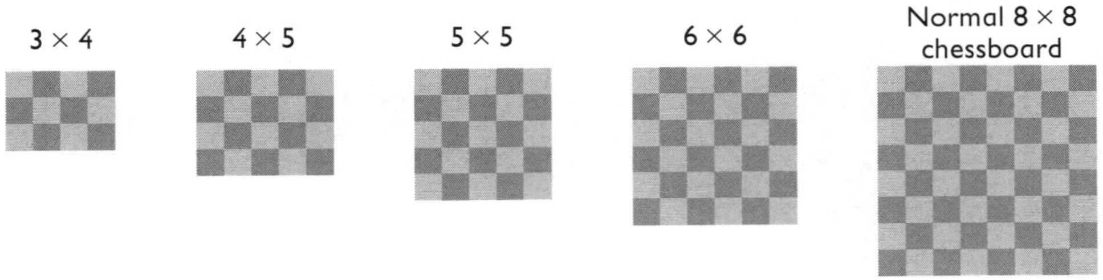

Let's Investigate

Look at this trail.

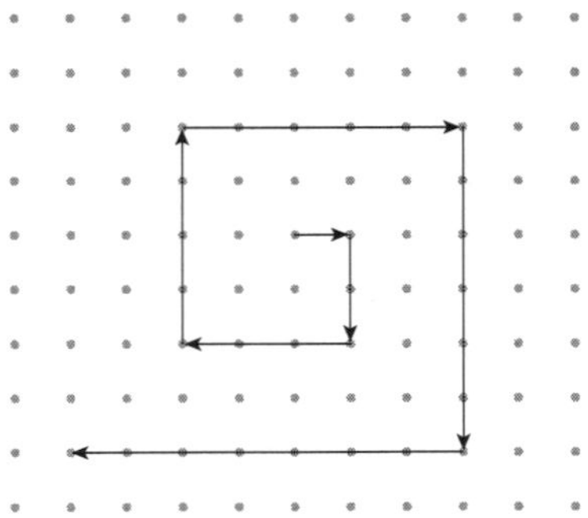

This is a 1, 2, 3… turn pattern. It is made from one unit of track, a clockwise turn of 90°, two units of track, a clockwise turn of 90°, three units of track, a clockwise turn of 90°, and so on.

Investigate trails using triangular dot paper.

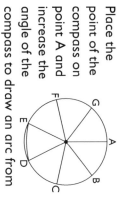

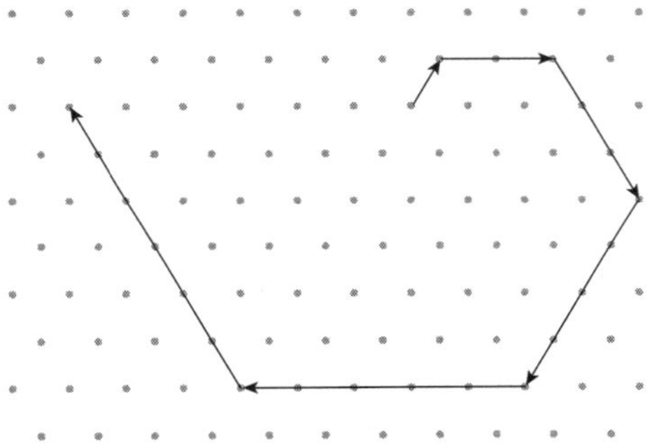

The Arts Roundup

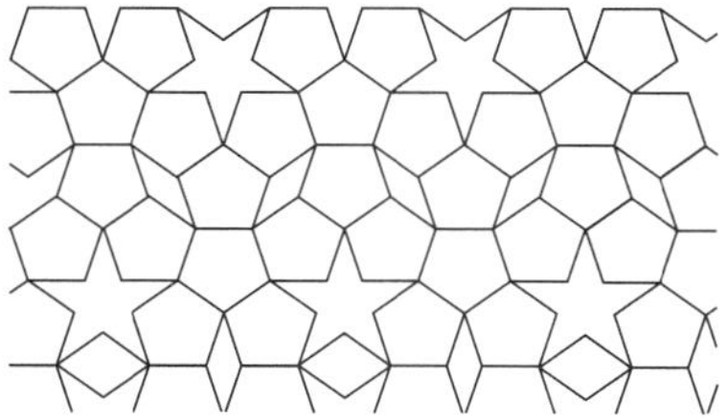

Devise a design that has:

- a repeating pattern
- and a regular pentagon
- and two lines of reflective symmetry (horizontal and vertical)
- and a shape that has been rotated
- and a shape that has been translated horizontally and vertically.

Draw your design.

Technology Today

Devise a design similar to that described in The Arts Roundup activity above but construct it using a computer program.

Construct

Follow these steps.

1. Using a pair of compasses, draw a circle with a radius of 9 cm.
2. Lightly mark a point at the top of the circle and label it A.
3. Then without changing the compass setting, place the compass point on point A and lightly mark another point (point B) on the circle.
4. Place the compass point on point B and mark another point (point C).
5. Continue until you have marked six points on the circle (A–F).
6. Using your ruler, draw a geometric design.

Here is one very simple design.

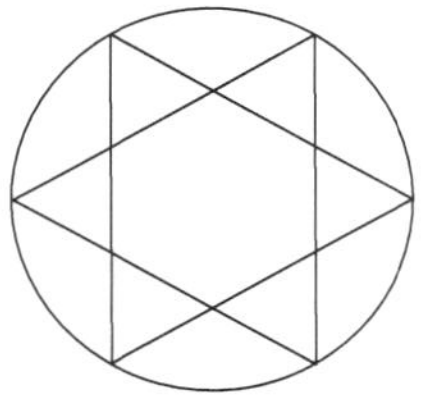

Make a more elaborate design of your own.

Then colour your design to show examples of reflective symmetry, rotational symmetry and translations.

Name:

The Maths Herald

Volume 6

Date:

The Language of Maths

Look carefully at this pattern.

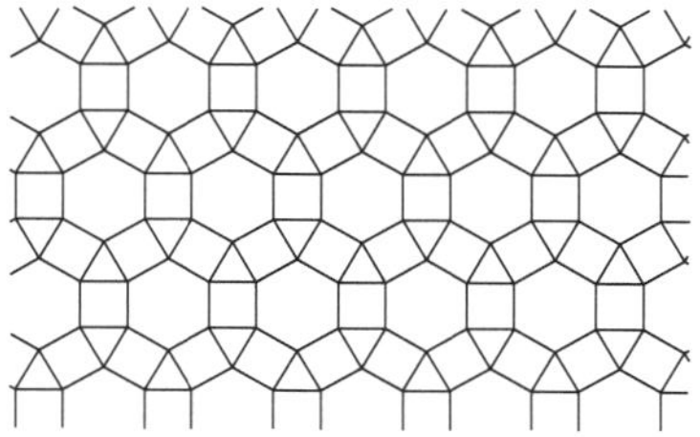

Imagine you had to explain to someone how to draw this pattern without them seeing it.

Write a detailed set of instructions explaining what to do.

Find a friend. Don't show them this pattern. Give them your set of instructions.

Can they accurately draw the diagram?

What's the Problem?

In the game of chess, the queen is extremely useful at defending squares.

She can move in a straight line, any number of squares, in any direction, i.e. vertically, horizontally and diagonally.

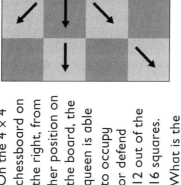

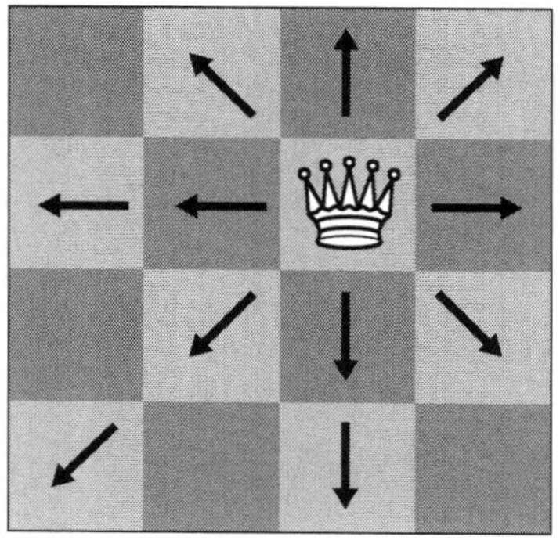

On the 4 × 4 chessboard on the right, from her position on the board, the queen is able to occupy or defend 12 out of the 16 squares.

What is the fewest number of queens you can place on a 4 × 4 chessboard so that all 16 squares are either occupied or defended? How many different solutions are there? Record your results on squared paper.

What is the fewest number of queens you can place on a 5 × 5 chessboard so that all 25 squares are either occupied or defended?

How about on a 6 × 6 chessboard?

What about a full-size chessboard of 8 × 8?

Around the World

Investigate reflective and rotational symmetry in flags.

Write a brief statement about each flag's symmetry.

What are some flags with no symmetry?

The Puzzler

Try the Eight Queens Puzzle.

Place eight chess queens on an 8 × 8 chessboard so that no two queens can attack, or capture, each other.

Record your results on squared paper.

How many different solutions can you find?

Let's Investigate

The two straight lines drawn through this circle are called *chords*.

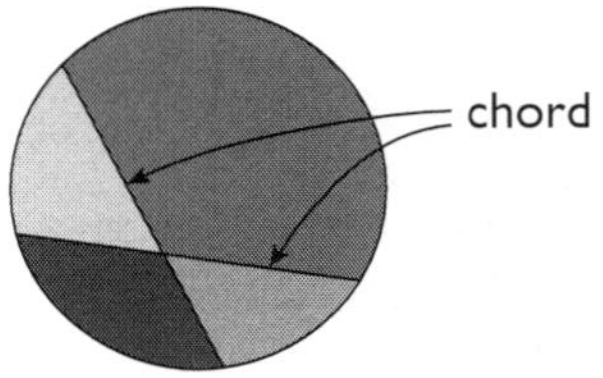

The four shaded areas that they have created are called *segments*.

Can you draw two chords through a circle so that there are only three segments?

How many different numbers of segments can you make by drawing three chords?

How about all those for four and five chords?

What patterns do you notice?

What is the maximum number of segments you can make for a particular number of chords?

Write a formula for the maximum number of segments you can make for a particular number of chords.

Famous Mathematicians

These diagrams are called *networks*. Which networks can you travel without taking your finger off the paper and without retracing any line?

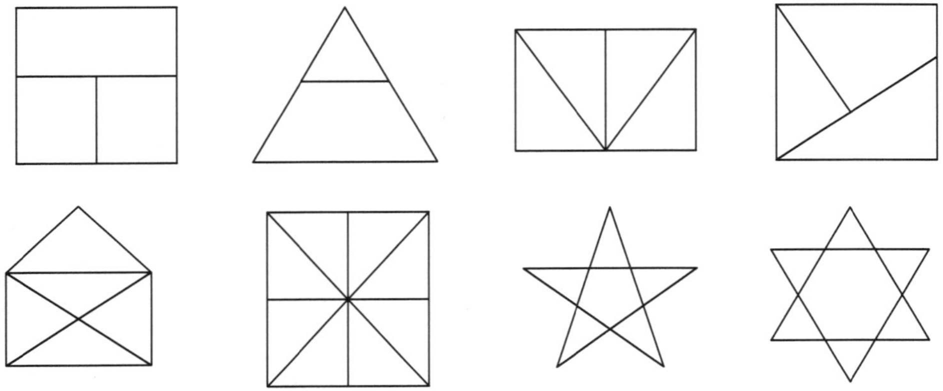

Leonhard Euler (1707–1783) was a Swiss mathematician.

He discovered some important rules about networks.

Clue

Networks can only be travelled like this if they have fewer than a certain number of odd vertices.

An *odd vertex* has an odd number of lines meeting at it.

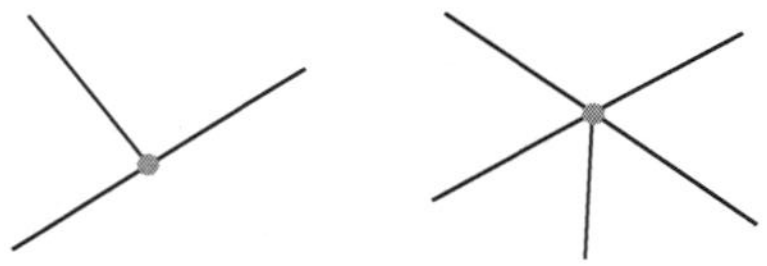

An *even vertex* has an even number of lines meeting at it.

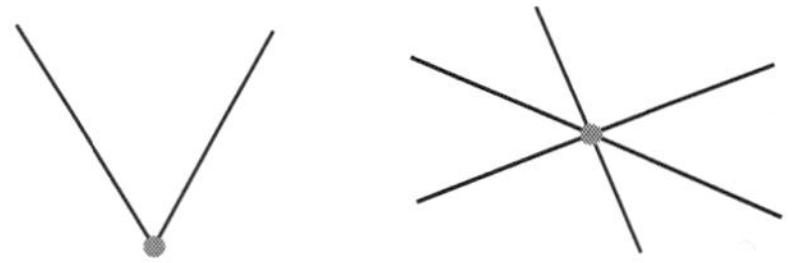

For each of the above networks think about the following:

- total number of vertices
- number of even vertices
- number of odd vertices
- whether can it be travelled.

Use this information to discover Euler's rules.

Now draw some of your own networks and say whether or not they can be travelled without lifting a finger or retracing any line.

Around the World

The distance around the equator is 40 000 km or approximately 25 000 miles. Estimate how long it would take to travel round the equator.

What is your estimation based on? Write a report to justify your estimation.

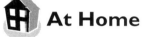

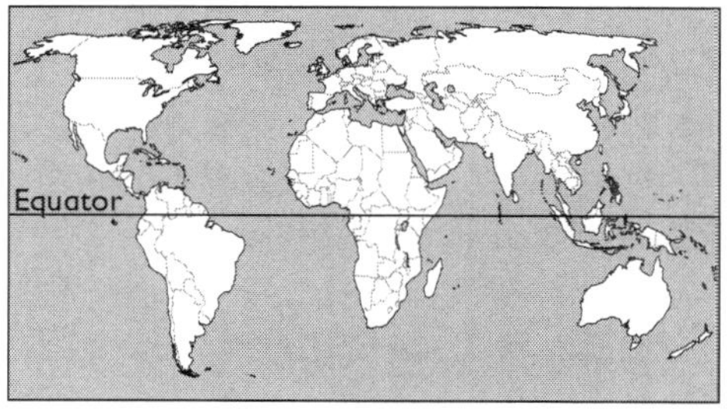

Money Matters

10p coins are placed one on top of the other to make a tower.

What would be the value of a 1 kilometre tower of 10p coins?

The Language of Maths

20,000 Leagues Under the Sea is a classic science-fiction novel by French writer Jules Verne published in 1869. It tells the story of Captain Nemo and his submarine Nautilus.

What is a league?

What is it equivalent to?

What may be an alternative title for *20,000 Leagues Under the Sea?*

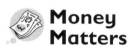

At Home

Estimate the distance from school to your home. Write down how you arrived at this estimate.

Now write down how you could most accurately measure this distance.

Can you do it? If so, do it!

Name:

The Maths Herald

Volume 6

Date:

Around the World

Usually a map cannot be drawn life-size. It has to fit onto a piece of paper. So in most cases maps are drawn to *scale*.

Something that is actually 5 km away may be drawn as 1 cm away on a map. In this case 1 cm represents 5 km. The scale is 1 cm : 5 km.

Using a map that has a scale on it, compare the distances between different landmarks.

Try and be as accurate as possible with your measurements.

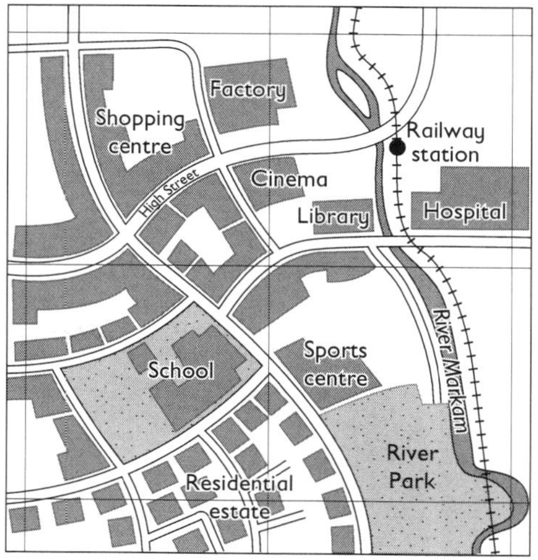

Construct

Just as most maps are drawn to scale, so too are different plans. Plans are drawn for whole buildings, individual rooms, pieces of machinery or furniture, or anything where it is not possible to have a life-size drawing.

Draw a simple plan of your classroom including the most important features, e.g. desks, whiteboard, cupboards, door, …

Measure these features and record them on your plan.

Now work out a scale for your plan and draw another plan of your classroom to scale.

Draw a simple plan of a piece of furniture in your classroom, e.g. desk or cupboard.

Measure all its features and record them on your plan.

Now work out a scale for your plan and draw another plan of the piece of furniture to scale.

Focus on Science

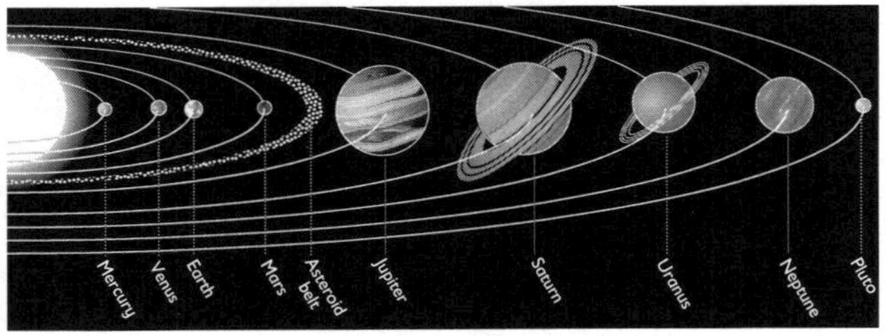

The diameter of the Earth is approximately 13 000 km.
The diameter of Pluto is approximately 2000 km and the diameter of the Sun approximately 1 400 000 km.

Find out the approximate diameters of all the planets in the solar system and draw them to the same scale.

For example, you may decide to draw the Earth with a diameter of 13 mm and Pluto with a diameter of 2 mm.

Around the World

The horizon is the line at which the Earth's surface and the sky appear to meet.

How far away is the horizon if you were standing on the seashore?

Use these formulas to find out:

d = distance to the horizon

h = your height above sea level

An approximate formula when measuring in kilometres and metres is:

$$d = \sqrt{12{\cdot}7h}$$

An approximate formula when measuring in miles and feet is:

$$d = \sqrt{1{\cdot}50h}$$

Measure your height from ground to eye level.

Then calculate how far the horizon appears to you.

Choose some friends and find out how far the horizon appears to them.

Why not try this out for someone at home (or your teacher)!

Let's Investigate

Each step on an ordinary flight of stairs has a vertical *riser* which is the height of the step, and a horizontal *tread*, which is the depth of the step that you walk on.

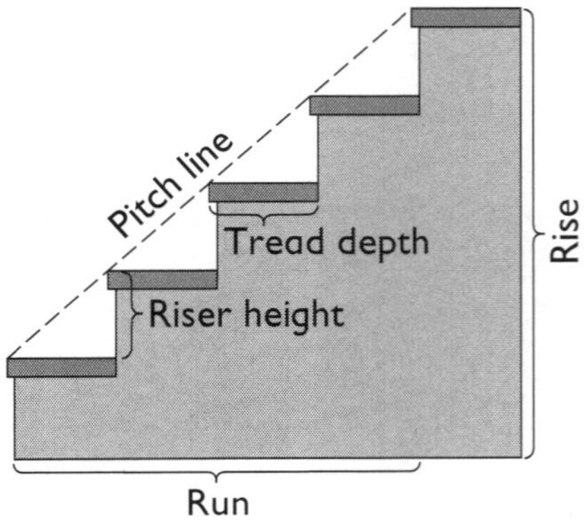

The *slope* or *pitch* of the stairs is the total rise divided by the total *run*. It is sometimes called the *rake* of the stairs. The *pitch line* is the imaginary line along the tip of the treads.

Investigate different staircases.

- What is the height of an average riser?
- What is the depth of an average tread?
- Is there a ratio between the height of the riser and the depth of the tread?
- What is the average slope of a staircase?

Sports Update

Most sports are played on areas of a particular shape and with specific dimensions.

Investigate the dimensions used for playing different sports such as:

- football
- cricket
- rugby union
- tennis
- basketball
- baseball

Draw a diagram showing the shape and dimensions for a sport of your choice.

Make sure that your diagram is to scale.

Let's Investigate

Give eight children in your class a slip of paper.

Ask them to write their name on the paper and draw a line they estimate to be 10 cm long.

Collect the slips of paper and measure each line to the nearest millimetre and record the results.

What was the percentage error for each child?

From the results, do most children tend to overestimate or underestimate short lengths?

At Home

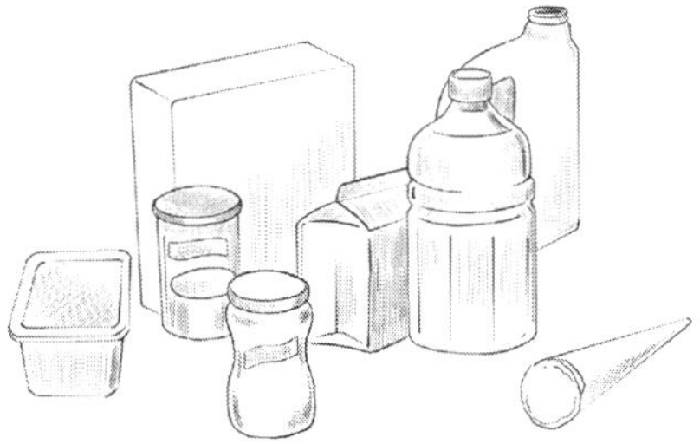

Most packaged food is sold by weight. For example, pasta, nuts, dried beans. Even fruit and vegetables are often sold in packets according to weight.

Investigate the approximate number of different food items that are equivalent to one kilogram.

What, for example, is the average number of oranges you get for a kilogram? What about pasta shells, potatoes, carrots . . ?

Remember, you are only after an approximate number, and the average.

Write a report about what you found out and how you went about it.

What's the Problem?

If someone weighs 63 kg, what is their approximate weight in stones and pounds?

Hint

You need to know about the relationship between the imperial measures (stones and pounds) and their metric equivalent.

Write an explanation of how you worked out the answer.

What's the Problem?

If someone weighs 12 st 8 lb, what is their approximate weight in kilograms?

Hint

You need to know about the relationship between the imperial measures (stones and pound) and their metric equivalent.

Write an explanation of how you worked out the answer.

Name:

The Maths Herald

Volume 6

Date:

Around the World

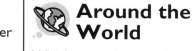

Throughout many parts of the world traders buy and sell raw materials or primary agricultural products such as wheat (flour), sugar, rice, tea and coffee. These are called *commodities*.

The table below shows the number of sacks of flour that eight different traders bought and the average weight of each sack of flour. Use the information in the table to answer the questions.

Trader	A	B	C	D	E	F	G	H
Number of sacks of flour bought	5	8	3	4	7	6	4	5
Average weight of sack (kg)	240	160	280	200	180	220	225	250

- Altogether, how much flour did Trader E buy in kg?
- Who bought more flour: Trader A or Trader B? How much more flour did they buy?
- Which trader bought $\frac{3}{4}$ of the total amount of flour as Trader A?
- Which trader bought a total of $1\frac{1}{4}$ tonnes of flour?
- Which two traders together bought a total of 2160 kg?
- Which trader bought the least amount of flour? How much flour was this?
- Which trader bought the most amount of flour? How much flour was this?
- Write the total amount of flour that each trader bought, starting with the trader that bought the least.

Around the World

Which countries are the biggest producers of these different commodities:

- wheat
- sugar
- rice
- tea
- coffee?

How much do they produce each year? How is it measured?

Draw a table, graph or chart showing the world's top producers of wheat, sugar, rice, tea and coffee.

Write a report of what you have found out.

Looking for Patterns

In each of these problems, the first two sets of scales balance. Work out how many ◯s are needed to balance the third set.

Puzzle 1

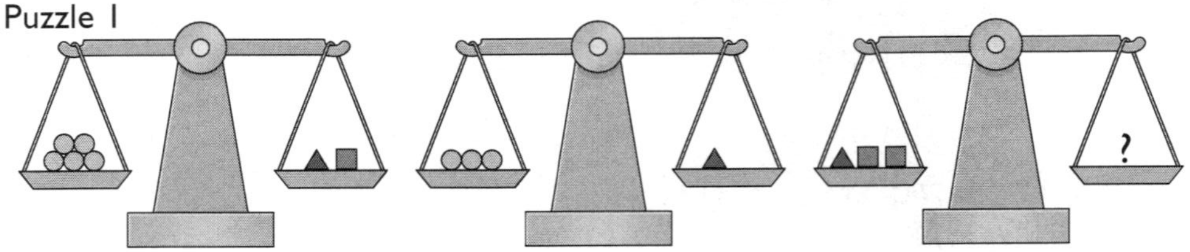

Puzzle 2

Puzzle 3

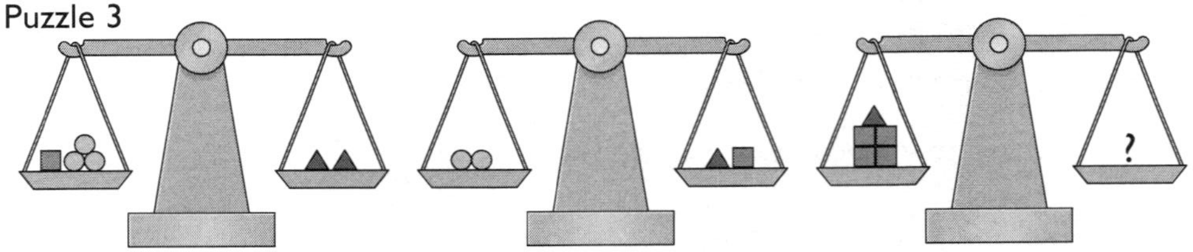

Write a statement about how you worked out how many ◯s were needed to balance the third sets of scales.

Now make up a similar problem of your own.

The Language of Maths

Design a poster describing the difference between mass and weight.

Focus on Science

A cube 1 m × 1 m × 1 m (1 cubic metre / 1 m^3) filled with water has a mass of 1000 kg.

Investigate the mass of each of the following:

- balsa wood
- gold
- lead
- pine wood
- silver
- aluminium

Issue 26 Mass and weight

Focus on Science

Every time you jump, you experience gravity – it pulls you back down to the ground. Without gravity, you'd float off into the atmosphere, along with all of the other matter on Earth.

Planet	Gravity Factor
Mercury	0·38
Venus	0·88
Earth	1
Mars	0·38
Jupiter	2·53
Saturn	1·19
Uranus	0·91
Neptune	1·13
Pluto	0·06

All the planets in the solar system have different gravitational pulls.

As a result, you would weigh more on some planets and less on others.

Find out your approximate weight on each of the planets, by multiplying your Earth weight by these gravity factors.

Find the Earth weight of other objects and then calculate their approximate weight on each of the other planets.

Let's Investigate

What is the mass and volume of rubbish that your class produces in a week? How much of this rubbish is recycled?

What are you going to have to do to find out?

Present your information using tables, graphs and / or charts.

What inferences can you make from your investigation about the following?

- the amount of rubbish your class produces in a term / year
- the amount of rubbish that is produced by the entire school in a week / term / year
- the amount of rubbish that is recycled by your class, and the entire school, each term / year
- on average, how much rubbish each person in the school produces in a term / year.

Famous Mathematicians

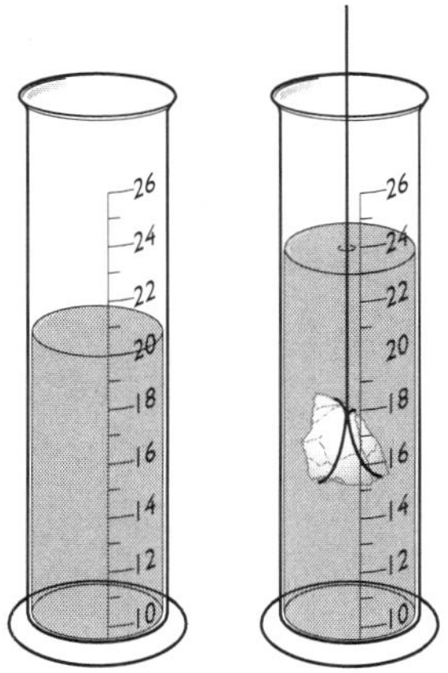

Sometimes we need to find the volume of irregular solids for which there is no mathematical formula we can use.

Archimedes, a Greek mathematician, physicist, engineer and astronomer was born in Sicily in 287 BC. It is said that one day he got into a full bath and the water overflowed. When he realised that the volume of water that had overflowed was equal to the volume of his body, he jumped out and ran through the streets shouting 'Eureka!'

We can use a measuring cylinder like the one shown above to measure the volume of irregular solids. The markings on the measuring cylinder are in cubic centimetres (cm^3).

volume of solid shape immersed in water = total volume of water and solid − volume of water

Activity

1. Pour some water into a measuring cylinder and record the water-level mark.
2. Place the solid object into the water and record the new water-level mark.
3. The increase in height of the water-level is the volume of the solid object.

You need:
- measuring cylinder
- water
- collection of small solid objects, e.g. small stone, coin, ball of modelling clay

Follow steps 1–3 above for each of the solid objects.
Record your results in a table stating the following information:

- name of solid object
- volume of water
- volume of water and solid object
- volume of solid

Let's Investigate

What is the volume of your classroom?

Which classroom in your school is the largest by volume? What is its volume?

Which classroom in your school is the smallest by volume? What is its volume?

Which are the largest and smallest rooms by volume in your school? What are their volumes?

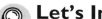

Name:

The Maths Herald

Volume 6

Date:

Around the World

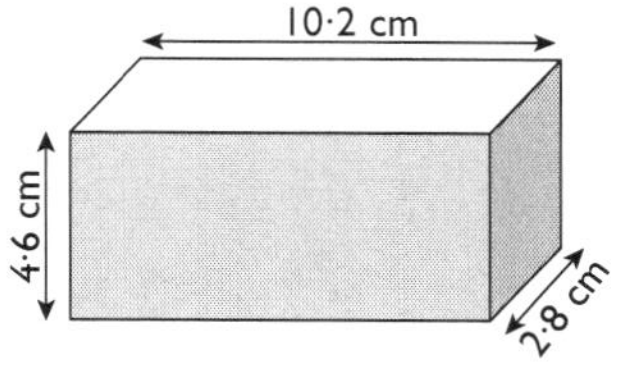

Volume is the amount of space that something occupies.

Look at the cuboid on the right.

Its dimensions are 10·2 cm × 2·8 cm × 4·6 cm.

Its volume is 131·376 cm^3.

To find the volume of any cube or cuboid we multiply the length by the width by the height.

We can write this as:

volume of a cuboid = length × width × height

or = l × w × h

or = lwh

Knowing the exact volume is extremely important to freight companies that transport parcels all round the world. Calculate the volume of each of these parcels.

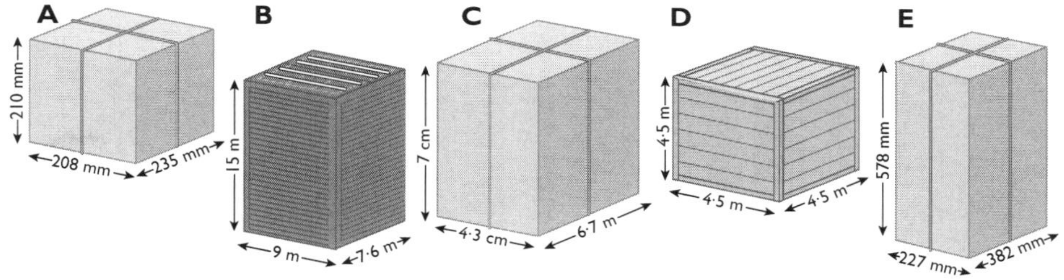

A rectangular parcel has a volume of 462 000 cm^3.
Its height is 80 cm. What might be the other dimensions of the parcel?

Around the World

Investigate different freight companies.

What are their rates? How do they differ between national and international rates?

How does the volume of a parcel affect pricing?

Let's Investigate

A *prism* is a 3-D solid with its two ends the same size and shape and parallel to each other. A prism is the same size and shape all the way through its length.
It does not get wider or narrower.

Look at these prisms.

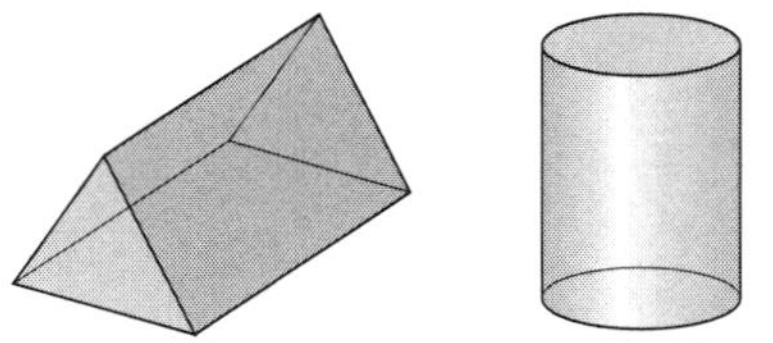

If you cut across these prisms, you will get two smaller prisms.

Such a cut across a shape is called a *cross-section*.

The shape of a cross-section of a triangular prism is a triangle.

The shape of a cross-section of a cylinder is a circle.

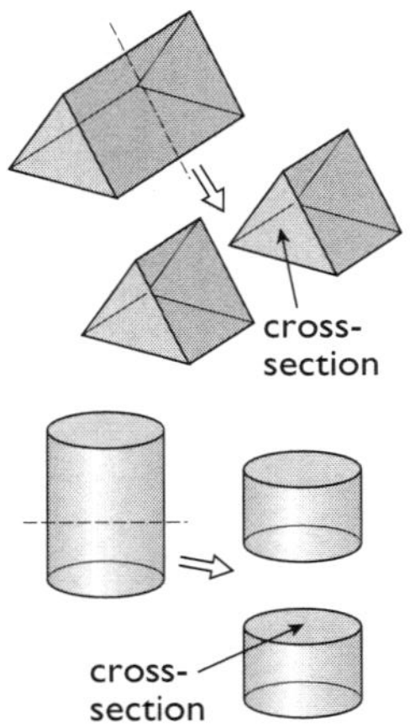

To find the volume of any prism we use the formula:

volume of a prism =
area of cross-section × length

So to find the volume of a cylinder the formula is:

volume = area of circle × length

$V = \pi r^2 \times l$ (or $V = \pi r^2 l$)

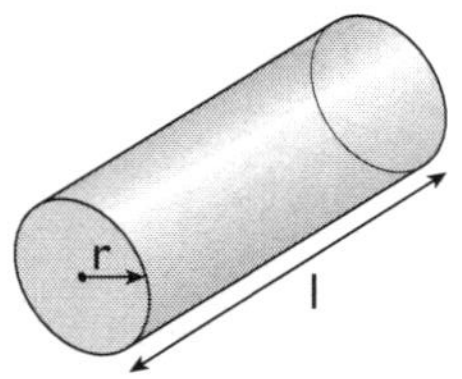

Hint:

Remember pi (π) is the ratio of a circle's circumference to its diameter. It is approximately 3·14.

So to find the volume of a triangular prism the formula is:

volume = area of triangle × length

$V = \frac{1}{2}bh \times l$ (or $V = \frac{1}{2}bhl$)

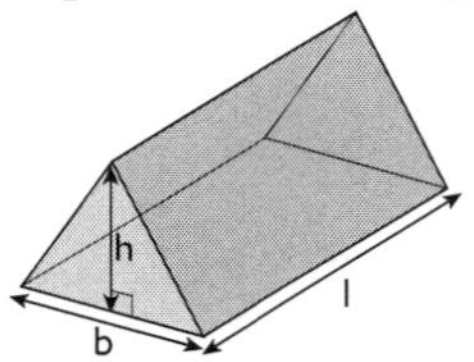

Calculate the volume of these prisms.

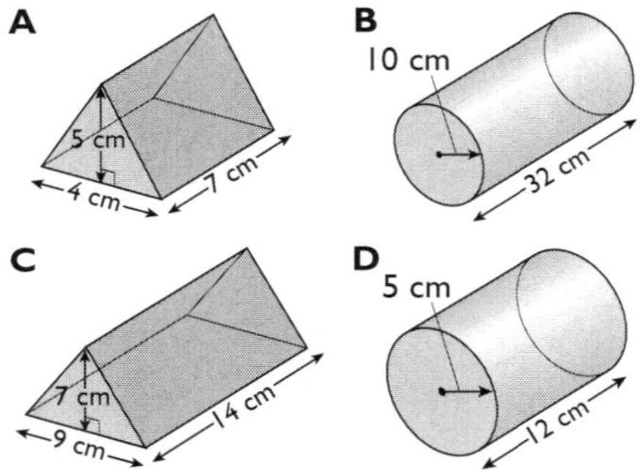

At Home

Gather together a collection of cylinders.

Using the formula from Let's Investigate on page 2 calculate the volume of each cylinder.

Focus on Science

Try the following experiment to compare the volume of a cone with the volume of a cylinder, both having the same radius and height.

Make a paper cone that just fits inside a can (100 ml can size is best).

Using sand or rice, find out how many conesful fill the can.

So, how does the volume of a cone compare with that of a cylinder, both with the same radius and height?

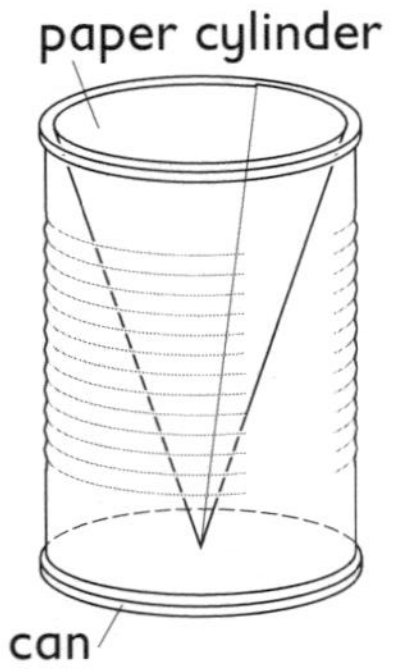

Sports Update

This is the formula for finding the volume of a sphere.

$\frac{4}{3}\pi r^3$

If these are the radii for different sporting balls, what are the volumes of the balls to the nearest 1 cm³?

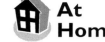

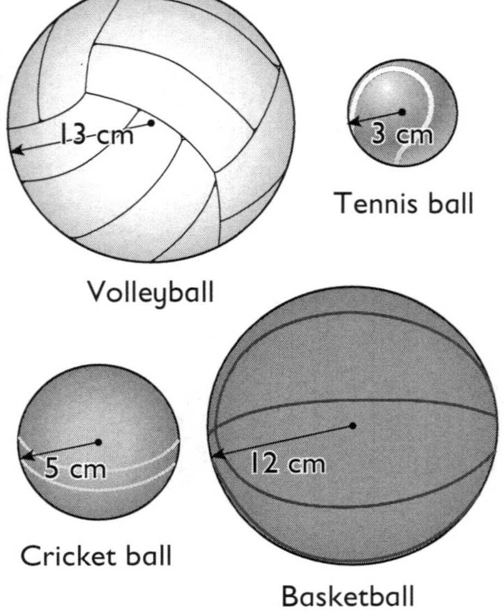

The Language of Maths

Design a poster describing the difference between volume and capacity.

Let's Investigate

On what day of the week were you born? Don't know? Use this formula known as Zeller's Rule to find out (unless you were born before 1760 – sorry!).

$$f = k + \left[\frac{(13 \times m - 1)}{5}\right] + D + \left[\frac{D}{4}\right] + \left[\frac{C}{4}\right] - 2 \times C$$

f = day of the week in which the person was born

k = day of the month in which the person was born

m = month in which the person was born

D = the last two digits of the year in which the person was born

C = the first two digits of the year in which the person was born

The following rules also apply to the formula:

Rule 1: Round down each number inside the brackets [ ].

For example, 2·7 rounds down to 2.

Rule 2: Months have to be counted specially for Zeller's Rule: March is 1, April is 2, and so on. Which means January is 11 and February is 12. (This makes the formula simpler, because on leap years February 29 is counted as the last day of the year.) Because of this rule, January and February are always counted as the 11th and 12th months of the *previous* year. Using the date 29 January 2002, for example, m = 11 and D = 01 (the last two digits of the year previous to 2002).

What is your date of birth?

Use the formula above to get a day of the week number (f).

Once you have calculated the day of the week number (f) here's what to do to find out on which day of the week you were born.

Step 1: Divide the day of the week number (f) by 7: $\frac{f}{7}$

Rules:

- Use pencil and paper to do the division calculation so that the remainder is expressed as a whole number and not a decimal.
- If the remainder is negative, add 7.

Step 2: The remainder you get from the division calculation is the day of the week (0 = Sunday, 1 = Monday, 2 = Tuesday...)

On which day of the week were you born?

Find out the year, month and date in which ten people were born.

They can be friends, family members or famous people. However, they must have been born after 1760 and not in a leap year.

Use the formula to find out on which day of the week each person was born.

FEBRUARY
M T W T F S S
1 2 3 4 5 6
7 8 9 10 11 12 13
14 15 16 17 18 19 20
21 22 23 24 25 26 27
28
MY BIRTHDAY

Name:

The Maths Herald

Volume 6

Date:

The Puzzler

The hour hand of a clock is pointing to 29 minutes past the hour.

What is the minute hand pointing to?

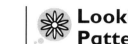

Looking for Patterns

Morcella has a town clock with two bells – a high-pitched bell and a low-pitched bell.

The low-pitched bell strikes the number of hours at each quarter hour using the 12-hour clock.

The high-pitched bell strikes at quarter past, half past and quarter to the hour – one strike for quarter past the hour, two strikes for half past and three strikes for quarter to the hour. For example, at 4:30 p.m. the low-pitched bell strikes four times and the high-pitched bell strikes twice.

How many strikes do each of the bells make in a 24-hour day?

Let's Investigate

This is how each of the ten digits appears on a digital clock.

Imagine that a 12-hour digital clock was placed in front of a mirror, so that for example, 2 looks like 5 and vice-versa.

At what times would the reflection show the same as the digital clock itself?

What about if it were a 24-hour digital clock?

Sports Update

The marathon is a race of 42·195 km. It commemorates the run made by Pheidippides from Marathon to Athens in 490 BC to announce the victory of the Greeks over the invading Persians.

Many cities throughout the world run their own marathon event every year. The marathon is also one of the most important events in the Olympics.

This table shows the male and female marathon world record holders.

Name	Nationality	Location of marathon	Year	Time (h:min:s)
Haile Gebrselassie	Ethiopia	Berlin, Germany	2008	2:03:59
Paula Radcliffe	UK	London, UK	2003	2:15:25

The 100-metre race is one of the world's most famous athletic events. This table shows the male and female 100-metre world record holders.

Name	Nationality	Location of race	Year	Time (s)
Usain Bolt	Jamaica	Berlin, Germany	2009	9:58
Florence Griffith Joyner	USA	Indianapolis, USA	2003	10:49

Imagine if both the male and female 100-metre record holders were able to run the marathon at the same speed as they ran 100 metres. Calculate, in hours and minutes, how long it would take each of them to complete the 42·195 km race.

An activity for two

You need:
- tape measure
- some friends
- stopwatch
- pencil and paper

1. Use the tape measure to measure out a distance of 100 metres. Mark a 'Start' line and a 'Finish' line on the ground.
2. Using the stopwatch, time how long it takes each person to run 100 metres. Record your results in a table.
3. When you have recorded the results, discuss them with your partner.
4. Decide how best to represent the data – perhaps as a table, line graph or bar chart.
5. When you have represented the data, write five statements about your results.
6. Compare your results with the results of the male and female 100-metre world record holders.

Focus on Science

Speed is how fast someone or something moves. It is often measured in *kilometres per hour* (km/h) or *metres per second* (m/s).

If you run on average 7 km/h, you run 7 kilometres in every hour.

In 2 hours you would travel 14 km (2 h × 7 km).

In 3 hours you would travel 21 km (3 h × 7 km).

In $\frac{1}{2}$ hour you would travel 3·5 km ($\frac{1}{2}$h × 7 km).

When travelling, it is very difficult to keep exactly the same speed all the time. When we talk about speed, we normally mean the *average speed*.

To find the average speed someone or something travels at, we divide the total distance travelled by the total amount of time taken:

$$\text{average speed} = \frac{\text{total distance travelled}}{\text{total time taken}}$$

If the average speed and the total time taken are known, we can find the total distance travelled by:

$$\text{total distance travelled} = \text{average speed} \times \text{total time taken}$$

In the same way, if the average speed and the total distance travelled are known, we can find the total time taken by:

$$\text{total time taken} = \frac{\text{total distance travelled}}{\text{average speed}}$$

- Barry drives 525 km on business. The journey takes him 7 hours. What is Barry's average speed?
- A man cycles 7·5 km in half an hour. How far could he cycle in $3\frac{1}{2}$ hours at this speed?

  How long would it take him to cycle 60 km at this speed?
- Copy and complete the table.

Total distance travelled	Total time taken	Average speed
	4 h	40 km/h
60 km	30 min	
315 km		90 km/h
93 km	$7\frac{3}{4}$h	
21 km		5 km/h

The Puzzler

Write down today's date, and the time it is right now to the nearest second!

How many months, days, hours, minutes and seconds until the start of your birthday?

Famous Mathematicians

Another lesser-used scale for measuring temperature is called the *Rankine*, named after the Scottish engineer and physicist William Rankine, who proposed it in 1859. Like Fahrenheit and Celsius, the Rankine is measured as a degree and is written as '°R'.

Just as the Kelvin scale has a relationship to the degrees Celsius, the Rankine has a correlation with degrees Fahrenheit. A temperature of ⁻459·67°F is exactly equal to 0°R.

In order to convert Celsius (C) and Fahrenheit (F) temperatures into Rankine (°R) use these formulas:

$°R = (°C + 273{\cdot}15) \times \frac{9}{5}$

$°R = °F + 459{\cdot}67$

- Choose some of the temperatures for the four cities in the Around the World activity on page 2 and convert the temperatures from Celsius into Rankine.
- Choose some of the temperatures you converted in the Let's Investigate activity on page 2 and convert these temperatures from Fahrenheit into Rankine.

Another method for converting Celsius to Rankine, is to first convert to Fahrenheit, then convert to Rankine using the Fahrenheit formula above.

Does this work? Which method is easier? Why?

Focus on Science

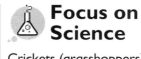

Crickets (grasshoppers) can tell the temperature. It's incredible but true!

Scientists have worked out that crickets chirp slower when the temperature is cooler and faster when it gets warmer.

These are the formulas that scientists have devised to calculate the approximate temperature using crickets.

temperature in degrees Fahrenheit = number of chirps in 15 seconds + 40

$$\text{temperature in degrees Celsius} = \frac{\text{number of chirps in 15 seconds} + 13}{2}$$

Here are two activities to do using crickets as thermometers.

An activity to do if there are some crickets around

Count how many chirps the cricket makes in 15 seconds then use one or both of the formulas to calculate the temperature.

- Use a thermometer to find the temperature.
- How do the two readings compare?

An activity to do if there aren't any crickets around

- Use a thermometer to find the temperature.
- Think about how you would need to alter the formulas to find out how many chirps a cricket would make in 15 seconds at that temperature (in degrees Fahrenheit and degrees Celsius).

Name:

The Maths Herald

Volume 6

Date:

Around the World

These climate graphs show the average annual rainfall and temperature for four different cities.

Imagine you work for a travel agency. Write a report of each city recommending which months of the year are best for tourists to visit each one, and which months they should avoid. Provide a rationale for each of your recommendations.

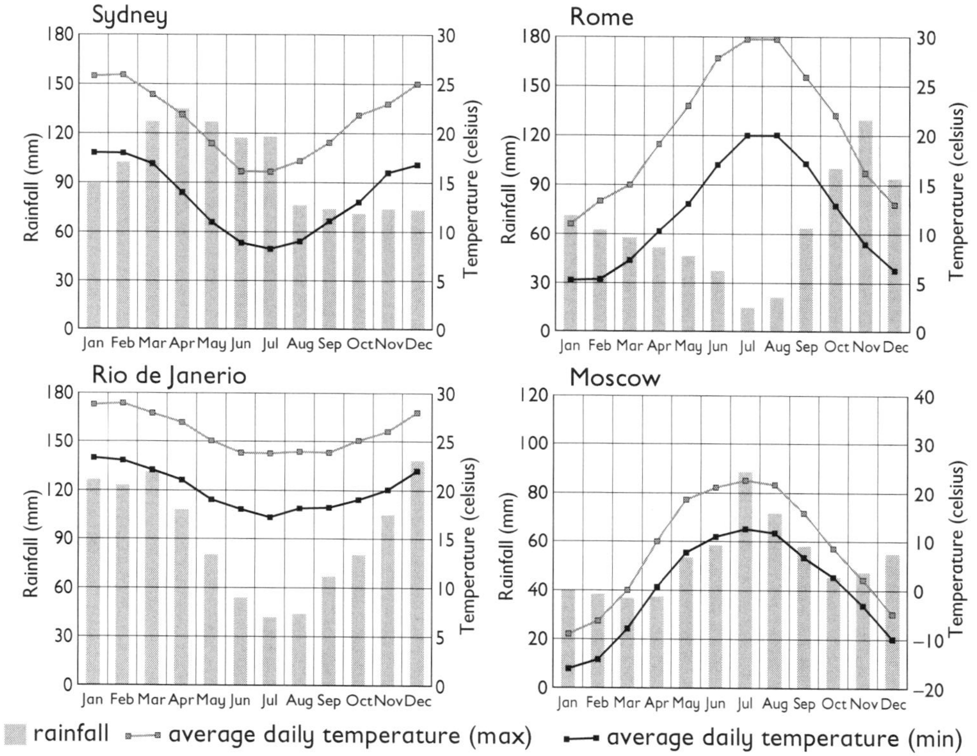

Let's Investigate

Both Fahrenheit and Celsius are two temperature scales based on the freezing conditions of water.

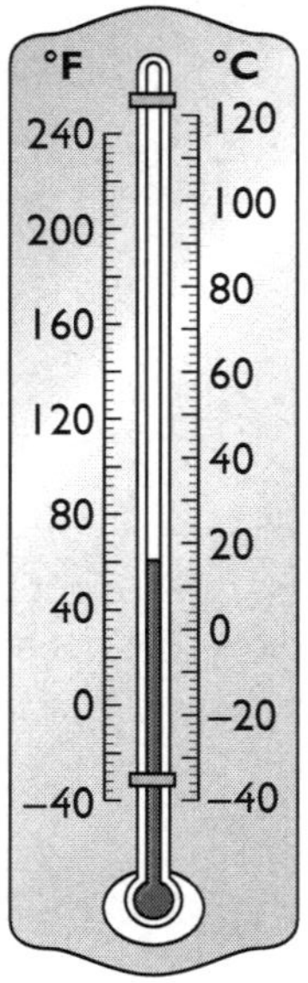

On the Fahrenheit scale, the freezing point of water is 32 degrees and the boiling point is 212 degrees. On the Celsius scale, the freezing point of water is 0 degrees and the boiling point is 100 degrees.

In order to convert the Celsius (C) temperature into Fahrenheit (F) use this formula:

$F = \frac{9}{5}C + 32$

Choose some of the temperatures for the four cities in the Around the World activity on the right and convert the temperatures from Celsius into Fahrenheit.

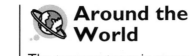

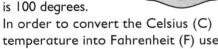

The Language of Maths

Investigate the origins of the terms Fahrenheit and Celsius.

Around the World

The temperatures in seven cities are 16°C, 21°C, 9°C, 33°C, 14°C, 10°C and 30°C.

The seven cities are London, Auckland, Rome, New York, Paris, Edinburgh and Melbourne.

Use the clues to match the temperatures with the cities.

1. The two cities that begin with a vowel have the hottest and coldest temperatures.
2. Rome's temperature is between New York's and Melbourne's temperatures.
3. Paris and London have a temperature difference of 4°C.
4. Rome's temperature is greater than New York's and less than Melbourne's.
5. Paris and Edinburgh have a temperature difference of 5°C.

Looking for Patterns

Facts: 0°C = 32°F
100°C = 212°F
$F = \frac{9}{5}C + 32$

Given the facts, write a formula for converting Fahrenheit to Celsius.

Check to see that your formula is correct.

Famous Mathematicians

Fahrenheit and Celsius are not the only two units of measure for temperature. Scientists often used other scales to measure temperature.

In 1848 a Belfast-born physicist and engineer by the name of William Thomson (later Lord Kelvin) developed a scale for measuring temperature. It is known as the *Kelvin Thermodynamic Temperature Scale*. Unlike Fahrenheit and Celsius, the Kelvin is not measured as a *degree* (°C or °F), instead it is written as 'K'.

The Kelvin and the degree Celsius are often used together, as 0 Kelvin equals ⁻273·15 degrees Celsius.

In order to convert Celsius (C) and Fahrenheit (F) temperatures into Kelvin (K) use these formulas:

$K = °C + 273{\cdot}15$

$K = (°F + 459{\cdot}67) \times \frac{5}{9}$

- Choose some of the temperatures for the four cities in the Around the World activity on page 2 and convert the temperatures from Celsius into Kelvin.
- Choose some of the temperatures you converted in the Let's Investigate activity on page 2 and convert these temperatures from Fahrenheit into Kelvin.

Another method for converting Fahrenheit to Kelvin, is to first convert to Celsius, then convert to Kelvin using the Celsius formula above.

Does this work? Which method is easier? Why?

Sports Update

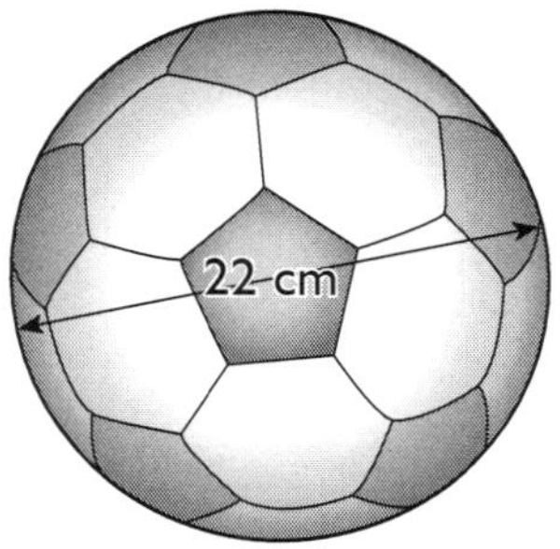

A football measures 22 cm across.

Design a method for working out the approximate total surface area of the football.

The Puzzler

- If the area of tangram piece C is one square unit, what are the areas of all of the other pieces?
- What is the area of the whole tangram puzzle?

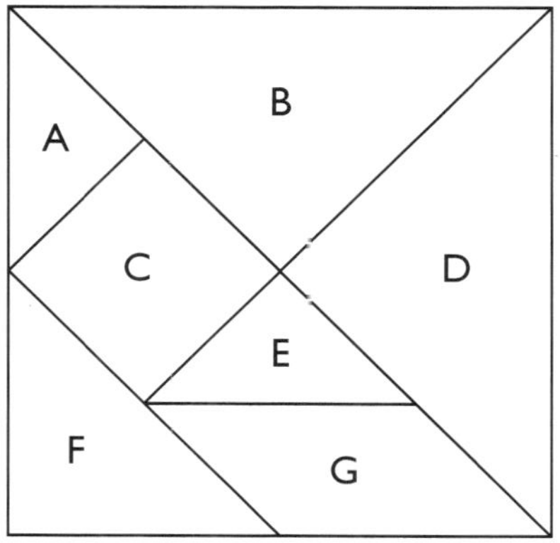

At Home

Choose two pages from a daily newspaper that have both news and advertisements.

- Look at these same two pages in the paper every day for four days.
- Work out how much of the area of each page is news and how much is adverts.
- Do these areas change from day to day?
- On the fourth day, work out the four-day average for both news and advertisements. Write about anything you notice.

Issue 30 Area

Name:

The Maths Herald

Volume 6

Date:

Looking for Patterns

This is area a.

This is area b.

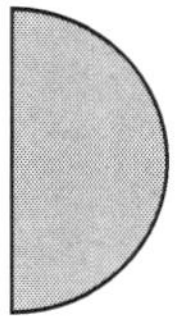

This is $a + b$.

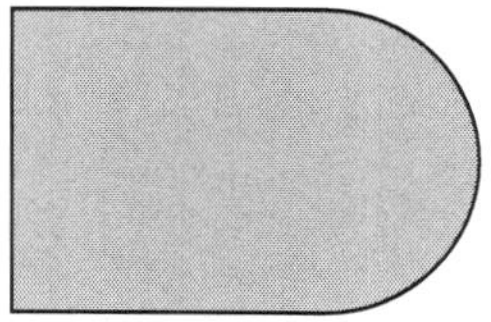

What is the area of this shape?

What are the areas of these shapes?

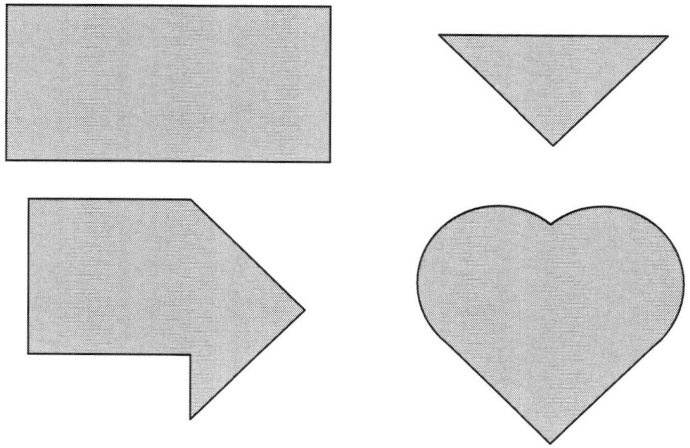

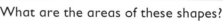

Draw some different shapes with areas which are $2a + b$.

In the Past

Tutankhamun is the most famous of all ancient Egyptian pharaohs. Known as the 'Boy King', he was born in c. 1341 BC and ruled Egypt from c. 1333 BC until his death in c. 1323 BC. Very little was known about Tutankhamun until 1922 when an English archaeologist by the name of Howard Carter discovered his tomb in the Valley of the Kings.

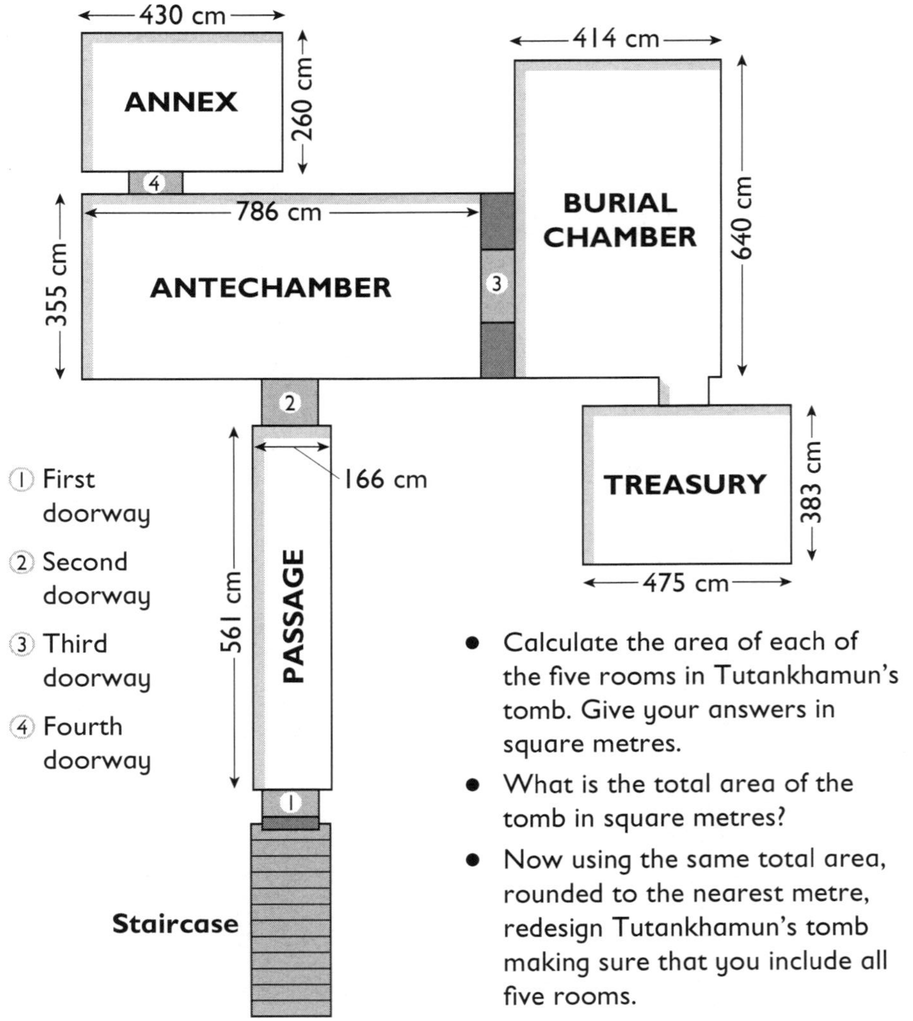

- Calculate the area of each of the five rooms in Tutankhamun's tomb. Give your answers in square metres.
- What is the total area of the tomb in square metres?
- Now using the same total area, rounded to the nearest metre, redesign Tutankhamun's tomb making sure that you include all five rooms.

Let's Investigate

Make two polygons on a geoboard or draw them on squared dot paper.

Use a formula or count square units inside the polygons to calculate the area of each shape.

Now use Pick's Formula to calculate the area of the two polygons you made.

Pick's Formula

For any polygon made on a geoboard or graph paper, the area of the polygon is equal to the sum of the pins (or intersections) on the perimeter of the polygon, divided by 2, plus the pins (or intersections) inside the polygon, minus one.

$A = (p \div 2) + i - 1$

(A = area, p = perimeter, i = interior pins)

Compare the areas you got using Pick's formula with the areas you got using a different formula or counting. What do you notice?

Try Pick's Formula using other polygons.

For what types of polygons does this formula work best?

What's the Problem?

If the diameter of the circle is 16 cm what is the area of the square?

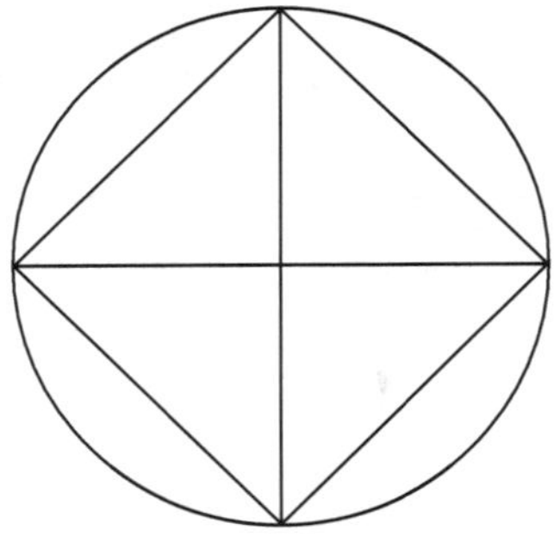

Let's Investigate

Using an 11 × 11 geoboard, make the largest octagon you can.

What fraction of the area of the geoboard is outside the octagon?

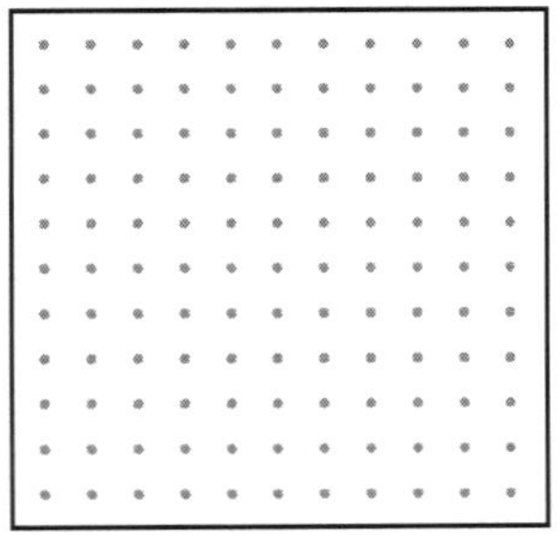

Looking for Patterns

Look at each of these matchstick patterns.

Draw the next two shapes in each sequence.

For each sequence:

- How many squares and matches are added each time?
- What is the formula for calculating the total number of matches used to make *n* number of squares?
- What is the formula for calculating the total number of matches around the perimeter of *n* number of squares?

Try some matchstick patterns of your own. Describe the different relationships.

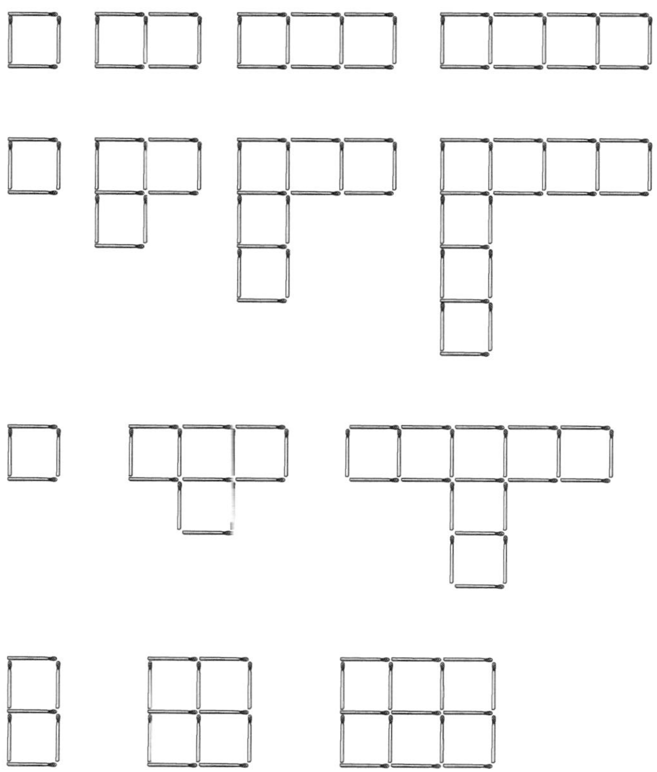

Let's Investigate

Measure and calculate the total perimeter of the plot of land that your school is on (see the Around the World activity on page 1).

Then measure and calculate the perimeter of the school building. If you have more than one building find the perimeters of all the buildings.

Draw to scale a simple plan that shows your measurements.

Name:

The Maths Herald

CN PM

Volume 6

Date:

Construct

In the middle of tiling her bathroom, Alice noticed that she could remove one of the tiles without changing the overall perimeter of the tiled area.

Which tile is this?

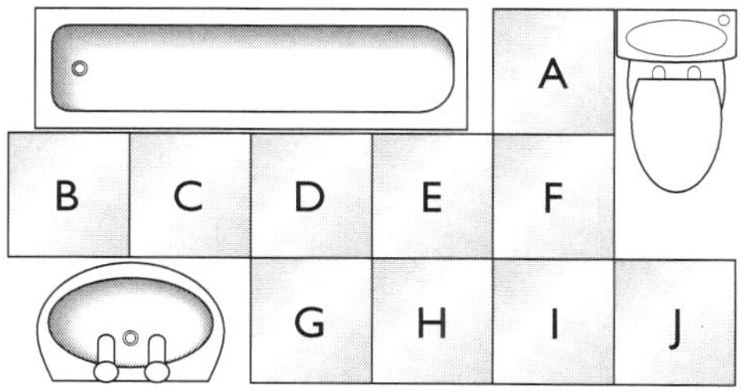

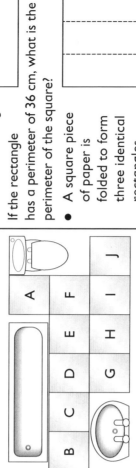

Around the World

Draw a plan, to scale, of the land on which your school is built.

Label the dimensions of the land on your plan.

What is the school's perimeter?

What's the Problem?

- A square piece of paper is folded in half horizontally to form a rectangle.

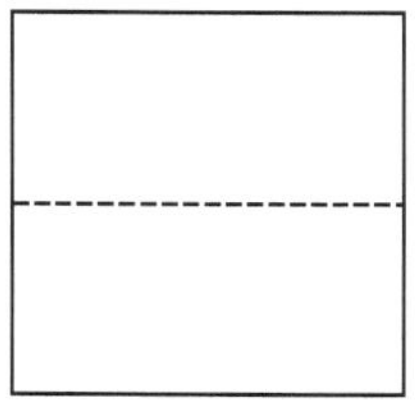

If the rectangle has a perimeter of 36 cm, what is the perimeter of the square?

- A square piece of paper is folded to form three identical rectangles.

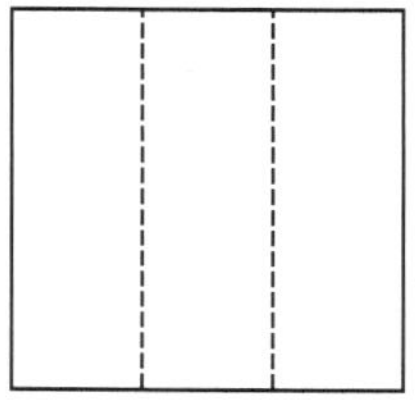

If the perimeter of one of the rectangles is 40 cm, what is the perimeter of the square?

The Language of Maths

Prove or disprove the following statement.

> Shapes that are congruent have the same perimeter, and shapes that have the same perimeter are congruent.

Around the World

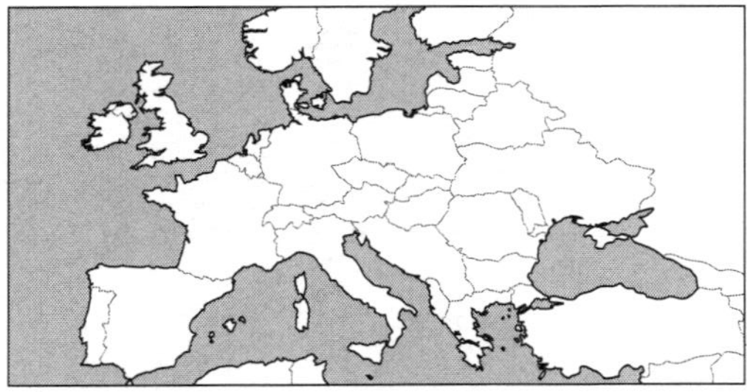

All countries of the world have borders. These borders are lines that officially separate one country from another. A border can either be a physical line such as a wall, fence or coast line, or it can be an invisible line that exists only on maps and official records.

There is, for example, a physical line – a fence, that separates the United States from Mexico. However, in many parts of continental Europe, between France and Italy for example, apart from road signs, you would not realise that you were crossing a border from one country into another.

A country's borderline acts as the country's perimeter.

Investigate the perimeters of different countries.

Which countries have the largest perimeter? Which have the smallest? Which countries are different in shape but have a similar perimeter?

www

Construct

Graham's Hotel recently installed a rectangular swimming pool.

For health and safety reasons they need to put a fence around the pool and some of the surrounding land. The total area that they need to fence off is 80 square metres. If the length of the fencing on each side can only measure a whole number of metres, what are all the different lengths of fencing the hotel can use?

Let's Investigate

- Can you make a shape on a geoboard that has a perimeter and area that are numerically equal? If you can, draw your shape on squared dot paper.
- What about making two different shapes on a geoboard where the two perimeters are the same and the two areas are the same? If you can, draw your shapes on squared dot paper. Can you make different pairs of shapes?

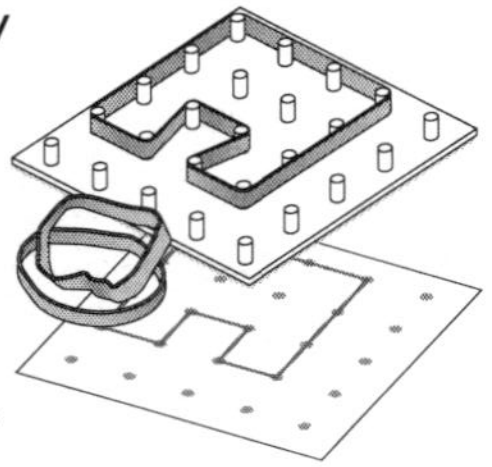

What's the Problem?

Brian is putting a wallpaper frieze onto the walls around his rectangular sitting room.

The perimeter of the room is 12·6 metres.

If the length of the sitting room is double its width, what are the dimensions of the sitting room?

Let's Investigate

The perimeter of each of these rectangles is less than its area.

Can you draw any rectangles whose perimeters are greater than their areas?

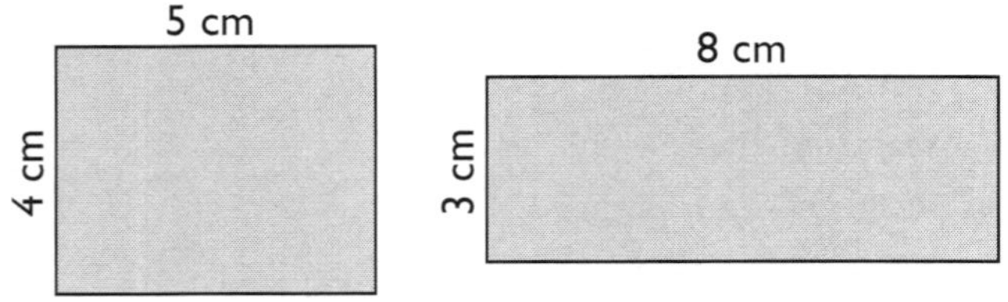

perimeter = 18 cm
area = 20 cm²

perimeter = 22 cm
area = 24 cm²

The Language of Maths

For each of the following shapes, write a formula or rule for working out the perimeter.

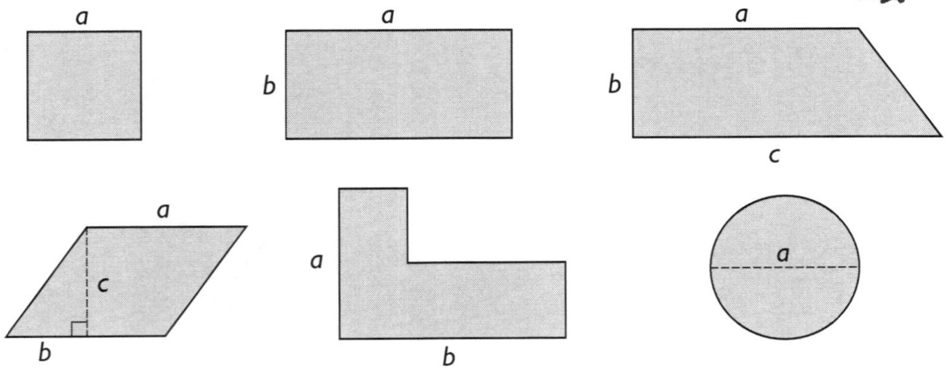

Let's Investigate

The *kilometre* is the most commonly used metric unit for expressing distances.

However, in the UK, we still use the imperial measurement *mile* to measure distance.

1 mile ≈ 1·6 kilometres

The most commonly used formula for converting miles (mi.) to kilometres (km) is:

km = mi. × 1·6

Another formula for converting miles to kilometres is:

km = mi. + $\frac{1}{2}$ mi. + $\frac{1}{10}$ mi.

or

km = mi. + 0·5 mi. + 0·1 mi.

Use both formulas to convert miles to kilometres.

Do both formulas give the same answer?

Which formula do you find easier? Why?

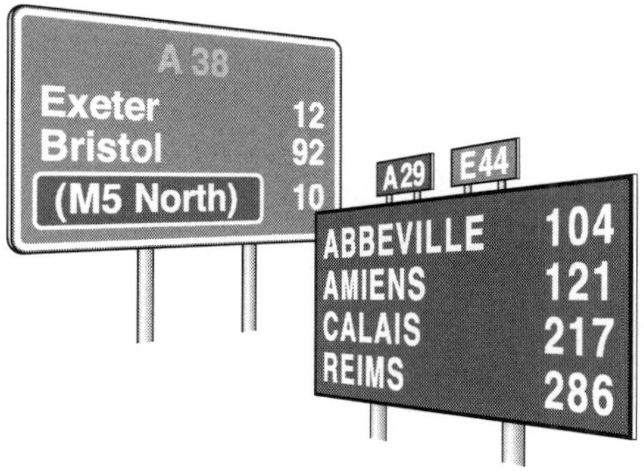

Let's Investigate

Sad news! Your school is closing down.

It has been decided to sell the land and subdivide it into housing lots.

Calculate the total area of the plot of land your school is on, including all playing fields.

Work out how many housing lots will fit into the area of the school.

Draw, to scale, your proposal for redeveloping the land.

Things to think about:

- What is your interpretation of the term 'housing lots'?
- What type of housing are you proposing – bungalows, semidetached, terraced, flats...?
- What type of housing is in keeping with the local area?
- What are the minimum dimensions required for each type of housing?

Write a report stating the reasoning behind all the decisions you have made.

Be prepared to justify your decisions.

Name:

The Maths Herald

Volume 6

Date:

Famous Mathematicians

Archimedes was a Greek mathematician, physicist, engineer and astronomer, who was born in Sicily in 287 BC. Among his greatest discoveries was the *Law of the Lever.*

The centre of a see-saw, the point of balance, is called the *fulcrum*.

Imagine a see-saw 4 m long, with a child weighing 24 kg sitting 2 m from the fulcrum and a child weighing 32 kg sitting at the other end of the see-saw.

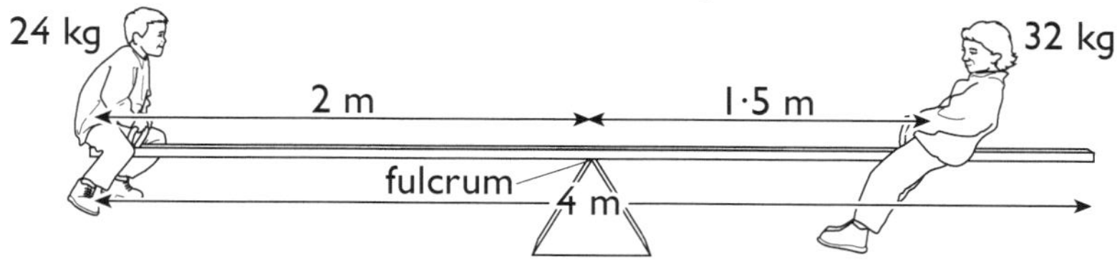

According to Archimedes' Law of the Lever in order for the see-saw to balance, the child weighing 32 kg will need to sit 1·5 m from the fulcrum.

Here are some measurements that, according to Archimedes' Law of the Lever, mean that the see-saw will balance.

Look at the measurements and work out a formula for Archimedes' Law of the Lever. Try using the symbols W1, D1, W2 and D2 to express your formula.

Person 1		Person 2	
Weight (W1)	Distance from fulcrum (D1)	Weight (W2)	Distance from fulcrum (D2)
24 kg	2 m	32 kg	1·5 m
40 kg	1 m	20 kg	2 m
20 kg	1·5 m	24 kg	1·25 m
80 kg	0·5 m	20 kg	2 m
	2 m	60 kg	1·5 m
70 kg		35 kg	2 m
36 kg	1·25 m	30 kg	
52·5 kg	2 m		1·25 m

Now use your formula to complete the table.

Famous Mathematicians

Galileo was born in 1564 in Italy. He made many amazing discoveries in science and mathematics. Before Galileo, people thought that heavy objects fell faster than lighter objects. To prove that this was not true, Galileo dropped a cannonball and a pebble from the leaning Tower of Pisa. Both objects hit the ground at the same time.

Galileo discovered that there was a relationship between the time it takes an object to fall to the ground and the distance it travels during the fall. The table below shows this relationship.

Time of fall (seconds)	Distance (m)
1	4·8
2	19·2
3	43·2
4	76·8
5	120

Use the table to discover the formula for Galileo's discovery.

At 828 m, the world's tallest building is the Burj Khalifa in Dubai. Using your formula, work out approximately how long it would take for an object to fall from the top of the building.

Focus on Science

Decibel is a unit used to measure the degree of loudness of sound. The softest sound that humans can hear is 0 decibels. The normal tone of a speaking voice is around 60 decibels. If a sound is more than about 100 decibels, humans find it very uncomfortable to listen to.

Investigate five different sounds. Find out what their decibel rating is.

Draw a decibel scale and show where your five sounds belong on the scale.

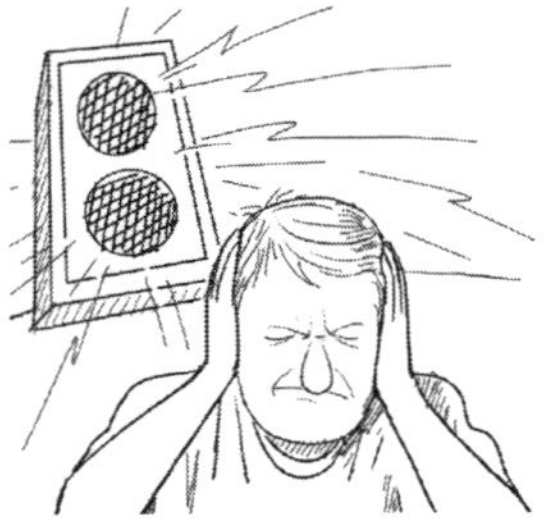

Around the World

Using a globe and a piece of string, work out the approximate sailing distances from:

- London to New York
- London to Sydney via the Suez Canal

Choose two other places and work out their sailing distance.

Find out the actual sailing distances (in kilometres) between these places.

Compare these with your approximations.

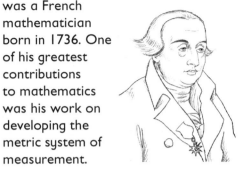

Let's Investigate

Decibels are used to measure the level of sound.

Investigate other unusual units of measure for measuring specific things.

What, for example, are each of these units of measure used for? Do they have an equivalent metric measurement? If so, what is it?

- fathom
- hand
- knot
- furlong
- quintal

What other unusual units of measure can you find? If they have an equivalent metric measurement, what is it?

Famous Mathematicians

Joseph Lagrange was a French mathematician born in 1736. One of his greatest contributions to mathematics was his work on developing the metric system of measurement.

Make a list of all the different metric units for length, mass and capacity.

Investigate the imperial unit equivalents for each of the metric units on your list.

Around the World

Many countries around the world, including most countries in continental Europe, use the metric system of measurement exclusively.

In the UK, we use a mixture of the imperial and metric systems.

Write a short report about the advantages and disadvantages of using just one system of measurement.

If the UK decided to convert entirely to just using the metric system, what things would need to change?

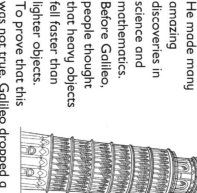

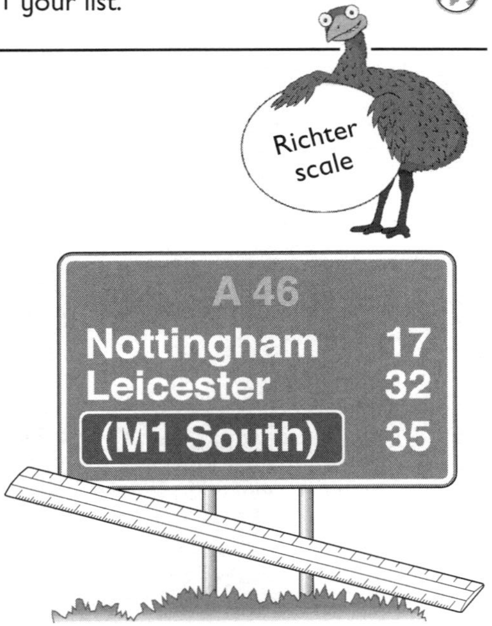

Looking for Patterns

A *scatter graph* is a graph that compares results in a set of data. It can also be used to look for connections or a relationship between the two sets of data.

Write a report explaining the results of this scatter graph. In particular comment on the results for children A, B, C and D.

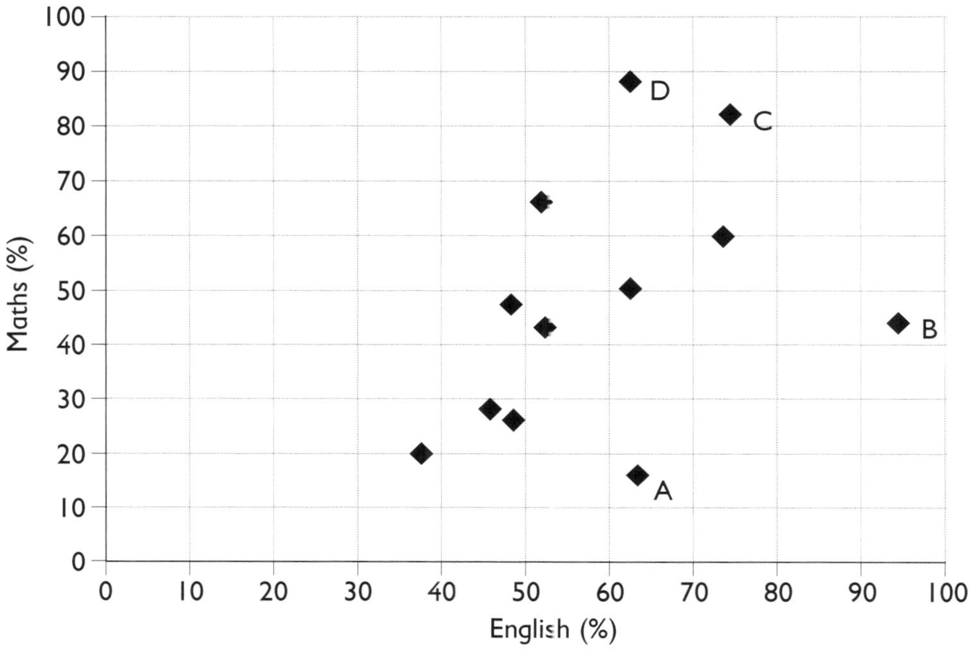

The Language of Maths

Look through a newspaper to find examples of information displayed as a graph or a table.

Re-represent the data in a pie chart.

Hint:

It may be helpful to convert the data in the graph or table into percentages before presenting the information in the pie chart.

Name:

The Maths Herald

Volume 6

Date:

The Arts Roundup

- Oliver is the director of a week-long arts festival. Each year, after the festival, Oliver draws a graph to show the results of the festival.

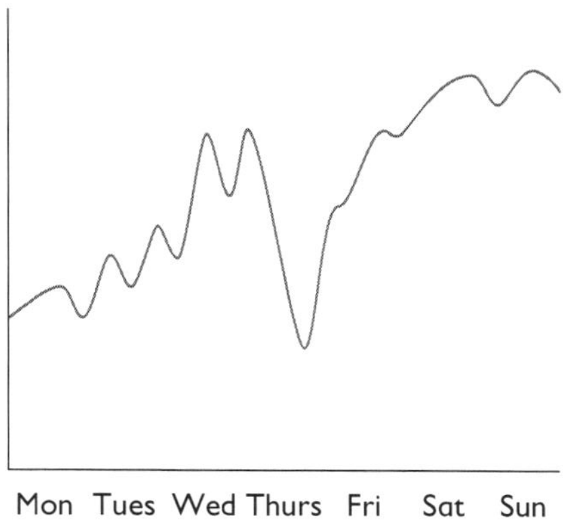

This year however, Oliver didn't fully label the graph.

Use Oliver's graph to write a short description about this year's arts festival.

- Make a graph of your own similar to the one above. Partly label your graph with some information.

Then write three broad questions based on the information on your graph.

Give your graph to a friend and ask them to answer your questions and to write a further two or three statements about your graph.

When your partner has finished, discuss their answers and statements. Do your interpretations and your friend's interpretations of the graph make sense?

Focus on Science

Find out the sunrise and sunset times of a place near to where you live.

Use the data for the first of the month only to draw a bar chart or graph of daylight hours.

In which month is the longest / shortest day?

What is the average length of a day?

SUNRISE AND SUNSET

Birmingham	4:25p.m. to 8:07a.m.
Bristol	4:32p.m. to 8:06a.m.
Dublin	4:38p.m. to 8:29a.m.
Glasgow	4:19p.m. to 8:33a.m.
Leeds	4:18p.m. to 8:12a.m.
London	4:23p.m. to 7:57a.m.
Manchester	4:22p.m. to 8:14a.m.
Newcastle	4:12p.m. to 8:17a.m.

Focus on Science

What is the nearest coastal town to where you live?

Find out about the tidal times for the previous month.

Use the data to draw a bar chart or graph of low and high tides.

Can you combine the data concerning both low and high tides on the same chart or graph?

Write a report on the results.

TODAY'S TIDES

SEAPORT	HIGH	LOW
Virginia Beach	06:45 a.m.	05:55 p.m.
Nags Head	07:00 a.m.	06:01 p.m.
Hatteras	07:04 a.m.	05:58 p.m.
Wrights Beach	08:05 a.m.	06:03 p.m.
Myrtle Beach	08:12 a.m.	07:04 p.m.
Charleston	08:25 a.m.	07:35 p.m.
Hilton Head	08:25 a.m.	07:50 p.m.
Brunwick	08:45 a.m.	07:45 p.m.
Jacksonville	08:50 a.m.	07:50 p.m.

Let's Investigate

You will need the sports section from a newspaper for this activity.

Look for the results for a sport that you are interested in.

Ask yourself different questions about the results. Then display your results in a graph, chart or table.

If your favourite sport is football, for example, you may think about things such as:

- goals scored
- draws
- home wins
- goal scorers
- away wins
- attendance figures

LEAGUE ONE

Brighton (Wood 25, 55; Bennett 27)	3	Peterborough Utd (Tomlin 66)	1	(Att 7,233)
Carlisle Utd (Berrett 44; Pen 57, 82; Cooper 73)	4	Peterborough U.	0	(Att 4,229)
Hartlepool Utd	0	Peterborough U. (Tomlin 86)	1	(Att 7,233)
Plymouth Argyle	0	Oldham Ath. (Stephens 47; Tounkara 72)	2	(Att 8,106)
Rochdale (Forbes 35 OG)	1	Leyton Orient (Chorley 60)	1	(Att 2,731)

The Language of Maths

Look at these three graphs about the Lane family.

Write statements comparing the age, height and weight of the members of the Lane family.

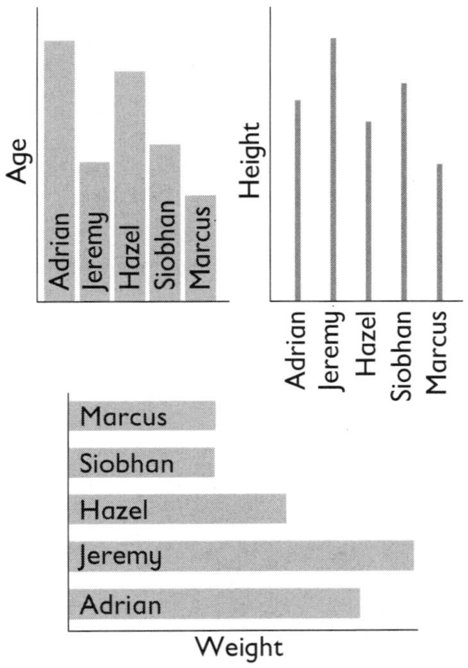

The Puzzler

This table shows the number of children that live in each of the flats in Rickety Towers.

Are there more flats or more children?

Write about how you worked it out.

Number of children	Number of flats
0	7
1	5
2	4
3	3
4 or more	1

In the Past

The line graph on the right shows, in thousands of kilometres, the average number of kilometres travelled by car per person from 1970 to 2000.

Write a detailed report describing the change in car use per person from 1970 to 2000.

What reasons can you give for these changes?

What conclusions can you draw?

What might the graph look like for the years 2000 to 2010? Why?

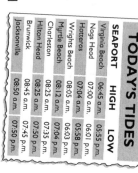

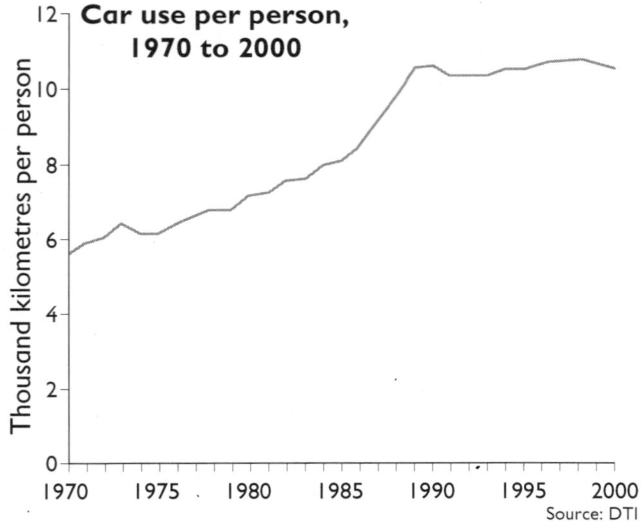

The Maths Herald

CN PM

Volume 6

Name:

Date:

Let's Investigate

'Rock-paper-scissors' is a hand game played by two people.

Players start with one hand behind their backs.

At a given signal, each player shows either a closed fist (rock), a flat hand (paper) or two fingers (scissors).

rock

paper

scissors

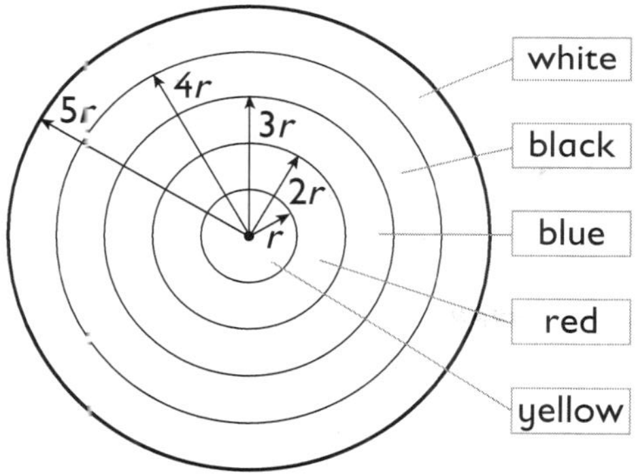

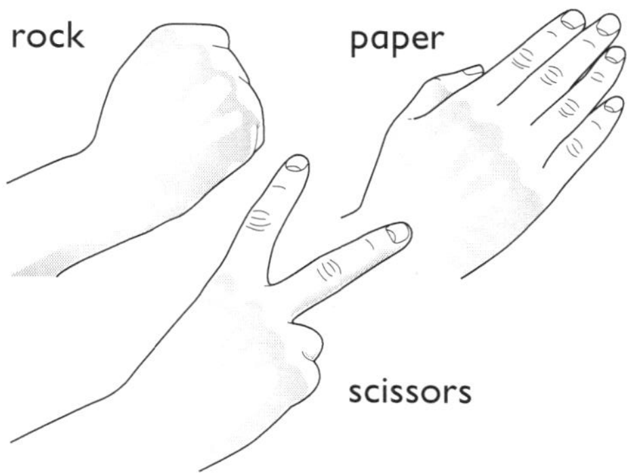

The winner of each round is determined as follows:

- Rock blunts scissors: so rock wins
- Scissors cut paper: so scissors wins
- Paper covers rock: so paper wins

If both players choose the same gesture, the game is tied and the players go again.

Find a partner and play 20 rounds of Rock-paper-scissors.

Record your game wins in a table.

Player	Tally	Total score	Percentage wins
A			
B			

After playing 20 rounds, work together to calculate the percentage of wins for each player.

Below is a tree diagram showing one of the possible outcomes of the game.

Player A	Player B	Winner
	rock	Tie
rock	paper	Player B
	scissors	Player A

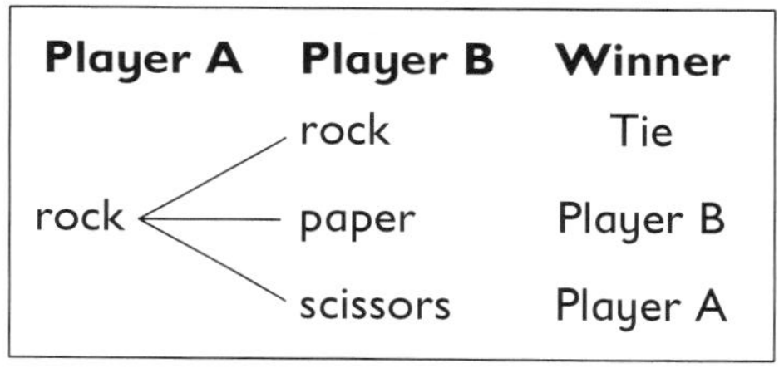

Draw tree diagrams showing all the other possible outcomes for the game.

Based on all your results, is Rock-paper-scissors a fair game? Justify your answer.

probability scale

Money Matters

Marcus has these coins in his pocket.

He takes four coins out of his pocket without looking.

- What is the probability that he will take a total of 50p out of his pocket?
- What is the probability that he will take a total of 25p out of his pocket?
- What is the probability that he will take more than 50p out of his pocket?

Sports Update

Archery is a sport in which competitors shoot at a target using a bow and arrow.

An archery board consists of five concentric circles.

To work out the area of the archery board, use Pythagoras' theorem

Remember:

$$\pi \text{ (pi)} = \frac{22}{7}$$

Area of a circle $= \pi \times (\text{radius of circle})^2$

Therefore, the area of the archery board on the right $= \pi \times (5r)^2 = 25\pi r$

Using Pythagoras' theorem, calculate the areas of each of the five different coloured rings below giving your answers in the same way.

Now use these areas to work out the probabilities of hitting each of the five colours.

white

black

blue

red

yellow

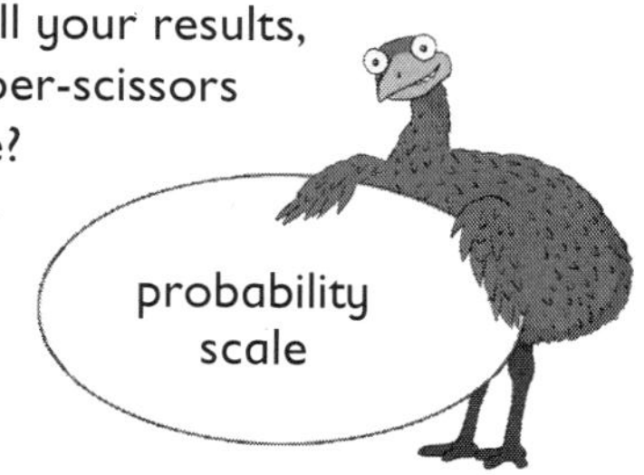

Let's Investigate

Consider the following:

ENRICHINGMATHSENRICHIN
GMATHSENRICHINGMATHS...

The words 'Enriching Maths' have been written over and over again.

- What is the 12th letter?
- What is the 53rd letter?
- What is the 175th letter?
- What is the probability that the letter is a 'T'?
- What is the probability that the letter is an 'I'?

How did you work out the answers to the second and third questions?

Now repeat the activity, this time using your name.

Write some statements about probabilities for different letters in your name.

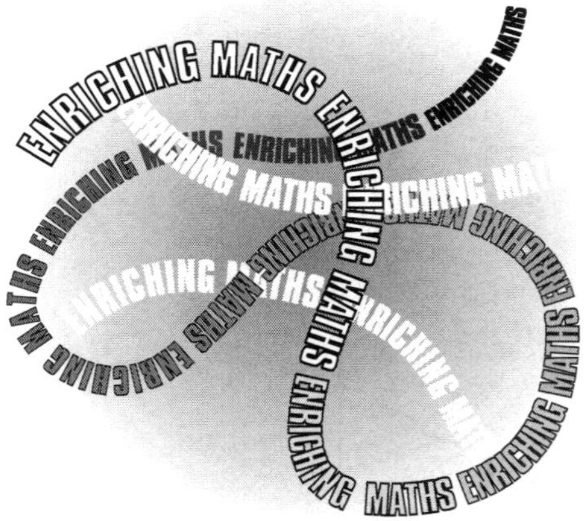

Construct

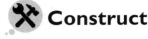

Work with a partner to design and construct two different board games.

One game must be a 'fair' game, and the other an 'unfair' game.

You may want to:

- use dice or spinners
- mark some spaces on your board as special
- have a pile of cards to give instructions
- make rules about what you do when you get a particular number on the dice or spinner.

Before asking others to play your games, make sure that you have tested them out to ensure that they are either 'fair' or 'unfair'.

Also, you need to ensure that the 'unfair' game is subtly, not obviously, 'rigged'.

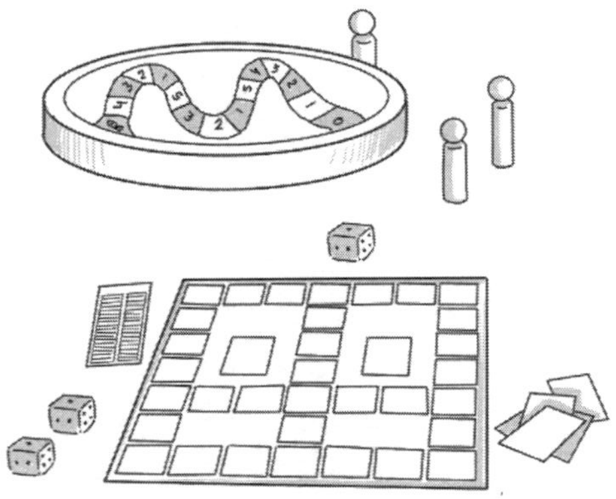

The Puzzler

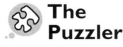

Scott catches the 07:50 train to work each morning.

The probability that he misses the train when he has overslept is $\frac{9}{10}$.

The probability that he misses the train when he has not overslept is $\frac{2}{5}$.

The probability that Scott oversleeps is $\frac{1}{20}$.

What is the probability that Scott misses the train tomorrow morning: likely, equal chance, unlikely?

How did you work it out?

The Language of Maths

When finding out the probability of something it is important to consider not just the mathematical likelihood, but all the factors that may affect the outcome of a situation.

Answer each of these questions giving justifications for your decisions.

What is the probability that, in any five-letter word:

- it will contain a vowel?
- it will contain the letter 'e'?
- it will contain more vowels than consonants?
- it will begin with a vowel?
- it will begin with the letter 'c'?
- the last letter will be a consonant?
- it will contain the same letter more than once?

Sports Update

Most sports are games of skill. The better your skill, the better chance you have of winning. The level of skill can depend on many factors including natural ability and the amount of practice.

In some sports individual competitors are given an advantage or disadvantage in an attempt to give every contestant an equal chance – this is called a *handicap*. Amateur golf is one such sport where handicaps are common.

Investigate how fairness is built into these sports through handicaps.

Let's Investigate

Investigate whether different types of newspapers use words or sentences of different lengths.

Follow these steps:

Step 1: Plan

Step 2: Collect data

Step 3: Process the data

Step 4: Represent the data

Step 5: Interpret and discuss the data.

Focus on Science

The time it takes someone to react to different stimuli can be measured in many ways.

Here is one way:

- Hold a ruler just over a person's outstretched thumb and forefinger.
- Drop the ruler at random and measure the distance it falls before the person catches it.
- Use the following formula to determine the person's reaction time:

$$t = \sqrt{\frac{d}{490}}$$

t = time in seconds

d = distance in centimetres

- Take five measurements and then average the five reaction times.

Who in your class has the fastest reactions?

Name:

The Maths Herald

Volume 6

Date:

Let's Investigate

Traffic lights are programmed to work differently at different times of the day. For example, a set of traffic lights near a group of shops may be programmed to turn red 30 times an hour between 8:00 a.m. and 8:00 p.m., whereas between the hours of 10:00 p.m. and 5:00 a.m. they are programmed to turn red only 15 times an hour.

What do you think are the reasons why traffic lights are programmed differently at different times of the day? Why aren't all sets of traffic lights programmed the same?

Locate an intersection near your school and collect traffic data.

Consider these questions:

- What type of data do you need to collect?
- How are you going to collect it?
- Over how long a period of time do you need to collect the data so that it is reliable?
- How are you going to present the data?

If you were planning to recommend to the local council how they should programme a set of traffic lights near your school, do you think that the mean, range, mode or median would be the most significant statistic to consider? Why?

Write your recommendations providing as much relevant statistical evidence as possible.

Sports Update

Keith has three dart scores with a mean of 30 and a range of 44.

His first dart scored 10.

What were his other two scores?

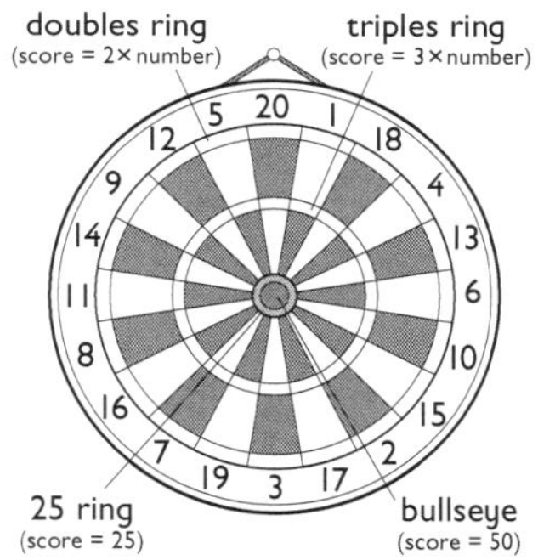

Around the World

There are approximately 7 billion (7 000 000 000) people in the world.

It is difficult to comprehend such a large number. So imagine that the world is reduced to a village of just 100 people.

Work with a partner or in a group to make a display about the information on the right.

Show how these statistics compare with your class, your school, your local area.

Also show what these statistics mean for the entire world population.

People in the village who:	Number (%)
are male	50
are unable to read or write	18
are under the age of 15	27
are over the age of 64	7
own a computer	1
have access to the internet	7
are Asian	61
are European	12
do not have electricity	24
do not have clear safe drinking water	17
are undernourished	16
are Christian	31
are Muslim	21
are Hindu	14
speak a Chinese dialect	17
speak English	8

Let's Investigate

What is the average number of crisps in a bag of crisps?

What are you going to do to find out?

Make sure that your data methods are statistically reliable.

Sports Update

At the end of a 15-game season, a basketball player calculated his statistics on his own goal shooting.

His mean score was 6. The median was 5 and the mode was 7.

What might his scores have been in each of the games?

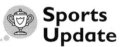

Sports Update

A school football team has played a total of 5 matches so far this season.

- Their mean score is 5.
- Their mode score is 6.
- Their median score is 6.
- Their range of scores is 6.

What could their scores have been for each match?

What will the team need to score in the next match to raise the mean score to 6?

The Puzzler

There are six people in the Hughes family.

If their average age is 15, what might their ages be?

What is the average age of your family?

At Home

Many different types of packaged food have printed on the packaging a notice stating the average number of servings.

What does this mean?

How do you think the manufacturers calculated this average?

What do you think they base their average on?

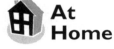

Around the World

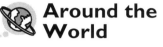

Keep a record of the pollution levels in the nearest location to your school where such data is collected.

Investigate what effect factors such as wind, rain and holidays have on pollution levels.

Sports Update

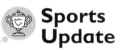

What is the distance of your average walking stride?

Construct a line conversion graph to illustrate the number of strides you take to cover a certain distance.

Check your graph's accuracy by walking and measuring the distances covered.

Construct a similar graph for someone whose walking stride is very different from yours.

Sports Update

Find out your average walking speed in:

- metres per second
- metres per minute
- meters per hour
- kilometres per hour

Using these results, estimate how fast you run.

Then measure to find out.

How does your running speed compare with Olympic and World record holders?

Name:

The Maths Herald

Volume 6

Date:

Around the World

The table below shows the average total monthly rainfall for each month of the year in Sydney, Australia.

	J	F	M	A	M	J	J	A	S	O	N	D
Average rainfall (mm)	102	118	130	126	121	131	98	82	69	77	84	78

The table on the right shows the seasons of the year in Sydney.

Summer	Dec, Jan, Feb
Autumn	Mar, Apr, May
Winter	June, July, Aug
Spring	Sep, Oct, Nov

The information on the amount of rain that usually falls in each season can be shown on a pie chart.

To do this, convert the fraction of the total rainfall for each season to a part of 360 degrees.

The calculation for summer is:

$$\text{Angle representing summer} = \frac{\text{total rainfall for summer}}{\text{total yearly rainfall}} \times 360°$$

$$= \frac{298}{1216} \times 360°$$

$$= 88{\cdot}223\ldots$$

$$= 88° \text{ (rounded to the nearest whole degree)}$$

Use the same method to find the angles representing the total average rainfall for the other three seasons.

Draw a pie chart showing the average seasonal rainfall for Sydney.

What would a pie chart showing the average seasonal rainfall for London look like?

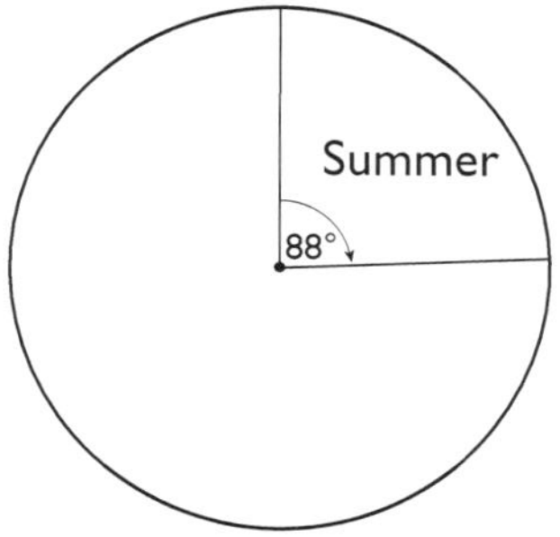

Construct

There are 21 dots on an ordinary 1–6 dot dice.

How could you rearrange these 21 dots so that in a game of highest roll wins, your new dice will beat an ordinary 1–6 dice?

NOTE: Draws are not counted, e.g.

The Language of Maths

Look through several newspapers to find examples of information displayed as a graph, chart or a table.

For each example, write a sentence or two describing the main conclusions of the data.

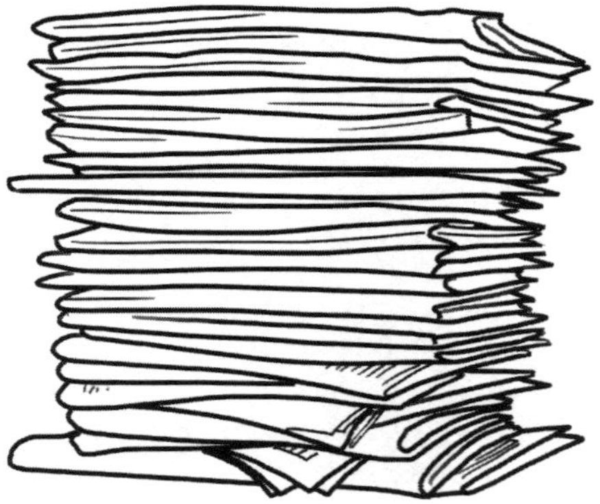

Focus on Science

The pie charts below show how much fuel was consumed in 1990 and 2001.

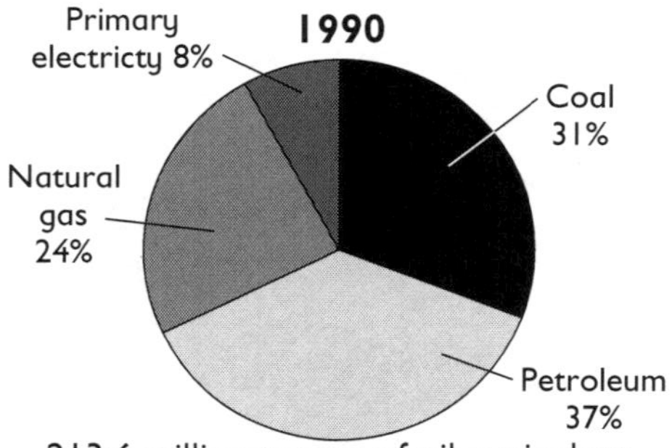

213·6 million tonnes of oil equivalent

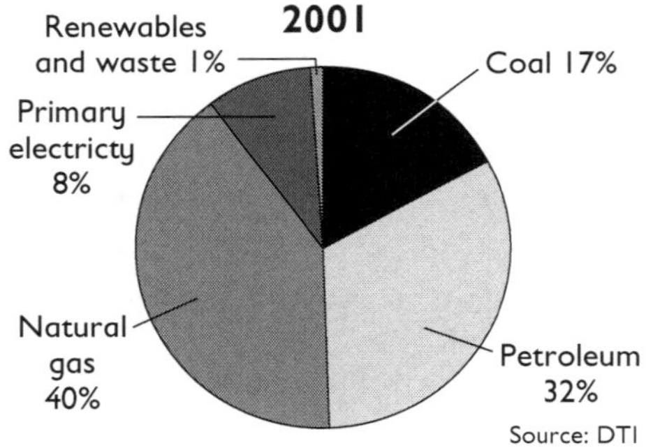

Source: DTI

237·7 million tonnes of oil equivalent

Write a detailed report describing these changes.

Draw another pie chart predicting how much of each fuel might be consumed in 2020. Justify your predictions.

Focus on Science

A *Watt* is a unit for measuring electric power.

1 kW (kilowatt) = 1000 watts

1 kWh (kilowatt-hour) = 1000 watts of electricity used for one hour

The average electricity consumption in the UK is 4800 kWh per household per year.

Excluding heating, average domestic electricity use can be accounted for as follows:

cold appliances	18%
cooking appliances	15%
wet appliances	15%
lighting	19%
consumer electronics	19%
domestic ICT	9%
other	5%

Calculate how many kilowatt-hours the average household uses on each of the above categories.

Find out how many kilowatt-hours you use at home – you should find this on an electricity bill.

Calculate how many kilowatt-hours your family uses on each of the above categories.

Sports Update

The Modified Harvard Step Test is a way of measuring levels of fitness.

What to do:

1. Step up and down from a chair or bench for a period of 5 minutes (300 seconds).
2. Rest for 1 minute.
3. Take your pulse rate for 30 seconds.
4. Use this formula to calculate the Fitness Factor.

$$\text{Fitness Factor} = \frac{\text{duration of exercise in seconds} \times 100}{5{\cdot}5 \times \text{pulse count}}$$

The Fitness Factor ratings are:

- below 50: poor
- 50–80: average
- 80–95: good
- above 95: excellent

How fit is your class?

Follow these steps:

Step 1: Plan

Step 2: Collect data

Step 3: Process the data

Step 4: Represent the data

Step 5: Interpret and discuss the data

Teacher's notes

Issue 1 Whole numbers

Prerequisites for learning

- Recognise and continue number sequences formed by counting on or back in steps of constant size
- Identify prime numbers
- Recognise and use proper factors
- Use tests of divisibility
- Construct and use simple expressions and formulae in words and symbols

Resources pencil and paper; RCM 2: My notes (optional); RCM 3: Pupil self assessment booklet (optional); RCM 5: 2 cm squared paper; range of different theatre plans – available on the internet (optional); computer with internet access

Teaching support

Page 1

Looking for Patterns

- Briefly discuss each of the sequences with the children. What patterns do they notice?

The Puzzler

- Children investigate consecutive numbers with two proper factors (14 and 15; 21 and 22; 26 and 27; 33, 34 and 35; 38 and 39; 57 and 58; 85, 86 and 87; 93, 94 and 95).

Let's Investigate

- Children investigate which prime numbers to 1000 are also prime numbers when their digits are reversed (101, 107, 113, 131, 149, 151, 157, 167, 179, 181, 191, 199, 311, 313, 337, 347, 353, 359, 373, 383, 389, 701, 709, 727, 733, 739, 743, 751, 761, 769, 787, 797, 907, 919, 929, 937, 941, 953, 967, 971, 983, 991)

Let's Investigate

- Children investigate pairs of consecutive odd numbers between 200 and 400 that are both primes (227 and 229; 239 and 241; 269 and 271; 281 and 283; 311 and 313; 347 and 349).

Page 2

Looking for Patterns

- Encourage the children to work out how many sides there are in a row of 4 and 5 greenhouses, if necessary, drawing a diagram.

  When devising a formula, encourage the children to look for the relationship between the number of greenhouses in a row and the total number of sides.

Looking for Patterns

- When writing a formula for the rule, discuss with the children the algebraic convention of referring to a number in the sequence as the *n*th term. Also explain the convention of omitting the multiplication sign when writing an algebraic expression, i.e. how: $n \times (n + 1) \times (n + 2)$ can be expressed as: $n(n + 1)(n + 2)$.

Looking for Patterns

- Assist the children in seeing the following patterns:
  - the units and thousands digits are even numbers
  - the sum of all four digits is divisible by 3, e.g.
    2112 = 2 + 1 + 1 + 2 = 6; 4554 = 4 + 5 + 5 + 4 = 18

The Puzzler

- Tell the children that there are three different combinations for making four square numbers (one one-digit number, one two-digit number and two three-digit numbers) and only one combination for making three square numbers (one two-digit number, one three-digit number and one four-digit number).

Page 3

The Arts Roundup

- Discuss the activity with the children and, if appropriate, have available a range of different theatre plans.

  Children need to design the auditoriums with exactly the number of seats given. Encourage them to think about the factors of 840 and 1260, and to ensure that the seating in the auditoriums is 'symmetrical'.

Looking for Patterns

- Children investigate which two-digit numbers have exactly ten factors (48 and 80).

What's the Problem?

- The key to identifying the correct number of factors is based on factor pairs and whether or not the number is a square number. If it is not a square number, then there should be an even number of factors. If it is a square number, then its square root is paired with itself and there are an odd number of factors.

Teaching support continued

Page 4

Sports Update

- Discuss with the children why the final score of 4 – 3 could also be a possible half-time score.
- Some children may need assistance in identifying the formula. When writing a formula for the rule, discuss with the children the algebraic convention of assigning a letter to represent a term, and also for omitting the multiplication sign when writing an algebraic expression, i.e. how: $(a + 1) \times (b + 1)$ can be expressed as: $(a + 1)(b + 1)$.

The Puzzler

- Tell the children that there are six possible three-digit numbers for each puzzle. Can they find them all?

In the Past

- There are a range of different number systems that the children could investigate such as: Babylonians, Ancient Egyptian, Ancient Greek, Ancient Chinese, Ancient Japanese and Hebrew.

AfL

- What are all the different possibilities? How can you be sure that you have accounted for them all?
- What is happening in this sequence?
- What pattern do you notice? What is the rule?
- How would you express this rule in words? What about using symbols?
- How else can you express this rule?

Answers

Page 1

Looking for Patterns
Sequence D will be the first to reach 1000 or more.
A = 32nd term is 1024 (Rule: increase the difference by 2 each time – sequence of square numbers)
B = 46th term is 1081 (Rule: increase the difference by 1 each time – sequence of triangular numbers)
C = 18th term is 1597 (Rule: add the previous two terms – Fibonacci sequence)
D = 11th term is 1024 (Rule: double the previous term)

The Puzzler
44 and 45
98 and 99

Let's Investigate
11, 13, 17, 31, 37, 71, 73, 79, 97

Page 1 continued

Let's Investigate

101 and 103
107 and 109
137 and 139
149 and 151
179 and 181
191 and 193
197 and 199

Page 2

Looking for Patterns

There would be 41 sides in a row of 10 houses.
Answers will vary for the formula, e.g. if n = number of houses in the row and s = total number of sides then $s = 4n + 1$.

Looking for Patterns

336, 504
Answers will vary for an explanation in words, e.g.
each number in the sequence is obtained by multiplying its position number in the sequence by the next two position numbers, i.e. $6 = 1 \times 2 \times 3$; $24 = 2 \times 3 \times 4$; …
Answers will vary for the formula, e.g. if n = the position in the sequence then *nth term* $= n \times (n + 1) \times (n + 2)$
or $n(n + 1)(n + 2)$.
So, the 6th term $= 6 \times 7 \times 8 = 336$.

Looking for Patterns

In each number:

- the units and thousands digits are the same
- the tens and hundreds digits are the same.

There are ten other numbers that are divisible by 66 and have the same units / thousands and tens / hundreds patterns: 2442, 2772, 4224, 4884, 6006, 6336, 6996, 8118, 8448, 8778.

The Puzzler

There are three different combinations for making four square numbers:
9, 81, 324, 576
9, 25, 361, 784
1, 36, 529, 784
There is only one combination for making three square numbers:
25, 841, 7396

Page 3

The Arts Roundup

Designs will vary.

Looking for Patterns

60, 72, 90 and 96

Answers continued

Page 3 continued

What's the Problem? 42 is missing.
If 1008 (or any number) is not a square number, then there should be an even number of factors. If the number is a square number, then its square root is paired with itself and there is an odd number of factors.
As 1008 is not a square number there should be an even number of factors. By pairing up the factors, e.g. 1 × 1008, 2 × 504 … it can be seen that one of the factors does not have a pair, i.e. 24.
Therefore 42 is missing.

Page 4

Sports Update There are 20 possible half-time scores:

0 – 0	1 – 0	2 – 0	3 – 0	4 – 0
0 – 1	1 – 1	2 – 1	3 – 1	4 – 1
0 – 2	1 – 2	2 – 2	3 – 2	4 – 2
0 – 3	1 – 3	2 – 3	3 – 3	4 – 3

If a = one team's final score and b = the other team's final score then the formula for calculating the number of possibilities is:
$(a + 1) \times (b + 1)$ or $(a + 1)(b + 1)$
So for a final score of 4 – 3
$(4 + 1)(3 + 1) = 5 \times 4 = 20$

The Puzzler 123, 132, 213, 231, 312, 321
257, 275, 527, 572, 725, 752

In the Past Results of the investigation will vary.

EMU

natural number

A whole number greater than zero.

Issue 2 Negative numbers

Prerequisites for learning

- Relate numbers to their position on a number line
- Recognise negative numbers in context, including temperature and how it is measured
- Recognise and continue number sequences formed by counting on or back in steps of constant size, including beyond zero when counting backwards
- Understand and use simple algebraic conventions
- Construct and interpret frequency tables, bar charts and line graphs

Resources pencil and paper; RCM 2: My notes (optional); RCM 3: Pupil self assessment booklet (optional); RCM 4: 1 cm squared paper; ruler; bowl of ice; thermometer; empty frozen food packages, e.g. packet of peas, ice-cream carton, fish fingers box … (optional); calculator; computer

Teaching support

Page 1

Let's Investigate

- At first, encourage the children to use a number line. However, after they have successfully demonstrated that they can add and subtract three (and four) positive and negative numbers, ask them to just write down the calculation.
- Discuss with the children what rules they can identify for adding and subtracting positive and negative numbers. This will assist them with the Technology Today activity on page 2.

Focus on Science

- This activity requires the children to measure and record the temperature increase of a bowl of ice. It is advised therefore, that the children do this activity on a suitable day, i.e. a day without PE or an assembly.
- Children could repeat this activity at a different time of the year and compare the two different rates of temperature increase.
- Children can write their report using ICT.

Page 2

Let's Investigate

- Ensure that children are familiar with letters used to represent numbers. Discuss with the children what rules they can identify for adding and subtracting a pair of positive and negative numbers. This will assist them with the Technology Today activity.

Teaching support continued

Page 2 continued

At Home

- Ensure that children have access to frozen foods at home and / or are able to visit a supermarket during out-of-school hours. If this is not possible, then bring to school some empty frozen food packages as examples.
- Once the children have completed the activity at home, ensure that there is an opportunity in class for pairs or groups of children to discuss and compare the results. What conclusions can they make?

Technology Today

- Explain to the children that their poster will go on display in the classroom and that it should be designed to help other children when adding and subtracting positive and negative numbers.

Page 3

Around the World

- Ensure that children understand the terms 'average minimum temperature' and 'record minimum temperature'.
- It may be necessary to assist some children in starting off their line graph, particularly with the numbering of the temperature axis. However, the Around the World activity on page 4 should give most children a clue as to how this can be done.

Looking for Patterns

- When creating their own number sequences involving negative numbers, encourage the children to make them as challenging as possible.
- Children can rewrite their number sequences omitting some of the numbers, then swap their incomplete sequences with a partner. Pairs then discuss the different sequences.

Page 4

Around the World

- Ensure the children understand the terms 'average daily temperature (max)' and 'average daily temperature (min)'.
- When writing their report, also ensure that children correctly identify the four seasons and make comparisons not only between seasons but also across the entire year.
- Children can write their report using ICT.

Page 4 continued

Looking for Patterns

- Suggest the children draw a number line to more easily identify those pairs of numbers with a difference of 0·2, i.e.

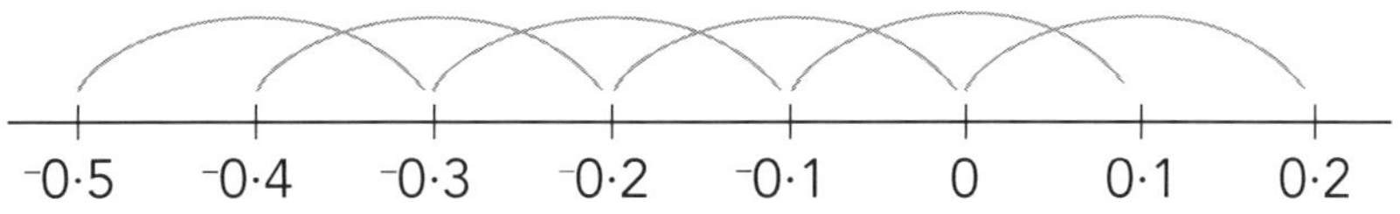

AfL

- What is the difference between these two numbers?
- What is the rule for finding the difference between a positive and a negative number? What about the difference between two negative numbers?
- What about adding together a positive number and a negative number?
- How does a number line help when adding and subtracting positive and negative numbers?
- What does this graph tell us? Is this the best way to show this? How else could you have displayed the information?

Answers

Page 1

Let's Investigate Calculations will vary.

Focus on Science Results and reports will vary.

Page 2

Let's Investigate Answers will vary. Examples may include:

$a + b = 12\ ({}^-5 + 17,\ 20 + {}^-8)$

$a - b = 15\ (10 - {}^-5,\ 7 - {}^-8)$

$a + b = {}^-8\ ({}^-11 + 3,\ 10 + {}^-18)$

$a - b = {}^-16\ ({}^-9 - 7,\ {}^-13 - 3)$

At Home Findings and conclusions will vary.

Technology Today Posters will vary.

Answers continued

Page 3

Around the World The line graph should look something similar to the following:

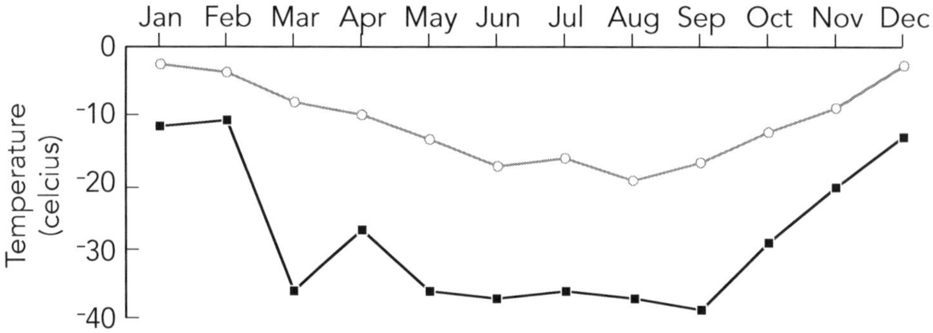

Reports will vary.

Looking for Patterns

37, 25, 13, 1, -11, -23, -35, -47, -59, -71, -83 Rule: subtract 12

-41, -33, -25, -17, -9, -1, 7, 15, 23 Rule: add 8

150, 80, 10, -60, -130, -200, -270, -340 Rule: subtract 70

-154, -117, -80, -43, -6, 31, 68, 105 Rule: add 37

Children's own number sequences will vary.

Page 4

Around the World Reports will vary.

Looking for Patterns -0·5 – -0·3; -0·4 – -0·2; -0·3 – -0·1; -0·2 – 0; 0 – 0·2; -0·1 – 0·1

EMU

$^{-}5^2$

$= {^{-}5} \times {^{-}5}$

$= 25$

Issue 3 Fractions

Prerequisites for learning

- Understand and use the term 'highest common factor' (HCF)
- Find equivalent fractions
- Simplify fractions by cancelling common factors
- Order a set of fractions by converting them to fractions with a common denominator
- Express a smaller whole number as a fraction of a larger one
- Relate fractions to multiplication and division
- Tabulate systematically the information in a problem

Resources pencil and paper; RCM 2: My notes (optional); RCM 3: Pupil self assessment booklet (optional); fraction wall (optional)

Teaching support

Page 1

Famous Mathematicians

- Demonstrate how to use Euclid's Algorithm using question 1 as an example:

```
        1
162 ) 189
      162        6
      ---     ------
       27  ) 162
        ↑      162
        |      ---
                 0
```

HCF is 27.

$$\frac{162 \div 27}{189 \div 27} = \frac{6}{7}$$

The Puzzler

- Ask the children to make their own puzzle similar to the one given.

The Puzzler

- Tell the children the position of one or two of the digits in the fraction, e.g.

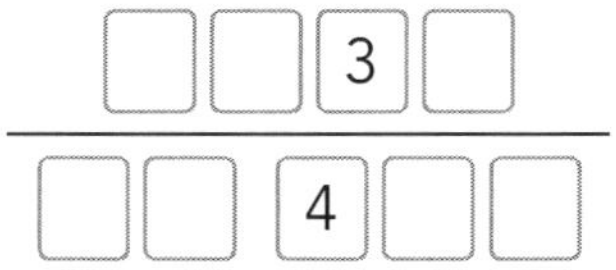

Teaching support continued

Page 2

Looking for Patterns

- Discuss with the children the relationship between the sequence number, i.e. F_1, F_2, F_3 … and the numbers that appear as denominators in those sequences, i.e. F_1: 1; F_2: 1 and 2; F_3: 1, 2 and 3.
- Also draw children's attention to the layout of the fractions that highlights which fractions have been added to each subsequent sequence. This will help them identify the pattern and then continue it, i.e.

$$F_1 = \frac{0}{1}, \frac{1}{1}$$
$$F_2 = \frac{0}{1}, \frac{1}{2}, \frac{1}{1}$$
$$F_3 = \frac{0}{1}, \frac{1}{3}, \frac{1}{2}, \frac{2}{3}, \frac{1}{1}$$
$$F_4 = \frac{0}{1}, \frac{1}{4}, \frac{1}{3}, \frac{1}{2}, \frac{2}{3}, \frac{3}{4}, \frac{1}{1}$$
$$F_5 = \frac{0}{1}, \frac{1}{5}, \frac{1}{4}, \frac{1}{3}, \frac{2}{5}, \frac{1}{2}, \frac{3}{5}, \frac{2}{3}, \frac{3}{4}, \frac{4}{5}, \frac{1}{1}$$
$$F_6 = \frac{0}{1}, \frac{1}{6}, \frac{1}{5}, \frac{1}{4}, \frac{1}{3}, \frac{2}{5}, \frac{1}{2}, \frac{3}{5}, \frac{2}{3}, \frac{3}{4}, \frac{4}{5}, \frac{5}{6}, \frac{1}{1}$$

- Ensure that children understand how to check their Farey sequences using the given formula.
- Ask the children to extend the sequence to F_{10}.

Page 3

What's the Problem?

- Ask prompting questions such as:
  - What if Cloe got £6 pocket money? What would a third of that be?
  - Can you think of an amount for Taylah so her half is the same as Cloe's third?
  - Can you think of an amount for Taylah so her half is less than Cloe's third?

Let's Investigate

- Provide the children with a fraction wall to assist them when comparing and ordering the fractions, i.e.

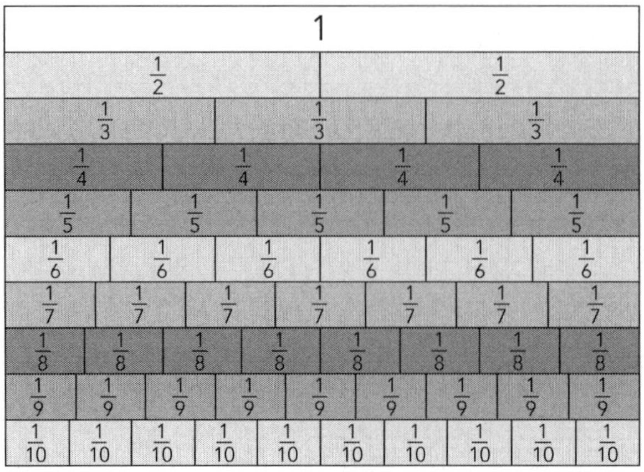

Page 3 continued
The Arts Roundup

- Children need to first convert $\frac{1}{8}$ and $\frac{2}{3}$ into equivalent fractions, i.e. $\frac{3}{24}$ and $\frac{16}{24}$. That leaves $\frac{5}{24}$ remaining. Therefore $\frac{5}{24}$ equals the fraction of musicians, $\frac{3}{24}$ the technicians and $\frac{16}{24}$ the singers – which means the total number of people in The Reggio Opera Company is 24.

Page 4
Looking for Patterns

- A possible method for working out the answer is by tabulating systematically the information, for example:

Teacher announcement	Number of children in the hall	Number of children who left the hall	Number of children remaining in the hall
1	190	96	94
2	94	48	46
3	46	24	22
4	22	12	10
5	10	6	4
6	4	3	1

What's the Problem?

- Answers will obviously vary. However possible calculations may be:
  - fraction of life so far spent asleep:

    $$\frac{8 \text{ hours}}{24 \text{ hours}} = \frac{1}{3}$$
  - fraction of life so far spent eating:

    $$\frac{2 \text{ hours}}{24 \text{ hours}} = \frac{1}{12}$$
  - fraction of life so far spent in school:

    (11 years old × 365 days) + 3 leap year days = 4018 days

    4018 days × 24 hours a day = 96 432 hours

    $$\begin{matrix}\text{7 years in} \\ \text{school}\end{matrix} \times \begin{matrix}\text{36 weeks} \\ \text{a year}\end{matrix} \times \begin{matrix}\text{5 days} \\ \text{a week}\end{matrix} \times \text{6 hours} = \text{7560 hours}$$

    $$\frac{7560 \text{ hours}}{96\,432 \text{ hours}} = \frac{45}{574} \approx \frac{1}{13}$$

AfL

- What patterns do you notice?
- What is the next fraction in the sequence? How do you know?
- Is there another way to work that out?
- How did you work that out? What clues did you use? How did they help?

Answers

Page 1

Famous Mathematicians

$\frac{162}{189} = \frac{6}{7}$ (HCF = 27) $\quad$ $\frac{68}{153} = \frac{4}{9}$ (HCF = 17) $\quad$ $\frac{65}{91} = \frac{5}{7}$ (HCF = 13)

$\frac{38}{95} = \frac{2}{5}$ (HCF = 19) $\quad$ $\frac{72}{135} = \frac{8}{15}$ (HCF = 9) $\quad$ $\frac{424}{477} = \frac{8}{9}$ (HCF = 53)

The Puzzler

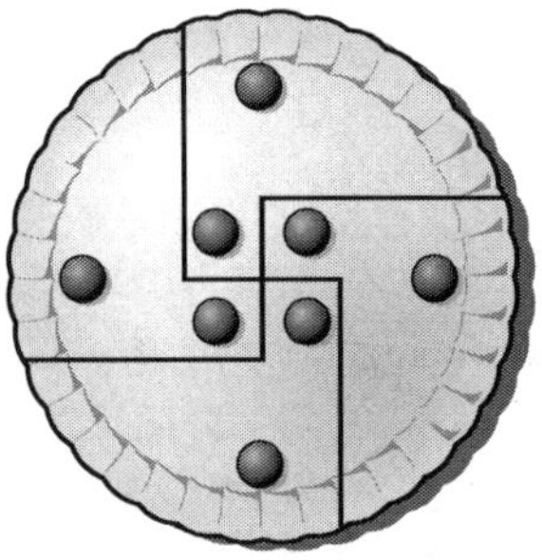

The Puzzler

$$\frac{5832}{17\,496} = \frac{1}{3}$$

Page 2

Looking for Patterns

$F_4 = \frac{0}{1}, \frac{1}{4}, \frac{1}{3}, \frac{1}{2}, \frac{2}{3}, \frac{3}{4}, \frac{1}{1}$

$\frac{1}{4}$ and $\frac{3}{4}$ are in F_4 but not in F_3.

$F_5 = \frac{0}{1}, \frac{1}{5}, \frac{1}{4}, \frac{1}{3}, \frac{2}{5}, \frac{1}{2}, \frac{3}{5}, \frac{2}{3}, \frac{3}{4}, \frac{4}{5}, \frac{1}{1}$

$F_6 = \frac{0}{1}, \frac{1}{6}, \frac{1}{5}, \frac{1}{4}, \frac{1}{3}, \frac{2}{5}, \frac{1}{2}, \frac{3}{5}, \frac{2}{3}, \frac{3}{4}, \frac{4}{5}, \frac{5}{6}, \frac{1}{1}$

Page 3

What's the Problem?

Half of Taylah's money can be less than a third of Cloe's. If, for example, Taylah has £1 and Cloe has £3, then half of Taylah's pocket money is 50p and a third of Cloe's is £1.
Amounts will vary.

Let's Investigate

Results of the investigation will vary.

The Arts Roundup

3 technicians.
16 singers.
24 people are in The Reggio Opera Company.

Page 4

Looking for Patterns

There were 190 children in the hall to start with.

What's the Problem?

Answers will vary. However most approximations should be similar to the following:
asleep: $\frac{1}{3}$ $\quad$ in school: $\frac{1}{13}$ $\quad$ eating: $\frac{1}{12}$

EMU

non-unitary fraction

A non-unitary fraction is a fraction with a numerator of 2 or more, e.g. $\frac{2}{3}, \frac{3}{4}, \frac{4}{5} \ldots$

Fractions with a numerator of 1, e.g. $\frac{1}{2}, \frac{1}{3}, \frac{1}{4} \ldots$ are called unitary (or unit) fractions.

Issue 4 Decimals

Prerequisites for learning

- Calculate mentally with integers and decimals
- Use efficient written methods to add and subtract decimals with up to two places
- Use understanding of place value to multiply and divide decimals by 10, 100 or 1000
- Use a calculator to solve problems, including those involving decimals
- Select and use standard metric units of measure and convert between units using decimals to two places
- Use the order of operations, including brackets

Resources pencil and paper; RCM 2: My notes (optional); RCM 3: Pupil self assessment booklet (optional); RCM 4: 1 cm squared paper (optional); ruler; section from a newspaper showing exchange rates; calculator; cheques from a range of different banks; material for making a poster; computer with internet access

Teaching support

Page 1

Money Matters

- Either provide the children with the section from a newspaper that shows exchange rates (financial and / or travel section) or access exchange rates from the internet.
- Ensure that children understand the difference between imports and exports.
- The most important aspect of this activity is the last section – drawing conclusions about the affects of exchange rates on the prices of imported and exported goods.
- Ask the children to draw a conversion graph showing the relationship between the pound and another major currency such as the Euro or US dollar.

Let's Investigate

- Using two, three or four digits it is possible to make the following combinations of decimals with one, two or three places:
    - decimals with one place: U·t, TU·t, HTU·t
    - decimals with two places: U·th, TU·th
    - decimals with three places: U·tht^{h}

Teaching support continued

Page 1 continued

Let's Investigate

- Ensure that children understand the difference between a terminating decimal and a recurring decimal.
- Children also need to be confident with using a calculator and understand the error display 'e'.

Page 2

Money Matters

- The main purpose of this activity is for the children to investigate for themselves how cheques work, what are their advantages and disadvantages, and how they are designed to ensure security.
- Ensure that there is a range of cheques from different banks available for the children to refer to when designing their school's cheque.

At Home

- After children have completed the activity at home, ensure that there is an opportunity in class for pairs or groups of children to compare and discuss their lists, and to draw conclusions about the usage of decimals with different decimal places.

The Language of Maths

- Encourage the children to be as detailed as possible when defining the word 'decimal'.

Page 3

Let's Investigate

- Ensure that children are confident in using the order of operations, including brackets.

Looking for Patterns

- Remind the children that they are designing a poster with the purpose of explaining to others how to effectively and efficiently convert between different metric units for length, mass and capacity. Therefore, the poster needs to be easy to read and follow, and illustrated with examples.

The Language of Maths

- Children should be able to infer the meaning of the prefixes 'centi', 'milli' and 'deci' from their association with words such as centimetre, millimetre and decimal. Likewise, they should be able deduce the meaning of the words 'decimetre', 'centigram', 'centilitre' and 'decilitre'.

Page 4

The Puzzler

- The amount of money in each envelope can be found by subtracting the total of the other two pairs of envelopes from £10. For example, Envelope E = £10 – (£5.20 + £3.40) = £1.40.

The Puzzler

- Tell the children that the common total is 3·4.

AfL

- What did you find out? How did you find this out? What does it mean?
- How do you know that you have found all the different possibilities?
- How did you organise your work?
- Explain to me how you worked that out. What strategies did you use? How did they help you?

Answers

Page 1

Money Matters Results of the investigation will vary.

Let's Investigate Results of the investigation will vary.

Let's Investigate $\frac{1}{2}, \frac{1}{4}, \frac{1}{5}, \frac{1}{8}, \frac{1}{10}, \frac{1}{16}, \frac{1}{20}, \frac{1}{25}, \frac{1}{32}, \frac{1}{40}, \frac{1}{50}, \frac{1}{64}, \frac{1}{80}$

Page 2

Money Matters Results of the investigation will vary.

At Home Results of the investigation will vary.

The Language of Maths 'Decimal' means using the number ten as a base. Numbers are expressed in a counting system that uses units of ten.

Page 3

Let's Investigate Results of the investigation will vary.

Looking for Patterns Results will vary.

The Language of Maths *centi* – one hundredth *milli* – one thousandth *deci* – one tenth
decimetre – metric unit of length that is equal to one tenth of a metre
centigram – metric unit of mass that is equal to one hundredth of a gram
decilitre – metric unit of capacity that is equal to one tenth of a litre
centilitre – metric unit of capacity that is equal to one hundredth of a litre

Answers continued

Page 4

The Puzzler A = £2.70
B = £2.50
C = £1.80
D = £1.60
E = £1.40

The Puzzler

1·6	0·3	0·2	1·3
0·5	1	1·1	0·8
0·9	0·6	0·7	1·2
0·4	1·5	1·4	0·1

Each row, column and diagonal totals 3·4.
Other solutions are possible.

EMU 

10^{-3}

= 0·001 (milli)

Issue 5

Percentages

Prerequisites for learning

- Understand percentage as the number of parts in every 100
- Express tenths and hundredths as percentages
- Express one quantity as a percentage of another
- Recognise approximate proportions of a whole and use percentages to describe and compare them

Resources pencil and paper; RCM 2: My notes (optional); RCM 3: Pupil self assessment booklet (optional); ruler; pair of compasses; protractor; newspapers, magazines and catalogues; data-handling software; calculator (optional); computer with internet access

Teaching support

Page 1

Let's Investigate

- Discuss with the children all the different regular activities they do in a weekday. Encourage the children to organise all the activities into six to ten different categories. This will make it easier for the children to draw their pie chart.
- It is advised that children create their pie chart using ICT.
- Children draw their pie chart using a pair of compasses, a protractor and a ruler.

The Puzzler

- Ensure children are familiar with magic squares.

  Ask the children to create a 4 × 4 magic percent square.

Focus on Science

- Children will need to use the internet for this activity.

Page 2

The Language of Maths

- Briefly introduce the children to the terms 'deposit', 'down-payment' and 'balance'. Ensure that they are secure in their understanding of these terms before setting them to work on the activity.

Teaching support continued

Page 2 continued

Let's Investigate

- At this stage, children should be able to recognise approximate proportions of a whole and use percentages to describe and compare them. Encourage the children to make comparisons between three, four or more groups.

Money Matters

- Most children should be able to calculate successfully the VAT on goods and services and the new price once VAT has been added.
- It will be easier to find prices in magazines and catalogues that are VAT inclusive. Services, as opposed to goods, are often quoted without VAT. To find prices of goods and services that do not include VAT refer to appropriate websites.
- If the price of an item already includes VAT, some children may need assistance in calculating the cost of the item before VAT (see Answers).

Page 3

Money Matters

- Below are the VAT rates for some European countries:

  18% – Russia and Spain
  19% – Germany
  20% – Austria and Italy
  21% – Belgium and Ireland
  22% – Poland
  23% – Portugal and Finland
  25% – Denmark, Norway and Sweden

  Note: Rates current at the end of 2010

The Language of Maths

- This activity requires children to be able to recognise approximate proportions of a whole and use percentages to describe and compare them.
- Explain to the children that each sector of the pie chart is a multiple of 5%.

Money Matters

- You may wish to provide children with appropriate clippings from newspapers rather than have them look for them themselves.

Page 4

Money Matters

- Draw children's attention to the illustrations displaying different percentages and talk about what they all have in common (they are multiples of 10% or 25%).

Page 4 continued

Technology Today

- To be able to answer this problem, children need to be able to express successfully one quantity as a percentage of another.
- Work through one or more examples with the children. If appropriate, provide the children with a calculator.

e.g. 58 out of 80.

$$\frac{58}{8\not{0}} \times \frac{10\not{0}}{1} = \frac{580}{8} = 72{\cdot}5\%$$

AfL

- What did you find out? What does it mean? How did you go about this?
- How did you go about working out the percentage? How would you do this on a calculator?
- What calculation did you do? What does the answer tell you?
- Approximately what percentage of the pie chart is this sector? Why do you think it is that percent?

Answers

Page 1

Let's Investigate Results of the investigation will vary.

The Puzzler

60%	10%	80%
70%	50%	30%
20%	90%	40%

The magic percent is 150%.
Other solutions are possible.

Focus on Science A humidity meter measures the amount of moisture in the air. RH% refers to the percentage of relative humidity in the air. Relative humidity is the amount of water vapour in the air expressed as a percentage of the maximum amount of water vapour that can exist in the air at that temperature.

Page 2

The Language of Maths Results of the investigation will vary.

Let's Investigate Results of the investigation will vary.

Answers continued

Page 2 continued

Money Matters

VAT stands for Value-Added Tax. It is a tax added to the value of a product at its production or distribution and is paid by the consumer when they purchase the product. Every quarter, the producer (or distributor) pays to the government the VAT they receive from consumers. The rate of VAT in the UK as of 1 January 2011 is 20%.

To calculate the price of an item including VAT:
(price of item before VAT x percentage rate of VAT) + price of item
e.g. price of item before VAT costs £24
VAT rate is 20%
(£24 × 0·2) + £24 = £28.80

To find the price of an item before VAT: $\frac{\text{price of item including VAT} \times 100}{100 + \text{percentage rate of VAT}}$

e.g. price of item including VAT costs £28.80
VAT rate is 20%

$$\frac{£28{\cdot}80 \times 100}{100 + 20} = \frac{2880}{120} = £24$$

Page 3

Money Matters Results of the investigation will vary.

The Language of Maths Answers will vary. However, they should be similar to the following:

Sector 1: 25%	Sector 2: 10%	Sector 3: 5%
Sector 4: 5%	Sector 5: 5%	Sector 6: 5%
Sector 7: 15%	Sector 8: 10%	Sector 9: 20%

Money Matters Results of the investigation will vary.

Page 4

Money Matters Results of the investigation will vary. However, most sales have discounts of multiples of 10% (or 25%). This is because such percentage discounts are easy to calculate, which means consumers can quickly work out how much money they are saving.

Technology Today Hector did best on Friday. He did worst on Wednesday.
Gomez did best on Tuesday and Friday. He did worst on Saturday.

EMU

‰
'Per mil' means parts per thousand. It is a tenth of a percent.

Issue 6

Ratio and proportion

Prerequisites for learning

- Use sequences to scale numbers up or down
- Solve problems involving ratio and proportion
- Understand and use ratio notation

Resources pencil and paper; RCM 2: My notes (optional); RCM 3: Pupil self assessment booklet (optional); recipe books; material for making a poster; computer with internet access

Teaching support

Page 1

The Puzzler

- Using direct proportion, assist the children in seeing the relationship between the two ratios, e.g.

  7 parts orange juice mixed with 3 parts water

  $$= \frac{7 \times 4}{3 \times 4} = \frac{28}{12}$$

  8 parts orange juice mixed with 4 parts water

  $$= \frac{8 \times 3}{4 \times 3} = \frac{24}{12}$$

At Home

- Children should not only write male and female ratio and proportion statements about their extended family but also about other topics. For example, the ratio and proportion of family members that are:
  - under the age of 40 and over the age of 40
  - married or not married
  - live in the same city / town as they do or live elsewhere.

  Discuss with the children other suitable topics.
- After children have completed the activity at home, ensure that there is an opportunity in class for pairs or groups of children to compare and discuss the different ratio and proportion statements they wrote about their families.

Teaching support continued

Page 1 continued

The Language of Maths

- Children should be familiar with the term 'direct proportion'. However you may need to spend some time discussing and providing examples of 'inverse proportion'.
- Work through the first problem with the children, i.e.

  As there are fewer men, the work will take longer.

  The ratio of men has decreased 6 : 8 or 3 : 4.

  So, the number of hours is increased in the ratio 4 : 3.

  The inverse of 3 : 4 is 4 : 3. The amount of time is in inverse proportion to the number of men.

  Number of hours $= 12 \times \frac{4}{3}$

  $= \frac{48}{3} = 16$ hours

Page 2

What's the Problem?

- Work through the first problem with the children.

What's the Problem?

- Ensure that children are familiar with ratio notation, e.g. 2 : 3, and how this can be extended to include three-part ratios such as 5 : 1 : 2.

Sports Update

- Some children may need assistance in working out the answer to the problem and in particular organising their work. One example may be:

  8 people in the stadium = 7 Nawra Rovers supporters

  9 Nawra Rovers supporters = 1 Nawra Rovers season ticket holder

  819 Nawra Rovers supporters = 91 Nawra Rovers season ticket holders

  819 Nawra Rovers supporters × $\frac{8}{7}$ ($1\frac{1}{7}$) people in the stadium = 936 people in the stadium

Page 3

Let's Investigate

- This is an open-ended investigation where, depending on the amount of time and effort children are prepared to invest in the activity, they can be as detailed and as accurate as they wish.
- The important aspect of this activity is the justifications that children give for the decisions that they made during the investigation.

Page 3 continued

Let's Investigate

- Either provide the children with a recipe book or direct them to a suitable website.
- When children are rewriting the quantities needed of each ingredient, suggest that one is for fewer people than given in the recipe, i.e. scaling down the recipe; and the other is for more people, i.e. scaling up the recipe.

Page 4

What's the Problem?

- For this problem, children need to find out, on average, how many children each day have school dinners as opposed to packed lunches. A precise number is not essential for this activity.

The Language of Maths

- Explain to the children that their poster will go on display in the classroom and that it should be designed so that other children can easily understand both the difference and relationship between ratio and proportion.

AfL

- What does the word 'ratio' mean? How do you write a ratio?
- What is the difference between 'direct proportion' and 'inverse proportion'?
- How do you write a proportion? How else can you express a proportion? Which do you prefer? Why?
- What does scaling have to do with ratio and proportion? Can you give me an example?
- Give me some other examples of when and how we use ratio and proportion.

Answers

Page 1

The Puzzler 7 parts orange juice mixed with 3 parts water is stronger.

At Home Answers and statements will vary.

The Language of Maths 16 hours
6 days
37 minutes 30 seconds

Answers continued

Page 2

What's the Problem?
15 men
7·5 days
Explanations will vary.

What's the Problem?
Books = 1235
CDs = 247
DVDs = 494

Sports Update
There are 936 people in the stadium.

Page 3

Let's Investigate
Results of the investigation will vary.

Let's Investigate
Results of the investigation will vary.

Page 4

What's the Problem?
Results will vary.

The Language of Maths
Posters will vary. However, they should convey the idea that ratio compares part to part (using terms such as *to every*), and proportion compares part to whole (using terms such as *in every*). The relationship between ratio and proportion can be explained through examples such as: *'two to every three' (a ratio) is equivalent to 'two in every five' (a proportion).*

EMU

a : b = b : a

Using ratio notation, a : b shows the relationship between two numbers or quantities. It can also be expressed in the form b : a. For example, in a class of 30 children, 14 boys and 16 girls, the ratio of boys to girls is 14 : 16 (or 7 : 8) and is equal to the ratio of girls to boys, i.e. 16 : 14 (or 8 : 7).

Issue 7

Counting and understanding number – General

Prerequisites for learning

- Count from any given number in whole-number and decimal steps, extending beyond zero when counting backwards
- Express a smaller whole number as a fraction of a larger one
- Relate fractions to their decimal representations
- Explain what each digit represents in whole numbers and decimals with up to three places
- Understand percentage as the number of parts in every 100 and express tenths and hundredths as percentages
- Solve problems involving ratio and proportion

Resources pencil and paper; RCM 2: My notes (optional); RCM 3: Pupil self assessment booklet (optional); computer with internet access

Teaching support

Page 1

The Language of Maths

- Ensure that children fully understand how the numbers 1 to 12 have been written in the ternary numeral system, and are confident in using and applying this knowledge in writing the numbers 13 to 20 in base 3.
- Once you are sure that children are secure in their understanding of writing numbers in the ternary numeral system, then ask them to investigate writing the numbers 1 to 20 in other bases.
- As children will be investigating the binary numeral system in the next activity Technology Today tell them not to look at the base 2 numeral system in this activity.

Technology Today

- The binary system works in base 2, so instead of 10s, 100s, 1000s … the place value of these numbers works in doubles: 1, 2, 4, 8, 16, 32, 64, 128 …. If you placed these in columns as in our number system, it would look something like this:

(128)	(64)	(32)	(16)	(8)	(4)	(2)	(1)
1	1	1	1	1	1	1	1

If you take the number 18, for example, it can be made from one lot of 16 and 2, so in binary it would appear as 1 0 0 1 0.

Teaching support continued

Page 1 continued

Technology Today continued

- You may wish to suggest that the children write the numbers 1 to 20 using binary notation.
- Children write several numbers as binary numerals and ask a friend to rewrite the numbers in base 10.

Number	Binary numeral				
	16	8	4	2	1
1					1
2				1	0
3				1	1
4			1	0	0
5			1	0	1
6			1	1	0
7			1	1	1
8		1	0	0	0
9		1	0	0	1
10		1	0	1	0
11		1	0	1	1
12		1	1	0	0
13		1	1	0	1
14		1	1	1	0
15		1	1	1	1
16	1	0	0	0	0
17	1	0	0	0	1
18	1	0	0	1	0
19	1	0	0	1	1
20	1	0	1	0	0

Page 2

Technology Today

- Choose other numbers between 1 and 20 and work with the children to calculate their value in modulo 3.
- Once the children are confident with writing numbers in modulo 3, they can they investigate writing numbers in modulo 4 and modulo 5.
- The numbers 19 and 34 are 'congruent modulo 5'; ask the children to explain what this means:

  (19 mod 5 = 19 ÷ 5 = 3 R 4, so 19 mod 5 = 4

  34 mod 5 = 34 ÷ 5 = 6 R 4, so 34 mod 5 = 4).

  Ask the children to suggest other pairs of congruent modulo 5 / modulo 4 / modulo 3 numbers.

Let's Investigate

- Most children will probably be familiar with Pascal's Triangle. If not, you may need to spend some time discussing it with the children.
- The important part of this activity is not identifying the rule and extending Pascal's Triangle, rather it is expressing it in modulo 3 and identifying different patterns.

Page 3

Around the World

- The two most important aspects of this activity are getting the children to think about how and when the different types of numbers are used in different jobs, and also thinking about those jobs that use a combination of all the different types of numbers.

Page 3 continued

Around the World continued

- Ask the children to think about the times when they are calculating with numbers that are not whole numbers (not integers), and whether they prefer to work with fractions, decimals, percentages or ratio and proportion. Why?

Money Matters

- You may wish to suggest that the children differentiate their two lists further by indicating those effects that would be advantageous and those that would not.

Around the World

- You will need to discuss the notion of a census with the children before they undertake this activity. You may also need to locate suitable websites to offer as suggestions to the children when they investigate the 2010 Chinese census.

Around the World

- Children investigate other censuses including, if appropriate, the 2011 census in England and Wales.

Page 4

Around the World

- Flags that are suitable for children to use when describing the proportion of the different colours used include:
  - Malta and Monaco ($\frac{1}{2}$)
  - France, Germany, Italy and Ireland ($\frac{1}{3}$)
  - Austria ($\frac{2}{3}$ red, $\frac{1}{3}$ white)
  - Portugal (approx. 60% red and 40% green)
  - Thailand (approx. 30% red, 30% blue and 40% white)
  - United Arab Emirates (approx. 25% red, 25% green, 25% white and 25% black)

The Puzzler

- Tell the children that the mathematical symbol needed is not in the illustration.

The Language of Maths

- The children should write a different description for each of the examples of how they would work out an approximate number.

AfL

- What did you find out about different numeral systems?
- Why do you think we use the base 10 numeral system rather than another numeral system?
- What did you notice about the values of numbers written in modulo 3 / modulo 4 / modulo 5?
- What patterns did you notice?
- What did you find as a result of your investigation?
- Tell me about your lists. What conclusions can you draw from them?
- When is it useful to use estimations and approximations? Why?

Answers

Page 1

The Language of Maths

base 10	13	14	15	16	17	18	19	20
base 3	111	112	120	121	122	200	201	202

Other base numeral systems will vary.

Technology Today Results of the investigation will vary. However the children should mention the fact that the binary numeral system is a number system with 2 as its base, and numbers are expressed as sequences of the digits 0 and 1.

Page 2

Technology Today Answers will vary.

Let's Investigate In Pascal's Triangle, each number is produced by adding the two numbers above:

1 2
↘ ↙
3

The next two rows of Pascal's Triangle are:

1
1 1
1 2 1
1 3 3 1
1 4 6 4 1
1 5 10 10 5 1
1 6 15 20 15 6 1
1 7 21 35 35 21 7 1

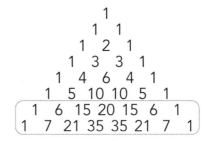

Answers continued

Page 2 continued

Let's Investigate (continued)

Pascal's Triangle written with its values in modulo 3:

Answers will vary when commenting on the patterns that arise in a Pascal's Triangle written with its values in modulo 3.

```
                  1
                1   1
              1   2   1
            1   0   0   1
          1   1   0   1   1
        1   2   1   1   2   1
      1   0   0   2   0   0   1
    1   1   0   2   2   0   1   1
  1   2   1   2   1   2   1   2   1
1   0   0   0   0   0   0   0   0   1
```

Page 3

Around the World Lists will vary.

Money Matters Lists will vary.

Around the World Results of the investigation will vary.

Page 4

Around the World Results of the investigation will vary.

The Puzzler Decimal point, i.e. 1·2

The Language of Maths Answers will vary.

EMU

irrational number

Any number that cannot be written as a fraction or a decimal with an infinite number of decimal places. Examples include π and $\sqrt{2}$.

Issue 8 Addition

Prerequisites for learning

- Use approximations and inverse operations to estimate and check results
- Identify prime numbers to at least 100
- Use tests of divisibility

Resources pencil and paper; RCM 2: My notes (optional); RCM 3: Pupil self assessment booklet (optional); ruler; dominoes; calculator (optional)

Teaching support

Page 1

Looking for Patterns

- Tell the children the value of one (or more) of the shapes in each of the grids, i.e.

■ = 7	● = 6
△ = 5	□ = 5
⬢ = 4	▲ = 3
◆ = 3	⬟ = 8
○ = 2	◇ = 4
	▽ = 7

The Puzzler

- Tell the children the value of one of the numbers (see Answers).

The Puzzler

- Ensure that the children are familiar with the term 'consecutive' and can identify consecutive odd numbers, e.g. 1, 3, 5, 7, …
- Ask the children to show all their working as this will help them when writing about how they discovered what the numbers are.

The Puzzler

- Ensure that the children can identify prime numbers to at least 100. If not, provide them with a list:

2	3	5	7	11
13	17	19	23	29
31	37	41	43	47
53	59	61	67	71
73	79	83	89	97

Page 2

The Language of Maths

- Before the children work independently on this activity, ensure that they understand how to work out a numerical tautonym.
- Children can spend as much or as little time on this activity as is appropriate. You may want some children to find only one or two four-, six- or eight-letter tautonyms, while other children might be expected to find more.

Page 2 continued

Let's Investigate

- Expect the children to use the given method to make several whole number palindromes before working with decimal numbers.
- Children should discover that the method is the same for decimal numbers as it is for whole numbers, but that the position of the decimal point plays an important role in creating perfect decimal palindromes such as 19·91 and 18·81, as opposed to imperfect decimal palindromes such as 111·1 and 66·6.

Page 3

Famous Mathematicians

- Most children will probably be familiar with Pascal's Triangle. If not, you may need to spend some time discussing it with the children.
- The important part of this activity is not identifying the rule, rather it is in investigating other rules for producing triangles of numbers.
- If children have difficulty getting started with the investigation offer them some suggestions:
  - start with a different first number
  - find the difference between the two numbers above
  - find the product of the two numbers above
  - start with a sequence at the base of the triangle.
- Once two children have made their own triangle of numbers they can swap, identify the rule and write the next two lines of the pattern.

Let's Investigate

- Ask the children to give reasons why coins in the UK are 1p, 2p, 5p, 10p, 20p, 50p, £1 and £2. Would another set of eight coins be just as affective? Why? Why not?

The Arts Roundup

- The method, as opposed to the answer, is the most important aspect of this activity.
- Once the children have made a start on the activity, discuss with them their method of working.

Teaching support continued

Page 3 continued

The Arts Roundup continued

- If children have difficulty getting started, suggest they organise their thoughts in a table. One possible method for working out the answer is:

Gates open	200 enter	200 in grounds ↙ + 200 more enter ground	5:00 p.m.
1st hour	400 enter	600 in grounds (200 + 400) ↙ + 200 more enter ground	6:00 p.m.
2nd hour	800 enter	1400 in grounds (200 + 400 + 800) ↙ + 200 more enter ground	7:00 p.m.
3rd hour	1600 enter	3000 in grounds (200 + 400 + 800 + 1600) ↙ + 200 more enter ground	8:00 p.m.
4th hour	3200 enter	6200 in grounds (200 + 400 + 800 + 1600 + 3200)	9:00 p.m.

Page 4

Looking for Patterns

- Suggest the children record their findings in a table.

Sum of 2 consecutive numbers	Sum of 3 consecutive numbers	Sum of 4 consecutive numbers	Sum of 5 consecutive numbers
1 + 2 = 3	1 + 2 + 3 = 6	1 + 2 + 3 + 4 = 10	1 + 2 + 3 + 4 + 5 = 15
2 + 3 = 5	2 + 3 + 4 = 9	2 + 3 + 4 + 5 = 14	2 + 3 + 4 + 5 + 6 = 20
3 + 4 = 7	3 + 4 + 5 = 12	3 + 4 + 5 + 6 = 18	3 + 4 + 5 + 6 + 7 = 25
4 + 5 = 9	4 + 5 + 6 = 15	4 + 5 + 6 + 7 = 22	4 + 5 + 6 + 7 + 8 = 30

- A number is the sum of 2 consecutive numbers if the number is odd.

  A number is the sum of 3 consecutive numbers if the number is divisible by 3.

  A number is the sum of 4 consecutive numbers if the number is divisible by 4 after 10 has been subtracted from it.

  A number is the sum of 5 consecutive numbers if the number is divisible by 5 and is 15 or greater.

Page 4 continued

Looking for Patterns continued

- The rule for finding whether a number is the sum of consecutive numbers is:

  A is the sum of n consecutive numbers if

  $$\frac{A - n\text{th triangular number}}{n} = \text{whole number}$$

e.g.

18 is the sum of 4 consecutive numbers if

$$\frac{18 - 4\text{th triangular number (i.e. 10)}}{4} = \text{whole number}$$

$$\frac{18 - 10}{4} = \frac{8}{4} = 2$$

Therefore 18 is the sum of 4 consecutive numbers.

Let's Investigate

- Encourage the children to find more than one solution.

The Puzzler

- Most children will find this puzzle relatively easy. What is most important about this activity is how they went about it.

AfL

- How did you work out the answer to this puzzle? What strategies did you use? How else could you have gone about it?
- Did you use trial and improvement to help you work out the answer to this puzzle? How did you know where to start? Then what did you do?
- How did you organise your thoughts? Did this help? What else could you have done? Why might this have been more effective?

Answers

Page 1

Looking for Patterns

7	5	4	3	19
7	7	4	4	22
2	3	5	4	14
5	5	2	3	15
21	20	15	14	

6	5	3	8	22
3	4	6	5	18
6	7	3	8	24
5	8	4	7	24
20	24	16	28	

The Puzzler

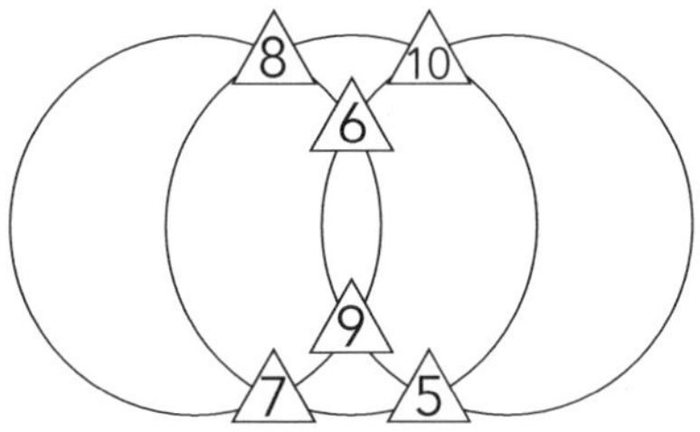

Other solutions are possible.

Answers continued

Page 1 continued

The Puzzler 17, 19, 21, 23, 25, 27, 29, 31, 33

The Puzzler

43	1	67
61	37	13
7	73	31

Page 2

The Language of Maths

Many words are possible.

Four-letter numerical tautonyms:
BUDS, BULK, CHEF, COME, DIAL, DONE, EXIT, FOIL, GRIP, HEAL, HUMP, LAID, LOVE, MEND, MOTH, NEAR, OKAY, PALE, PINK, RUST, SELL, SPOT, SPUN, TABS, TAIL, TAPE, THIS, TIDY, TOPS, UNTO, VAIN

Six-letter numerical tautonyms:
ASSENT, ASSUME, BOTTLE, BUTTER, CREATE, HUNTER, REPENT, SAVERS, SHADES, SMACKS, TIMERS, VACATE, WASTER

Eight-letter numerical tautonyms:
ANTIDOTE, BACKACHE, DISTILLS, FLOORING

Let's Investigate

The same method applies for decimal numbers as for whole numbers. However, with decimal numbers the position of the decimal point does not always create a perfect palindrome, e.g.

8·6	13·5
8·6 + 6·8 = 15·4	13·5 + 53·1 = 66·6
15·4 + 45·1 = 60·5	
60·5 + 50·6 = 111·1	

A perfect palindrome can be made by altering the position of the decimal point, e.g.

8·6	13·5
8·6 + 6·8 = 15·4	13·5 + 5·31 = 18·81
15·4 + 4·51 = 19·91	

Page 3

Famous Mathematicians

In Pascal's Triangle, each number is produced by adding the two numbers above:

Let's Investigate

10 = 7 + 2 + 1
16 = 8 + 7 + 1
20 = 8 + 7 + 5
The numbers 4 and 19 cannot be made using the given set.
The set of numbers {1, 2, 3, 7, 8} can make all the numbers 1 to 21 and none above.

Page 3 continued

The Arts Roundup The gates opened at 5 p.m.

Page 4

Looking for Patterns The numbers are consecutive.
The sums of two consecutive numbers are all odd numbers.
The sums of three consecutive numbers are all divisible by 3.
The sums of four consecutive numbers start at 10 and increase by 4 each time.
The sums of five consecutive numbers start at 15 and increase by 5 each time.

Let's Investigate

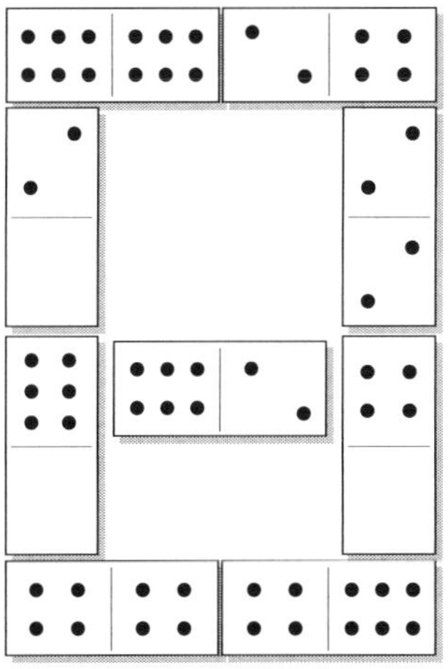

Other solutions are possible.

The Puzzler

AUGUST						
M	T	W	T	F	S	S
					1	2
3	4	5	6	7	8	9
10	11	12	13	14	15	16
17	18	19	20	21	22	23
24	25	26	27	28	29	30
31						

SEPTEMBER						
M	T	W	T	F	S	S
		1	2	3	4	5
6	7	8	9	10	11	12
13	14	15	16	17	18	19
20	21	22	23	24	25	26
27	28	29	30			

EMU

± plus or minus
The symbol is often used when describing a margin of error such as ±5 mm or ±2%.

Issue 9 Subtraction

Prerequisites for learning

- Use approximations and inverse operations to estimate and check results
- Identify prime numbers to at least 100
- Identify square roots of perfect squares to at least 12 × 12
- Find the square and square root of a number using a calculator

Resources pencil and paper; RCM 2: My notes (optional); RCM 3: Pupil self assessment booklet (optional); calculator (optional)

Teaching support

Page 1

Around the World

- Ensure that children understand the Yoruba number system, in particular the importance of the number 20 and how subtraction is used to express numbers.
- Rather than expressing all the numbers to 100 (or 200) using the Yoruba number system, ask the children to only write a selection of numbers less than 100 (or 200).

Let's Investigate

- By this stage most children should be able to identify prime numbers to at least 100. However, if they are unable to do so, tell the children to work in pairs. For this investigation do not give the children a list of prime numbers as it will make the activity too easy.

Page 2

Famous Mathematicians

- Ask the children to further investigate the life and work of DR Kaprekar.

Looking for Patterns

- Tell the children to use prime numbers less than 100.
- Tell the children to use prime numbers greater than 100.

Page 3

The Puzzler

- You may wish to use this activity as an opportunity to introduce the children to the terms 'minuend', 'subtrahend' and 'difference'.

587	minuend
– 369	subtrahend
218	difference

The Puzzler

- Ensure that children can find the square and square root of one-digit and two-digit numbers, including using a calculator.
- When working on the second puzzle, tell the children that the two-digit number is less than 50.

Let's Investigate

- This activity and the Let's Investigate activity on page 4, offers a written method of subtraction.

Page 4

Let's Investigate

- This activity and the Let's Investigate activity on page 3, offers a written method of subtraction.

What's the Problem?

- The most important aspect of this activity is not in calculating the answers to the four calculations but in the children's explanations as to which method of subtraction they prefer to use for each calculation and why.

AfL

- What is the answer to the puzzle? How did you work it out? What strategies did you use?
- Use your own words to explain to me this method of subtraction.
- Which of these methods of subtraction do you prefer? Why?
- How would you work out the answer to this calculation? Why would you use this method?

Answers

Page 1

Around the World Calculations will vary

Let's Investigate Pairs of consecutive primes less than 100 that have a difference of 2: 3 and 5, 5 and 7, 11 and 13, 17 and 19, 29 and 31, 41 and 43, 59 and 61, 71 and 73.
Pairs of consecutive primes less than 100 that have a difference of 4: 3 and 7, 7 and 11, 13 and 17, 19 and 23, 37 and 41, 43 and 47, 67 and 71, 79 and 83.

Page 2

Famous Mathematicians The largest number of subtraction calculations needed before the calculation starts repeating itself is five.
If you start with a four-digit number you will eventually end up with an answer of 6174 (known as Kaprekar's constant).

Looking for Patterns Different calculations are possible. For example, for consecutive prime numbers:
41 – 11 – 13 – 17 = 0
829 – 271 – 277 – 281 = 0

For non-consecutive prime numbers:
59 – 11 – 19 – 29 = 0
919 – 103 – 307 – 509 = 0

Page 3

The Puzzler

$$\begin{array}{r} 987654321 \\ -\ 123456789 \\ \hline 864197532 \\ \hline \end{array}$$

The Puzzler

4	36
$4^2 = 16$	$36^2 = 1296$
$\sqrt{4} = 2$	$\sqrt{36} = 6$
16 – 2 = 14	1296 – 6 = 1290

Let's Investigate The method always works including for calculations involving decimals, e.g.

37·8	9 – 1 = 8	37·8	123·4
– 14·3	9 – 4 = 5	+ 85·6	23·4 + 0·1 = 23·5
	9 – 3 = 6	123·4	

Page 4

Let's Investigate The method always works including for calculations involving decimals, e.g.

37·8	9 – 3 = 6	62·1	9 – 7 = 2	23·5
– 14·3	9 – 7 = 2	+ 14·3	9 – 6 = 3	
	9 – 8 = 1	76·4	9 – 4 = 5	

What's the Problem? Preferences and reasoning will vary.

EMU 

mathematical constant

A mathematical constant is a special number that occurs naturally in mathematics. Pi (π) is an example of a constant.

Issue 10 Multiplication

Prerequisites for learning

- Understand squares, cubes and other powers
- Understand how the commutative, associative and distributive laws, and the relationships between operations, including inverse operations, can be used to calculate more efficiently
- Use efficient written methods to multiply

Resources pencil and paper; RCM 2: My notes (optional); RCM 3: Pupil self assessment booklet (optional); ruler; calculator

Teaching support

Page 1

The Puzzler

- The grid method of multiplication will assist children in seeing the relationship between 41 × 51 = 2091 and the other two calculations:

41 × 51

	40	1	
50	2000	50	2050
1	40	1	41
			2091

41 × 52

	40	1	
50	2000	50	2050
2	80	2	82
			2132

41 × 52 = (41 × 51) + (40 + 1)
= 2091 + 41
= 2132

42 × 52

	40	2	
50	2000	100	2100
2	80	4	84
			2184

42 × 52 = (41 × 52) + (50 + 2)
= 2132 + 52
= 2184

- Discuss with the children the relationships between the numbers in each of the calculations, i.e.

34 × 202

34 = 2 × 17

Therefore:

34 × 202 = 2 × (17 × 202)
= 2 × 3434
= 6868

34 = 404

34 = 2 × 17

404 = 2 × 202

Therefore:

34 × 404 = 2 × 17 × 2 × 202
= (2 × 2) × (17 × 202)
= 4 x 3434
= 13 736

Teaching support continued

Page 1 continued

The Puzzler

- 3! (referred to as 'factorial 3') is the product of all the positive numbers less than and equal to 3, i.e. 3 × 2 × 1 = 6.

  Work through other examples such as 2! (2 × 1 = 2).

  When solving the equation (4 × 2)! remind the children of the order of operations, i.e. (4 × 2)! = 8! = 40 320.

Money Matters

- Discuss with the children that if one £1 is just over 3 mm, then £10 is just over 3 cm (encourage answers that have been rounded down).

  Therefore:

  £170 = 17 × 3 cm
  = 51 cm

  £174 = 51 cm + (4 × 3 mm)
  = 51 cm + 1·2 cm
  = 52·2 cm

Focus on Science

- Calculations for the three problems are:
  - How far is the Earth from the Sun?

    8 min and 9 sec is 489 sec

    Distance from Earth to Sun = 489 sec × speed of light
    = 489 × 299 792 km
    = 146 598 288 km
  - How far is Mercury from the Sun?

    3 min and 13 sec is 193 sec

    Distance from Mercury to Sun = 193 sec × speed of light
    = 193 × 299 792 km
    = 57 859 856 km
  - How far is Venus from the Sun?

    6 min and 1 sec is 361 sec

    Distance from Venus to Sun = 361 sec × speed of light
    = 361 × 299 792 km
    = 108 224 912 km

Page 2

Around the World

- Draw children's attention to the following aspects of the method:
  - partitioning the tens and units digits after multiplication, e.g. 7 × 8 = 56
  - the carry digits, e.g. 2 + 8 = 10

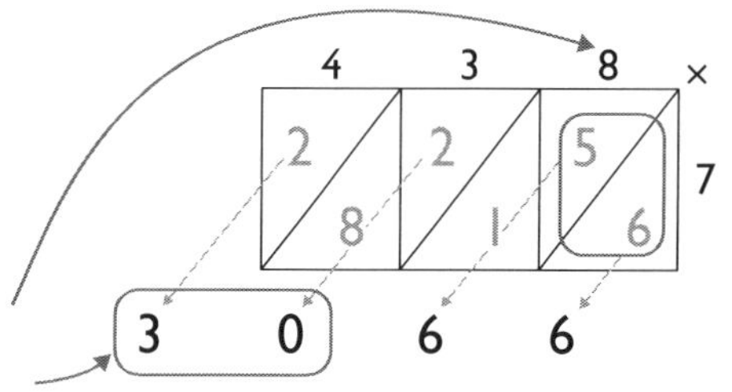

- Children write about the similarities and differences between this method and the grid method for multiplication.

Looking for Patterns

- Assist the children by giving them one or more of the missing digits, e.g

☆☆	8☆
× ☆7	× ☆☆
2880	☆☆5☆
336	☆☆☆7
3216	4☆☆☆

Let's Investigate

- Remind the children to pay careful attention to the rules.
- Tell the children that there are seven possible calculations.

Page 3

Let's Investigate

- Ask the children to write an explanation as to how they worked out what the greatest product is.
- What if the digits were 5, 6, 7, 8 and 9?
  (876 × 95 = 83 220)

Looking for Patterns

- If children have difficulty explaining what is happening, ask them to multiply 12 345 679 by 9 (answer: 111 111 111). Point out the relationship between these answers to the answers to the 11 times-tables. This should help them to identify the pattern.

Page 4

Looking for Patterns

- Draw children's attention to the two examples and discuss each line of the calculations, asking the children to comment on what they notice. If necessary, provide further examples, e.g. $5^3 \times 5^4 =$; $2^4 \div 2^2 =$

Let's Investigate

- When investigating whether or not the method works for similar pairs of three-digit and four-digit numbers, remind the children that pairs of numbers must be near multiples, e.g. 237×243 ($240^2 - 3^2$) and 1488×1492 ($1490^2 - 2^2$).

AfL

- What answer did you get for this puzzle? When you first looked at the puzzle how did you begin to work it out?
- What relationships / patterns did you notice? How did this help you?
- Talk me through your method of working out the puzzle.
- What do you think about this method? Is it a method that you might use? When? Why not?

Answers

Page 1

The Puzzler $41 \times 51 = 2091$

Explanations will vary. Possible explanations include:

$$\begin{aligned} 41 \times 52 &= (41 \times 51) + (41 \times 1) \\ &= 2091 + 41 \\ &= 2132 \\ 42 \times 52 &= (41 \times 52) + (1 \times 52) \\ &= 2132 + 52 \\ &= 2184 \end{aligned}$$

or

$$\begin{aligned} 42 \times 52 &= (41 \times 51) + (41 \times 1) + (1 \times 52) \\ &= 2091 + 41 + 52 \\ &= 2184 \end{aligned}$$

$17 \times 202 = 3434$

Explanations will vary. Possible explanations include:

$$\begin{aligned} 34 \times 202 &= 2 \times (17 \times 202) \\ &= 2 \times 3434 \\ &= 6868 \end{aligned}$$

$$\begin{aligned} 34 \times 404 &= 2 \times 17 \times 2 \times 202 \\ &= 2 \times 2 \times (17 \times 202) \\ &= 4 \times 3434 \\ &= 13\,736 \end{aligned}$$

The Puzzler $4! = 24$

$4! \times 2 = 48$

$(4 \times 2)! = 40\,320$

Page 1 continued

Money Matters 52·2 cm

Focus on Science 146 598 288 km
57 859 856 km
108 224 912 km

Page 2

Around the World
83 × 76 = 6308
537 × 49 = 26 313
886 × 356 = 315 416
73·9 × 34·6 = 2556·94

Looking for Patterns

48 × 67	89 × 53	*or*	83 × 59
2880	4450		4150
336	267		747
3216	4717		4897

Let's Investigate
5 × 5 = 25
5 × 7 = 35
3 × 25 = 75
3 × 75 = 225
5 × 55 = 275
5 × 75 = 375
7 × 75 = 525

Page 3

Let's Investigate 431 × 52 = 22 412

Looking for Patterns 9 × 12 345 679 = 111 111 111.

Therefore, it is the digit chosen in step 2 that creates the pattern.
For example, 7 × (9 × 12 345 679) = 777 777 777.
When 111 111 111 is multiplied by a one-digit number, the answer consists only of that digit. This pattern is similar to 11 multiplied by a one-digit number.

Similarly, when 9 × 12 345 679 (i.e. 111 111 111) is multiplied by a number less than 19, the pattern is similar to 11 multiplied by that number.

For example: 12 × 11 = 132
12 × 111 111 111 = 1 333 333 332

Page 4

Looking for Patterns The index laws for multiplication and division of positive integer powers are:

$n^a \times n^b = n^{a+b}$

e.g. $4^2 \times 4^3 = 4^{2+3} = 4^5 = 1024$

$n^a \div n^b = n^{a-b}$

e.g. $4^5 \div 4^3 = 4^{5-3} = 4^2 = 16$

Let's Investigate This method works for similar pairs of three-digit and four-digit numbers.

EMU

factorial

This is the product of all the positive numbers less than and equal to a specific number (n) and is written as 'n!'
For example, 3! means 3 × 2 × 1 = 6 (3! = 6).

Issue 11 Division

Prerequisites for learning

- Understand tests of divisibility
- Recognise and use multiples, factors, divisors, common factors, highest common factors and lowest common multiples in simple cases
- Make and justify estimates and approximations to calculations

Resources pencil and paper; RCM 2: My notes (optional); RCM 3: Pupil self assessment booklet (optional); calculator (optional); computer with internet access

Teaching support

Page 1

Focus on Science

- Discuss with the children how rounding will help with calculating approximations.

  For example,

  Light travels at 299 792 km per second, which rounds to 300 000 km per second

  Mercury is approximately 58 million km from the Sun.

  So:

  58 ~~000 000~~ km ÷ 3~~00 000~~ km per sec ≈ 193 sec

  193 sec ÷ 60 sec ≈ 3 min

Let's Investigate

- Ask the children to investigate whether or not the statement is also true for decimal numbers. Children should provide examples to justify their conclusions.

The Puzzler

- Give the children the order of the digits, i.e.

  1 5 2 3 4

  (152 x 3 ÷ 4)

Page 2

Around the World

- Ensure that children fully understand the concept of 'population density' and how; when referring to the population density of countries; is it expressed as the number of people per square kilometre (per km^2).
- Work through one of the calculations with the children, for example:

  Using a calculator

  Australia: 22 456 552 ÷ 7 682 300 = 2·92 …
  Therefore approx 3 people per km^2.

  Rounding

  Australia: 22 ~~000 000~~ ÷ 8 ~~000 000~~ = 2·75
  Therefore approx 3 people per km^2.

The Puzzler

- Tell children one or more of the numbers in each puzzle (see Answers).

Page 3

The Puzzler

- Puzzle 1: Assist the children in realising that by rewriting the three-digit number to create a six-digit number you have actually multiplied the three-digit number by 1001 (i.e. 527 × 1001 = 527 527).
- Puzzle 2: Ensure that children are confident with the previous puzzle before they embark on the second puzzle.
- For the second puzzle you may wish to give the children one of the divisors (see Answers).

Looking for Patterns

- Children should have no difficulties in writing divisibility tests for 3, 4, 6, 8 and 9. They may however, need some assistance with divisibility tests for 7, 11 and 12.

Page 4

The Puzzler

- Through discussion, help the children realise that the smallest number must be a multiple of 7 but not a multiple of 2, 3, 4, 5 or 6.

Looking for Patterns

- For one or two of the calculations, tell the children one of the digits in the other factor that is not 34, e.g.

  □ 8 × □ □ = 1972   2 □ × □ □ = 816

Teaching support continued

Page 4 continued

At Home

- If more appropriate, ask the children to calculate the population density of the school or the neighbourhood around the school. Discuss with the children how in such cases answers will more than likely need to be expressed as the number of people per square metre (m^2).
- Once the children have completed the activity at home, ensure that there is an opportunity in class for pairs or groups of children to discuss their results.

AfL

- How did you work out the answer? Did you make an approximation? What did you do?
- How accurate is your answer / approximation?
- Did you use trial and improvement to help you work out the answer to this puzzle? Where did you begin? Why did you start there?
- What do your results mean?
- How did knowing about multiples / factors / divisors help you with this activity?

Answers

Page 1

Focus on Science

Planet	Approximate time for light to travel from the Sun
Mercury	3 min
Venus	6 min
Earth	8 min
Mars	13 min
Jupiter	43 min
Saturn	1 hr 18 min
Uranus	2 hr 41 min
Neptune	4 hr 4 min
Pluto	5 hr 28 min

Explanation will vary.

Page 1 continued

Let's Investigate

The statement is true.

When you reverse the digits of any two-digit number to make a new number and find the total of the two numbers, the answer is always divisible by 11, e.g.

87 + 78	43 + 34
= 165 ÷ 11	= 77 ÷ 11
= 15	= 7

This only applies to numbers with an even number of digits, i.e. pairs of two-digit, four-digit, six-digit … numbers.

The Puzzler

152 × 3 ÷ 4 = 114

Page 2

Around the World

Country	Population density
Australia	3 people per km^2
India	362 people per km^2
Jamaica	247 people per km^2
United Kingdom	255 people per km^2
United States	32 people per km^2

The countries with the greatest population densities are:

- Macau – China (18 534 people per km^2)
- Monaco (16 923 people per km^2)
- Singapore (7021 people per km^2)

The countries with the smallest population densities are:

- Greenland (0·03 people per km^2)
- Mongolia (2 people per km^2)
- Namibia (3 people per km^2)

The Puzzler

6, 9, 12, 30, 45, 78   3, 6, 9, 24, 78, 105

Page 3

The Puzzler

Puzzle 1: The final answer will always be the three-digit number you started with. Dividing by 7, 11 and 13 is the same as dividing by 1001 (i.e. 7 × 11 × 13 = 1001). By rewriting the three-digit number to create a six-digit number you have actually multiplied the three-digit number by 1001 (i.e. 527 × 1001 = 527 527). Then by dividing by 1001 the result is the three-digit number you started with.

Puzzle 2: 686 868 ÷ 68 = 10 101.

Therefore you need to find three numbers that multiply together to make 10 101.

So, for the remainder of the puzzle many answers are possible:

Divide this number by:	13	7	7	3	3
Divide this number by:	21	37	13	37	13
Divide this number by:	37	39	111	91	259

Answers continued

Page 3 continued

Looking for Patterns

3: the sum of the digits is divisible by 3
4: the last two digits are divisible by 4
6: the number is even and divisible by 3 or the number is divisible by 2 and 3
8: the last 3 digits are divisible by 8
9: the sum of the digits is divisible by 9
7: Take the last digit, double it, and then find the difference between this answer and the rest of the number. Continue to do this until you come to a number you know is or is not, divisible by 7.

Example:

56: 6 × 2 = 12   12 – 5 = 7
539: 9 × 2 = 18   53 – 18 = 35

Since 35 is divisible by 7 then so also is 539.

11: Subtract the last digit from the rest of the number. Continue to do this until you come to a number you know is or is not, divisible by 11.

Example:

374: 37 – 4 = 33. Since 33 is divisible by 11, then so also is 374.

12: The number is divisible by 3 and 4.

Example:
336: 3 + 3 + 6 = 12, which is divisible by 3.
36 ÷ 4 = 9, which means it is divisible by 4.
So 336 is divisible by 12.

Page 4

The Puzzler 49

Looking for Patterns

34 is the two-digit factor
58 × 34 = 1972
24 × 34 = 816
79 × 34 = 2686

At Home Results and explanations will vary.

EMU

dividend
A number or quantity that is to be divided by another number or quantity.
For example, in the calculation 14 ÷ 7 = 2, 14 is the dividend (dividend ÷ divisor = quotient).

Issue 12 Mixed operations

Prerequisites for learning

- Represent information or unknown numbers in an equation
- Understand and use simple algebraic conventions
- Derive quickly squares of numbers to 10 × 10
- Use the order of operations, including brackets

Resources pencil and paper; RCM 2: My notes (optional); RCM 3: Pupil self assessment booklet (optional); ruler; calculator (optional)

Teaching support

Page 1

Sports Update

- Assist the children in deriving a formula for working out the total number of games played for any number of teams. NOTE: Every team plays every other team twice (once at home and once away).

Number of teams	Number of games
2	2
3	6
4	12
5	20
6	30
n	$n(n-1)$

- Introduce the children to the pattern in the relationship between the number of players and the number of games, for example.

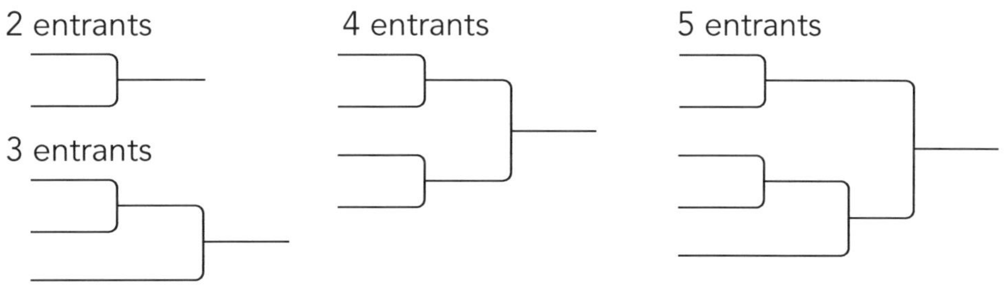

Sports Update

- Assist the children in deriving a formula for working out the total number of matches played.

Number of entrants	Number of matches
2	1
3	2
4	3
5	4
6	5
n	$n-1$

Teaching support continued

Page 1 continued

Let's Investigate

- Ensure children understand the diagram.
- Ask the children to present their results in a format different from that in the pupil issue.

Page 2

Sports Update

- Ensure children understand the information presented in the tables and the requirements of the activity.
- Work with the children to begin writing one of the programmes.

Page 3

Let's Investigate

- Children need to be confident with using the correct order of operations, including brackets. If necessary, draw children's attention to the BODMAS diagram.
- Ensure that children are also able to understand and use simple expressions in symbols, and substitute positive numbers into simple linear expressions. If necessary, go through one or two of the expressions with the children.

Let's Investigate

- Tell the children to find at least two different ways of making each of the numbers.

What's the Problem?

- As well as having a secure understanding of the points mentioned in the above activity, children also need to understand and use simple algebraic conventions for multiplication ($a \times b = ab$) and division ($a \div b = \frac{a}{b}$).

Page 4

Looking for Patterns

- Ensure that the children fully understand how the first number trick can be expressed using algebra. This will assist the children when using algebra to explain the second number trick and when writing their own.

Page 4

What's the Problem?

- If children are having difficulties in one or more of the calculations, tell them the correct position of one of the other digits (see Answers).

The Puzzler

- Ask the children to make their own puzzle, perhaps involving other shapes, e.g.

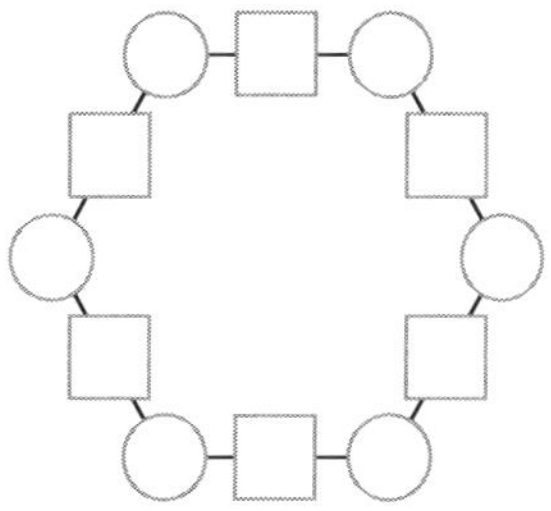

AfL

- Explain to me what this expression means.
- How would you write that using symbols rather than numbers or words?
- Can you find an alternative calculation / expression / formula?
- What relationships / patterns did you notice?
- Apply your formula to this situation. Does it work?

Answers

Page 1

Sports Update 90
Formula = $n(n - 1)$

Sports Update 11 matches
Formula = $n - 1$

Let's Investigate Results of the investigation will vary.

Page 2

Sports Update Children's programmes will vary.

Page 3

Let's Investigate

$41 = (4 \times 9) + 5$
$= (5 \times 9) - 4$

$87 = (7 \times 9) + (2 \times 7) + (2 \times 5)$
$= (2 \times 5 \times 9) - (6 \div 2)$

$120 = 6 \times 5 \times 4$
$= 3 \times 5 \times 2 \times 4$

$59 = (6 \times 9) + 5$
$= (7 \times 7) + (2 \times 5)$

$93 = (7 \times 9) + (4 \times 7) + 2$
$= (2 \times 42) + (6 \div 2)$

Other calculations are possible.

Page 3 continued

Let's Investigate

(5 + 7) – 10 = 2
5 + (7 – 10) = 2
(5 – 7) + 10 = 8
5 × (7 – 10) = $^{-}15$
(5 × 7) – 10 = 25
5 + 7 + 10 = 22
5 – (7 + 10) = $^{-}12$
(5 + 7) × 10 = 120
(5 – 7) × 10 = $^{-}20$

What's the Problem?

(3 × 5) – 8 + 24 = 31
34 + 5(8 – 5) = 49
(4 × 8) – 84 + (8 × 5) + 68 = 56
12(8 + 5) – 7(8 – 5) = 135
$\frac{40}{8} - \frac{15}{5} = 2$
6([4 × 5] – [2 × 8]) + (6 × 8) – (6 × 5) = 42

Page 4

Looking for Patterns

• Think of a number.	*n*
• Add 5.	*n* + 5
• Multiply the result by 2.	2*n* + 10
• Subtract 4.	2*n* + 6
• Halve it.	*n* + 3
• Subtract your original number.	3

Answers will vary. Check that the children's algebraic expressions work.

What's the Problem?

58 + 7 = 65
32 × 9 = 288
75 + 68 = 143
23 × 14 = 322
74 – 6 = 68
112 ÷ 7 = 16
107 – 59 = 48
468 ÷ 26 = 18

The Puzzler

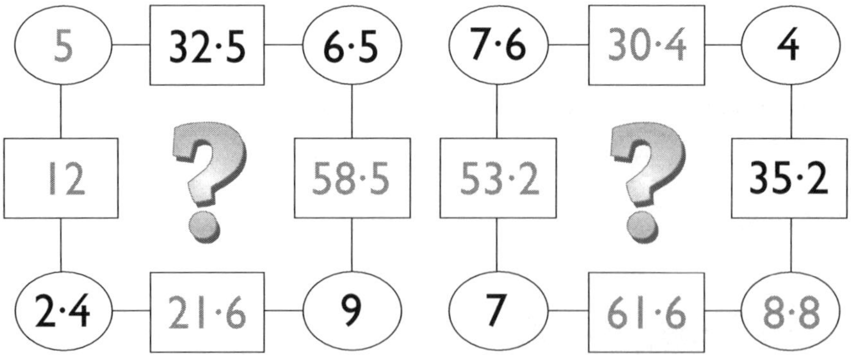

EMU

slide rule
A mechanical device for carrying out calculations particularly those involving multiplication and division.

Issue 13 Mixed operations – The Financial Issue

Prerequisites for learning

- Use efficient written methods to add, subtract, multiply and divide whole numbers and decimals with up to two places
- Find fractions using division
- Find percentages of numbers and quantities
- Use simple expressions and formulas in words and symbols

Resources pencil and paper; RCM 2: My notes (optional); RCM 3: Pupil self assessment booklet (optional); calculator (optional)

Teaching support

Pages 1–2
Money Matters

- Ensure that the children are familiar with the following terms and their abbreviations: 'principal' (P), 'fixed rate of interest' (R), 'fixed length of time' (T), 'per annum' (p.a.), 'fixed term deposit' and 'simple interest' (I).
- Children also need to understand and use the formulas to calculate simple interest and the total amount due. Therefore it is important that they fully comprehend the example provided.
- It is recommended that children work in pairs for the second part of this activity where they investigate savings rates in newspapers and offer advice as to the most favourable option available.

Teaching support continued

Pages 2–3
Money Matters

- As well as an understanding of the terms used in the Money Matters activity on page 1, children also need to understand the terms 'loan' and 'repayment'. Point out to the children that the expression 'how much money is being borrowed (P)' refers to the 'principal' as previously discussed.
- Children also need to understand and use the formulas to calculate simple interest, the total amount due and monthly repayments. Therefore it is important that they fully comprehend the example provided.
- It is recommended that children work in pairs for the second part of this activity where they investigate loan rates in newspapers and offer advice as to the most favourable option available.

Pages 3–4
Money Matters

- The concepts involved in this activity are more complex than in the previous two Money Matters activities. Therefore it is important that children fully understand the following terms: 'shares', 'investors / shareholders', 'nominal value', 'face value', 'market price', 'par', 'premium', 'discount' and 'dividend'.

  It is advised that time is spent with the children going through and discussing in detail the two examples provided.

AfL

- What have you learnt in this issue?
- Explain to me how savings / loans / shares work.
- Talk me through this formula.
- What does this mean?
- Do you think that this would be a good option? Why? Why not? What are the alternatives? How are these better / worse?

Answers

Pages 1–2

Money Matters

Mr J Brown
Simple interest = £120
Total amount = £2120

Mrs A Williams
Simple interest = £800
Total amount = £4800

Mr T Kanu
Simple interest = £2160
Total amount = £14 160

Mrs B Andersen
Simple interest = £9912.50
Total amount = £40 412.50

Options will vary.

Pages 2–3

Money Matters

Mr Charles
a. £3720
b. £96 720
c. £4030

Mr & Mrs Lee
a. £129 600
b. £489 600
c. £3400

Net Works
a. £1 687 500
b. £3 187 500
c. £10 625

Crystal Pools
a. £630 000
b. £1 530 000
c. £6375

Options will vary.

Pages 3–4

Money Matters

£20 000	£132	£20
£1650	£450 000	

EMU

economics
The study of how goods and services are produced and distributed.

Issue 14 Calculating with fractions

Prerequisites for learning

- Tabulate systematically the information in a problem or puzzle
- Recognise and use lowest common multiples
- Identify equivalent fractions
- Interpret mixed numbers
- Simplify fractions by cancelling common factors
- Order a set of fractions by converting them to fractions with a common denominator
- Use mental methods of calculation with fractions

Resources pencil and paper; RCM 2: My notes (optional); RCM 3: Pupil self assessment booklet (optional); calculator (optional)

Teaching support

Page 1

Let's Investigate

- You may wish to draw children's attention to the Let's Investigate activity on page 4 which sets out a method for multiplying a mixed number by a mixed number. This may help children in writing a method for multiplying a fraction by a fraction.

  Alternatively, discuss the following method with the children:

  1. If possible, simplify the numerators and denominators by cancelling.
  2. Multiply the numerators together to get the numerator.
  3. Multiply the denominators together to get the denominator.
  4. Reduce the fraction to its simplest form or change an improper fraction to a mixed number.

Money Matters

- Suggest the children record their working in a table that records what the girls did (Action) and how much money each girl had after each action.

  A possible method for working out the answer is:

	Lucy	Melinda
Action 1	£10.50	£1.50
	– £ 3.00	+ £3.00
Action 2	£ 7.50	£4.50
	+ £ 1.50	– £1.50
Action 3	£ 9.00	£3.00
	– £ 3.00	+ £3.00
	£ 6.00	£6.00

Page 2

Around the World

- An illustration of the problem may help children see the solution.

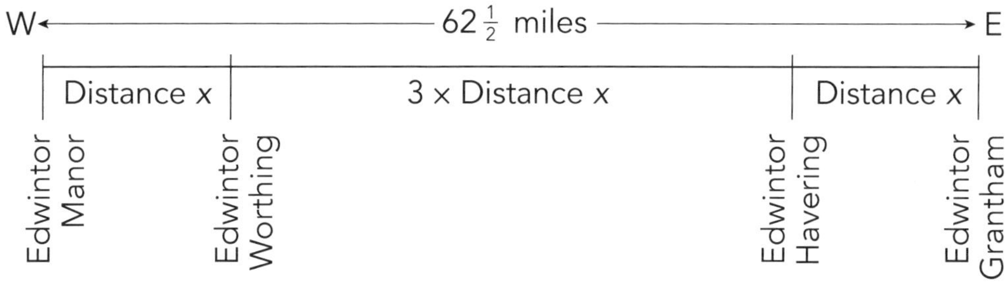

Money Matters

- Suggest the children record their working in a table that records how much money Greg spent at each shop and how much money he had left after spending each amount.

  A possible method for working out the answer is:

	Amount spent	Amount remaining
Florist	£14 ($\frac{1}{2}$)	£14 ($\frac{1}{2}$)
Dry cleaning	£20 ($\frac{1}{3}$ + £4)	£28 ($\frac{2}{3}$ – £4)
Supermarket	£60 ($\frac{1}{2}$ + £6)	£48 ($\frac{1}{2}$ – £6)

  Total started = £60 + £20 + £14 + £14 = £108

The Puzzler

- For this puzzle children need to be confident with adding and subtracting fractions.

  Tell the children that:

  - for the first puzzle all the mixed numbers are either halves or quarters (including $\frac{3}{4}$)
  - for the second puzzle all the mixed numbers are either halves or fifths (including $\frac{2}{5}$, $\frac{3}{5}$ or $\frac{4}{5}$)

Let's Investigate

- Draw children's attention to the Let's Investigate activity on page 1 which shows how a fraction calculation can be presented as a diagram.
- Suggest the children use shapes such as circles or rectangles to draw their diagrams.
- Ask children to draw two different diagrams to represent each of the fraction statements – perhaps one of the diagrams using shapes and the other diagram a completely different type of picture.
- If children have difficulty in knowing how to approach the puzzle, tell them that Greg spent £60 in the supermarket.

Teaching support continued

Page 3

Let's Investigate

- Ensure that children understand the method for adding fractions with different denominators. Therefore it is important that they fully comprehend the examples provided.

  Children also need to be able to identify equivalent fractions, simplify fractions, recognise and use lowest common multiples (L.C.M), and interpret mixed numbers.

  The degree of difficulty in this activity depends upon the fractions that children choose to add together. Adding unitary fractions in most cases will be easier than adding non-unitary fractions. Adding pairs of mixed numbers will probably be the most challenging.

In the Past

- Referring to the example of $\frac{3}{4}$, discuss with the children how $\frac{3}{4}$ can also be written as $\frac{1}{4} + \frac{1}{4} + \frac{1}{4}$, but that $\frac{1}{2} + \frac{1}{4}$ is more 'elegant' than $\frac{1}{4} + \frac{1}{4} + \frac{1}{4}$ because it has two terms rather than three, and because it starts with the largest fraction with a numerator of 1 ($\frac{1}{2}$) that can be taken out of $\frac{3}{4}$.

  Remind the children that they should aim to write each fraction as a sum with the least number of unitary fractions.

Page 4

Let's Investigate

- Ensure that children understand the method for subtracting fractions with different denominators. Therefore it is important that they fully comprehend the examples provided.

  Children also need to be able to identify equivalent fractions, simplify fractions, recognise and use lowest common multiples (L.C.M), and interpret mixed numbers.

  The degree of difficulty in this activity depends upon the fractions that children choose to subtract. Subtracting unitary fraction in most cases will be easier than subtracting non-unitary fractions. Finding the difference between pairs of mixed numbers will probably be the most challenging.

Let's Investigate

- This Let's Investigate activity deals with multiplying mixed numbers, and is an extension of the Let's Investigate activity on page 1 where children were asked to find a method for multiplying fractions.

- Explain to me how to add / subtract / multiply a pair of fractions. What about a pair of mixed numbers?
- How did you work out the answer to this problem / puzzle? Where did you start? How did you record your working? Did you draw a table / diagram? Did this help? How?

Answers

Page 1

Let's Investigate $\frac{3}{5} \times \frac{5}{6} = \frac{1}{2}$ $\quad \frac{1}{4} \times \frac{7}{8} = \frac{7}{32}$ $\quad \frac{2}{3} \times \frac{5}{9} = \frac{10}{27}$ $\quad \frac{5}{8} \times \frac{6}{7} = \frac{15}{28}$ $\quad \frac{5}{6} \times \frac{1}{4} \times \frac{3}{8} = \frac{5}{64}$

Money Matters Lucy £10.50
Melinda £1.50

Page 2

Around the World 12·5 miles

Money Matters £108

The Puzzler

$\boxed{3\frac{1}{2}} + \boxed{4\frac{1}{4}} - \boxed{3\frac{1}{4}} + \boxed{1\frac{1}{4}} - \boxed{2\frac{3}{4}} = \boxed{3}$

$\boxed{2\frac{3}{5}} + \boxed{4\frac{2}{5}} + \boxed{3\frac{1}{2}} - \boxed{1\frac{4}{5}} - \boxed{2\frac{1}{5}} = \boxed{6\frac{1}{2}}$

Other answers are possible.

Let's Investigate Diagrams will vary.

Page 3

Let's Investigate Results of the investigation will vary.

In the Past Results of the investigation will vary.

Page 4

Let's Investigate Results of the investigation will vary.

Let's Investigate Results of the investigation will vary.

EMU

L.C.M.
lowest or least common multiple
For example, the L.C.M. of 3 and 4 is 12.

Issue 15 Calculating with percentages

Prerequisites for learning

- Find percentages of numbers and quantities
- Express one quantity as a percentage of another
- Calculate percentage increases or decreases
- Make and justify estimates and approximations to calculations

Resources pencil and paper; RCM 2: My notes (optional); RCM 3: Pupil self assessment booklet (optional); calculator (optional); map of the local area and a contrasting area

Teaching support

Page 1

Money Matters

- Ensure that the children are familiar with the following terms: 'increment', 'original price', 'percentage increase', 'discount' and 'percentage decrease'.
- Children also need to understand and use the formulas to calculate a percentage increase or decrease.

  Work through the first problem with the children, i.e.

  original price = £60
  decrease in price (discount) = £60 – £42 = £18
  $= \frac{18}{60} \times 100\%$
  $= \frac{3}{10} \times 100\%$
  $= 30\%$
- It is recommended that children work in pairs for the second part of this activity.

Page 2

Money Matters

- Ensure that the children understand the concept of commission and can use the formulas to calculate a commission in pounds and a commission as a percentage. It is important that they fully comprehend the examples provided.

Page 3

Around the World

- Discuss with the children how they are only expected to provide approximate percentages of land that is allocated to each of the different categories.
- It is important that children are able to explain how they arrived at their approximations.

Focus on Science

- As the calculations in this activity require the children to find percentages of multiples of 100 (i.e. 2000, 1500 and 800) they should be encouraged to use mental and written methods to work out the answers, and not use a calculator.
- Do children identify and use the relationship between 9%, 18% and 36%?

Focus on Science

- As with the previous Focus on Science activity, the children should be encouraged to use mental and written methods to work out the percentages and not use a calculator.
- Can the children work out one of the percentages, i.e. for canines, and then use the relationship for the number of pairs of each different kind of teeth to work out the remaining percentages? For example,
  - Percentage of adult teeth that are molars is three times the percentage of adult teeth that are canine.
  - Percentage of adult teeth that are incisors or bicuspids is twice the percentage of adult teeth that are canine.

Page 4

Focus on Science

- Remind the children how they are only expected to provide approximate percentages. Discuss with them how rounding can help with their approximation, and also what degree of rounding is appropriate given the context of the problem.

What's the Problem?

- Children should be encouraged to use mental and written methods to work out the answers and not use a calculator.

Teaching support continued

Page 4 continued

The Arts Roundup

- Assist the children with working out the problem, i.e.

  the number of female musicians that also perform with smaller ensembles: $\frac{40}{100} \times \frac{30}{1} = \frac{1200}{100} = 12$.

  So, the total number of musicians that also perform with smaller ensembles: 12 + 16 = 28.

  So, the percentage of the 70 orchestra members that also perform with smaller ensembles: $\frac{28}{70} \times \frac{100}{1} = \frac{2800}{70} = 40\%$.

The Puzzler

- Provide the children with an example (see Answers).
- Ask the children to complete other statements such as:

  ☐ is ◯ % of 32

  ☐ is 14% of ◯

Alternatively, children can make up statements of their own.

AfL

- How did you work out that percentage?
- How did you work out that percentage increase / decrease?
- What is this expressed as a percentage?
- What did you use to help you work out that answer? Was there a percentage that you already knew that you used to help you? How did this help? Why did you do that?
- How did rounding help you with your calculation? What does that mean in terms of the accuracy of your answer?

Answers

Page 1

Money Matters 30% 15%
50% 20%

Page 2

Money Matters

Agent	Value of goods sold	Commission as a percentage	Commission in pounds
D Rogers	£34 000	6%	£2040
M Quincy	£194 000	5%	£9700
A Leech	£29 500	8%	£2360
W Ali	£67 800	4%	£2712
C T Adams	£45 350	3%	£1360.50

Best agent: M Quincy (sold the most value of goods yet has only the third-highest percentage commission).
Worst agent: A Leech (sold the least value of goods yet has the highest percentage commission).

Page 3

Around the World
Results of the investigation will vary.

Focus on Science

	Head and neck	Both arms and hands	Torso	Both legs and feet
Adult	180 cm^2	360 cm^2	740 cm^2	720 cm^2
Teenager	135 cm^2	270 cm^2	555 cm^2	540 cm^2
Child	72 cm^2	144 cm^2	296 cm^2	288 cm^2

Focus on Science
molars: 37·5%
incisors: 25%
bicuspids: 25%
canines: 12·5%

Page 4

Focus on Science
38·67%
72·34%
Answers may vary depending on the degree of rounding that children did.

What's the Problem?
The approximate total surface area of the Earth is 494 300 000 km^2. Approximately 346 000 000 km^2 of the Earth's surface is covered by water.

The Arts Roundup
40%

The Puzzler
Statements will vary. Examples may include:
5 is 10% of 50
12 is 15% of 80
18 is 30% of 60
55 is 44% of 125

EMU

percentage points
Percentage points refers to the difference between two percentages. For example, a percentage rise from 20% to 30% can be described as a rise of 10 percentage points.

Issue 16 Calculating – General

Prerequisites for learning

- Identify prime numbers to at least 100
- Find the prime factors of two-digit numbers
- Understand squares, cubes and other powers
- Understand square root and use the square root key on a calculator
- Use efficient written methods to add and subtract whole numbers
- Find fractions using division
- Find percentages of numbers and quantities
- Make and justify estimates and approximations to calculations

Resources pencil and paper; RCM 2: My notes (optional); RCM 3: Pupil self assessment booklet (optional); calculator

Teaching support

Page 1

Let's Investigate

- Discuss the two examples with the children. Emphasise how in each example the primes have been grouped together to make two identical numbers (squares), i.e.

$$2 \times 2 \times 11 \times 11 \rightarrow (2 \times 11) \times (2 \times 11) \rightarrow 22 \times 22$$

$$3 \times 3 \times 3 \times 3 \times 3 \times 3 \rightarrow (3 \times 3 \times 3) \times (3 \times 3 \times 3) \rightarrow 27 \times 27$$

- Provide the children with a list of all prime numbers to 100, i.e. 2, 3, 5, 7, 11, 13, 17, 19, 23, 29, 31, 37, 41, 43, 47, 53, 59, 61, 67, 71, 73, 79, 83, 89 and 97.
- Children comment on the strengths and limitations of this method.

Looking for Patterns

- The important aspect of this activity is for the children to write about how they worked out what each pair of numbers is.

Page 2

Famous Mathematicians

- Ensure that children are able to perform the different types of calculations needed to use Heron's method for finding the square root of a number.
- Children comment on the strengths and limitations of this method.

Page 2 continued

Money Matters

- Children need to realise that they are working with approximations. They also need to appreciate that when working out the quantities needed to make 180 cupcakes, given the quantities that each of the items are sold in, they will need to buy more of each item than is required to ensure that they have sufficient quantities.
- Discuss with the children that profit is calculated by finding the difference between the amount earned and the amount spent (£135 – £12.50 = £122.50).

Page 3

Around the World

- Ensure children are able to identify the pattern of numbers that are being subtracted, i.e. the pattern of odd numbers.

Let's Investigate

- The important aspect of this activity is for the children to write about which method for finding the square root of a number they prefer and why.
- Children comment on the strengths and limitations of their chosen method.

Page 4

The Language of Maths

- Children investigate other powers and index notation.

Money Matters

- There is a range of different income tax allowances in the UK. This activity has been simplified to only take into account the personal allowance. It makes no mention of the personal allowances for people aged 65–74 or aged 75 and over. Neither does it refer to the Married couple's allowance nor the Blind person's allowance. You may wish to discuss these and other allowances with the children if you feel it is appropriate.
- Discuss the example with the children and ensure that they realise that when calculating the income tax due, that if the taxable income is above £37,400, then tax will need to be calculated at different rates, i.e.

  Amount of tax due on £41 525
  = (£37 400 × 20%) + (£4125 × 40%)
  (taxable income = basic rate + higher rate)
  (Note: £41 525 – £37 400 = £4125)

AfL

- Which method for finding the square root of a number do you prefer? Why?
- What are the benefits of this method? What are its limitations?
- Which patterns did you identify? How did this help you?
- What approximations did you make? What does this mean about the level of accuracy of your answer?

Answers

Page 1

Let's Investigate

$\sqrt{576} = 24$ $\sqrt{676} = 26$ $\sqrt{841} = 29$
$\sqrt{961} = 31$ $\sqrt{1225} = 35$ $\sqrt{1444} = 38$

Looking for Patterns

27 and 62
276 and 523

Page 2

Famous Mathematicians

$\sqrt{28} \approx 5{\cdot}29$ $\sqrt{39} \approx 6{\cdot}24$ $\sqrt{46} \approx 6{\cdot}78$
$\sqrt{88} \approx 9{\cdot}38$ $\sqrt{73} \approx 8{\cdot}54$ $\sqrt{62} \approx 7{\cdot}87$

Money Matters

To make 180 cupcakes you would need the following quantities of each ingredient:

825 g butter
825 g sugar
15 drops vanilla essence
15 large eggs
825 g self-raising flour
$7\frac{1}{2}$ teaspoons baking powder

To make 180 cupcakes you would need to buy the following quantities of each ingredient:

4 × 250 g butter	4 × £1.10 = £4.40
1 × 1 kg sugar	1 × 95p = 95p
1 × 28 ml vanilla essence	1 × £1.20 = £1.20
3 × 6 large eggs	3 × £1.20 = £3.60
1 × 1 kg self-raising flour	1 × £1.50 = £1.50
1 × 170 g baking powder	1 × 85p = 85p

Therefore the approximate cost to make 180 cupcakes is £12.50.
If all the cupcakes are sold at 75p each you would take £135.
This is a profit of £122.50.

Page 3

Around the World

$\sqrt{289} = 17$ $\sqrt{576} = 24$ $\sqrt{361} = 19$
$\sqrt{529} = 23$ $\sqrt{961} = 31$ $\sqrt{784} = 28$

This method can only be used to find the square roots of perfect squares.

Let's Investigate Results of the investigation will vary depending on the child's preference.

Page 4

The Language of Maths $3^5 = 243$ $5^3 = 125$ $2^7 = 128$ $8^5 = 32\,768$ $7^4 = 2401$

Money Matters £56 000: £12 330 £82 000: £22 730 £195 000: £71 782.50

EMU

$\sqrt[3]{}$

cube root

A cube root is a number that when multiplied by itself twice gives the stated number.

e.g. $\sqrt[3]{8} = 2$ (i.e. $2 \times 2 \times 2 = 8$)

Issue 17 2-D shapes

Prerequisites for learning

- Recognise squares of numbers and the square roots of perfect squares
- Understand and identify properties of a circle, including centre, radius, diameter and circumference
- Understand pi (π) as the ratio of the circumference of a circle to its diameter, equal to 3·14
- Use a pair of compasses to draw circles
- Represent information or unknown numbers in an equation
- Understand and use simple algebraic conventions

Resources pencil and paper; RCM 2: My notes (optional); RCM 3: Pupil self assessment booklet (optional); RCM 5: 2 cm squared paper; ruler; set-square; matchsticks; calculator; at least six circular objects, all different sizes, e.g. plates of different sizes, wastepaper basket, analogue clock, geometric circular shape; tape measure

Teaching support

Page 1

Let's Investigate

- Ensure children understand what a 'chord' is.
- Suggest the children tabulate the information to help them identify the pattern and then write the formula, e.g.
- Some children may need assistance with writing the formula. This can either be written in words or using symbols.

Encourage children to write the formula using symbols.

Number of points (p)	Number of chords (c)
2	1
3	3
4	6
5	10
6	15
7	21
8	28

Page 2

Let's Investigate

- This is a practical activity where children discover pi (π) for themselves, and realise that the circumference of a circle is approximately 3·14 or $3\frac{1}{7}$ ($\frac{22}{7}$) times the diameter.
- Ensure that the children understand the terms 'circumference', 'diameter' and 'radius'.

Page 2 continued

Let's Investigate

- Ensure children understand that the word 'congruent' means that the pieces are identical in size and shape and that they can be exactly superimposed. Note: This is the EMU activity for this issue.

The Puzzler

- Diagonal BD is the same as diagonal AC. The diagonal AC is the radius of the circle. Therefore, the diameter of the circle is 12 cm.

Page 3

What's the Problem?

- Discuss with the children the formulas for calculating the circumference of a circle given the diameter or radius, and the diameter of a circle when given the circumference. Ensure that they understand that πd means $\pi \times d$ and that $2\pi r$ means $2 \times \pi \times r$.
- If necessary, work through the questions with the children, i.e.
  - Calculate the circumference of a circle with a diameter of 18 cm.

    $c = \pi d$
    $= 3{\cdot}14 \times 18$
    $= 56{\cdot}52$ cm
  - Calculate the circumference of a circle with a radius of 6 cm.

    $c = 2\pi r$
    $= 2 \times 3{\cdot}14 \times 6$
    $= 37{\cdot}68$ cm
  - To the nearest centimetre, calculate the diameter and radius of a circle with a circumference of 173 cm.

    diameter = circumference $\div \pi$
    $= 173 \text{ cm} \div \frac{22}{7} = 173 \text{ cm} \times \frac{7}{22}$
    $= \frac{173 \times 7}{22}$
    $= \frac{1211}{22}$
    = approximately 55 cm
    radius = diameter $\div$ 2
    $= 55 \div 2$
    = approximately $27{\cdot}5$ cm

The Puzzler

- Children make some matchsticks puzzles of their own.

Teaching support continued

Page 4

Famous Mathematicians

- Ensure children fully understand Pythagoras' theorem, i.e.

$$c^2 = a^2 + b^2$$
$$\therefore c = \sqrt{a^2 + b^2}$$

Because $c^2 = a^2 + b^2$

then $a^2 = c^2 - b^2$ or $b^2 = c^2 - a^2$

$\therefore a = \sqrt{c^2 - b^2}$ $\therefore b = \sqrt{c^2 - a^2}$

- If necessary, provide an example substituting two of the letters for numbers, e.g.

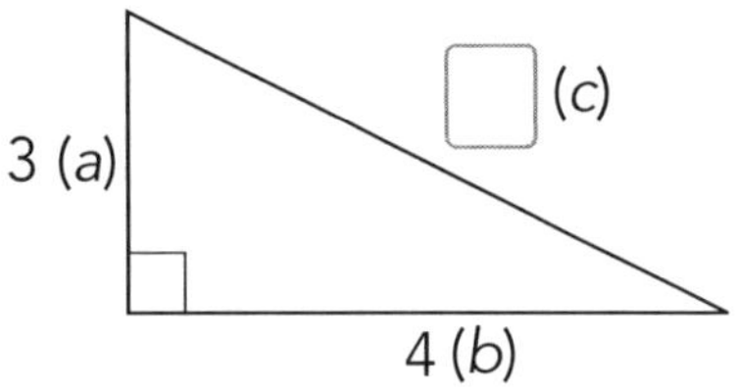

$$c^2 = a^2 + b^2$$
$$= 3^2 + 4^2$$
$$= 9 + 16$$
$$c = \sqrt{25}$$
$$= 5$$

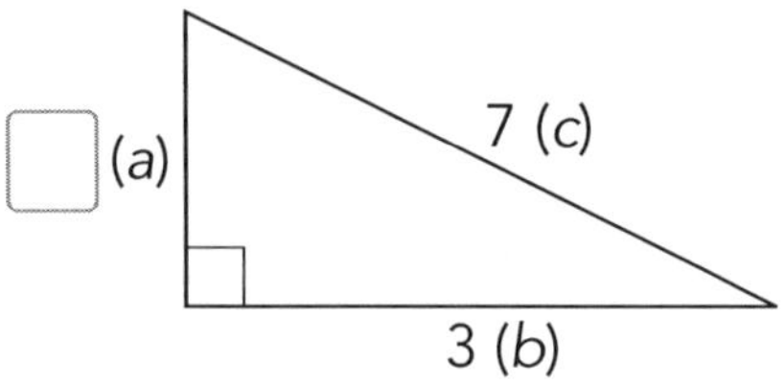

$$a^2 = c^2 - b^2$$
$$= 7^2 - 3^2$$
$$= 49 - 9$$
$$a = \sqrt{40}$$
$$\approx 6{\cdot}3$$

Sports Update

- Remind the children that the lengths given are approximates, but that they should aim to draw and label their diagrams as accurately as possible.
- Work with the children as they draw their first triangle, e.g.

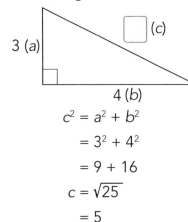

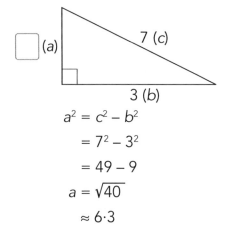

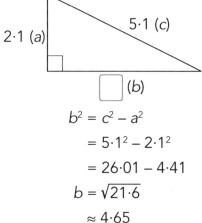

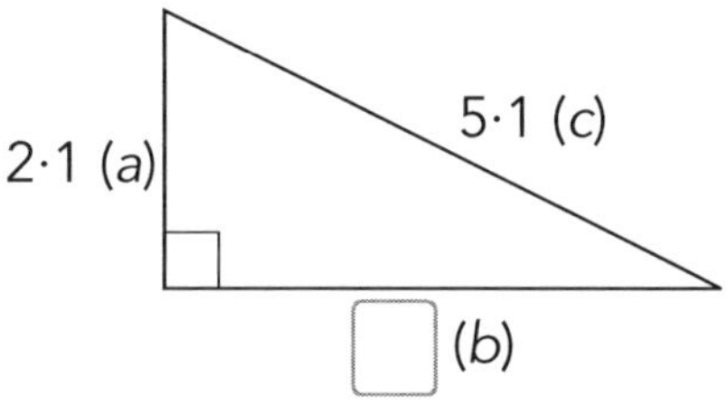

$$b^2 = c^2 - a^2$$
$$= 5{\cdot}1^2 - 2{\cdot}1^2$$
$$= 26{\cdot}01 - 4{\cdot}41$$
$$b = \sqrt{21{\cdot}6}$$
$$\approx 4{\cdot}65$$

AfL

- Explain the formula to me in your own words.
- How might we write this using symbols rather than words?
- What did you find out as a result of your investigation? What does this mean? Can you make a generalisation?
- How did you work out the answer to that puzzle? What patterns / relationships did you notice?

Answers

Page 1

Let's Investigate

5 points = 10 chords
6 points = 15 chords
7 points = 21 chords
8 points = 28 chords

The sequence of chords for circles with 2, 3, 4, 5, 6, 7 and 8 points is the sequence of triangular numbers.

Formula

$$\text{no. of chords} = \frac{\text{no. of points (no. of points} - 1)}{2}$$

$$c = \frac{p\,(p-1)}{2}$$

24 points = 276 chords

Page 2

Let's Investigate The average should be approximately equal to the value of pi (π), i.e. 3·14.

Let's Investigate Squares will vary. Some possibilities may include:

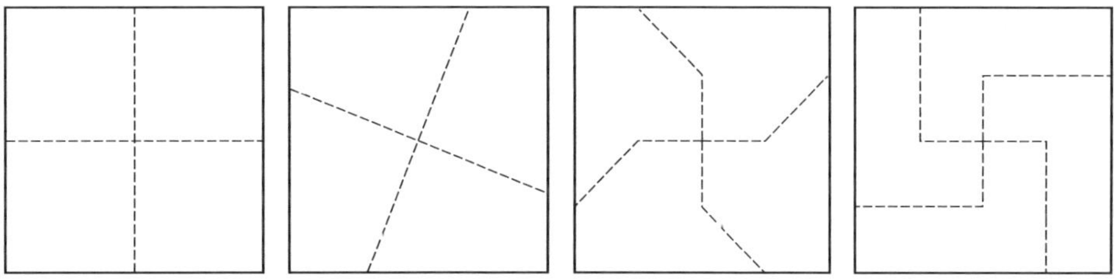

The Puzzler The diameter of the circle is 12 cm.
Explanations will vary.

Page 3

What's the Problem? The circumference of a circle with a diameter of 18 cm is 56·52 cm.
The circumference of a circle with a radius of 6 cm is 37·68 cm.
The diameter of a circle with a circumference of 173 cm is approximately 55 cm.
The radius of a circle with a circumference of 173 cm is approximately 27·5 cm.
Results of the investigation will vary.

Answers continued

Page 3 continued

The Puzzler

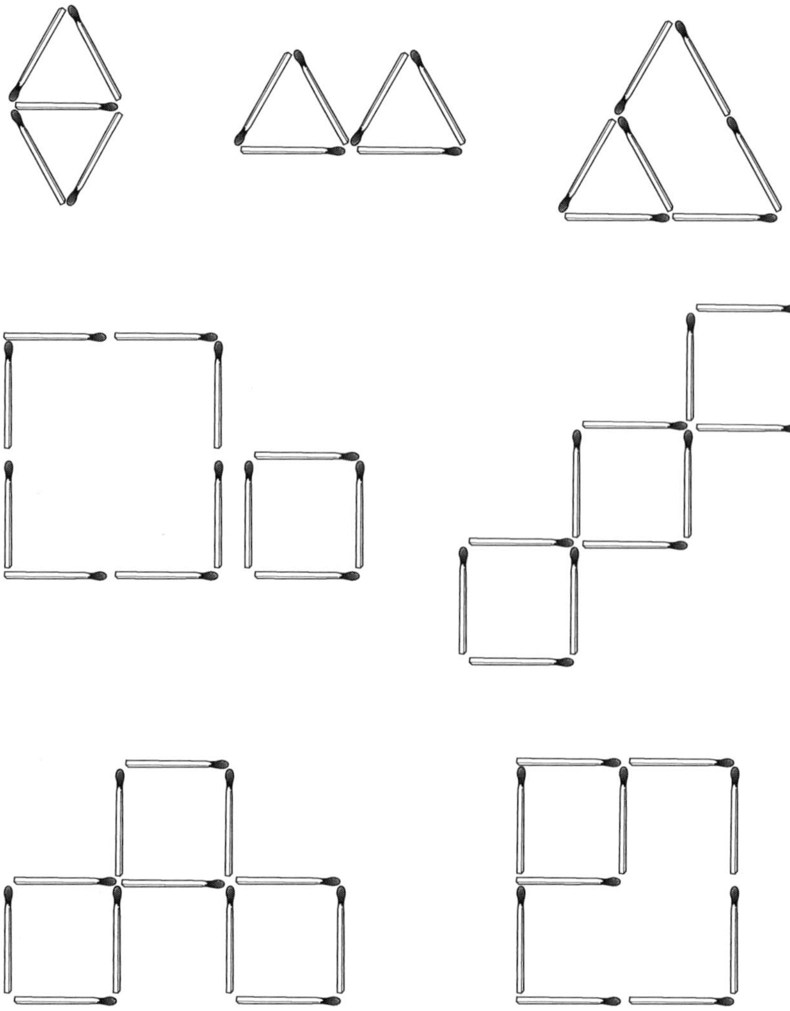

Page 4

Famous Mathematicians

13 miles

$$c = \sqrt{a^2 + b^2}$$
$$= \sqrt{5^2 + 12^2}$$
$$= \sqrt{25 + 144}$$
$$= \sqrt{169}$$
$$= 13$$

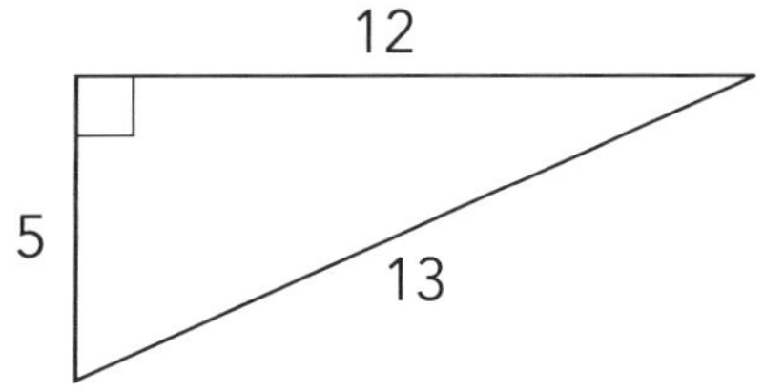

4 m

$$a = \sqrt{c^2 - b^2}$$
$$= \sqrt{5^2 - 3^2}$$
$$= \sqrt{25 - 9}$$
$$= \sqrt{16}$$
$$= 4$$

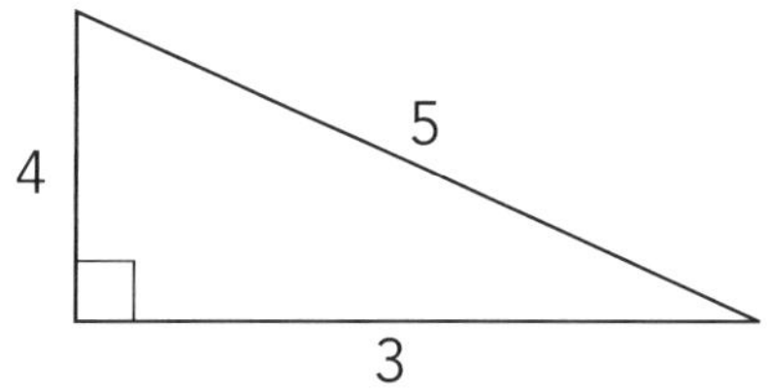

Sports Update Triangles should show the following measurements:

	Arm length (cm)	Body length (cm)	Ground level line length
Lisa	42 cm ÷ 20 = 2·1 cm	102 cm ÷ 20 = 5·1 cm	21·6 cm
Dan	64 cm ÷ 20 = 3·2 cm	150 cm ÷ 20 = 7·5 cm	41·6 cm
Michelle	36 cm ÷ 20 = 1·8 cm	84 cm ÷ 20 = 4·2 cm	14·4 cm
Joseph	48 cm ÷ 20 = 2·4 cm	112 cm ÷ 20 = 5·6 cm	25·6 cm
Ian	58 cm ÷ 20 = 2·9 cm	136 cm ÷ 20 = 6·8 cm	37·83 cm

EMU

congruent

Shapes are congruent if they are exactly the same size and shape and can be exactly superimposed.

Issue 18 3-D solids

Prerequisites for learning

- Identify, visualise and describe properties of 3-D solids
- Identify and draw nets of 3-D shapes
- Represent and interpret sequences, patterns and relationships involving shapes; suggest and test hypotheses; construct and use simple expressions and formulas in words then symbols

Resources pencil and paper; RCM 2: My notes (optional); RCM 3: Pupil self assessment booklet (optional); ruler; collection of different polyhedrons (optional); 12 straws; eight joiners; commercially produced skeletal construction kits, e.g. Frameworks Set (optional); six paper squares, ideally each a different colour; interlocking cubes (optional); stiff cardboard, scissors and colouring materials (optional); 1–6 dice (optional)

Teaching support

Page 1

Famous Mathematicians

- Provide the children with a collection of different polyhedrons including cube, cuboid, triangular-based pyramid, square-based pyramid, triangular prism, octahedron, dodecahedron and icosahedron. This will enable them to count the number of faces, vertices and edges and therefore more easily identify Euler's formula.

Construct

- This very practical activity enables children to create different cubes and cuboids.
- Suggest that children use more than 12 straws and eight joiners. This will enable them to make other polyhedrons.
- If available, provide the children with commercially produced skeletal construction kits.

Page 2

Let's Investigate

- Provide the children with eight interlocking cubes all of the same colour.
- If children cannot use the results of the 2 × 2 × 2 cube investigation to answer the same questions for the two other cubes, then provide them with 27 and 64 interlocking cubes all of the same colour so that they can create their own 3 × 3 × 3 and 4 × 4 × 4 cubes.

Page 2 continued

Construct

- Children use stiff cardboard, a ruler, scissors and colouring materials to construct their own calendar.

Page 3

Construct

- If appropriate, allow the children to work in pairs or groups to make their own origami cube.
- Children can investigate other origami shapes.

Page 4

The Puzzler

- Provide the children with a 1–6 dice.

Let's Investigate

- Discuss with the children different orientations of the same arrangements. For example, how these four $2 \times 2 \times 2$ cubes are considered to be the same:

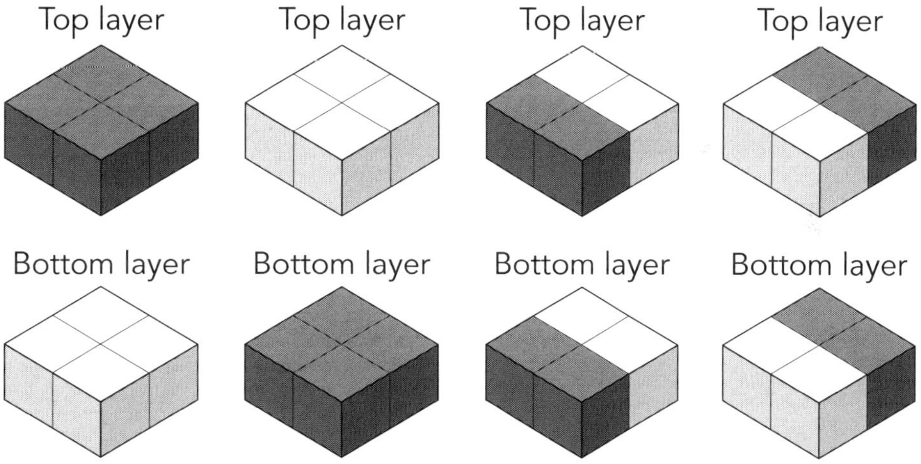

- Provide the children with four interlocking cubes of one colour and four of another colour.

AfL

- What is the rule / formula?
- What did you discover as a result of your investigation? What generalisations can you make?
- What mental image did you have? How did this help you? How do you know that you are correct?

Answers

Page 1

Famous Mathematicians

$F + V = E + 2$ or $F + V - 2 = E$

Polyhedron	Faces (F)	Vertices (V)	Edges (E)
cube (hexahedron)	6	8	12
cuboid	6	8	12
triangular-based pyramid (tetrahedron)	4	4	6
square-based pyramid	5	5	8
triangular prism	5	6	9
octahedron	8	6	12
dodecahedron	12	20	30
icosahedron	20	12	30

A football has 60 vertices.

Construct Results of the investigation will vary.

Page 2

Let's Investigate 8 small cubes make up the large 2 × 2 × 2 cube

3 yellow faces: 8
2 yellow faces: 0
1 yellow face: 0
0 yellow faces: 0

The total of the answers to the second questions (8) is equal to the answer to the first question (8).

27 small cubes make up the large 3 × 3 × 3 cube

3 yellow faces: 8
2 yellow faces: 12
1 yellow face: 6
0 yellow faces: 1

64 small cubes make up the large 4 × 4 × 4 cube

3 yellow faces: 8
2 yellow faces: 24
1 yellow face: 24
0 yellow faces: 8

Regardless of the size of the large square, the number of small squares with 3 yellow faces is always 8.

Page 2 continued

Construct Many answers are possible. However the digits 0, 1 and 2 must appear on both cubes. The remaining faces must have the digits 3–8 on them (the digit 6 is used upside down as the digit 9). One possible solution is:

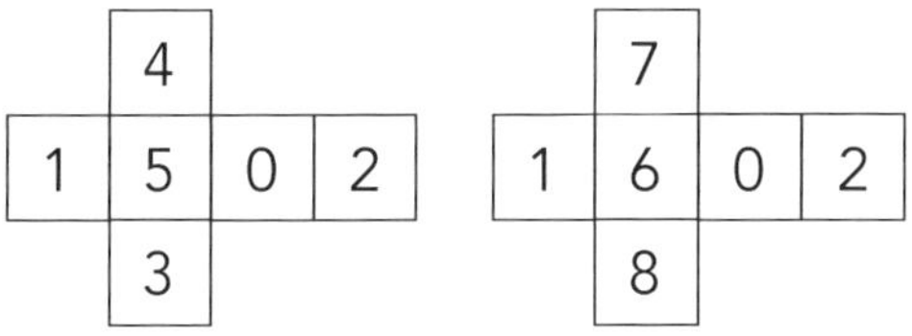

Page 3

Construct No answer required.

Page 4

The Puzzler

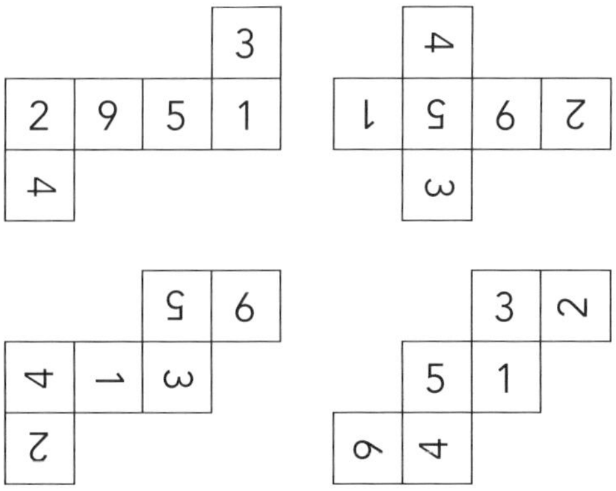

Other answers are possible.

Let's Investigate There are four completely different arrangements possible.

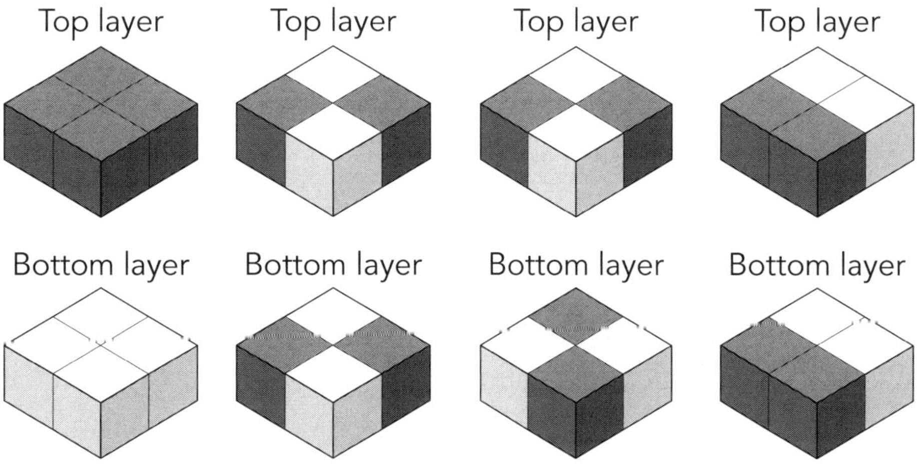

Results of the investigation will vary for using different numbers of each colour.

EMU 

icosidodecahedron

A polyhedron with 20 triangular faces and 12 pentagonal faces. It has 30 identical vertices, with two triangles and two pentagons meeting at each. It has 60 edges, each separating a triangle from a pentagon.

Issue 19 Reflective symmetry

Prerequisites for learning

- Understand and identify properties of a circle, including: centre, radius, diameter and circumference
- Use a pair of compasses
- Recognise reflective symmetry
- Complete patterns with up to two lines of symmetry
- Draw the position of a shape after a reflection

Resources pencil and paper; RCM 2: My notes (optional); RCM 3: Pupil self assessment booklet (optional); RCM 5: 2 cm squared paper; ruler; postcards, travel brochures, books and magazines showing examples of reflective symmetry; camera (optional); pair of compasses; coloured pencils; wallpaper samples showing examples of reflective symmetry (optional); computer with internet access

Teaching support

Page 1

Construct

- Allow the children to use the school camera to take photos of examples of reflective symmetry in and around the school.

  Encourage the children to look for examples of reflective symmetry in architecture from different cultures.

Around the World

- There are two aspects to this investigation. Firstly, investigating Ndebele art and culture, and secondly designing a Ndebele mural.
- After children have designed their mural, ask them to write a statement describing what makes it an example of Ndebele art and commenting on its symmetry.

Page 2

Around the World

- Similar to the Around the World activity on page 1, there are two aspects to this investigation. Firstly, investigating Akan art and culture, and secondly drawing a design for an Akan stool.
- After children have designed their stool, ask them to write a statement describing what makes it an example of an Akan stool and commenting on its symmetry.

Page 2 continued

The Arts Roundup

- Patterns based on equilateral triangles and hexagons are easy to draw using a compass because the radius of a circle divides its circumference into six equal parts.
- The steps of the pattern should look as follows:

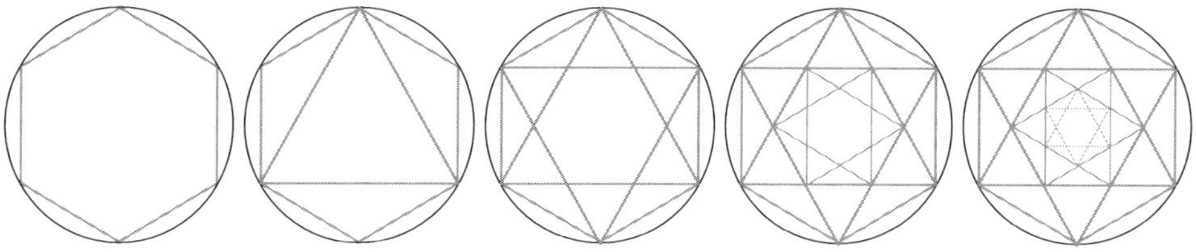

Page 3

Looking for Patterns

- If appropriate, children can create their designs using ICT.
- When children have finished their design they swap their design, but not their description, with another child. Each child then writes a description of their partner's design. When they have finished, they compare the descriptions of the same design.

Sports Update

- Children investigate symmetry in the designs of different sports fields, for example, football, rugby, basketball and tennis.

Page 4

In the Past

- There are two aspects to this investigation. Firstly, investigating mosaics from different civilisations and cultures, and secondly designing a mosaic pattern with reflective symmetry.
- Similar to the Looking for Patterns activity on page 3, children can create their patterns using squared paper or ICT.
- Ask the children to write a brief statement describing the symmetry in each design.

The Puzzler

- Suggest the children use squared paper to write their name in mirror lines placed at different angles.
- Children should not be limited to only horizontal, vertical and the diagonal angle shown. For example,

At Home

- You may wish for the children to undertake this activity in school rather than at home. If so, provide wallpaper samples showing examples of reflective symmetry or ask them to find examples on the internet.

Teaching support continued

Page 4 continued

At Home continued

- If the children do complete the activity at home, ensure that there is an opportunity in class for pairs or groups of children to discuss their results.
- Ask the children to write a brief statement describing the symmetry in each wallpaper design.

AfL

- Describe to me the symmetry in this building / mural / stool / wallpaper.
- Tell me how your design / pattern / mural / stool shows reflective symmetry.
- What type of symmetry is this?

Answers

Page 1

Construct Results of the investigation will vary.

Around the World Results of the investigation will vary.

Page 2

Around the World Results of the investigation will vary.

The Arts Roundup Children's patterns will vary.

Page 3

Looking for Patterns Children's patterns will vary.

Sports Update Statement will vary. However, all the moves show examples of vertical and horizontal symmetry.

Page 4

In the Past Children's patterns will vary.

The Puzzler Children's reflections will vary.

At Home Results of the investigation will vary.

EMU

plane of symmetry

Just as 2-D shapes have lines of symmetry, so 3-D solids have planes of symmetry.

Issue 20 Rotational symmetry

Prerequisites for learning

- Understand and identify properties of a circle, including centre
- Use a pair of compasses

Resources pencil and paper; RCM 2: My notes (optional); RCM 3: Pupil self assessment booklet (optional); RCM 4: Squared paper; RCM 7: Squared dot paper; RCM 8: Triangular dot paper; RCM 9: Isometric paper; ruler; camera (optional); coloured pencils; pair of compasses; scissors; computer

Teaching support

Page 1

Around the World

- Children make a poster / display of symmetrical Rangoli patterns found on the internet. They write a brief description of each pattern describing its rotational symmetry.

Looking for Patterns

- Extend the activity by asking the children to draw a larger triangle and to use nine different colours, i.e.

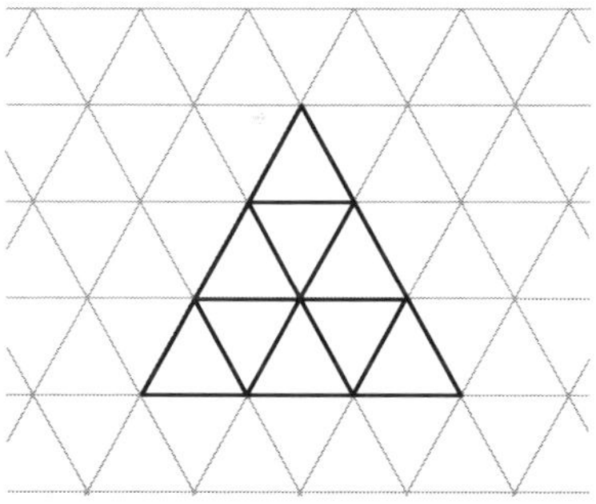

Page 2

Looking for Patterns

- Referring to the example, discuss with the children how the shape has not only been rotated through a half turn, but also translated.
- Instruct the children to create their half-turn rotation tessellating patterns using ICT.

Let's Investigate

- Rather than drawing the hubcaps, allow the children to use the school camera to take photos of the hubcaps.
- Ask the children to find other examples of rotational symmetry in and around the school, e.g. toys and equipment from the Foundation stage.

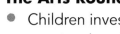

Teaching support continued

Page 3
The Arts Roundup

- Children investigate Islamic art, looking in particular for examples of rotational and reflective symmetry.

Page 4
Construct

- The numerous variations in this activity means that it is an extremely open-ended investigation that children can revisit several times. Encourage them to investigate:
  - different templates (shapes)
  - overlapping shapes that result from the rotations, i.e.

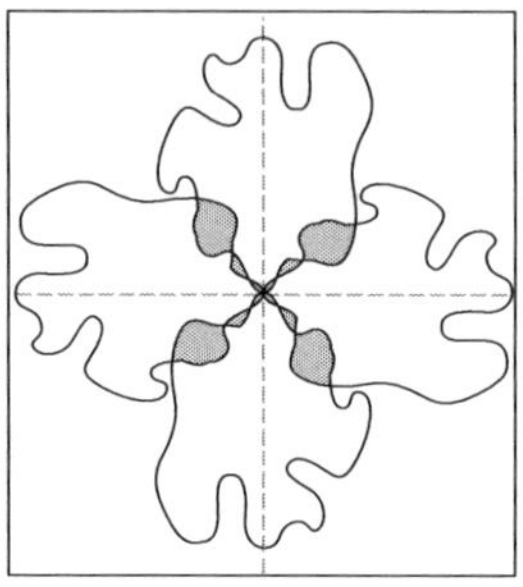

  - lines drawn at different angles, i.e.

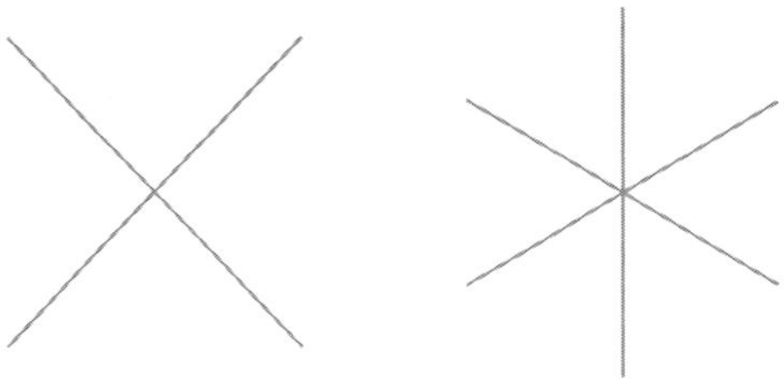

Let's Investigate

- There are 12 different pentominoes.

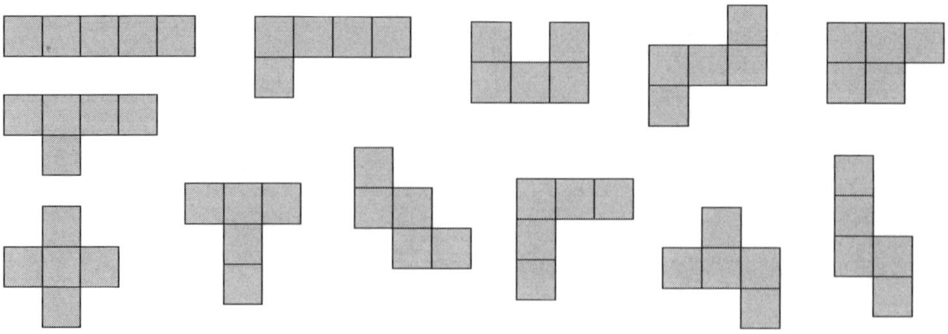

There are five different tetrominoes.

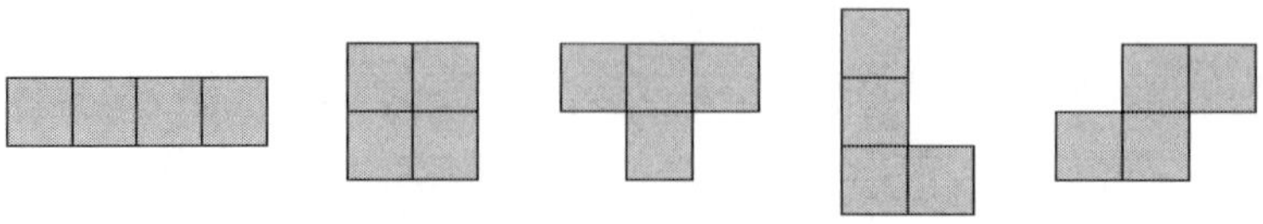

AfL

- Explain your pattern to me. How does it show rotational symmetry?
- How has this shape been rotated?
- Can you tell me some things that show rotational symmetry? How do they show it?
- What did you find out about Rangoli / Islamic patterns? How are they symmetrical?
- What can you tell me about tessellations? What makes this shape tessellate? Why doesn't this shape tessellate?

Answers

Page 1

Around the World Results of the investigation will vary.

Looking for Patterns Patterns will vary.

Page 2

Looking for Patterns

Tessellating patterns made from other shapes will vary.

Let's Investigate Results of the investigation will vary.

Page 3

The Arts Roundup Patterns will vary.

Page 4

Construct Templates and patterns will vary.

Let's Investigate A pentomino is a 2-D shape made from five congruent squares, connected along their edges.
Results of the investigation will vary.

EMU

order of symmetry

The order of symmetry of a shape is the number of times a shape can be fitted back onto its own outline during a complete turn. For example the order of symmetry of a square is 4, and a rectangle is 2.

Issue 21 Translations

Prerequisites for learning

- Understand tessellations
- Use coordinates in all four quadrants to draw, locate and complete shapes that meet given properties

Resources pencil and paper; RCM 2: My notes (optional); RCM 3: Pupil self assessment booklet (optional); RCM 5: 2 cm squared paper; RCM 7: Squared dot paper, RCM 8: Triangular dot paper; ruler; cardboard; scissors; sticky tape; coloured pencils; geoboard (optional); elastic bands (optional) computer with internet access

Teaching support

Page 1

Looking for Patterns

- Instruct the children to create their tessellating patterns using ICT.

The Arts Roundup

- Children make templates of greater complexity.

Page 2

The Arts Roundup

- Make a display of the work of MC Escher, including a brief description of how mathematics features in each of the works of art.

Construct

- Children make templates of greater complexity.

Page 3

In the Past

- There are two aspects to this investigation. Firstly, investigating mosaic border patterns from different civilisations and cultures, and secondly designing a mosaic border pattern made from a translated shape.
- Children can create their border pattern using mathematical paper or ICT.

Page 3 continued

Let's Investigate

- Remind the children that a translation is the movement of a shape from one position to another without any rotation, reflection or change in size, and moving only vertically or horizontally.
- Children investigate which triangles triangle 2 can land on exactly after one or two translations.

Page 4

Let's Investigate

- The numerous variations in this activity mean that it is an extremely open-ended investigation that children can revisit several times. Encourage them to investigate:
  - drawing other quadrilaterals and polygons
  - using different grids
  - using other types of transformations.

The Puzzler

- Provide the children with a geoboard and elastic bands.

AfL

- Explain your pattern to me. How does it show translations?
- How has this shape been translated?
- What happened when you translated your shape? What was similar / different about the shapes when they were translated onto different paper?
- Can you tell me some things that show a translating pattern? How do they show it?
- What did you find out about the work of MC Escher / mosaic border patterns? How do they show translations?
- What can you tell me about tessellations? What makes this shape tessellate? Why doesn't this shape tessellate?

Answers

Page 1

Looking for Patterns	Tessellating patterns will vary.
The Arts Roundup	Templates and tessellations will vary.

Answers continued

Page 2

The Arts Roundup Results of the investigation will vary.

Construct Templates and tessellations will vary.

Page 3

In the Past Children's border patterns will vary.

Let's Investigate One translation:

Shape A: 3
Shape B: 0
Shape C: 4 and 10
Shape D: 2
Shape E: 9

Two translations:

Shape A: 1
Shape B: 4
Shape C: 12
Shape D: 1, 3, 6 and 7
Shape E: 4, 5, 8 and 10

Page 4

Let's Investigate Results of the investigation will vary.

The Puzzler 3 × 3 geoboard: 1
4 × 4 geoboard: 5
5 × 5 geoboard: 11
Results of the investigation will vary if the size of the right-angled triangle is different, e.g. 1-unit by 1-unit.

EMU

transformation
Reflections, rotations and translations are all forms of transformation.

Issue 22 Position and direction

Prerequisites for learning

- Use coordinates in the first quadrant to draw, locate and complete shapes that meet given properties
- Identify, visualise and describe properties of triangles, quadrilaterals and other regular polygons; use knowledge of properties to draw 2-D shapes
- Use the eight compass points to describe direction
- Use simple expressions and formulas in symbols
- Understand squares and cubes of numbers
- Find the difference between a positive and a negative integer, or two negative integers

Resources pencil and paper; RCM 2: My notes (optional); RCM 3: Pupil self assessment booklet (optional); RCM 4: 1 cm squared paper; RCM 5: 2 cm squared paper; RCM 7: Squared dot paper; ruler; material for making a poster; map of the local area (optional); computer with internet access

Teaching support

Page 1
Famous Mathematicians

- Ensure that children understand the formula, and special case formula, for "The Witch of Agnesi".
- As children need to find the squares of negative numbers when using the formula (e.g. $^{-}10^{2}$), you may need to discuss with them the multiplication of two negative integers. An effective way of demonstrating this is by linking known multiplication tables to negative number multiplication tables. For example:

$2 \times 2 = 4$	$2 \times {}^{-}2 = {}^{-}4$
$1 \times 2 = 2$	$1 \times {}^{-}2 = {}^{-}2$
$0 \times 2 = 0$	$0 \times {}^{-}2 = 0$
${}^{-}1 \times 2 = {}^{-}2$	${}^{-}1 \times {}^{-}2 = 2$
${}^{-}2 \times 2 = {}^{-}4$	${}^{-}2 \times {}^{-}2 = 4$ (or ${}^{-}2^{2} = 4$)
${}^{-}3 \times 2 = {}^{-}6$	${}^{-}3 \times {}^{-}2 = 6$

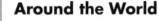

Teaching support continued

Page 2

Construct

- Along with their own mazes, children find other examples of mazes on the internet to make a display.

Around the World

- You may wish the children to work in pairs or as a group on this activity.

Page 3

The Puzzler

- Children write a similar puzzle of their own using the eight compass points to describe direction.

Let's Investigate

- Remind the children of the definition and properties of each of the following quadrilaterals:

  parallelogram: 2 pairs of opposite parallel sides / opposite sides and angles are equal

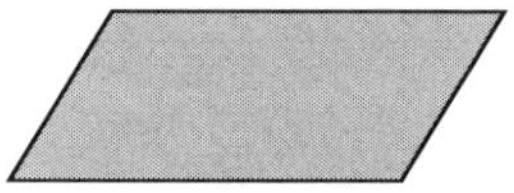

  rhombus: a special parallelogram / 4 equal sides / opposite sides equal and parallel / opposite angles equal / 2 lines of symmetry

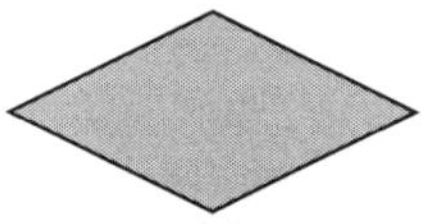

  rectangle: a special parallelogram / 4 right angles / opposite sides equal and parallel / 2 lines of symmetry

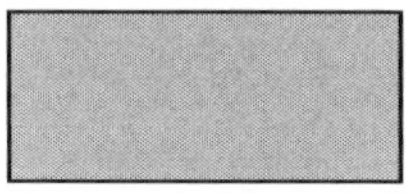

  square: a special parallelogram and a special rhombus / 4 equal sides / 4 right angles / opposite sides equal and parallel / 4 lines of symmetry

  kite: 2 pairs of adjacent sides equal / 1 pair of opposite angles equal / 1 line of symmetry

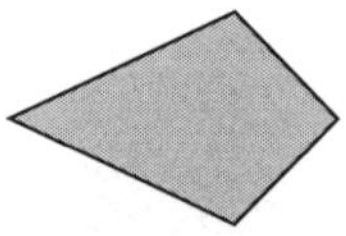

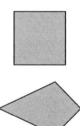

  trapezium: 1 pair of parallel sides

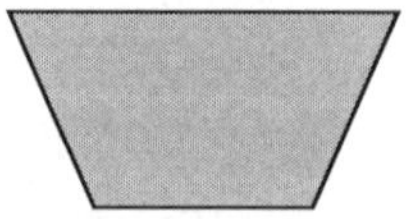

- Children may need to use more than one coordinates grid.
- Children find the perimeter and area of each of their quadrilaterals.

Around the World

- You may wish to provide the children with a map of the local area.

Page 4

Construct

- Ensure that children understand the formula for drawing a parabola using coordinates.
- As children need to calculate with negative numbers when using the formula, for example, $y = ({}^{-}1 - 1)^2 + 1$, you may need to remind them of how to find the difference between a positive and a negative integer and how to multiply together two negative integers (see Famous Mathematicians activity on page 187).
- Go through two examples with the children, one using a positive *x*-axis value, the other a negative *x*-axis value to work out the coordinates:

$y = (x - 1)^2 + 1$	$y = (x - 1)^2 + 1$
$= (5 - 1)^2 + 1$	$= ({}^{-}2 - 1)^2 + 1$
$= 4^2 + 1$	$= {}^{-}3^2 + 1$
$= 16 + 1$	$= 9 + 1$
$= 17$	$= 10$
(5, 17)	(⁻2, 10)

AfL

- Tell me some of your coordinates.
- What patterns do you notice in this list of coordinates?
- If you were to continue this curve what would be the next set of coordinates?
- How did you make your list of instructions as clear as possible? How did you ensure that your map conveyed all the necessary information while not being too detailed?

Answers

Page 1

Famous Mathematicians (⁻10, 1) (⁻9, 1·2) (⁻8, 1·4) (⁻7, 1·7) (⁻6, 2) (⁻5, 2·5) (⁻4, 3) (⁻3, 3·7) (⁻2, 4·3) (⁻1, 4·8) (0, 5) (1, 4·8) (2, 4·3) (3, 3·7) (4, 3) (5, 2·5) (6, 2) (7, 1·7) (8, 1·4) (9, 1·2) (10, 1)

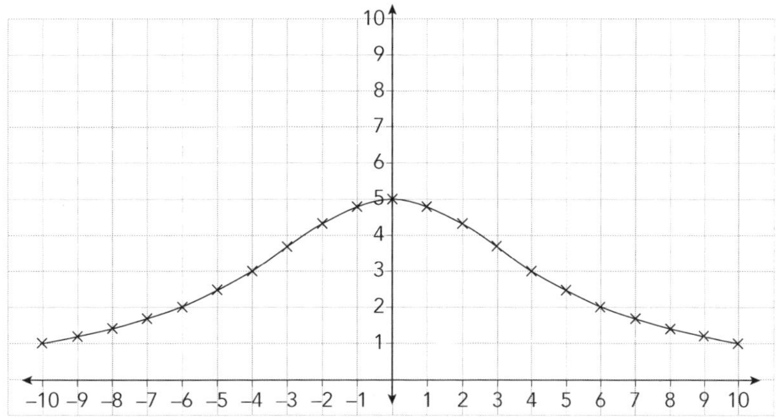

Page 2

Construct Mazes and conclusions will vary.

Around the World Posters will vary.

Page 3

The Puzzler 10 km

Let's Investigate Coordinates of quadrilaterals, perimeters and areas will vary.

Around the World Instructions will vary.

Page 4

Construct

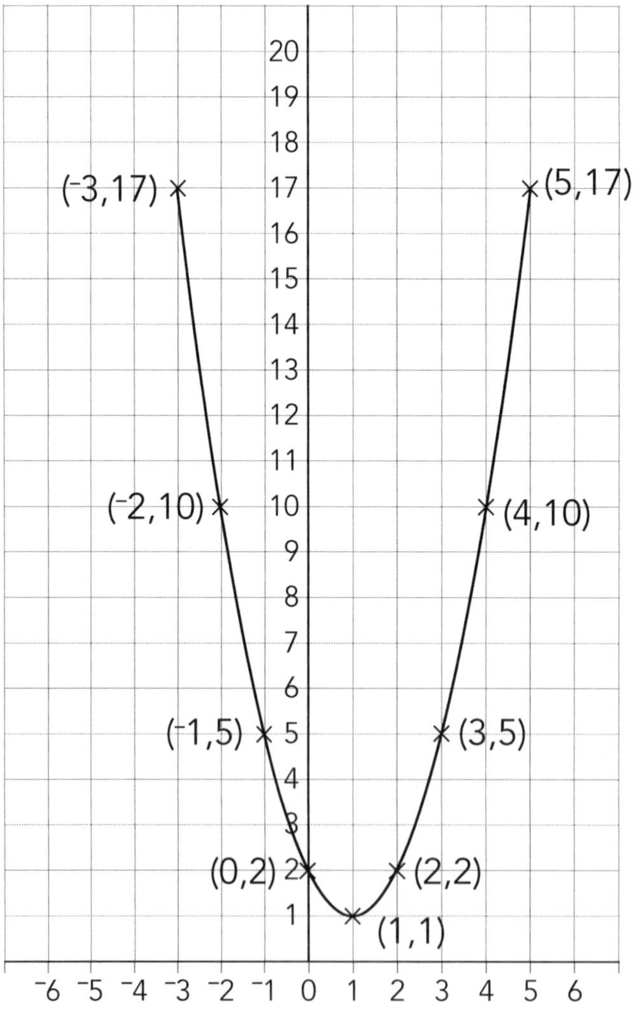

EMU

GPS

Global Positioning System is a navigational and surveying facility which is based on receiving signals from different satellites.

Issue 23 Movement and angle

Prerequisites for learning

- Know that angles are measured in degrees and that one whole turn is 360°; compare and order angles
- Estimate, draw and measure acute and obtuse angles using an angle measurer or protractor to a suitable degree of accuracy
- Use a pair of compasses to draw circles
- Understand and identify properties of a circle, including centre, radius and arc
- Collect, select, process, present and interpret data

Resources pencil and paper; RCM 2: My notes (optional); RCM 3: Pupil self assessment booklet (optional); RCM 4: 1 cm squared paper; magnetic / orienteering compass; RCM 5: 2 cm squared paper; RCM 7: Squared dot paper; RCM 8: Triangular dot paper; RCM 9: Isometric paper; RCM 10: Diamond paper; ruler; pair of compasses; protractor; floor robot; chessboard (optional); coin, 1–6 dice, 1–8 digit cards; a random number generating function on a computer, e.g. Number Spinners Interactive Teaching Program (ITP) or similar; torch; tape measure; computer with internet access

Teaching support

Page 1

Sports Update

- Children investigate the importance of angles in other sports, e.g. football, golf (golf clubs), tennis …

Let's Investigate

- This activity is about knowing the size of interior angles in different polygons.
- Discuss with the children that if n represents the number of sides of a polygon, the formula for calculating the sum of interior angles is $180 \times (n - 2)$.

  So, the sums of angles in regular polygons are:

  - 3-sided shape (triangle): 180° ∴ Interior angle is 60°.
  - 4-sided shape (square): 360° ∴ Interior angle is 90°.
  - 5-sided shape (pentagon): 540° ∴ Interior angle is 108°.
  - 6-sided shape (hexagon): 720° ∴ Interior angle is 120°.
  - 7-sided shape (heptagon): 900° ∴ Interior angle is 128·5°.
  - 8-sided shape (octagon): 1080° ∴ Interior angle is 135°.

Teaching support continued

Page 1 continued

Let's Investigate continued

- 9-sided shape (nonagon): 1260° ∴ Interior angle is 140°.
- 10-sided shape (decagon): 1440° ∴ Interior angle is 144°.
- 12-sided shape (dodecagon): 1800° ∴ Interior angle is 150°.

Children need this information when writing their instructions.

- Use a diagram to show the children the angle of turn in the example, i.e.

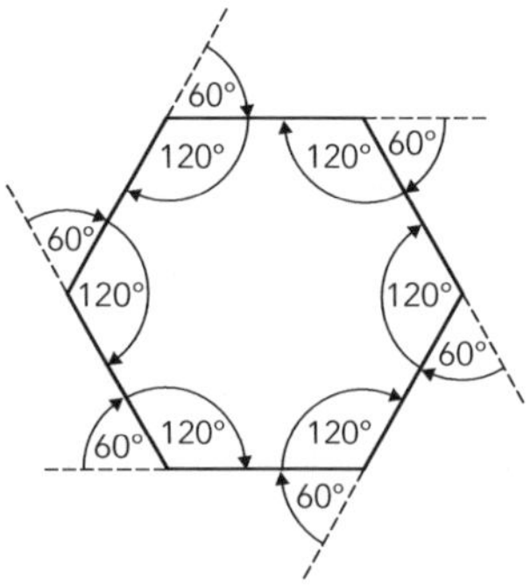

Page 2

Technology Today

- Pairs of children can compare the sets of instructions they wrote for the Let's Investigate activity on page 1, choose one set of instructions for each shape and use a floor robot.

Construct

- To draw the shape of a 50p coin, children need to repeat step 6 a further five times.
- Knowing which two points form an arc depends on continuing the pattern in step 4 and step 5. If children cannot identify the pattern, suggest they tabulate the information.

Point	Arc drawn between points:
A	D and E
B	E and F
C	F and G
D	G and A
E	A and B
F	B and C
G	C and D

Around the World

- Ensure that children understand how bearings work.
- When giving bearings of places outside, it is recommended that children work in pairs.
- Children investigate the sport of orienteering.

Page 3

The Puzzler

- Explain to the children that there are different solutions possible for each board.
- Some children may find it helpful to refer to an actual chessboard and knight piece.
- Using the 3 × 4 board as an example, work with the children to record one of the possible solutions onto squared paper, i.e.

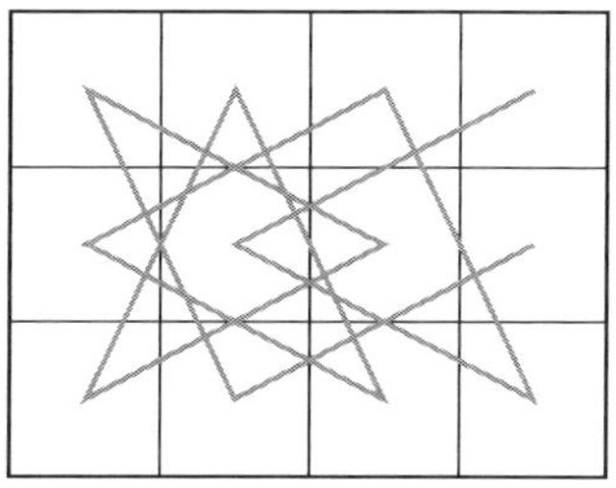

- Some children may find the 6 × 6 and 8 × 8 boards too challenging. If this is the case, suggest they only find solutions for the smaller boards.

  You may wish to discuss with the children that a possible solution to the 8 × 8 chessboard can be made by using two 3 × 4 boards and two 4 × 5 boards, i.e.

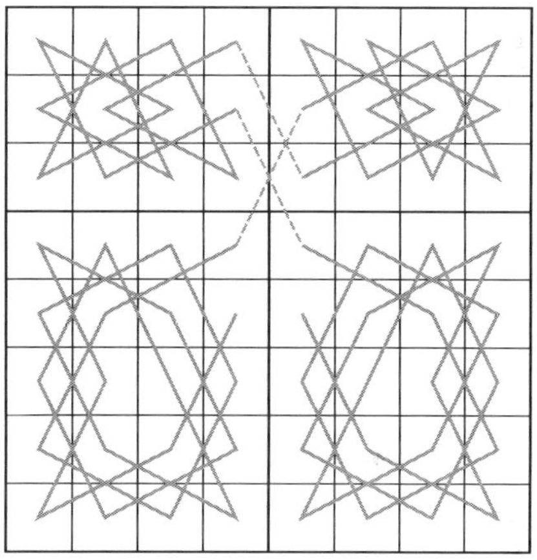

Let's Investigate

- Ensure children use a range of different dot paper.

Page 4

Let's Investigate

- Ensure children use a range of different dot paper and if available, a random number generating function on a computer, e.g. Number Spinners ITP or similar.

Focus on Science

- Suggest that one method of measuring the angle is to measure the distance of the light source from the object and the height of the light source above the object. From this children can draw a scale triangle and measure the angle of the light source.

Teaching support continued

Page 4 continued

At Home

- After children have completed the activity at home, ensure that there is an opportunity in class for pairs or groups of children to discuss their results.

AfL

- How did you work out / calculate what the size of the angle was?
- Describe your route to me.
- What instructions did you write?
- Where did you stand in the playground? Tell me an object that you chose. Give me the compass bearings for this.
- How did you work out the solution to the puzzle? Did you find another route?
- Tell me what you did in your experiment. What are the results? What does this tell us?

Answers

Page 1

Sports Update
2×1 table: Pocket E
3×2 table: Pocket F
4×1 table: Pocket B
7×3 table: Pocket D

Let's Investigate
Instructions will vary. However, they should be similar to the following:

- equilateral triangle: 3 angles each of 60°
- rectangle: 4 angles each of 90°
- regular pentagon: 5 angles each of 108°
- regular octagon: 8 angles each of 135°

Page 2

Technology Today
Instructions will vary depending on the ICT robotic equipment available.

Construct
No answer required.

Around the World
The arrow of a magnetic compass is a magnet. Therefore it always rotates to point to magnetic north.
Results of the investigation will vary.

Page 3

The Puzzler Solutions will vary. One solution for each chessboard is:

3 × 4

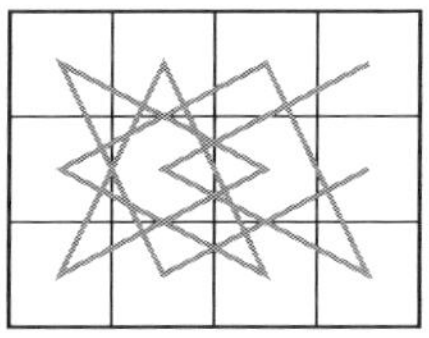

4 × 5

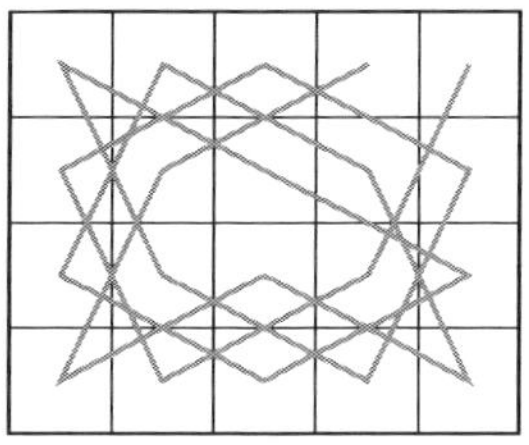

5 × 5

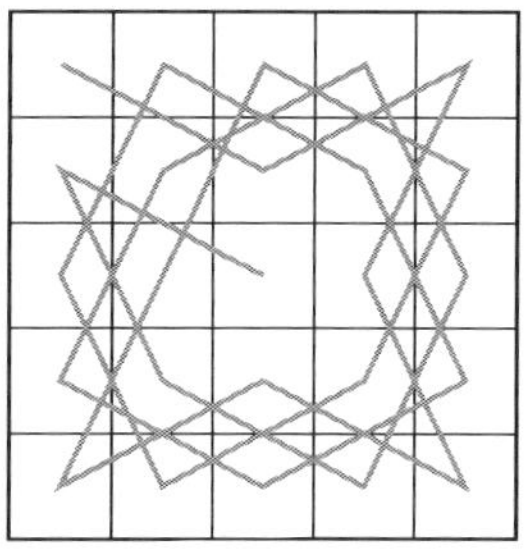

6 × 6

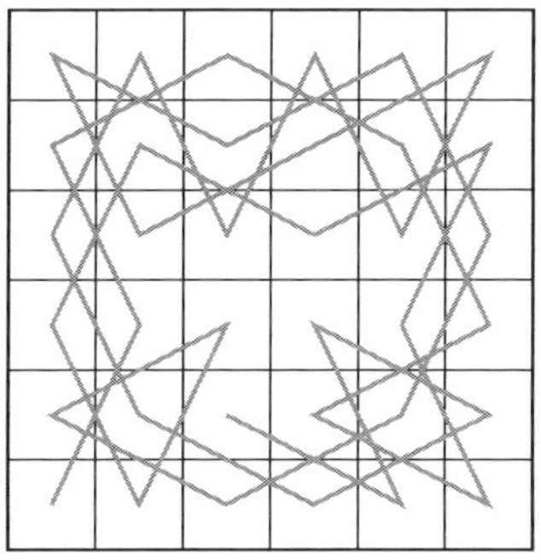

Normal 8 × 8

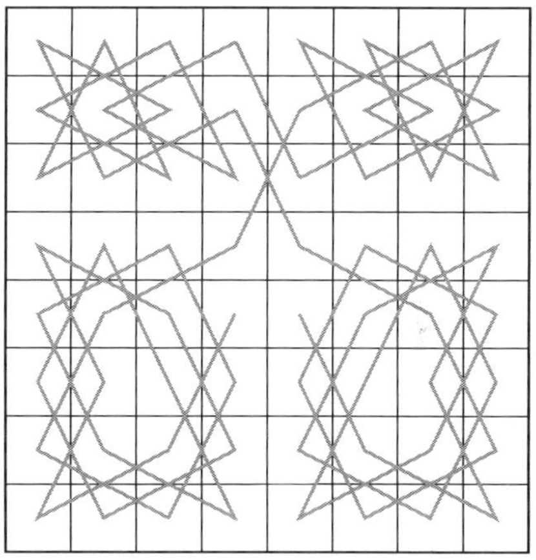

Let's Investigate Trails will vary.

Page 4

Let's Investigate Paths will vary.

Focus on Science Reports, graphs and conclusions will vary.

At Home Lists of angles will vary.

EMU

radian

A unit of angle, equal to an angle at the centre of a circle whose arc length is equal to the length of the radius.

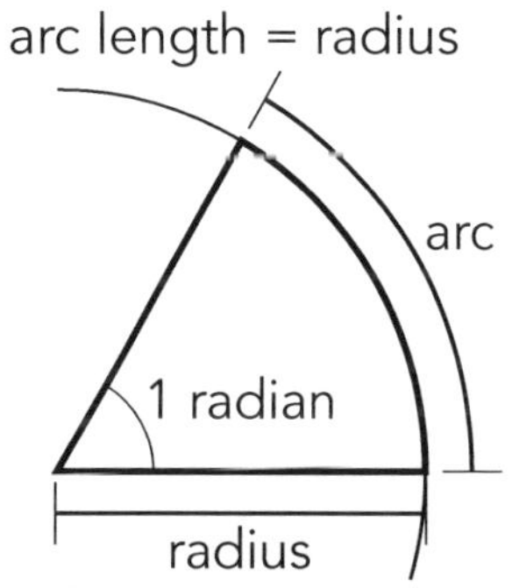

Understanding shape – General

Prerequisites for learning

- Understand and identify properties of a circle, including circumference, chord and segment
- Use a pair of compasses to draw circles
- Understand and use simple algebraic conventions
- Represent information or unknown numbers in an equation

Resources pencil and paper; RCM 2: My notes (optional); RCM 3: Pupil self assessment booklet (optional); RCMs: 4–10 mathematical papers; ruler; chessboard (optional); pair of compasses; coloured pencils; computer with internet access

Teaching support

Page 1

The Language of Maths

- Some children may see this as a pattern made up of 12-sided shapes (dodecagons). However it is easier to describe the pattern by seeing it as a series of interconnecting regular hexagons, each one surrounded by rotated triangles and squares that form the hexagons' vertices and sides.
- Remind the children of the word 'regular' as it relates to 2-D shapes. The use of this term is important to describe the pattern successfully.

What's the Problem?

- Explain to the children that rotations are not considered different, i.e. the following are all the same solution.

- If children have difficulty identifying similarities suggest that they turn their sheet of squared paper around.

Page 1 continued

What's the Problem? continued

- Tell the children the fewest number of queens necessary to defend the chessboard:
  - 4 × 4 chessboard: 2 queens
  - 5 × 5 chessboard: 3 queens
  - 6 × 6 chessboard: 3 queens
  - 8 × 8 chessboard: 5 queens.
- Some children may find it helpful to refer to an actual chessboard and queen piece (they will need to use additional chess pieces as substitute queens).

Page 2

Around the World

- State and country flags that are suitable for children to use when investigating different types of symmetry include:
  - vertical symmetry: Canada and India
  - horizontal symmetry: Norway and France
  - vertical and horizontal symmetry: United Kingdom and Jamaica
  - rotational symmetry: European Union and Hong Kong
  - no symmetry: Australia and USA.

The Puzzler

- Explain to the children that the solution to this puzzle means that no two queens can share the same row, column, or diagonal.
- Tell the children that not allowing for repetitions of rotation and symmetry, there are 12 unique solutions. How many of them can they find?
- Some children may find it helpful to refer to an actual chessboard and queen piece (they will need to use additional chess pieces as substitute queens).

Let's Investigate

- Suggest the children draw a table to assist them in identifying the rule, i.e.

Number of chords (C)	Number of segments (S)	
2	4	
3	7	+3
4	11	+4
5	16	+5
6	22	+6

Page 2 continued

Let's Investigate continued

- You may need to provide some children with assistance when devising a formula for the maximum number of segments you can make for a particular number of chords:

$$S = \frac{C(C + 1)}{2} + 1$$

- Some children may also need reminding of the order of operations, and that $C(C + 1)$ is the same as $C \times (C + 1)$.

Page 3

Famous Mathematicians

- Ensure that children understand the difference between an odd and an even vertex.
- Children investigate the Konigsberg Bridge Problem.

Page 4

The Arts Roundup

- Children choose the mathematical paper that is best suited to their design.

Technology Today

- If appropriate, children could reproduce on the computer the design they created in The Arts Roundup above.

Construct

- Children follow steps 1 to 5. Then, without changing the compass settings, they draw six new circles using the six points around the circumference of the original circle for the centres. Children then colour their design to show examples of symmetry, rotation and translation.

AfL

- Describe this design / pattern to me. What words are important in describing the design / pattern?
- How did you work out the solution to this problem / puzzle? Did you find more than one solution?
- What is the rule? Can you use this rule to write a formula?
- What was one of Euler's discoveries?

Answers

Page 1

The Language of Maths Instructions will vary.

What's the Problem?

4 × 4

5 × 5 (other solutions are possible)

6 × 6

8 × 8

Page 2

Around the World Results of the investigation will vary.

The Puzzler There are 12 unique solutions. However, if allowing different orientations of the same unique solution, i.e. rotation and reflection, there are a total of 92 solutions. This is one solution.

Page 2 continued

Let's Investigate

S = maximum number of segments

C = number of chords

$$S = \frac{C(C + 1)}{2} + 1$$

Page 3

Famous Mathematicians

Can the networks be travelled?

No	Yes	No	No
Yes	No	Yes	Yes

Euler's rules:

- A network can be travelled if it has two odd vertices. However, the travelling must begin at one of the odd vertices and finish at the other.
- A network with more than two odd points cannot be travelled without retracing a line twice.
- A network with no odd vertices (only even vertices) can be travelled along each line once, and only once.
- The journey can start at any point and will always finish at the same point as it started.

Children's own networks will vary.

Page 4

The Arts Roundup Designs will vary.

Technology Today Designs will vary.

Construct Designs will vary.

EMU

surveying

To make a detailed map of an area of land, including its boundaries, area and elevation. It involves the use of, among other elements, geometry (including angles) and finding distances.

Issue 25

Length and distance

Prerequisites for learning

- Recognise the square roots of perfect squares
- Understand and use simple algebraic conventions
- Represent information or unknown numbers in an equation
- Understand the word 'scale' in the contexts of maps and in drawing enlargements and reductions
- Understand and identify properties of a circle, including radius, diameter and circumference
- Solve simple problems involving ratio
- Collect, select, process, present and interpret data

Resources pencil and paper; RCM 2: My notes (optional); RCM 3: Pupil self assessment booklet (optional); RCM 4: 1 cm squared paper; ruler; selection of maps showing different scales; calculator; pair of compasses; eight slips of paper; tape measure; trundle wheel; computer with internet access

Teaching support

Page 1

Around the World

- Show the children how to measure the distance between two places on the map and then use the scale to calculate the actual distance.
- You may wish to discuss with the children the difference between the actual distance between two places on a map and the distance 'as the crow flies'.

Construct

- This activity involves measuring, converting and drawing. Encourage the children to be as accurate as possible throughout each stage of the activity.

Teaching support continued

Page 2

Focus on Science

- The second column in the table below shows the diameter (in kilometres) of each of the planets. You may wish to provide this information for the children rather than have them find it out for themselves. The final column offers a possible scale drawing size for each of the planets.

Planet	Diameter in km	Diameter in km (rounded)	To scale
Sun	1 391 000	1 400 000	140 cm
Mercury	4879	5000	5 mm
Venus	12 104	12 000	12 mm
Earth	12 756	13 000	13 mm
Mars	6794	7000	7 mm
Jupiter	142 984	140 000	14 cm
Saturn	120 536	120 000	12 cm
Uranus	51 118	51 000	51 mm
Neptune	49 528	50 000	5 cm
Pluto	2390	2000	2 mm

- Some of the planets will either be too large or too small to draw if they are all based on the same scale, e.g. Sun (too large), Pluto, Mercury and Mars (too small). For such planets suggest children just write the diameter.

Around the World

- Work through an example with the children, e.g.

Metric units

For a height of 1·5 metres

$d = \sqrt{12{\cdot}7h}$

$d = \sqrt{12{\cdot}7 \times 1{\cdot}5}$

$d = 4{\cdot}36$ km

Imperial units

For a height of 5 feet

$d = \sqrt{1{\cdot}50h}$

$d = \sqrt{1{\cdot}50 \times 5}$

$d = 2{\cdot}74$ miles

Page 3

Let's Investigate

- Ensure that children understand all the terms involved with staircases.

Sports Update

- The degree of complexity of this activity depends on how detailed the children make their scale drawing.

Page 3 continued

Let's Investigate

- Assist children to work out the percentage error, i.e.

$$\frac{\text{Actual error (cm)}}{10\text{ cm}} \times \frac{100}{1}$$

- Repeat the activity, only this time asking the children to cut a piece of string as close to 30 cm long as possible.

Page 4

Around the World

- The answer to this activity will depend on the mode of transportation children use. They need to find out kilometres per hour or miles per hour for their chosen mode of transport and calculate accordingly, i.e.
  - plane: average cruising speed = 800 km/h or 500 MPH
  - running: 10 km/h or 6 MPH
  - walking: 5 km/h or 3 MPH
  - boat: average cruising speed = 35 knots or 65 km/h or 40 MPH.

The Language of Maths

- You may wish to discuss with the children how in the book, the reference to 20 000 leagues (or 111 120 kilometers or 69 047 miles) does not mean depth. It actually refers to the distance travelled underwater. 20 000 leagues / 111 120 kilometers / 69 047 miles is almost three times the circumference of the Earth.
- Children investigate maths in books / stories.

Money Matters

- A 10p coin is 1·85 mm thick.

  Methods will vary. One method is:

  1 km = 1 000 000 mm

  1 000 000 ÷ 1·85 = 540 541 coins – £54 054.10

At Home

- You may wish for the children to undertake this activity in school rather than at home.
- If the children do undertake this activity at home, once they have completed the task, ensure that there is an opportunity in class for pairs or groups of children to discuss their results.

AfL

- Tell me the scale of your map / diagram. What does this mean?
- What did you find out?
- What were the results of your investigation? What conclusions can you draw?
- What do your estimates / approximations mean? How accurate are they? What does this mean?

Answers

Page 1

Around the World Answers will vary.

Construct Plans will vary.

Page 2

Focus on Science Diagrams will vary.

Around the World Answers will vary depending on the unit of measure used and the children's heights.

Page 3

Let's Investigate Results will vary depending on the staircases children investigate.

Sports Update Diagrams will vary depending on the chosen sport.

Let's Investigate Results of the investigation will vary.

Page 4

Around the World Answers will vary depending on the mode of transport used.

The Language of Maths A league is a unit of length.
1 league = 5·55600 kilometres or 3·45233834 miles
Alternative titles for *20,000 Leagues Under the Sea* could be *111 120 Kilometres Under the Sea* or *69 047 Miles Under the Sea*.

Money Matters £54 054.10

At Home Results of the investigation will vary.

EMU

nanometre
One billionth of a metre.

Issue 26 Mass and weight

Prerequisites for learning

- Understand logic puzzles
- Calculate mentally with integers and decimals
- Measure and calculate using imperial units and know their approximate metric values
- Collect, select, process, present and interpret data

Resources pencil and paper; RCM 2: My notes (optional); RCM 3: Pupil self assessment booklet (optional); RCM 4: 1 cm squared paper; ruler; material for making a poster; calculator; selection of food packaging (optional); computer with internet access

Teaching support

Page 1

Around the World

- Most children will find this activity relatively easy. Ensure children know that 1 tonne is equivalent to 1000 kg.

Around the World

- Children can produce their results in a graph or chart using ICT.
- Children investigate other commodities such as gold, iron-ore, zinc, rubber and copper.

Page 2

Looking for Patterns

- These logic problems can be solved in various ways. However, all methods are based on identifying patterns and relationships. One way of solving such problems is to assign values to the shapes. For example, in the first problem:

  By looking at the second set of scales, we can see that:

  $3 \times \bigcirc = 1 \times \triangle$

  $\therefore \bigcirc = 1$ and $\triangle = 3$

  By looking at the first set of scales, we can work out using what we have discovered above that:

  $2 \times \bigcirc = 1 \times \square$

  $\therefore \bigcirc = 1$ and $\square = 2$

  So, $\triangle\square\square = 3 + 2 + 2\bigcirc$

  $\therefore 7 \times \bigcirc$ balance the third scale.

Teaching support continued

Page 2 continued

Possible values for the other puzzles are:

Puzzle 2:

○ = 3

□ = 5

△ = 7

∴ 5 × ○ balance the third scale.

Puzzle 3:

○ = 3

□ = 1

△ = 5

∴ 3 × ○ balance the third scale.

The Language of Maths

- Explain to the children that their poster should include a combination of words and illustrations to explain the difference between mass and weight.

Focus on Science

- Children comment of the buoyancy of each of the objects. What conclusions can they draw from their investigation?

Page 3

Focus on Science

- You may prefer to leave out the first part of the activity where children find out their own weight on each of the planets. If so, tell the children to go straight onto finding the Earth weight of other objects and then to calculate their approximate weight on each of the other planets.

Let's Investigate

- Ensure children understand the difference between mass and volume, and are able to calculate (and / or approximate) volume (see Issue 27).
- The important aspect of this activity is the inferences that children make as a result of their investigation.

Page 4

At Home

- Remind the children that they are only expected to make approximations in this activity. Discuss with the children how they might arrive at these approximations and averages.
- You may wish for the children to undertake this activity in school rather than at home. If so, have available a selection of food packaging.
- If the children do undertake this activity at home, once they have completed the task, ensure that there is an opportunity in class for pairs or groups of children to discuss their results.

Page 4 continued

What's the Problem?

- Explain to the children the relationship between stones and pounds, and their metric equivalent, i.e.
  1 pound (lb) = 0·454 kg
  14 pounds = 1 stone (st)
- One method of working out the answer is:
  If 1lb = 0·454 kg, then 63 kg ÷ 0·454 ≈ 139 lb
  If 14 lb = 1 st, then 139 lb ÷ 14 = 9 st 13 lb

What's the Problem?

- Explain to the children the relationship between stones and pounds, and their metric equivalent, i.e.
  1 pound (lb) = 0·454 kg
  14 pounds = 1 stone (st)
- One method of working out the answer is:
  If 14 lb = 1 st, then (12 st × 14) + 8 lb = 176 lb
  If 1 lb = 0·454 kg, then 176 lb × 0·454 ≈ 80 kg

AfL

- What did you find out? How did you record your results? Why did you decide to present them in this way?
- What conclusions can you draw from your investigation?
- How did you work out these puzzles? What strategies did you use?
- What calculations did you do?

Answers

Page 1

Around the World
1260 kg
Trader B / 80 kg
Trader G
Trader H
Traders C and F
Trader D / 800 kg
Trader F / 1320 kg
Trader D (800 kg), Trader C (840 kg), Trader G (900 kg), Trader A (1200 kg), Trader H (1250 kg), Trader E (1260 kg), Trader B (1280 kg) and Trader F (1320 kg)

Answers continued

Page 1 continued

Around the World

Presentation and reports will vary however, the top three producers of each commodity are shown in the table below:

Commodity	Top three producers (tonnes) (*million tonnes)
wheat	China (115*) / India (81*) / USA (71*)
sugar	Brazil (36*) / China (8*) / India (16*)
rice	China (187*) / India (144*) / Indonesia (57*)
tea	China (1*) / India (930 000) / Kenya (310 000)
coffee	Brazil (2*) / Vietnam (960 000) / Cambodia (700 000)

Page 2

Looking for Patterns

Puzzle 1: 7 × ○ balance the third scale.
Puzzle 2: 5 × ○ balance the third scale.
Puzzle 3: 3 × ○ balance the third scale.

The Language of Maths

Posters will vary. However definitions should be similar to the following:

- The mass of an object is how much matter it contains.
- The weight of an object is the force caused by gravity pulling down on the mass of an object.

Focus on Science

The mass of the materials are:

- balsa wood: 170 kg/m^3
- gold: 19 320 kg/m^3
- lead: 11 340 kg/m^3
- pine wood*: 560 kg/m^3
- silver: 10 490 kg/m^3
- aluminium*: 2600 kg/m^3

Note: kg/m^3 refers to the number of kilograms per cubic metre.
* Answers may vary depending on the type of material used.

Page 3

Focus on Science Results of the investigation will vary.

Let's Investigate Results of the investigation will vary.

Page 4

At Home Results of the investigation will vary.

What's the Problem? 9 st 13 lb

What's the Problem? 80 kg

EMU

inference
An inference is a conclusion drawn from evidence or reasoning.

Issue 27 Volume and capacity

Prerequisites for learning

- Understand the concept of volume
- Understand and use simple algebraic conventions
- Use simple expressions and formulas in symbols
- Understand pi (π) as the ratio of the circumference of a circle to its diameter and is equal to 3·14

Resources pencil and paper; RCM 2: My notes (optional); RCM 3: Pupil self assessment booklet (optional); collection of cylinders, e.g. tin can, tube of sweets, drinking glass, toilet roll … (optional); material for making a poster; 100 ml can; sand or rice; measuring cylinder with scale in cubic centimetres; water; collection of small solid objects, e.g. small stone, coin, ball of modelling clay …; calculator (optional); computer with internet access

Teaching support

Page 1

Around the World

- Ensure children understand and can use the formula for calculating the volume of a cuboid.

Around the World

- Rates for both national and international freightage can easily be found on the internet.
- The important aspect of this activity is how the volume of a parcel, as opposed to distance, affects pricing.
- Suggest the children record their results in a table.

Page 2

Let's Investigate

- This activity introduces children to the formulas for calculating the volume of a cylinder and a triangular prism. Ensure that they understand and can use these formulas before working independently on this activity and the At Home activity on page 3. You may also need to remind / introduce children to pi (π).

Teaching support continued

Page 2 continued

Let's Investigate continued

Volume of a cylinder

$$
\begin{aligned}
V &= \pi r^2 l \\
&= 3{\cdot}14 \times 10^2 \times 32 \\
&= 3{\cdot}14 \times 100 \times 32 \\
&\approx 10\,048^3
\end{aligned}
$$

Volume of a triangular prism

$$
\begin{aligned}
V &= \tfrac{1}{2} bhl \\
&= \tfrac{1}{2} \times 4 \times 5 \times 7 \\
&= \tfrac{140}{2} \\
&= 70 \text{ cm}^3
\end{aligned}
$$

Page 3

At Home

- You may wish for the children to undertake this activity in school rather than at home. If so, have available a collection of cylinders, e.g. tin can, tube of sweets, drinking glass, toilet roll …
- If the children do undertake this activity at home, once they have completed the task, ensure that there is an opportunity in class for pairs or groups of children to discuss their results.

Sports Update

- Ensure children understand and can use the formula for calculating the volume of a sphere.

  Tennis ball with a radius of 3 cm

  $\frac{4}{3}\pi r^3$

  $\frac{4}{3} \times 3{\cdot}14 \times 3^3$

  $= \frac{4}{3} \times 3{\cdot}14 \times 27$

  $= \frac{339}{3}$

  $\approx 113 \text{ cm}^3$

Focus on Science

- Remind the children that the formula for calculating the volume of the cylinder is $V = \pi r^2 h$. Ask them to find out what the formula is for calculating the volume of a cone ($V = \frac{1}{3}\pi r^2 h$).
- Given that both the cylinder and cone have the same radius and height then three conesful should fill the can.

The Language of Maths

- Explain to the children that their poster should include a combination of words and illustrations to explain the difference between volume and capacity.

Page 4

Famous Mathematicians

- Be sure to provide children with measuring cylinders with scales in cubic centimetres.

Let's Investigate

- This investigation assumes that most classrooms will be cuboid in shape and therefore children will be able to use the formula $V = lwh$. However, classrooms do come in shapes other than cuboids. In such cases children will need to make approximations. When doing so, children should write about the assumptions they have made when arriving at their approximations.

AfL

- How do you calculate volume? What about for a different solid?
- Explain this formula to me in your own words.
- What were the results of your experiment? What conclusions can you make?
- What did your investigation discover? Why do you think this is?

Answers

Page 1

Around the World

10 264 800 mm^3
1026 m^3
201·67 cm^3
91·125 m^3
50 120 692 mm^3
One possible answer is 50 cm × 115·5 cm, but there are endless possibilities.

Around the World

Results of the investigation will vary.

Page 2

Let's Investigate

70 cm^3
10 048 cm^3
441 cm^3
942 cm^3

Answers continued

Page 3

At Home Results of the investigation will vary.

Sports Update Tennis ball = 113 cm^3
Volley ball = 9198 cm^3
Cricket ball = 523 cm^3
Basket ball = 7235 cm^3

Focus on Science Three conesful should fill the can.
The volume of the cone is $\frac{1}{3}$ that of the cylinder.

The Language of Maths Posters will vary. However the definition should be similar to the following:

Volume and capacity measure the same thing: three-dimensional space, but they are slightly different in usage. Capacity refers to how much a container can hold (with contents measured commonly in litres or its derived units); while volume is the space actually occupied by an object or the bulk of some substance.

Page 4

Famous Mathematicians Results of the investigation will vary.

Let's Investigate Results of the investigation will vary.

EMU

SI

SI is the International System of Units (abbreviated SI from the French Le Système International d'Unités). It is the world's most widely used system of measurement.

It is based on the metric system and the number ten and involves seven 'base' units: metre, kilogram, second, ampere, kelvin, candela, mole. Litre is also an SI unit but is not considered a 'base' unit.

Issue 28 Time

Prerequisites for learning

- Understand and use simple algebraic conventions
- Use simple expressions and formulas in symbols

Resources pencil and paper; RCM 2: My notes (optional); RCM 3: Pupil self assessment booklet (optional); Telling Time Interactive Teaching Program (ITP) or similar (optional); digital clock (optional); mirror (optional); tape measure; stopwatch; calculator (optional)

Teaching support

Page 1

The Puzzler

- If children have an analogue wristwatch, they may find this activity very easy.
- You may wish to show the children the answer using the ITP: Telling Time or similar.
- Children investigate what number the minute hand is pointing to when the hour hand is pointing to 9, 19, 39, 49 or 59. What about if the hour hand is pointing to 1, 11, 21, 31, 41, 51?

Looking for Patterns

- A method for working out each answer is:

  Low-pitched bell

  Every hour the low-pitched bell strikes four times – on the hour, at 15 minutes past, 30 minutes past and 45 minutes past. Given that there are two 12-hour periods in 24 hours the calculation is $[(1 \times 4) + (2 \times 4) + (3 \times 4) \ldots (12 \times 4)] \times 2$ which totals 624 strikes.

  High-pitched bell

  Every hour the high-pitched bell strikes once at quarter past the hour, twice at half past the hour and thrice at quarter to the hour. Given that there are 24 hours a day the calculation is $24 \times (1 + 2 + 3)$ which totals 144 strikes.

Let's Investigate

- A digital clock and a mirror may help children to see which digits, and subsequently which times, are affected by reflection.

Teaching support continued

Page 2

Sports Update

- One method for working out how long it would take the male and female 100-metre record holders to run the marathon at the same speed as they ran 100 metres is:

  42·195 km × 1000 = 42 195 m

  42 195 m ÷ 100 m = 421·95

  ∴ Usain Bolt would take 421·95 × 9·58 sec to run this distance

  = 4042·28 sec

  = 67 min 22 sec

  = 1 h 7 min 22 sec
- Give the children time to discuss the results of the racing activity back in the classroom.
- Ask the children to work out how long it would take them to run a marathon if they ran the whole distance at this speed.

Page 3

Focus on Science

- Work through the first two problems with the children, i.e.

  total distance travelled = 525 km

  total time taken = 7 hours

  $$\text{average speed} = \frac{\text{total distance travelled}}{\text{total time taken}} = \frac{525\text{ km}}{7\text{ hours}} = 75\text{ km/h}$$

  total distance travelled = 7·5 km

  total time taken = $\frac{1}{2}$ hour

  $$\text{average speed} = \frac{\text{total distance travelled}}{\text{total time taken}} = \frac{7{\cdot}5\text{ km}}{30\text{ min}} = \frac{15\text{ km}}{1\text{ h}}$$

  average speed = 15 km/h

  time taken = $3\frac{1}{2}$ hours

  total distance travelled = average speed x total time taken

  = 15 km/h x $3\frac{1}{2}$ hours

  total distance travelled in $3\frac{1}{2}$ h = 52·5 km

Page 3 continued
Focus on Science continued

total distance travelled = 60 km

$$\text{total time taken} = \frac{\text{total distance travelled}}{\text{average speed}}$$

$$= \frac{60 \text{ km}}{15 \text{ km/h}}$$

total time taken = 4 hours

The Puzzler

- Suggest children work in pairs doing the calculations for both birthdays together.

Page 4
Let's Investigate

- Remind the children of the order of operations.
- Work through an example with the children.

For example, 29 January 2002.

$$f = k + \left[\frac{(13 \times m - 1)}{5}\right] + D + \left[\frac{D}{4}\right] + \left[\frac{C}{4}\right] - 2 \times C$$

$$= 29 + \left[\frac{(13 \times 11 - 1)}{5}\right] + 1 + \left[\frac{1}{4}\right] + \left[\frac{20}{4}\right] - 2 \times 20$$

$$= 29 + \left[(28{\cdot}4)\right] + 1 + \left[0{\cdot}25\right] + \left[5\right] - 40$$

$$= 29 + 28 + 1 + 5 - 40$$

$$= 23$$

To find the day of the week divide f by 7: $\frac{f}{7}$

$$= \frac{23}{7}$$

= 3 R 2 (2 = Tuesday)

So, 29 January 2002 was a Tuesday.

AfL

- How did you work out the answer to the puzzle? What conclusions can you draw from it? Is there a rule? If so, what is it?
- Explain the formula to me.
- Talk me through your calculation. How did you work that out?

Answers

Page 1

The Puzzler 48 minutes past

Looking for Patterns Low-pitched bell: 624 strikes
High-pitched bell: 144 strikes

Let's Investigate 12-hour digital clock

01:10 02:50 05:20
10:01 11:11 12:51

24-hour clock – the six times above and the following:

00:00 15:21 20:05
21:15 22:55

Page 2

Sports Update Usain Bolt: 1 h 7 min 22 sec
Florence Griffith Joyner: 1 h 13 min 46 sec
Answers will vary for the paired activity.

Page 3

Focus on Science Barry's average speed is 75 km/h.
The man could cycle 52·5 km in 3 $\frac{1}{2}$ hours.
It would take it him 4 hours to cycle 60 km.

Total distance travelled	Total time taken	Average speed
160 km	4 h	40 km/h
60 km	30 min	120 km/h
315 km	3 h 30 min	90 km/h
93 km	7 $\frac{3}{4}$ h	12 km/h
21 km	4 h 12 min	5 km/h

The Puzzler Answers will vary.

Page 4

Let's Investigate Answers will vary.

EMU 

horology
The study or science of measuring time.

Issue 29 Temperature

Prerequisites for learning

- Interpret and compare graphs and diagrams that represent data
- Understand and use simple algebraic conventions
- Use simple expressions and formulae in symbols
- Relate fractions to multiplication and division
- Find fractions of whole-number quantities

Resources pencil and paper; RCM 2: My notes (optional); RCM 3: Pupil self assessment booklet (optional); computer with internet access; thermometer; calculator (optional)

Teaching support

Page 1

Around the World

- Ensure children are able to read and interpret bar charts and line graphs.
- The important aspect of this activity is the rationales that children give for their recommendations based on the data provided.

Page 2

Let's Investigate

- Explain the meaning of the formula $F = \frac{9}{5}C + 32$, i.e.
  - multiply the Celsius temperature by 9
  - divide the answer by 5
  - add 32 to the answer.

Around the World

- Children write their own logic puzzle.

The Language of Maths

- Encourage the children to find out as much as they can about the terms Fahrenheit and Celsius, including after whom each of the scales are named.

Teaching support continued

Page 3

Looking for Patterns

- Assist the children by expressing a formula in words for converting Fahrenheit to Celsius, i.e.
  - subtract 32 from the Fahrenheit number
  - divide the answer by 9
  - multiply that answer by 5.

Famous Mathematicians

- Ensure that the children understand and can use the formulas to convert Fahrenheit and Celsius into Kelvin.
- Ask the children to investigate the application of the Kelvin scale in science and industry.

Page 4

Famous Mathematicians

- Ensure that the children understand and can use the formulas to convert Fahrenheit and Celsius into Rankine.
- Ask the children to investigate the application of the Rankine scale in science and industry.

Focus on Science

- It is more than likely that children will complete the second activity, i.e. when there aren't any crickets around. If this is the case, then you may need to discuss with the children how to rewrite the two formulas.

AfL

- Explain to me why you made those recommendations. What are your recommendations based on?
- How do you convert this temperature of … into … ?
- What does this formula mean?
- Do these formulas work? Which do you prefer? Why?
- Do the answers vary at all depending upon which formula you use? Why is this? Does it matter?

Answers

Page 1

Around the World Reports and rationales will vary.

Page 2

Let's Investigate Answers will vary depending on the temperatures chosen.

Around the World London 10°C, Auckland 33°C, Rome 21°C, New York 16°C, Paris 14°C, Edinburgh 9°C, Melbourne 30°C

The Language of Maths Results of the investigation will vary. However:

- Fahrenheit was named after the German physicist Gabriel Daniel Fahrenheit (1686–1736)
- Celsius was named after the Swedish astronomer Andres Celsius (1701–1744).

Page 3

Looking for Patterns $C = \frac{5}{9}(F - 32)$

Famous Mathematicians Answers and explanations will vary.

Page 4

Famous Mathematicians Answers and explanations will vary.

Focus on Science Crickets activity: Answers will vary

No crickets activity: Answers will vary, however the inverse formulas are:

number of chirps in 15 seconds = temperature in degrees Fahrenheit – 40

number of chirps in 15 seconds = (temperature in degrees Celsius × 2) – 13

EMU 

meteorology

The scientific study of the Earth's atmosphere, especially its patterns of weather and climate.

Issue 30 Area

Prerequisites for learning

- Use simple expressions and formulas in symbols
- Understand and use simple algebraic conventions
- Use fractions to describe and compare proportions
- Calculate the area of rectilinear shapes
- Understand and identify properties of a circle, including diameter and radius
- Understand pi (π) as the ratio of the circumference of a circle to its diameter which is equal to 3·14

Resources pencil and paper; RCM 2: My notes (optional); RCM 3: Pupil self assessment booklet (optional); RCM 7: Squared dot paper; ruler; scissors (optional); 11 × 11 geoboard; elastic bands; calculator, (optional); access to a range of measuring equipment; access to a daily supply of newspapers at home

Teaching support

Page 1
Looking for Patterns

- Suggest that the children draw and cut out several squares and semi-circles and label them *a* and *b* accordingly. They can then use these to construct the shapes on the page. This will provide a useful visual cue.
- Drawing lines to separate the compound shapes may assist in identifying the individual shapes, e.g.

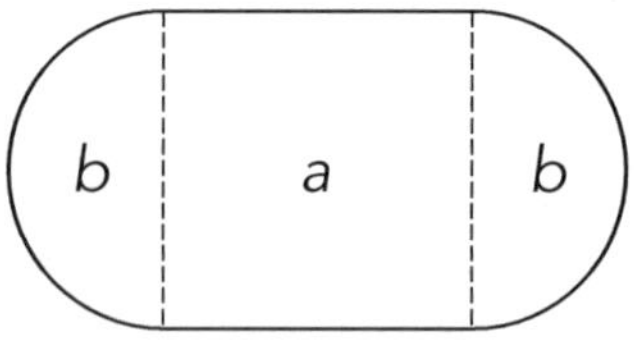

- Discuss with the children some algebraic conventions. For example, that $a + b + b$ can be expressed as $a + 2b$, or that $a \div 2$ can be written as $\frac{1}{2}a$.

Page 2

In the Past

- Most children should require little or no assistance in answering questions 1 or 2.
- Some children may require help in redesigning Tutankhamun's tomb. If this is the case, allow the children to work in pairs to discuss and reason appropriate alternatives.

Page 3

Let's Investigate

- Ensure that the children fully understand Pick's Formula before setting them off to work independently.
- Using a geoboard is an easier alternative to using squared paper.

What's the Problem?

- There are different methods to solve this problem. One possible method is to imagine the four right-angled triangles put together as two squares, each with sides 8 cm. Therefore, the area of each square is 64 cm^2 and $2 \times 64\ cm^2 = 128\ cm^2$.

Let's Investigate

- Discuss the difference between regular and irregular polygons. The largest octagon that can be made on the geoboard is an irregular octagon.

Page 4

Sports Update

- The shape of a soccer ball is not a sphere. It is actually a truncated icosahedron. It is made from 32 polygons: 12 regular pentagons and 20 regular hexagons.
- Most children will probably solve this problem using an informal method. However if appropriate, introduce the children to the formula for finding the area of a sphere: $A = 4\pi r^2$. In order to be able to apply this formula the children will need to be familiar with the meaning of both pi (π) and radius (r).

Teaching support continued

Page 4 continued

The Puzzler

- Encourage the children to use what they know, i.e. that C is one square unit, to work out what they don't know, e.g. that A and E are both half the size of C.

At Home

- Ensure that the children have access to a daily supply of newspapers. If this is not possible, try and provide them with a daily (preferably free) paper.
- Once children have completed the home activity, provide them with an opportunity to share what they did with others. What conclusions can they make?

AfL

- How would you express this in words? What about using letters and symbols?
- How did you work that out? Is there another way you could have arrived at that answer? What is the most effective and efficient method? Why is this the best method?
- Is there another answer / possibility? Are there any more?
- What have you discovered? How might this help you in the future?

Answers

Page 1

Looking for Patterns

$a + b + b$ or $a + 2b$
$a + a$ or $2a$
$a \div 2$ or $\frac{1}{2}a$
$a + \frac{1}{2}a$ or $1\frac{1}{2}a$
$a + b + b$ or $a + 2b$
Answers will vary for different shapes whose areas are $2a + b$.

Page 2

In the Past

Passage = 931·26 m^2
Antechamber = 2790·3 m^2
Annex = 1118 m^2
Burial Chamber = 2649·6 m^2
Treasury = 1819·25 m^2
Total area = 9308·41 m^2
Answers will vary for the redesigned tomb.

Page 3

Let's Investigate Results of the investigation will vary.

What's the Problem? 128 cm^2

Let's Investigate

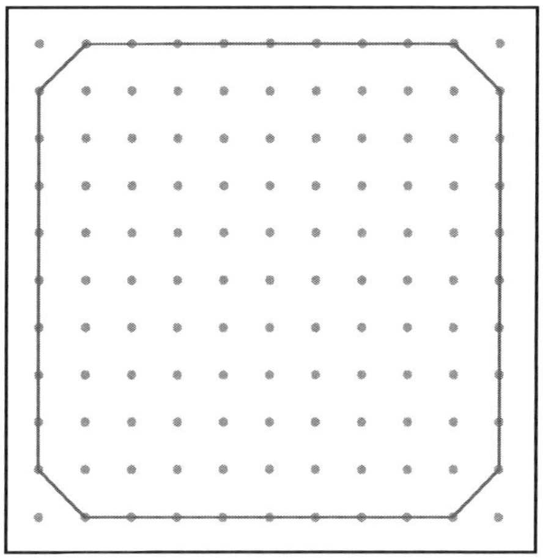

$\frac{2}{100}$ or $\frac{1}{50}$ of the geoboard is outside of the octagon.

Page 4

Sports Update Answers will vary for informal methods.
If using the formula $A = 4\pi r^2$,
then: $A = 4 \times 3{\cdot}14 \times 121 = 1520$ cm^2

The Puzzler Tangram pieces A and E = 0·5 square unit
Tangram pieces B and D = 2 square units
Tangram pieces F and G = 1 square unit
Total = 8 square units

At Home Results and comparisons will vary.

EMU

hectare

A metric unit of area equal to 100 acres or 10 000 square metres (2·471 acres).

Issue 31 Perimeter

Prerequisites for learning

- Calculate the area and perimeter of rectilinear shapes
- Understand and use simple algebraic conventions
- Represent information or unknown numbers in an equation

Resources pencil and paper; RCM 2: My notes (optional); RCM 3: Pupil self assessment booklet (optional); RCM 4: 1 cm squared paper; RCM 7: Squared dot paper; ruler; world atlas; trundle wheel; geoboard; elastic bands; matchsticks; computer with internet access

Teaching support

Page 1

Construct

- Most children should find this activity relatively easy. When they have worked out which tile can be removed without changing the overall perimeter, ask them to explain their thinking.

What's the Problem?

- Assist the children in seeing the squares as follows:

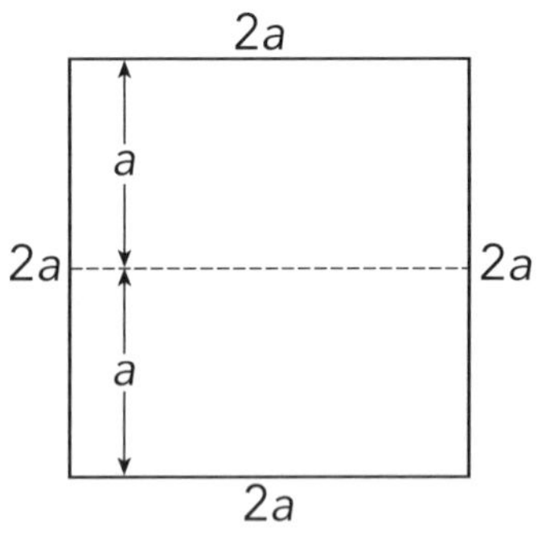

As the square was folded in half, the length of the rectangle is half the width.

So, perimeter of the rectangle
$= (2a \times 2) + (a \times 2) = 36$ cm
$\therefore 4a + 2a = 36$ cm
$\therefore 6a = 36$ cm
$\therefore a = 6$ cm

So, perimeter of the square
$= 2a \times 4$
$= 12$ cm $\times 4$
$= 48$ cm

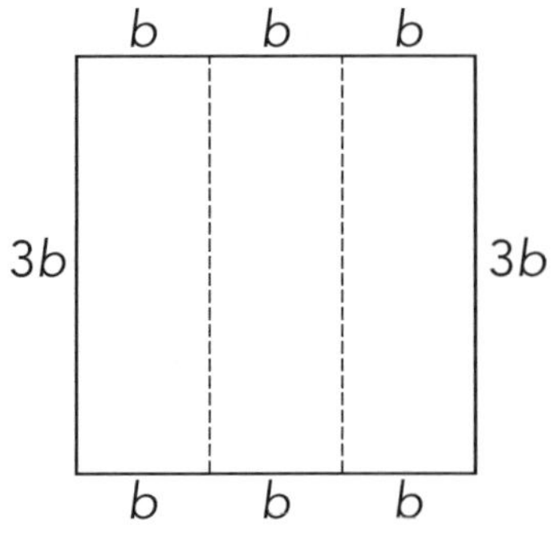

The perimeter of one rectangle
$= (3b \times 2) + (b \times 2) = 40$ cm
$\therefore 6b + 2b = 40$ cm
$\therefore 8b = 40$ cm
$\therefore b = 5$ cm

So, perimeter of the square
$= 3b \times 4$
$= 15$ cm $\times 4$
$= 60$ cm

Page 1 continued

Around the World

- This activity is best suited for pairs or small groups of children.
- A trundle wheel is an excellent resource for measuring the dimensions of the land on which the school is built. Ensure that children are familiar with, and are able to use, a trundle wheel before they start on this activity.
- The Let's Investigate activity on page 4 depends on children having successfully completed this activity.

The Language of Maths

- Remind the children that shapes are congruent if they are exactly the same size and shape.

Page 2

Around the World

- Children can find out about borders either on the internet or using a world atlas. Prior to the activity, you may wish to discuss these options with the children and decide which one is most appropriate.
- For either option, you will probably need to discuss with the children how their borders / perimeters will be approximates.

Construct

- Explain to the children that there are five different lengths of fencing possible.

Let's Investigate

- Suggest children move straight onto using squared dot paper.

Page 3

What's the Problem?

- One method of working is:

  12·6 ÷ 6 = 2·1
  2·1 × 1 = 2·1
  2·1 × 2 = 4·2
  (2·1 + 4·2) × 2 = 12·6

Let's Investigate

- Children investigate other polygons whose perimeters are greater than their areas.

Teaching support continued

Page 3 continued

The Language of Maths

- Children will easily be able to offer formulas for the square and rectangle.
- To write the formulas for the two other quadrilaterals and the circle, children need to understand and use both Pythagoras' theorem and the formula for calculating the circumference of a circle. Both these concepts are covered in Issue 17.

Page 4

Looking for Patterns

- Children should have no difficulty in drawing the next two shapes in each sequence. Nor should they have trouble in stating the number of extra squares and the number of matches used to make them.
- Some children may need help in writing the formulas and may benefit from drawing a table of the number of squares and the number of matches used, e.g. for the first sequence:

No. of squares (*n*)	1	2	3	4	5
No. of matches used	4	7	10	13	16
No. of matches in perimeter	4	6	8	10	12

- When working out the formula for number of matches used: each increase in n increases the number of matches by 3. Therefore for n extra squares, the number of extra matches is $3n$. The total number of matches needed for one square is 4 ($= 3n + 1$). Therefore $3n + 1$ is the formula.
- When working out the formula for the number of matches in the perimeter: each increase in n increases the number of matches by 2. Therefore for n extra squares, the number of extra matches is $2n$. The total number of matches needed for one square is 4 ($= 2n + 2$). Therefore $2n + 2$ is the formula.
- Discuss with the children why the formulas for the first three sequences are the same.

Let's Investigate

- Children should use the measurements they made in the Around the World activity on page 1.

AfL

- What relationships do you notice? What is the rule / pattern? How can you express this as a formula?
- Is this statement completely true? Why?
- What is the answer to this problem / puzzle? How did you work it out?
- What are the results of your investigation?

Answers

Page 1

Construct Tile G

What's the Problem? 48 cm
60 cm

Around the World Plans will vary.

The Language of Maths Shapes that are congruent do have the same perimeter, however shapes that have the same perimeter are not necessarily congruent.

Page 2

Around the World Results of the investigation will vary. However Canada has the largest combined land and sea border and the Vatican City has the smallest border. Cuba and the Bahamas have similar sized borders, as do the Philippines and China.

Construct

Sides of rectangle (m)		Total length of fencing (m)
1	80	162
2	40	84
4	20	48
8	10	36
16	5	42

Let's Investigate A 4 × 4 square has a perimeter and area that are numerically equal. This is also true for a 3 × 6 rectangle.
There are many possible pairs of shapes where the two perimeters are the same and the two areas are the same, e.g.

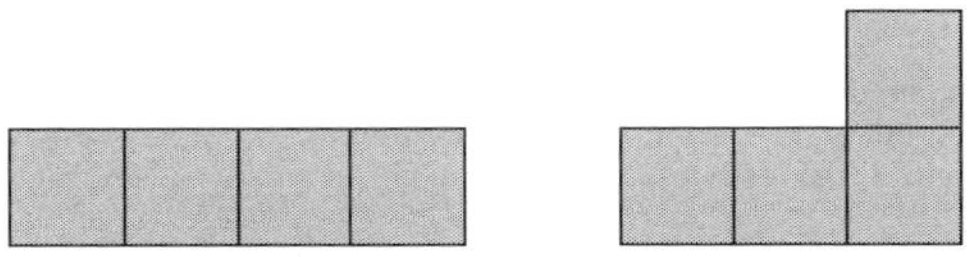

Answers continued

Page 3

What's the Problem?

Length: 4·2 m
Width: 2·1 m

Let's Investigate

Answers will vary. However, rectangles whose perimeters are greater than their areas include 2 × 3, 2 × 4, 2 × 5, 2 × 6 … rectangles.

The Language of Maths

Formulas or rules will vary, However possible formulas are:

- for a square: $4a$
- for a rectangle: $2(a + b)$
- for the irregular quadrilateral: $a + b + c + \sqrt{b^2 + (c - a)^2}$
- for the parallelogram: $2a + 2\sqrt{b^2 + c^2}$
- for the irregular hexagon: $2(a + b)$
- for the circle: πa

Page 4

Looking for Patterns

NOTE: For each formula below n = number of squares

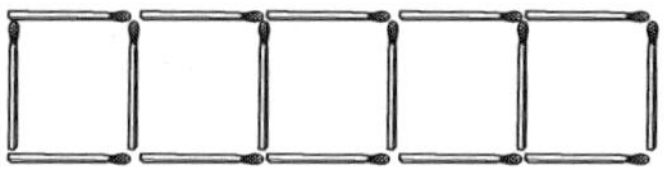

1 square using 3 matches are added each time.

The formula for the number of squares and the number of matches used: $3n + 1$

The formula for the number of squares and the number of matches around the perimeter: $2n + 2$.

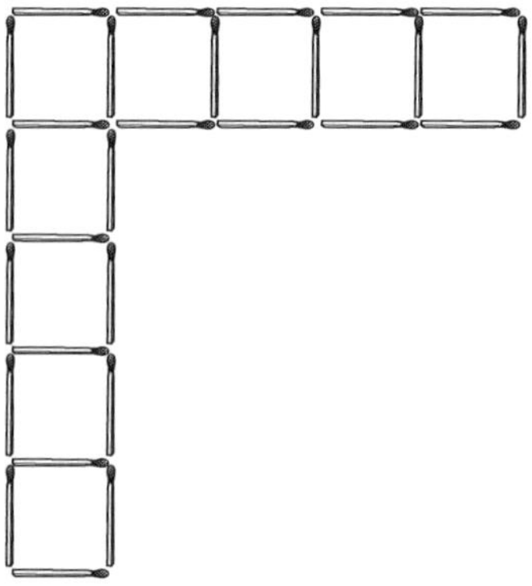

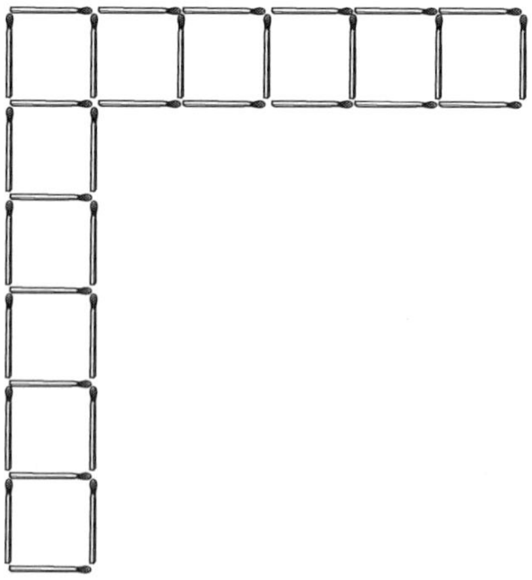

2 squares using 6 matches are added each time.

The formula for the number of squares and the number of matches used: $3n + 1$.

The formula for the number of squares and the number of matches around the perimeter: $2n + 2$.

Page 4 continued

Looking for Patterns continued

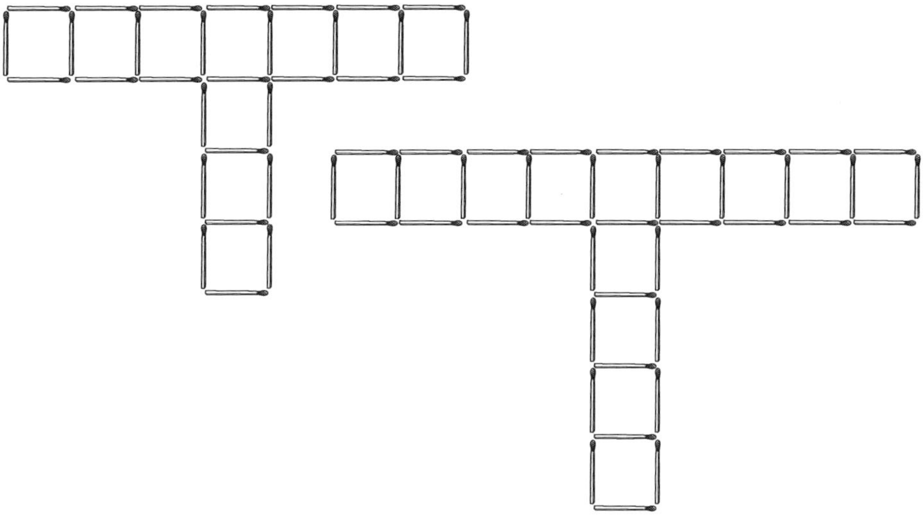

3 squares using 9 matches are added each time.

The formula for the number of squares and the number of matches used: $3n + 1$

The formula for the number of squares and the number of matches around the perimeter: $2n + 2$.

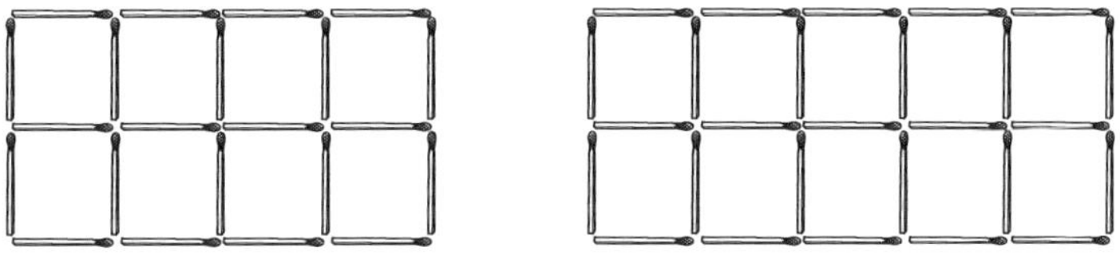

2 squares using 5 matches are added each time.

The formula for the number of squares and the number of matches used: $\frac{5n}{2} + 2$

The formula for the number of squares and the number of matches around the perimeter: $n + 4$

Let's Investigate Plans will vary.

EMU

circumference

The distance around a closed curve. It is a special perimeter.

Issue 32 Measuring – General

Prerequisites for learning

- Understand and use simple algebraic conventions
- Represent information or unknown numbers in an equation
- Know and use imperial measures still in everyday use and their metric equivalents

Resources pencil and paper; RCM 2: My notes (optional); RCM 3: Pupil self assessment booklet (optional); RCM 4: 1 cm squared paper; ruler; globe or world atlas, string; calculator (optional); road atlas; computer with internet access

Teaching support

Page 1
Famous Mathematicians

- By referring to the first four rows in the table, children should be able to easily identify the relationship between the measurements for Person 1 and Person 2, and therefore the rule and formula (i.e. W1 × D1 = W2 × D2).
- Children investigate further the life and discoveries of Archimedes.

Page 2
Famous Mathematicians

- By referring to the table, children should be able to identify the relationship between the time it takes an object to fall to the ground and the distance it travels during the fall.

  However, you may need to discuss with the children how to represent this as a formula, i.e. $4{\cdot}8 \times t^2$ or $4{\cdot}8t^2$. Depending on how the formula is expressed, you may also need to remind the children of the order of operations (i.e. find t^2 first then multiply the result by 4·8), and the algebraic convention of omitting the multiplication sign.
- Children investigate further the life and discoveries of Galileo.

Focus on Science

- This activity, EMU and the Let's Investigate activity on page 3 are all aimed at introducing children to unusual and very specific units of measures.
- You may wish to discuss with the children that the decibel scale is a logarithmic scale, i.e. 20 decibels is 10 times louder than 10 decibels; 30 decibels is 100 times louder than 10 decibels; 40 decibels is 1000 times louder than 10 decibels, …

Page 2 continued

Around the World

- In order for children to make their approximations, the globe will need to have some form of scale. If such a globe is not available, then suggest to the children that they use a world atlas.
- Children work out the distances in nautical miles.

  1 km = 0·54 nautical miles

  1 nautical mile = 1·852 km

Page 3

Let's Investigate

- This activity, EMU and the Focus on Science activity on page 2 are all aimed at introducing children to unusual and very specific units of measures.
- The most important aspect of this activity is finding, where appropriate, the equivalent metric measurement.

Famous Mathematicians

- In Issue 27, EMU required the children to investigate SI – the International System of Units. This system is based on the metric system and is an ideal starting point for the first part of this activity.
- Children should know the imperial unit equivalents for some of the metric units. They should be encouraged to investigate those equivalents they do not yet know.

Around the World

- Children can continue this activity at home by asking their parents or grandparents about what they consider to be the advantages and disadvantages of both the metric and imperial systems.

Page 4

Let's Investigate

- Most UK road atlases include a chart that shows the distances in miles by road between various cities. Provide children with such a chart and ask them to draw their own chart for just five different cities with the measurements given in kilometres.

Let's Investigate

- Children may be able to use the measurements they made in the Around the World activity on page 1 of Issue 31 to help them calculate the total area of the plot of land that the school is on.

Teaching support continued

Page 4 continued

Let's Investigate continued

- As there are various tasks involved in this activity, you may want the children to work on this in groups, with individuals or pairs working on different aspects. Children then share their results with the group before writing their report.

AfL

- What patterns did you notice? What is the relationship? Is there a rule?
- What formula did you discover? Describe this to me in words. What about using symbols?
- Show me an example that applies this formula.
- What did you find out about this investigation?
- What was your reasoning for making these decisions? Why are they valid reasons?

Answers

Page 1

Famous Mathematicians

Archimedes' formula is W1 × D1 = W2 × D2.

Person 1		Person 2	
Weight (W1)	Distance from fulcrum (D1)	Weight (W2)	Distance from fulcrum (D2)
24 kg	2 m	32 kg	1·5 m
40 kg	1 m	20 kg	2 m
20 kg	1·5 m	24 kg	1·25 m
80 kg	0·5 m	20 kg	2 m
45 kg	2 m	60 kg	1·5 m
70 kg	1 m	35 kg	2 m
36 kg	1·25 m	30 kg	1·5 m
52·5 kg	2 m	84 kg	1·25 m

Page 2

Famous Mathematicians

Galileo's formula is $4{\cdot}8t^2$ ($4{\cdot}8 \times t^2$).

It would take approximately 13 seconds for an object to fall to the ground from the top of Burj Khalifa.

Focus on Science

Answers will vary.
However, a decibel scale may look something like:

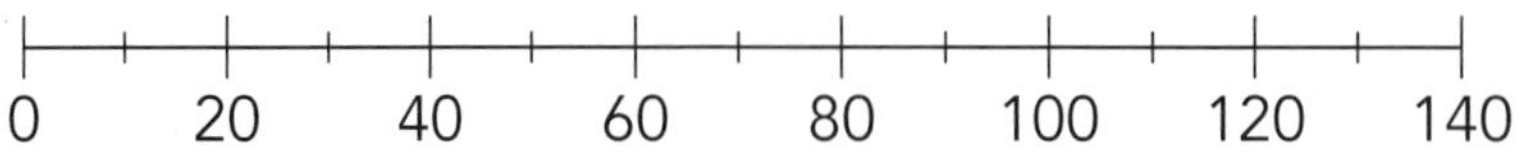

Page 2 continued

Around the World Estimated sailing distances will vary.
The actual sailing distance from:

- London to New York is 6189 km (3342 nautical miles)
- London to Sydney via the Suez Canal is 21 351 km (11 529 nautical miles).

Page 3

Let's Investigate

Fathom: depth of water.	1 fathom = 8 feet or 1·8 m
Hand: height of a horse.	1 hand = 4 inches or 10·2 cm
Knot: speed of a boat.	1 knot = 1·15 mph =1·852 km/h
Furlong: measure of distance.	1 furlong = one-eighth of a mile, 220 yards or 201·2 m
Quintal: measure of mass.	1 quintal = 100 base units of either pounds or kilograms

Results of the investigation will vary.

Famous Mathematicians Answers will vary. However some of the common equivalents may include the following:

Length	1 millimetre = 0·03937 inches 1 centimetre = 0·3937 inches 1 metre = 3·281 feet 1 metre = 1·0936 yards 1 kilometre = 0·6214 miles
Mass	1 gram = 0·0352 ounces 1 kilogram = 2·2046 pounds
Capacity	1 millilitre = 0·035 ounces 1 litre = 1·76 pints 1 litre = 0·22 gallons

Around the World Reports will vary, however, things that would need to change include road signs, weight information on packaging, weather reporting …

Page 4

Let's Investigate Both formulas give the same answer.
Reasons as to which formula children prefer will vary.

Let's Investigate Results of the investigation will vary.

EMU

Richter scale

A scale from 1 to 10 used to measure the severity of earthquakes according to the amount of energy released. The larger the number, the stronger the earthquake.

Issue 33 Organising and interpreting data

Prerequisites for learning

- Solve problems by collecting, selecting, processing, presenting and interpreting data, using ICT where appropriate
- Construct and interpret frequency tables, bar charts, line graphs and pie charts
- Recognise approximate proportions of a whole and use percentages to describe and compare them

Resources pencil and paper; RCM 2: My notes (optional); RCM 3: Pupil self assessment booklet (optional); RCM 4: 1 cm squared paper; ruler; newspapers; pair of compasses; protractor; calculator (optional); data handling software; computer with internet access

Teaching support

Page 1

The Arts Roundup

- This activity highlights the different interpretations that different people can have of the same set of data. What is important however is that children are able to recognise and logically explain the trends that the line graph displays. Therefore, once the children have completed the first part of this activity, conduct a group discussion providing an opportunity for each child to describe their interpretation of Oliver's graph.
- The second part of this activity provides the children with an opportunity to create their own partly labelled graph, and to answer questions and interpret similar graphs constructed by other children.

Focus on Science

- Children will need to have access to the internet to complete this activity.
- If appropriate, ask the children to construct their bar chart or graph using ICT.

Page 2

Focus on Science

- Children will need to have access to the internet to complete this activity.
- If appropriate, ask the children to construct their bar chart or graph using ICT.

Page 2 continued

Let's Investigate

- Depending on the sport and aspect of the investigation, children may need to have access to the internet to complete this activity. However, if the children are finding out the results from a newspaper, they may need to have access to newspapers over a period of time.
- If appropriate, ask the children to construct their bar chart or graph using ICT.

The Language of Maths

- Similar to The Arts Roundup activity on page 1, this activity involves children recognising and explaining the trends that each of the graphs display. Once the children have completed the activity, conduct a group discussion providing an opportunity for children to read and compare statements.

Page 3

The Puzzler

- Most children should find this puzzle relatively easy to solve. The important aspect of this activity is the children writing about how they worked it out.

In the Past

- This activity is concerned with interpreting data displayed in a line graph, drawing reasonable conclusions, and making and justifying likely predictions based on the trends displayed in the graph.

Page 4

Looking for Patterns

- For some children, this may be the first time that they have come across a scatter graph. If this is the case, you may need to spend some time with the children briefly highlighting the connections, relationships and trends displayed in the graph.

The Language of Maths

- Some children may need assistance in converting the data in the graph or table into percentages before presenting the information in the pie chart.
- Children can either draw the pie chart or use ICT.

AfL

- What can you tell me about the information displayed in the graph / chart / table?
- What relationships / connections / trends do you notice?
- What conclusions can you draw from this data?
- Explain to me the results of your investigation.
- Why did you decide to present your data in this way? How else could you have displayed the data?
- What predictions can you make in light of the trends that this graph shows?

Answers

Page 1

The Arts Roundup Descriptions, graphs, questions and statements will vary.

Focus on Science Results of the investigation will vary.

Page 2

Focus on Science Results of the investigation will vary.

Let's Investigate Results of the investigation will vary.

The Language of Maths Statements will vary.

Page 3

The Puzzler More children live in Rickety Towers than there are flats.

In the Past Reports, reasoning, conclusions and predictions will vary.

Page 4

Looking for Patterns Reports will vary.

The Language of Maths Pie charts will vary depending on the data used.

EMU

spreadsheet

A computer program that displays numerical data in cells in rows and columns, in which computer formulas can perform calculations on the data.

Issue 34 Probability

Prerequisites for learning

- Solve problems by collecting, selecting, processing, presenting and interpreting data, using ICT where appropriate
- Write a short report of a statistical enquiry, justifying choices and conclusions
- Construct and interpret frequency tables, bar charts, line graphs and pie charts
- Recognise approximate proportions of a whole and use percentages to describe and compare them

Resources pencil and paper; RCM 2: My notes (optional); RCM 3: Pupil self assessment booklet (optional); dice; spinners; material for making board games; selection of different types of books; newspapers; computer with internet access

Teaching support

Page 1

Let's Investigate

- In this activity pairs of children investigate the fairness of the game 'Rock-paper-scissors'. Ensure that children understand the rules of the game and how the possible outcomes of the game can be expressed using tree diagrams.

  The important aspect of this activity is the reasoning children give as to whether or not 'Rock-paper-scissors' is a fair game.

Page 2

Let's Investigate

- The letters in ENRICHING MATHS are repeated in sets of 14. So:
  - to work out the 53rd letter: 53 = (14 × 3) + 11.
    So the 11th letter in ENRICHING MATHS is 'A'.
  - to work out the 175th letter: 175 = (14 × 12) + 7.
    So the 7th letter in ENRICHING MATHS is 'I'.

Teaching support continued

Page 2 continued

Construct

- Discuss board games the children know and the rules of these games. There are general conventions that apply to all games, such as taking turns in order, and specific rules that apply to particular games.
- The children should consider how these rules contribute to the game's fairness. Clearly, in a game of chance, as long as everyone plays to the same rules, it feels as if everyone has the same chance of winning.
- When children make their unfair game, encourage them to change something very small about their game, so that it isn't quite clear whether or not it is fair.

Page 3

The Puzzler

- The probability that Scott oversleeps and misses the train is $\frac{9}{10} \times \frac{1}{20} = \frac{9}{200}$.

  The probability that Scott does not oversleep and misses the train is $\frac{2}{5} \times \frac{19}{20} = \frac{38}{100} = \frac{76}{200}$.

  Therefore the probability that Scott misses the train is $\frac{9}{200} + \frac{76}{200} = \frac{85}{200} = \frac{17}{40}$.

  So it is unlikely that Scott will miss the train.

The Language of Maths

- This activity considers how different factors can affect the outcome of a situation and therefore the probability.
- Children should investigate a selection of different types of books such as picture books, children's books, novels, newspapers etc.

Sports Update

- Sports that use handicaps include golf, horse-racing and sailing. The way in which handicaps operate vary depending on the sport. In golf for example, a person subtracts their handicap from their score. In horse-racing, horses are placed certain distances behind the scratch line.

Page 4

Money Matters

- Suggest the children make a table to work out the possible combinations and totals of coins that Marcus could take. From this the children should be able to work out the probabilities.

20p coin	10p coin	5p coin	Totals
3	1		70p
3		1	65p
2	2		60p
2		2	50p
2	1	1	55p
1	3		50p
1		3	35p
1	2	1	45p
1	1	2	40p
	3	1	35p
	2	2	30p
	1	3	25p

Sports Update

- Some children may find this activity difficult without knowing the value of r. Encourage them to work out the areas as multiples of π and r. It is the relative sizes of the areas that are important.

  Children have used pi (π) in other Issues to calculate perimeters and diameters of circles. If the children have not yet completed these Issues you may need to spend time talking about this mathematical constant.

  A method of working out the areas and probabilities are below:

  The area of the white ring = the total area of the target – the area of the black circle ($25\pi r - 16\pi r = 9\pi r$).

  The area of the black ring = the area of the black circle – the area of the blue circle ($16\pi r - 9\pi r = 7\pi r$).

  The area of the blue ring = the area of the blue circle – the area of the red circle ($9\pi r - 4\pi r = 5\pi r$).

  The area of the red ring = the area of the red circle – the area of the yellow circle ($4\pi r - \pi r = 3\pi r$).

  The area of the yellow circle = πr.

Teaching support continued

Page 4 continued

Sports Update continued

Therefore:

The probability of hitting the white ring:

$$= \frac{\text{area of white ring} \times 100}{\text{total area of the target}} = \frac{9\pi r \times 100}{25\pi r} = \frac{900}{25} = 36\%$$

The probability of hitting the black ring:

$$= \frac{\text{area of black ring} \times 100}{\text{total area of the target}} = \frac{7\pi r \times 100}{25\pi r} = \frac{700}{25} = 28\%$$

The probability of hitting the blue ring:

$$= \frac{\text{area of blue ring} \times 100}{\text{total area of the target}} = \frac{5\pi r \times 100}{25\pi r} = \frac{500}{25} = 20\%$$

The probability of hitting the red ring:

$$= \frac{\text{area of red ring} \times 100}{\text{total area of the target}} = \frac{3\pi r \times 100}{25\pi r} = \frac{300}{25} = 12\%$$

The probability of hitting the yellow ring:

$$= \frac{\text{area of yellow ring} \times 100}{\text{total area of the target}} = \frac{\pi r \times 100}{25\pi r} = \frac{100}{25} = 4\%$$

AfL

- Is this a fair or unfair game? Why?
- What is the probability / likelihood of that happening?
- How did you work out that probability? What does it mean?
- Tell me the results of your investigation. How does probability help you explain your results?

Answers

Page 1

Let's Investigate

Player A	Player B	Winner
paper	rock	player A
	paper	tie
	scissors	player B

Player A	Player B	Winner
scissors	rock	player B
	paper	player A
	scissors	tie

Rock-paper-scissors is a fair game with each player having an equal chance of winning, losing or tying.
Justifications will vary.

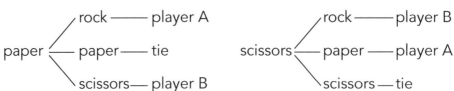

Page 2

Let's Investigate

The 12th letter is T.
The 53rd letter is A.
The 175th letter is I.
The probability that the letter is a T is $\frac{1}{14}$.
The probability that the letter is an I is $\frac{1}{7}$.
Explanations as to how children worked out the answers to the second and third questions will vary.
Check children's probability statements for their own name.

Construct

Board games will vary.

Page 3

The Puzzler

It is unlikely that Scott will miss the train.

The Language of Maths

Answers and justifications will vary.

Sports Update

Results of the investigation will vary.

Page 4

Money Matters

Probability of taking 50p is $\frac{1}{6}$.
Probability of taking 25p is $\frac{1}{12}$.
Probability of taking more than 50p is $\frac{1}{3}$.

Sports Update

Area of the white ring = $9\pi r$.
Area of the black ring = $7\pi r$.
Area of the blue ring = $5\pi r$.
Area of the red ring = $3\pi r$.
Area of the yellow circle = πr.

Probability of hitting the white ring is 36%.
Probability of hitting the black ring is 28%.
Probability of hitting the blue ring is 20%.
Probability of hitting the red ring is 12%.
Probability of hitting the yellow ring is 4%.

EMU

probability scale

For a finite number of possible outcomes, a probability scale is a way of recording the chance or likelihood of a particular outcome. On a scale from 0 to 1, the lowest probability is zero (impossible) and the highest probability is 1 (certain).

Issue 35 Statistics

Prerequisites for learning

- Describe and interpret results and solutions to problems using the mode, range, median and mean
- Solve problems by collecting, selecting, processing, presenting and interpreting data, using ICT where appropriate
- Construct and interpret frequency tables, bar charts, line graphs and pie charts
- Write a short report of a statistical enquiry, justifying choices and conclusions
- Understand the concept of and symbol for square root, and use the square root key on a calculator

Resources pencil and paper; RCM 2: My notes (optional); RCM 3: Pupil self assessment booklet (optional); RCM 4: 1 cm squared paper; ruler; selection of food packages showing recommended number of servings, e.g. cereal boxes, orange juice container, ground coffee (optional); selection of different types of newspaper, i.e. broadsheets and tabloids; calculator; data handling software; computer with internet access

Teaching support

Page 1

Let's Investigate

- This activity is best undertaken as a group task as it involves children collecting traffic data at an intersection near the school.
- Children can present their statistical evidence using ICT.

Sports Update

- The total of the scores is 90, i.e. 3 × 30 (number of darts × mean). Therefore the two other darts must total 80 (90 – 10).
- Draw children's attention to the dartboard and how scores greater than 20 are achieved using the double and triple rings, and the two centre rings.

Page 2

Around the World

- "If the world was a village of just 100 people" is a concept that children may have come across before. If not, it is worth spending time before children work independently on this activity discussing it with them.

Page 2 continued

Around the World continued

- Encourage the children to use the information in the table to display the information that is most relevant to them. They should also compare the village of 100 people with populations that mean something to them.
- Investigate "If the UK was a village of just 100 people".

Let's Investigate

- If crisps are sold in school, you may want to discuss with the children how they could involve other children in the class / school to help them with the investigation.

Page 3

Sports Update

- Ensure children understand the meaning of mode, median and mean.
- The total of the scores is 90, i.e. 15×6 (number of games × mean).
- Children write a similar problem of their own.

The Puzzler

- Children give more than one answer.

Sports Update

- Tell the children that there are two possible sets of scores and ask them to find both sets.

At Home

- You may wish for the children to undertake this activity in school rather than at home. If so, have available a selection of food packages showing recommended number of servings, e.g. cereal boxes, orange juice container, ground coffee …
- If the children do undertake this activity at home, once they have completed the task, ensure that there is an opportunity in class for pairs or groups of children to discuss their results.

Page 4

Let's Investigate

- Children should investigate different types of newspapers, e.g. broadsheets and tabloids, as well as different newspapers, e.g. *The Daily Telegraph*, the *Times* and *The Guardian*.

Focus on Science

- Ensure children understand and can use the formula to determine a person's reaction time.
- Children present their results using ICT.

AfL

- What are the results of your investigation? How did you go about collecting the necessary data? What do your results tell you?
- Are your results reliable? How can you be sure?
- What is the answer to this problem / puzzle? How did you work it out?

Answers

Page 1

Let's Investigate Results of the investigation will vary.

Sports Update Keith's other two scores were 26 (double 13) and 54 (triple 18).

Page 2

Around the World Results of the investigation will vary.

Let's Investigate Results of the investigation will vary.

Page 3

Sports Update Answers will vary for the scores of the 15 games. One possible combination is: 1, 2, 2, 3, 3, 4, 4, 5, 7, 7, 7, 10, 11, 12, 12

The Puzzler Answers will vary for the different ages of the family members. One possible answer is 32, 35, 10, 7, 5, 1.

Sports Update Scores for each match could be either: 2, 3, 6, 6, 8 or 1, 5, 6, 6, 7. The team need to score 11 goals in the next match to raise their mean score to 6.

At Home Results of the investigation will vary.

Page 4

Let's Investigate Results of the investigation will vary.

Focus on Science Results of the investigation will vary.

EMU

primary and secondary sources

A primary source is data collected first-hand through observations, tests, experiments or other similar methods. A secondary source is data collected from reference books, newspapers, websites, CD-ROMs and so on.

Issue 36 Handling data – General

Prerequisites for learning

- Find percentages of whole-number quantities
- Solve problems by collecting, selecting, processing, presenting and interpreting data, using ICT where appropriate
- Construct and interpret frequency tables, bar charts, line graphs and pie charts
- Write a short report of a statistical enquiry, justifying choices and conclusions

Resources pencil and paper; RCM 2: My notes (optional); RCM 3: Pupil self assessment booklet (optional); RCM 4: 1 cm squared paper; ruler; selection of newspapers; pair of compasses; protractor; calculator; electricity bill (optional); stopwatch; tape measure; data handling software; computer with internet access

Teaching support

Page 1
Around the World

- Total rainfalls are:

  Summer: 78 + 102 + 118 = 298 mm

  Autumn: 130 + 126 + 121 = 377 mm

  Winter: 131 + 98 + 82 = 311 mm

  Spring: 69 + 77 + 84 = 230 mm

  Yearly: 1216 mm

  Therefore, angles are:

  Summer: $\frac{298}{1216} \times 360 = 88{\cdot}223 \ldots (88°)$

  Autumn: $\frac{377}{1216} \times 360 = 111{\cdot}611 \ldots (112°)$

  Winter: $\frac{311}{1216} \times 360 = 92{\cdot}072 \ldots (92°)$

  Spring: $\frac{230}{1216} \times 360 = 68{\cdot}092 \ldots (68°)$

- Children can either draw the pie chart or use ICT.

Teaching support continued

Page 2

Construct

- In working out which arrangements of the 21 dots are better than an ordinary 1–6 dice, it is the ratio of wins to loses that is important, not the proportion of wins to the total number of rolls.
- One method of working out alternatives is to use a 6 × 6 grid similar to those below to show all the possible outcomes of a particular pair of dice.

2 ordinary 1–6 dice:

1/1	1/2	1/3	1/4	1/5	1/6
2/1	2/2	2/3	2/4	2/5	2/6
3/1	3/2	3/3	3/4	3/5	3/6
4/1	4/2	4/3	4/4	4/5	4/6
5/1	5/2	5/3	5/4	5/5	5/6
6/1	6/2	6/3	6/4	6/5	6/6

Wins: 15 Lossses : 15

1 ordinary dice / winning dice with 21 dots arranged as 0, 0, 5, 5, 5, 6

1/0	2/0	3/0	4/0	5/0	6/0
1/0	2/0	3/0	4/0	5/0	6/0
1/5	2/5	3/5	4/5	5/5	6/5
1/5	2/5	3/5	4/5	5/5	6/5
1/5	2/5	3/5	4/5	5/5	6/5
1/6	2/6	3/6	4/6	5/6	6/6

Wins: 17 Lossses : 15

Key: win | draw | lose

The Language of Maths

- Children may need to look through several newspapers before they find information displayed as a graph, chart or table. Encourage the children to find information that has meaning and relevance to them.

Focus on Science

- The first part of this activity is concerned with interpreting and comparing data presented in two pie charts. The second part involves the children using the information presented in the pie charts to make and justify predictions, and drawing an appropriate pie chart.
- Children can either draw the pie chart or use ICT.

Page 3

Focus on Science

- For the second part of this activity children need to bring an electricity bill into school. Alternatively, children can complete this part of the activity at home, or you could bring in an electricity bill of your own.

Page 3 continued

Sports Update

- Some sensitivity may need to be taken into consideration with this activity. However, results can still be presented ensuring anonymity, and conclusions made.
- Suggest the children present their results in a graph chart or table, using ICT if appropriate.

Page 4

Around the World

- Children will need to have access to the internet to complete this activity.

Sports Update

- Ensure children are familiar with line conversion graphs, e.g. converting from metric to imperial units or from degrees Fahrenheit to degrees Celsius, and exchange rate conversion graphs.
- Children construct their line conversion graphs using ICT.

Sports Update

- Discuss with the children how they are going to find out their average walking speed in m/sec, m/min, m/hr, km/h. Are they going to work out one or two and use these to calculate the others?
- Children can investigate for themselves the Olympic and World record holders. Limited data is available in Issue 28.

AfL

- Talk me through how you drew your pie chart. How did you work out the angles?
- Tell me the results of your investigation.
- Why did you present the information in this way? Why did you think it was the best way?
- What do these graphs / charts show? What conclusions can you draw from them? What predictions can you make? How can you justify your predictions?
- Why is this data best presented in this way? What benefits does it have over other types of graphs / charts?

Answers

Page 1

Around the World

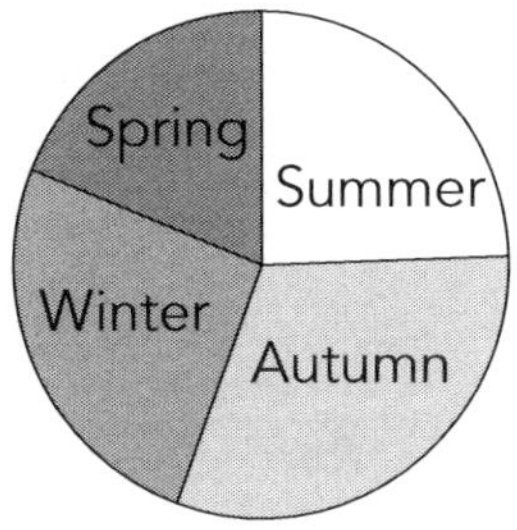

Answers continued

Page 2

Construct

The two best arrangements are:
0, 0, 5, 5, 5, 6
0, 0, 4, 5, 6, 6.
One better arrangement than an ordinary 1–6 dice is 0, 1, 4, 5, 5, 6.
Other answers are possible.

Focus on Science

Report and pie chart will vary. However continuing the trend from 1990 to 2001, the 2020 pie chart should show a greater percentage of 'Renewables and waste'.

The Language of Maths

Conclusions will vary depending on the data used.

Page 3

Focus on Science

cold appliances	864 kWh
cooking appliances	720 kWh
wet appliances	720 kWh
lighting	912 kWh
consumer electronics	912 kWh
domestic ICT	432 kWh
other	240 kWh

Results of the investigation at home will vary.

Sports Update

Results of the investigation will vary.

Page 4

Around the World

Results of the investigation will vary.

Sports Update

Conversion graphs will vary.

Sports Update

Results of the investigation will vary.

EMU

grouped frequency distribution

When there is a large set of data it can often be difficult to show every data value as there will be too many to display in a table or on a graph. So the data can be grouped into class intervals (or groups) to help us organise, interpret and analyse the data.

Enriching Maths 6 Record of completion

Class/Teacher ______________________

Strand	Topic	*Enriching Maths* Issue	Names									
Counting and understanding number	Whole numbers	1										
	Negative numbers	2										
	Fractions	3										
	Decimals	4										
	Percentages	5										
	Ratio and proportion	6										
	General	7										
Calculating	Addition	8										
	Subtraction	9										
	Multiplication	10										
	Division	11										
	Mixed operations	12										
	Mixed operations	13										
	Calculating with fractions	14										
	Calculating with percentages	15										
	General	16										

Strand	Topic	*Enriching Maths* Issue	Names									
Understanding shape	2-D shapes	17										
	3-D solids	18										
	Reflective symmetry	19										
	Rotational symmetry	20										
	Translations	21										
	Position and direction	22										
	Movement and angle	23										
	General	24										
Measuring	Length and distance	25										
	Mass and weight	26										
	Volume and capacity	27										
	Time	28										
	Temperature	29										
	Area	30										
	Perimeter	31										
	General	32										
Handling data	Organising and interpreting data	33										
	Probability	34										
	Statistics	35										
	General	36										

My notes

EMU

Name: ____ Issue: ____

The Maths Herald

Volume 6

Date of starting Issue: ____ Date of finishing Issue: ____

My notes

My notes

My notes

Any other comments?

Your teacher's comments

Name: ____________ Issue: ____________

The Maths Herald

Volume 6

Date of starting Issue: ____________ Date of finishing Issue: ____________

What have you learned?

What did you use to help you?

What did you enjoy the most?

What did you enjoy the least?

Did you find the work:

too easy? ☐

just about right? ☐

too hard? ☐

What would you like to learn next about this topic and why?

1 cm squared paper

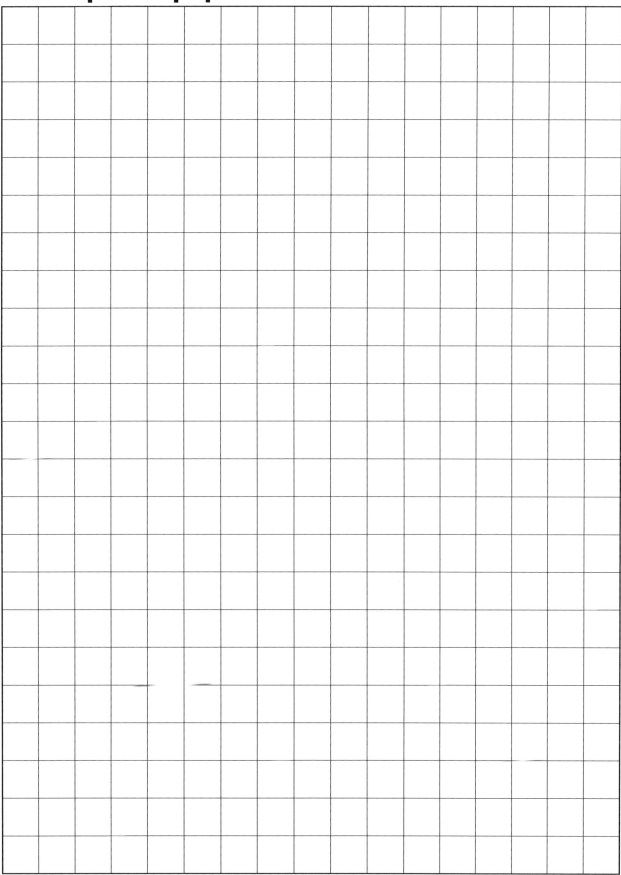

2 cm squared paper

0·5 cm squared paper

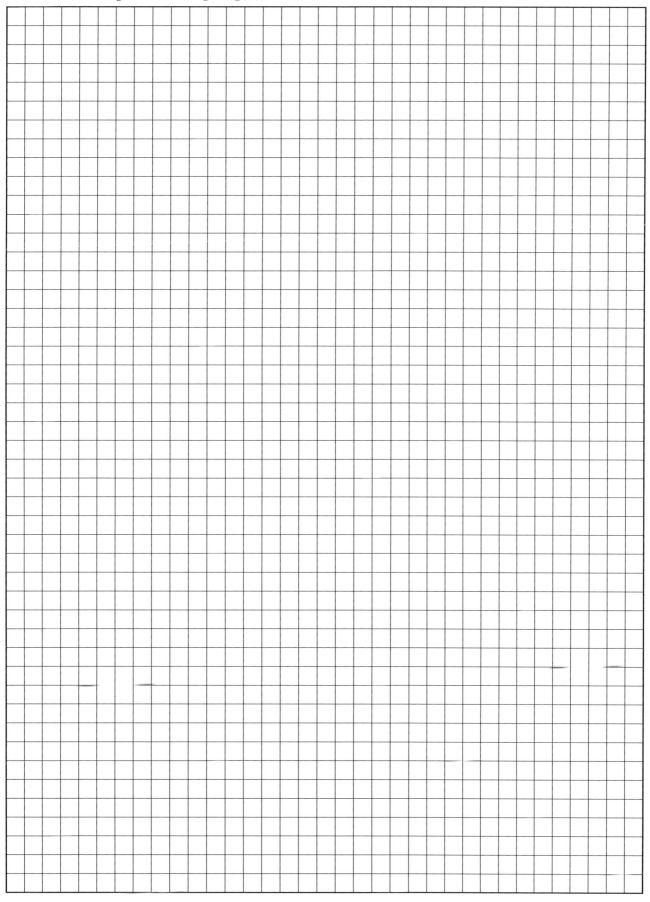

Squared dot paper

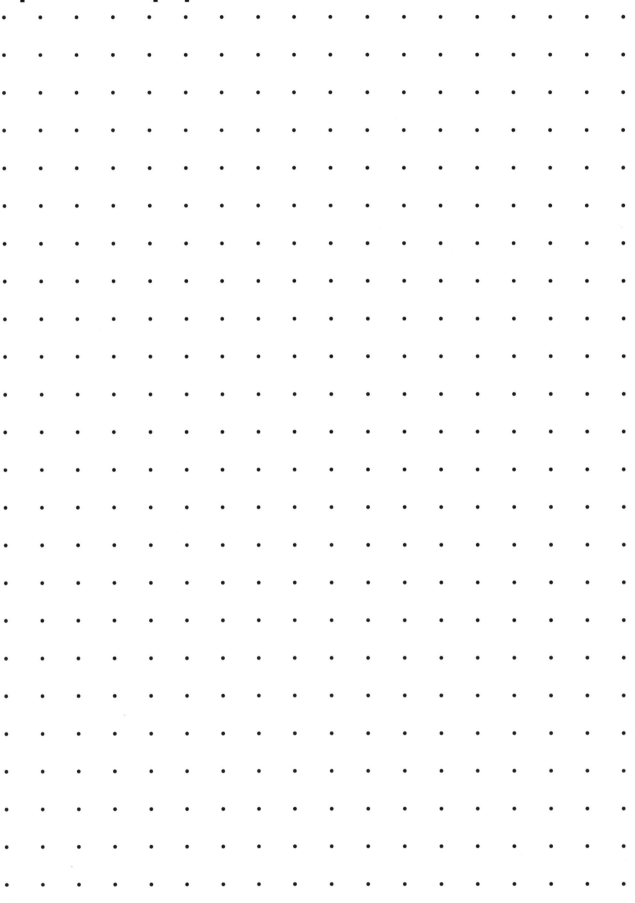

Triangular dot paper

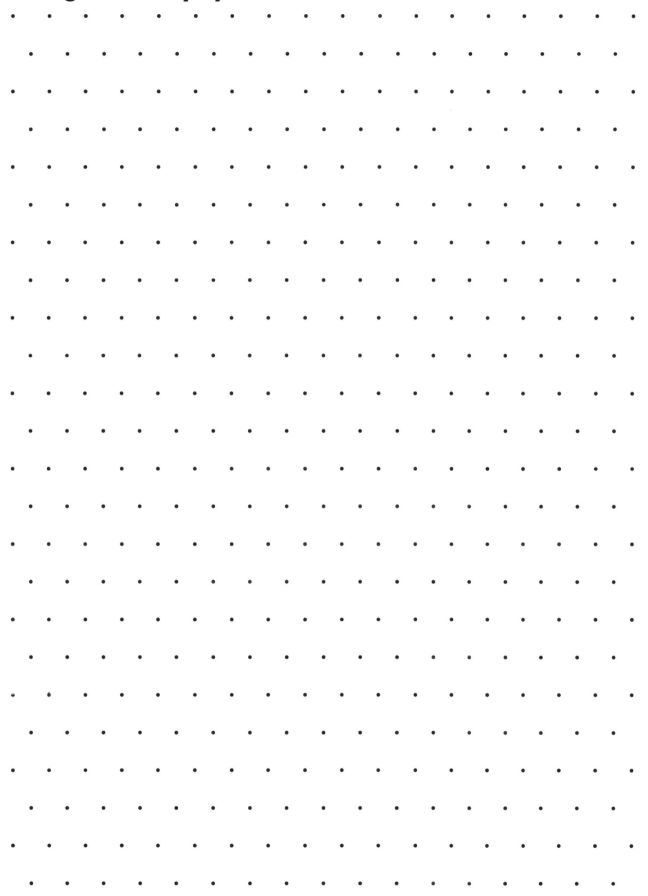

Isometric paper

Diamond paper

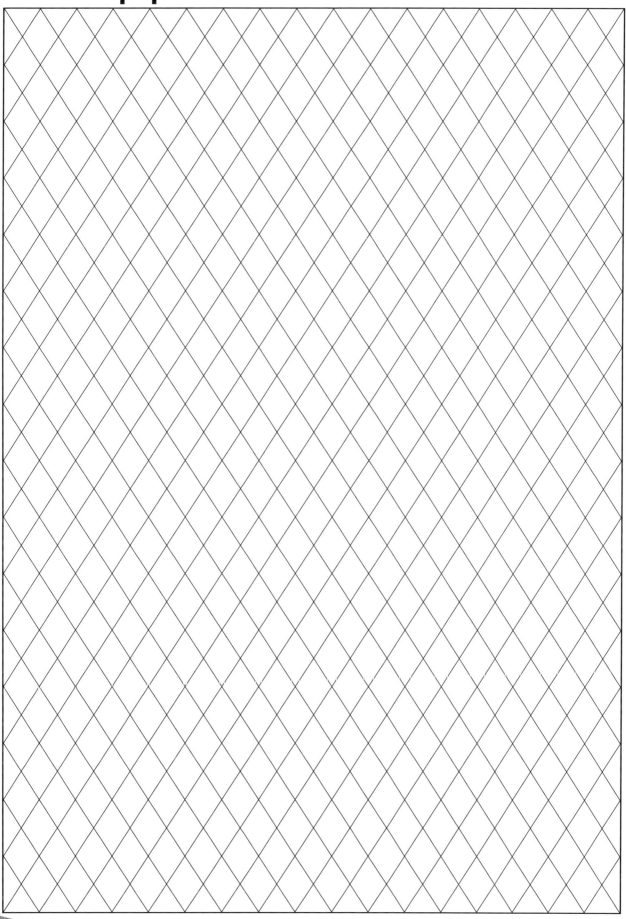